RESIDENTIAL SCHOOLS AND RECONCILIATION

Canada Confronts Its History

Residential Schools and Reconciliation

Canada Confronts Its History

J.R. MILLER

UNIVERSITY OF TORONTO PRESS
Toronto Buffalo London

© University of Toronto Press 2017
Toronto Buffalo London
www.utppublishing.com
Printed in Canada

ISBN 978-1-4875-0218-8

Printed on acid-free, 100% post-consumer recycled paper with
vegetable-based inks.

Library and Archives Canada Cataloguing in Publication

Miller, J. R. (James Rodger), 1943–, author
Residential schools and reconciliation : Canada confronts
its history / J.R. Miller.

Includes bibliographical references and index.
ISBN 978-1-4875-0218-8 (cloth)

1. Native peoples – Canada – Residential schools.   2. Native peoples –
Canada – History.   3. Truth and Reconciliation Commission of Canada.
4. Truth commissions – Canada.   5. Canada – Ethnic relations – History.
I. Title.

E96.5.M53 2018   371.829'97071   C2017-904303-X

University of Toronto Press acknowledges the financial assistance to its
publishing program of the Canada Council for the Arts and the Ontario Arts
Council, an agency of the Ontario Government.

Canada Council   Conseil des Arts
for the Arts   du Canada

Funded by the   Financé par le
Government   gouvernement
of Canada   du Canada

ONTARIO ARTS COUNCIL
CONSEIL DES ARTS DE L'ONTARIO
an Ontario government agency
un organisme du gouvernement de l'Ontario

To Christian

Contents

Part Three: Redress and Reconciliation

Illustrations

Acknowledgments

As is usually the case, the preparation of this volume depended on the assistance of many people and institutions. I am grateful to the institutions and programs that have supported the research for this study. The most important of them have been the Canada Research Chairs Program, the Social Sciences and Humanities Research Council (SSHRC), and the Killam Program. Since the late 1990s, I have benefited from a number of awards, formerly called Standard Research Grants, from SSHRC on treaties, reconciliation, and Indigenous policy generally. As well, I have been the beneficiary of a generous grant that accompanied SSHRC's Gold Medal for achievement in research in 2010. From 2001 until I retired in 2014, I also held the Canada Research Chair in Native-Newcomer Relations, a position that greatly facilitated my own research while also conferring the benefit of working with a number of talented graduate students and postdoctoral fellows. And in 2014, I was fortunate to receive the Killam Prize in the Humanities from the Canada Council. This award, too, was accompanied by a money prize. As well, I would be remiss if I did not acknowledge the many ways in which the University of Saskatchewan facilitated and encouraged my research.

As with any historical research, mine has benefited greatly from the hard and effective work of archivists and librarians. Among the latter, I would especially note the professional librarians at the University of Saskatchewan's Murray Library. The professional staff of denominational archives – the United Church of Canada Archives (Nicole Vonk and staff), the General Synod Archives of the Anglican Church of Canada (Nancy Hurn and Laurel Parson), and the Archives of the Presbyterian Church in Canada (Kim Arnold and Bob Anger) – unfailingly were as cheerful and friendly as they were professional and efficient.

And until it deteriorated into an environment that was not particularly helpful to individual researchers, I also benefited from the advice and assistance of staff at Library and Archives Canada.

By no means did all the help I received come from institutions and their employees. Jonathan Dewar, formerly with the Aboriginal Healing Foundation and Algoma University, was invaluable in providing advice about illustrations, especially artwork for the cover. Numerous staff associated with the Shingwauk Project at Algoma University were also helpful, as well as welcoming and convivial when I joined them at reunions of the Shingwauk school on numerous occasions. Mike Cachagee, Shirley Horn, Don Jackson, Ed Sadowski, and Krista McCracken were gracious and informative. Donald B. Smith, Professor Emeritus of History of the University of Calgary, was enormously generous with advice about sources and other matters relevant to this project, as he famously has been to so many researchers. The many individuals who generously made time in their schedules to be interviewed at the Shingwauk Project and across the country were critical to my understanding the forces in contention in a series of relatively recent events. The names of most of those informants are listed in the bibliography.

As well, the following people answered queries and/or provided sources for my consideration: Carling Beninger, Leonard Doell, Brian Gable, Meagan Hough, Peter Jull, Julianne Kasmer, Amber Kostuschenko, John F. Leslie, Jennifer Llewellyn, Tom McMahon, Cecilia Morgan, Donna and Jim Sinclair, Sylvia Smith, Kim Stanton, and Angela Wanhalla.

I also wish to thank my editor, Len Husband, managing editor Frances Mundy, and their colleagues at the University of Toronto Press for their careful work on the manuscript. As well, I would like to thank Adrian Mather, who prepared the index.

Closer to home, Bill Waiser read and provided valuable comments on earlier drafts of many of the chapters, as did my wife and colleague, Lesley Biggs.

Of course, none of these generous people is responsible for any of the errors in the work.

This study is dedicated to my son, Dr Christian A. Miller.

Note on Terminology

In an effort to provide the reader with some variety in wording, this volume employs a number of terms for the first peoples of Canada. *Indigenous*, *Aboriginal*, or *Native* is used to describe the first peoples as a group. *First Nation* refers more specifically to those peoples whom the federal government used to term "status Indians." *Métis* embraces Indigenous peoples of mixed ancestry, whether of partial French, Scottish, or English background.

The terms for the federal government department with constitutional responsibility for First Nations are also varied, although in this case the variety is the result of changes that the government has introduced from time to time. It was known as the Department of Indian Affairs (DIA) from its creation in 1880 until 1936. As part of economies introduced in response to the Great Depression, the department then downgraded to a branch – Indian Affairs Branch (IAB) – of the Department of Mines and Resources and then, in 1949, of the Department of Citizenship and Immigration. In 1966, the title was changed once more to the Department of Indian Affairs and Northern Development (DIAND), reflecting an emphasis on and interest in economic development on Indigenous lands. DIAND evolved for a time into INAC, Indian and Northern Affairs Canada. In 2011, the government of Stephen Harper altered the name to Aboriginal Affairs and Northern Development Canada (AANDC), recognizing that, for some time, Aboriginal peoples had expressed an aversion to the term *Indian*. Finally, late in 2015, the new government of Justin Trudeau ushered in the latest formulation, Indigenous and Northern Affairs Canada (INAC).

The need to bring ... Aboriginal peoples into our national consciousness, to deal fairly and equitably with them, to reconcile them as part
of the Canadian mainstream and to deal with their problems, [is] likely
the most important public policy issue of the 21st century.

John Crosbie, former Progressive
Conservative cabinet minister
to editor, *National Post*, 18 January 2003

Introduction
"We Did Not Hear You"

At Laurentian University one day in August 1986, a party of Native people waited patiently in the corner of a parking lot. They had been there for several hours when many non-Native people, some of them wearing a clerical collar or other marker of United Church of Canada clergy, made their way to join them from a nearby building where they had been holding discussions. This procession was headed by a man wearing a purple stole, the colour symbolizing penitence in Christian churches. They had left their deliberations only after protracted debate over the course of action they were to take when they met their Native brethren. Earlier in the meeting of the General Council, the national governing body of the United Church, Native delegates had called upon the church to issue an apology for its treatment of Native people during its missionary history. Members of the denomination had, for two years, been intensely debating issues concerning the relationship between the United Church and Native people. At the 1984 General Council meeting in Morden, Manitoba, Alberta Billy, a First Nation delegate from Cape Mudge, British Columbia, had demanded an apology for the church's treatment of Native people.[1] In the interim, individuals within the denomination had argued over whether an apology was justified, and whether issuing an apology would in effect repudiate the validity and worth of Christ's message to all peoples. Many of those arguments had been rehearsed again at the Sudbury meeting after the Native delegates had reiterated the call for an apology. Finally, the procession that wended its way from the meeting hall to the gathering of Native people nearby would deliver the church's answer.

The Reverend Bob Smith, moderator of the national body, spoke movingly about the delegates' regret about the treatment of Native people by the church. "We did not hear you when you shared your visions. In our zeal to tell you of the good news of Jesus Christ we were closed to the value of your spirituality." He also admitted that, in the past, missionaries "had confused Western ways and culture with the depth and breadth and length and height of the gospel of Christ." They had "imposed our civilization as a condition for accepting the gospel." Concluding, Smith said that he and his colleagues "ask you to forgive us and to walk together with us in the Spirit of Christ so that our peoples may be blessed and God's creation healed."[2]

The other Christian denominations that had had the closest involvement with Indigenous peoples, including the operation of residential schools for Indigenous children, in due course joined the movement to show contrition. Five years after the events at Laurentian University, two agencies of the Roman Catholic Church in Canada expressed their remorse. The Oblates of Mary Immaculate apologized for "the part we played in the cultural, ethnic, linguistic and religious imperialism" that missionaries had inflicted on Indigenous peoples after contact. In 1991, a meeting of sixteen Roman Catholic bishops, representatives of Catholic agencies, and First Nations adherents also conveyed the denomination's regret.[3] In 1993, Primate Michael Peers, the head of the Anglican Church of Canada, delivered a message to the National Native Convocation in northwestern Ontario. Referring to residential schools, he confessed that he "felt shame and humiliation as I have heard of suffering inflicted by my people, and as I think of the part our church played in that suffering." And he said, "I pledge to you my best efforts, and the efforts of our church at the national level, to walk with you along the path of God's healing."[4]

It was historically fitting that it was the religious denominations and organizations that had been most intimately involved with residential schooling that took the first steps towards reconciliation with residential school survivors by issuing apologies between 1986 and 1998. From the earliest settlement times of Europeans in the northern part of North America, the Christian churches had been major instruments of the state's interactions with Indigenous peoples. Beginning in seventeenth-century New France, one of the missionaries' key initiatives had been custodial schools in which the children of the First Nations with whom the Europeans dealt in trade and diplomacy had been housed and subjected to European schooling. Over the centuries, as the early frontiers of faith, commerce, and diplomacy had given way to an expanding settlement frontier, European newcomers had persistently tried to influence Indigenous society through such schools. In the late nineteenth century, the Canadian state had turned to residential schools operated by the Roman Catholics, Anglicans, Methodists, and Presbyterians to advance policies designed to change Indigenous societies culturally, economically, and socially. The churches and the Canadian state remained partners in the institutions for more than a century, until the residential schools were slowly closed one by one, the last of them abandoned only in 1996. As the final schools were being shuttered, church leaders were in the process of apologizing for the residential schools they had operated.

If the churches were the logical agency to begin what would develop into a movement to bring about reconciliation between Indigenous people and other Canadians, they did not remain the central players in the process for long. Canadian society would stumble forward slowly to engage with the legacy of residential schooling through the 1990s and early twenty-first century with a succession of overtures and efforts. Between 1992 and 1996, the federally appointed Royal Commission on Aboriginal Peoples (RCAP) increased awareness of the history of residential schools, completing its work with a call for a public inquiry into the schools and their impact. When the government responded to RCAP, it was not to create another inquiry but to offer a ministerial apology for the educational assault on Indigenous society and to create a major agency designed to assist individuals and communities to cope with the damage that the schools had done. While this Aboriginal Healing Foundation (AHF) did effective work to help Indigenous people for over a decade, by itself it did not respond to what Aboriginal leaders and former students wanted from the government. One manifestation of their disappointment was the development of a wave of litigation by residential school survivors seeking compensation for the damage that the schools had done to them. Eventually, the tide of litigation became so great that the federal government recognized that a different approach was needed. The result of the government's change of direction was negotiation of a massive Indian Residential School Settlement Agreement (IRSSA) in 2006, which provided for several programs designed to advance reconciliation. Today the Canadian state is still working through the several initiatives that the settlement agreement established.

This volume is a study of the various processes through which Canada over the past thirty years has moved haltingly towards reconciliation between Indigenous and immigrant peoples. The church apologies,

RCAP, the AHF, litigation, the IRSSA, a prime ministerial apology, and the Truth and Reconciliation Commission are key phases in the narrative of a society slowly waking up – or trying to rouse itself – from a sleep of ignorance about one of the darkest chapters in its history. As well, it is a study of how historical understanding has evolved and how Canadians have struggled to come to grips with the negative aspects of their country's past. And it is also the story of how Aboriginal people in Canada have responded since the mid-1980s to the royal commission, contention over litigation, programs of compensation, apologies, and a wide-ranging inquiry by Truth and Reconciliation commissioners.

A clue to the reaction of former school students and their communities can be found in the response in August 1986 and afterward to the church action that began the search for reconciliation. The Aboriginal delegates to the United Church's General Council at Laurentian University had, at the time, informed their colleagues that the apology the moderator had offered was not accepted, although it was "joyfully received and acknowledged." To mark the occasion, the Aboriginal delegates laid the beginnings of a stone cairn. They deliberately left the cairn incomplete, to be built upon as the church provided evidence of its intention to "live out" the apology.[5] One step in the process of living its apology occurred at the next General Council, at which the church created an All Native Circle Conference to represent Aboriginal people within the Church more effectively.[6] On behalf of the conference, one of its members, Edith Memnook, spelled out what Native people expected if the cairn was to be completed:

> The All Native Circle Conference has now acknowledged your Apology to Native People. Our people have continued to affirm the teachings of the Native way of life. Our spiritual teachings and values have taught us to uphold the Sacred Fire; to be guardians of Mother Earth, and strive to maintain harmony and peaceful coexistence with all peoples.
>
> We only ask of you to respect our Sacred Fire, the Creation, and to live in peaceful coexistence with us …
>
> The Native people of The All Native Circle Conference hope and pray that the Apology is not symbolic but these are the words of action and sincerity.[7]

Thus the United Church, the first to express regret for its treatment of Indigenous people, was put on notice that its actions would be scrutinized to see if they measured up to its words.

The response of Native people within the United Church encapsulates the reaction of residential school survivors and Indigenous people in general to the emerging movement for reconciliation that Canada has seen since the 1980s. First Nations and other Indigenous peoples have, at every stage, watched to see, not just what Canadian leaders and institutions have said, but what they have subsequently done. Would the various Christian denominations live out their apologies? Would the federal government respond meaningfully to the revelations and final report of the Royal Commission on Aboriginal Peoples? Tellingly, the federal government dragged the churches into litigation over residential school abuse, thus complicating the judicial process but also leading to more assertive actions by Indigenous organizations and people. Would the settlement agreement and the apology that Prime Minister Stephen Harper finally provided before Parliament in 2008 pave the way to substantial efforts to promote healing among survivors? Or would his subsequent behaviour suggest that the apology not be viewed as a step towards meaningful change and healing? Would Canadians respond to the Truth and Reconciliation Commission in ways that showed they were dedicated to making amends for the ills of residential schools and advancing the cause of reconciliation? Would the cairn at Laurentian University be completed?

Native survivors of the residential schools have responded to reconciliatory initiatives by waiting and watching to see if those making the gestures would continue to act in the same spirit. When they thought nothing meaningful had been done, they voiced that assessment. But when they decided that their non-Native partners were sincere in their words and were acting in the same spirit, they responded positively – and added more stones to the cairn that was begun in 1986. The events that are covered in this work illustrate that, while the cairn of reconciliation has been augmented and enhanced in some ways, it is still incomplete.

PART ONE

Exposing the Problem

1

The Churches Apologize

It was to be expected that the first Canadian social institutions to express remorse for residential schools were the Christian denominations that had operated the boarding schools. Governments in Canada had always chosen to deliver social policy related to Aboriginal peoples through the churches, and, for their part, the religious bodies historically had proved enthusiastic partners of the state in this endeavour. Within decades, however, both the churches that operated the schools and the state that authorized and largely financed them became disillusioned with their combined educational efforts. Increasing awareness of the shortcomings of residential schools by the middle of the twentieth century led to an abortive attempt to make changes in the delivery of schooling to Indigenous children. The forces that had begun to cast doubt on their role in Native education continued to work on the several Christian denominations, which slowly began to fashion a different approach to serving Indigenous peoples. Through the 1970s and 1980s, the churches moved from being a delivery vehicle for government-fashioned social policy to acting as supporters of Aboriginal communities and organizations, frequently in opposition to the economic development that the federal government favoured. By the 1980s, the time was ripe for the Christian denominations to take a further step by renouncing and expressing regret for their role as the handmaidens of the state in administering Native peoples.

Given the long history of state-church cooperation in Native affairs in Canada, the deep involvement of four of Christianity's major denominations

in residential schooling was not surprising. A Christian evangeliz-
ing mission, encouraged and aided by the state, was undertaken in the
eastern part of the country, where the impact of European contact was
felt first, from the earliest times after contact. In seventeenth-century
New France, the French monarchy insisted that fur-trading companies
work with Roman Catholic missionary orders to carry the message
of Christ to Indigenous populations. The state-encouraged program of
proselytization included other aspects of social policy, such as medical care and schooling. The French settlements was the site of no fewer
than four separate sectarian attempts to house Native youths in custodial schools, all of them notably unsuccessful. These early experiments
in residential schooling failed for two reasons. First, in a colony whose
principal purposes were commercial, military, and diplomatic, newcomers had little desire to bring about the cultural change that European
schooling was designed to effect. The First Nations of the northeastern
woodlands with whom the French interacted in the 1600s were profi-
cient fur-gatherers and -traders, as well as highly skilled forest diplomats
and warriors. There was little reason beyond the simply religious motive
that propelled the missionaries to try to change Native society through
schooling. Second, Indigenous people outnumbered the European newcomers by a large margin and did not see the need to adjust significantly
to accommodate the Europeans in commerce and diplomacy. Hence, the
seventeenth-century European missionary initiatives involved agents of
the Roman Catholic Church in many ways, but these evangelists did not
leave a legacy in residential schooling.[1]

Although conditions changed when Britain succeeded France as
the principal colonizer in early Canada, the social role of the Christian
churches remained unaltered. Following the French period, the earliest
experiments in education for First Nations children in the Maritimes,
southern Quebec, and Ontario were undertaken by Christian denominations, with the encouragement and support of the Britannic state.
In New Brunswick between the 1780s and early nineteenth century, a
nondenominational Protestant missionary organization called the New
England Company operated a residential school, which it termed an
"Indian College," at Sussex Vale. This institution proved a precursor
of Canadian residential schools in the problems it generated. Children were not well cared for in the school and were often exploited
and abused when sent out to local colonists as apprentice farmers and
housekeepers.[2] The New England Company nonetheless continued to
play an active role in colonial education, operating the longest-running

residential school in Canada near Brantford, Ontario, from the 1830s to the late years of the twentieth century. Throughout colonial British North America, including the future Quebec and the fledgling colonies on Vancouver Island and the British Columbia mainland, Roman Catholic orders and several Protestant denominations operated schools for Native children, many of them on the reserves that the state began to create in the early nineteenth century. Residential schools were not established in Prince Edward Island, Nova Scotia, or southern Quebec, but small boarding schools began to pop up in the southern portion of what was to become Ontario. In the 1840s and 1850s, the colonial government in Ontario created several residential schools for Aboriginal students, but without notable success. And, in the 1820s in the Hudson's Bay Company territory known as Rupert's Land, a small custodial school was operated by a cleric of the Church Missionary Society, the Church of England's principal evangelizer – again, without much success. Thus, by the time the Dominion of Canada was created in 1867, the country had a lengthy tradition of state and church combining to provide schooling for Native youth.[3] At best, these efforts were not successful.

The tradition continued in post-Confederation Canada, as the new central government turned to the task of providing schooling for the First Nations over whom it had acquired jurisdiction in the country's founding constitution. When Ottawa pondered schooling for First Nations in the West, the recommendations it received on the subject insisted that the residential schools should be denominational, not secular. It was unthinkable, said Nicholas Davin in his report to the federal government on schooling for Indigenous children, to deprive First Nations of "their simple Indian mythology" by subjecting them to "civilization" in the classroom, without providing something elevating in its place. As well, the churches could supply teachers fairly easily, thanks to the existence of volunteers with Christian training and evangelical zeal. "It must be obvious that to teach semi-civilized children is a more difficult task than to teach children with inherited aptitudes, whose training is, moreover, carried on at home." Missionary instructors were essential. "The advantage of calling in the aid of religion is, that there is a chance of getting an enthusiastic person, with, therefore, a motive power beyond anything pecuniary remuneration could supply. The work requires not only the energy but the patience of an enthusiast."[4] Thus, the die was cast from the earliest days of government-sponsored residential schooling. The first three industrial schools that

Canada set up in the West, in 1883, were operated by the churches, two
by the Oblates of the Roman Catholic Church and one by the Anglicans. As residential schools spread through the prairie West and British
Columbia in the 1880s and 1890s, and then into the more remote regions
of Ontario early in the twentieth century, the initial pattern of church-
state cooperation was maintained. This pattern was replicated over and
over again, as the system was extended to the North and, after 1929, to
the Maritimes in the form of a single Atlantic school at Schubenacadie,
Nova Scotia. For good or ill, the colonial partnership of church and state
prevailed in the Dominion of Canada.[5]

For their part, First Nations had not initially opposed schools operated by Christian missionaries. Their accommodating response to missionaries stemmed from their values and their approaches to dealing
with European newcomers. Throughout the lengthy history of Christian evangelization in Canada, one of the most striking features of the
interaction was the openness of Indigenous peoples to others' faiths.
Unlike Christians, they were ready to learn about the beliefs and sacred
practices of newcomers. Moreover, beginning noticeably in Ontario in
the 1830s and 1840s, some First Nations leaders adopted an instrumental approach to Euro-Canadian educational initiatives. Many of them
saw the schools that were being proposed, whether day or residential,
as potential aids for their communities in dealing with the large number
of Europeans who were taking over their lands. In fact, at a conference in
Orillia in 1846, a group of First Nations representatives not only agreed
to the creation of "manual labour schools," a nineteenth-century form
of residential schools, but pledged to support the institutions with one-
quarter of their annuities from the Crown for twenty-five years.[6] Similarly, when Canada negotiated treaties with First Nations on the plains
in the 1870s, government commissioners found that First Nations negotiators were interested in provisions that would guarantee their communities access to Euro-Canadian schooling in future. The leaders who
favoured non-Native schools, even though they were to be operated by
missionaries, had a clearly thought-out reason for doing so: they anticipated that these schools – including those established at Orillia in 1846
and Fort Carlton in the North-West Territories in 1876 – would equip
their children to deal with the newcomers, whose increasing numbers
otherwise represented a threat to Aboriginal survival.[7]

The history of Native denominational schooling shows as well that First
Nations quickly turned against church-run residential schools when the
institutions failed to deliver what Indigenous leaders expected of them.

The "manual labour schools" that chiefs at the 1846 Orillia Conference had pledged to support with a portion of their annuities soon alienated their Native supporters because the children were mistreated. The result was that First Nations communities in southern Ontario began to withhold their children and generally decline to cooperate with the missionaries. As early as the late 1850s, an inquiry by the colonial government found, for example, that the Chippewas of Sarnia, initially enthusiastic supporters of a residential school at nearby Munceytown, had come to oppose it. Although "the parents know well the great advantage which the education there obtained will be to their children, yet great difficulty is experienced by the Missionary and Superintendent to induce them to send them, or to allow them to remain a sufficient length of time to accomplish their education, and form new habits." Of the new "manual labour schools" the commissioners decided, "it is with great reluctance that we are forced to the conclusion that this benevolent experiment has been to a great extent a failure."[8]

In the post-Confederation period, the same pattern of Native response to custodial institutions continued in other regions. Although First Nations were often receptive to schooling for their children, the harsh regime and disappointing educational results that the young experienced soon turned the parents and home community against the schools. The care that students received at residential schools was often inadequate, in large part because the federal government began holding down expenditures on First Nations schooling as early as 1892. While the churches that operated the schools contributed to their maintenance from their own funds, the financial support that was available from the religious institutions and the government never seemed to stretch far enough. Accommodation, food, dress, health care, and recreation all were substandard. Moreover, although, as Davin had predicted, the staff might have been imbued with missionary zeal, frequently they were ill-qualified pedagogues. Classroom inadequacies were compounded by other considerations. Because the schools were run on the "half-day system," in which students spent half their day in a classroom receiving academic instruction and half working around the school, they were disadvantaged in learning, particularly from teachers who were not always well trained themselves. In addition, at some times of the year, such as harvest, most students who were big enough to help with farm labour might be pulled out of class for days or even weeks on end.[9] This sort of experience was not what parents had been led to expect of these schools. And, finally, children were subjected to an abusive teaching and

custodial regime in which their Aboriginal identity, culture, and practices were systematically denigrated.[10] It was little wonder that parents
who had been interested in Euro-Canadian schooling for its potential to
equip their offspring with useful knowledge and skills quickly turned
against the institutions and their operators who were the authors of such
mistreatment.

The missionaries who ran the residential schools found themselves
compromised by these developments. Most personnel who worked
in the schools were enthusiasts, even, in some cases, idealists, who
wanted to serve their God and help people they perceived as less fortunate than themselves. But if they experienced failure and resistance
from the students or their parents, most found it difficult to accept the
force of the implied criticisms and adjust their behaviour. Often, they
interpreted resistance as rejection of the secular and religious education they offered, something that missionaries found hard to accept. It
was easier to blame the students for the shortcomings of the schools
than to face up to the reality that the system the Canadian government
and the churches had created was not succeeding. As anthropologist
Noel Dyck has observed, "instead of wondering why aboriginal people do not do as they are told, in spite of the costs that this entails, tutelage agents and institutions obtusely ignore their own involvement
in the relationship and ask, 'why don't they help themselves?' The
motives of the tutor typically remain unexamined and unquestioned,
but only at the cost of demeaning aboriginal peoples and denying that
they have or ever will have the capacity to organize their own lives."[11]
The few missionary workers who did ask questions of, or protest to,
their church superiors found that their efforts were not appreciated
or heeded.

For their part, church authorities at the various denominational head
offices found themselves caught in the partnership they had forged
with the federal government. It was difficult to protest strenuously
against the actions of a Department of Indian Affairs, which provided
some of the funds needed to carry out the churches' evangelical mission. The government had the power to approve a new residential
school for a denomination or not, to increase the number of authorized
students in a school for which Ottawa would pay a per capita annual
grant, or to provide funding for major school maintenance and reno-
vation projects. The result of the government's dominance in financial
matters was that the denominations avoided criticizing Indian policy.
The contrast with the United States was striking. There, in the late

nineteenth and early twentieth century, it was often Christians, clerical and lay, who participated in the "Friends of the Indians" movement that criticized and pushed the Bureau of Indian Affairs to improve its policies and administration.[12] In Canada, the churches had made themselves complicit in policy through their partnership with government and, for the most part, they remained silent. The point was made implicitly by Indian Affairs deputy minister D.C. Scott when he told an American audience in 1916 that Canadians, unlike their southern neighbours, were satisfied with allowing government and churches to deal with Native people.[13]

The behaviour of the various churches involved in residential schooling illustrated the problems they faced in the twentieth century. The Anglicans' experience with their residential schools showed how conflicted some denominations were. Early in the new century, an energetic Anglican layman, Sam Blake, took over leadership of the denomination's Missionary Society of the Church in Canada. Blake's initial inquiries into the operation of the schools quickly convinced him that the residential institutions were a failure and should be closed down. A major reason for his negative view was the realization that accommodations and health care were so bad that the children in the schools on the prairies experienced horrific rates of morbidity and mortality. Blake's determination to eliminate the Anglican boarding schools was welcomed by the deputy minister of Indian Affairs, Frank Pedley, who also was interested in reducing the number of the institutions. But, when the Anglican head office in Toronto proposed closing some of its schools, church leaders in Winnipeg and other western centres rebelled and prevented the changes. It was left to the deputy minister to move instead to a new administrative regime that was supposed to improve the schools. So far as the health issues were concerned, Dr Peter Bryce, a government medical officer, uncovered and attempted to report on noxious conditions in prairie schools, but was dismissed and his damning report was never released by the government (he published it himself in 1922).[14] As Blake's abortive attempt to reform the Anglican schools illustrated, there were different points of view about the residential schools and how they should be handled within the denominations.

By the Great War, all the denominations involved in residential schools – Roman Catholic, Anglican, Methodist, and Presbyterian – were aware to some extent of problems in the establishments they ran. But there were sharp differences between them as to what should be done to counteract these problems. The Roman Catholics, who operated by far the largest number of schools, were the most attached to maintaining the system. Many of their schools were run by the missionary order the Oblates of Mary Immaculate, although several were operated by female religious, and all depended heavily on the labour of hundreds of nuns. The non-Catholic churches were losing their enthusiasm for Indigenous missions in general in the twentieth century. Most of them were more enamoured of other mission fields, such as the Indian subcontinent or East Asia. The Anglicans, who operated about one-third of the Canadian residential schools, were, as the experience of Sam Blake had shown, divided between missionaries in the field and a small group at head office in Toronto who considered phasing out schools. A similar situation prevailed with the Methodists, the third-largest player in residential schooling, where there was a division of opinion between missionaries in the West and their national superintendent, Dr Alexander Sutherland, in Toronto. The Presbyterians, who operated only a handful of residential schools, appeared not to hold strong views on the institutions. In any event, the differences of opinion among the Christian denominations that worked in uneasy partnership with government in Indian Affairs stood as an obstacle to any reduction or elimination of the institutions.

The churches' opposition to reform deterred government from doing anything about the problems. By the interwar period it was well known in both governmental and church circles that the schools were serving Native students poorly in accommodation and care, as well as in the classroom. Periodic investigations by both Indian Affairs and some of the denominations had turned up evidence of serious problems. The arrival of the Great Depression, with its crippling impact on government revenues and churches' donations, exacerbated the situation. The Department of Indian Affairs cut the annual per capita grants that supported the costs of maintaining and teaching Indigenous children by a drastic 15 per cent during the decade. As well, it appears that the government's straitened finances during the 1930s created either a reason or an excuse for refusing to build any more residential schools or replace any that had burned down.[15] On the eve of the Second World War, both government and churches were in an uneasy holding pattern. The churches' sole initiative at this time was to set aside their strong denominational rivalries to cooperate in lobbying Ottawa for an increase in the per capita grants to run the schools. Although the federal government restored the per capita grant in two stages by 1939, no changes occurred in other areas of schools policy prior to the 1940s.[16]

The Second World War and its aftermath would stimulate another attempt to deal with the issue of First Nations schooling. The war against Nazi Germany and Imperial Japan, with their virulently racist ideologies, had focused the attention of many Canadians on the issue of racism. When they pondered the damage that such beliefs could do, they could not easily avoid seeing the inherently racist foundation of Canadian Indian policy, including educational policy. Wallace Robb, an Ontario poet who was a parent with a strong interest in First Nations, wrote the *Globe and Mail* in 1944 to say, "We who have sons and daughters in the fight and who pray and work from dawn to dusk, that honor and right shall prevail in this struggle are not going to permit our own officials to act like Huns towards the Indians right under our noses."[17] In general, the political classes were conscious that change was needed. As an Alberta member of Parliament put it, "the Canadian people as a whole are interested in the problem of the Indians; they have become aware that the country has been negligent in the matter of looking after the Indians and they are anxious to remedy our shortcomings. Parliament and the country is [*sic*] 'human rights' conscious."[18] This heightened consciousness led in 1946 to the creation of a joint committee of senators and members of Parliament to recommend revisions of the Indian Act after considering briefs and oral representations from a variety of stakeholders. Naturally, Native education attracted a great deal of comment, including from representatives of the churches who delivered schooling in both day and custodial institutions.

On the whole, representatives of the churches who appeared before the Special Joint Committee on the Indian Act (SJC) supported the view of the Department of Indian Affairs that the ultimate goal of Native schooling was integration. The schools, whether day or residential, were to prepare the young to "join the mainstream" of Canadian society. In that sense, there was a consensus among the non-Native people who made representations to the SJC that the schools should be assimilative in character. Understandably, that was not the view of the Aboriginal groups who sent briefs and testified before the committee. Rather, they continued to emphasize, as Aboriginal peoples long had, that schooling should promote economic development, not cultural assimilation.

The Aboriginal spokespeople differed on whether the schools should continue to be denominationally operated or not, as well as whether there still was a role for residential institutions, but were united in their rejection of assimilation.[19] If a single opinion can be divined, the Native viewpoint was expressed by Joseph Dreaver of the Union of Saskatchewan Indians, who said flatly, "Our greatest need to-day is proper education."[20] As always, First Nations were not opposed to Euro-Canadian schooling, only to aspects of it that threatened their identity.

The testimony of the various churches before the SJC revealed that views were shifting within their ranks. (By this time, the Methodist Church and most of the Presbyterian Church had joined with the Congregational Church to form the United Church of Canada. The churches involved in residential school remained four: Roman Catholics, Anglicans, the United Church, and a small group of continuing Presbyterians.) Although all the churches expressed public support for the Department of Indian Affairs' preferred goal of education for integration, privately the Roman Catholics, Anglicans, and Presbyterians had reservations about that plan. As the head of the Oblate schools commission explained, the fear was that the reduction in the emphasis on religion in Native schools that the government favoured would lead to their failure. Such a failure would bring about Native children's attendance at integrated public schools that would prove so uncongenial that they would drop out even earlier than they did in schools run by the religious organizations.[21] Otherwise, all the churches agreed on integration as at least a long-term goal. The biggest deviation from the church consensus came from the United Church of Canada, which informed the SJC that "the time has come seriously to consider the establishment of Indian education on a completely non-sectarian basis."[22]

The underlying differences among the denominations became more obvious in the aftermath of the SJC. While the committee was deliberating, Father Plourde of the Oblate schools administration worked energetically to encourage First Nations who were on reserves served by Roman Catholic priests to lobby against the elimination of denominational control of and religious instruction in the schools.[23] When the SJC reported its recommendations to the government, the opponents of secularization found that they had more work to do. The committee recommended changes to "those sections of the Act which pertain to education in order to prepare Indian children to take their place as citizens. Your committee, therefore, recommends that wherever and whenever possible Indian children should be educated in association with other children."[24] Once more Father Plourde and the Oblates mounted a vigorous lobbying effort against any drastic changes to schooling, securing the support of the Catholic hierarchy to put pressure on the cabinet of Prime Minister St Laurent. Partly as a consequence of this political arm-twisting, the overhaul of the Indian Act in 1951 left Native education still under denominational administration.[25]

The experience of the Special Joint Committee was revealing. Its hearings indicated that all the churches recognized the necessity to be less oppressive in schooling, although most of them still favoured using the schools for some form of cultural assimilation. Now, the assimilative policy bore the less obnoxious label "education for citizenship." The SJC experience also highlighted sharp and growing differences among the denominations. At one end of the spectrum, the United Church had taken a stand for non-sectarian education; at the other, the Roman Catholics had stood strongly for the continuation of denominational residential schooling. No one seemed to notice or care that these positions did not reflect the views that most First Nations representations had espoused.

The twin processes of evolution and differentiation among the churches continued in the next phase of educational policy aimed at First Nations. By the time the Special Joint Committee reported, Indian Affairs had come down strongly in favour of what it termed "integrated schooling." This policy, which was consistent with the goals of education for citizenship and preparing Native youth for integration into non-Native society and economy, was based on both fiscal and ideological considerations, as far as bureaucrats were concerned. The policy anticipated de-emphasizing residential schooling in favour of negotiated agreements with local, publicly supported school boards to accommodate Native students in off-reserve schools. It had the virtue of moving away from the practice of segregation that had long characterized Native schooling policy but that, by the mid-1940s, was in disfavour. Another point in integration's favour was the fact that its pursuit would allow Indian Affairs to continue its policy of not building more residential schools, thereby reducing the capital costs of Native schooling for the government. Because the Native birth rate had begun to accelerate dramatically by the 1940s, a policy that avoided larger annual outlays for capital construction was attractive to the government. The "icing on the cake" for supporters was the fact that integration had been endorsed by the eminent anthropologist Diamond Jenness when he appeared before the Special Joint Committee. For Jenness, integrated schooling was one item in his revealingly titled "Plan for Liquidating Canada's Indian Problems within 25 Years." Other elements included the eventual elimination of the reserve system and total integration of Native people into Canadian society.[26]

The issue of integration revealed growing differences in the churches' views on education. As could be expected, the United Church, which had advocated non-sectarian schools for Aboriginal children, was strongly supportive of integration. In most provinces, Aboriginal children who attended state-supported schools would attend public schools that officially did not have a religious affiliation or character. The Anglicans decided to move the administrative headquarters for their missions and schools (the Indian School Administration – ISA) to Ottawa to ensure better communication with bureaucrats. By 1961 the head of that administration was reporting that

> the Anglican Church officially is supporting the Federal Government in its plan to integrate native pupils into white school classrooms as soon as reasonably possible and with the full knowledge and co-operation of the parents. This plan, in principle, is, we believe, to the ultimate good of the Indian children. However, some of the I.S.A. Principals as well as the Superintendent are becoming alarmed at the form this integration is taking. It had been anticipated that integration would be of a "selective" nature but in some areas it has become "indiscriminate" and we feel the success of the integration programme is being hazarded by the zeal of those who want to do too much too quickly. Our Church ought to watch very carefully the development of the integration programme and, if it becomes necessary, be bold enough to change its policy.[27]

The Roman Catholics were the naysayers in this chorus on integration. For Catholics, exposing their charges to non-Aboriginal children in integrated, public schools was equivalent to endangering their souls. Catholic social philosophy strongly favoured schooling the young in denominational institutions under clerical direction. Moreover, missionaries and school administrators who worked in the schools noted that First Nations children felt ill at ease in integrated classrooms for a number of social reasons, ranging from their lack of exposure to the opposite sex in residential schools to the fact that they did not have the same kind of clothes that non-Native children sported and usually did not have pocket money either. And then there was the ugly reality, which First Nations high school students at the Jesuit residential school in Spanish, Ontario, pointed out: the non-Aboriginal students would not accept the Aboriginal students.[28] The Oblates who administered Catholic residential schools tried to warn Indian Affairs officials that integrated schooling would be a disaster, but without any success. Unfortunately, their warnings were proved all too accurate.

The social and ideological currents that had helped push the Department of Indian Affairs to adopt integrated schooling also worked on the Canadian churches involved with Native missions through the 1950s and 1960s. Increasing awareness of international developments such as the decolonization movement that swept the Global South after the Second World War stimulated both Aboriginal groups and missionaries within Canada. Among First Nations, the current would culminate in the adoption of the notion of a Fourth World of Indigenous peoples linked by a shared experience of recent or ongoing colonialism. The Fourth World was a collectivity of peoples beyond the traditional three: capitalist, communist, and "developing." Like others in this Fourth World, First Nations leaders began to see themselves as dependent, internal colonies within the state. Shuswap leader George Manuel, who served as national chief of the pan-Canadian National Indian Brotherhood for the period 1970–6, was the founding president of the World Council of Indigenous Peoples in 1975–82. Manuel's era of prominence marked the cresting of the Fourth World concept in Indian Country.[29]

Within the Department of Indian Affairs, the postwar fashion that had the greatest currency was the use of social science methods to survey and analyse the conditions that prevailed within First Nations. It had been obvious for a long time that Indigenous peoples in Canada were not faring well. In the 1960s, bureaucrats sponsored a wide-ranging examination, under the leadership of anthropologist Harry Hawthorn of the University of British Columbia, of the social and economic conditions that prevailed among First Nations. The Hawthorn Report, as his research team's 1965–6 final report became known, revealed the stark reality of poverty, poor health, wretched housing, and other marks of marginalization. Hawthorn underlined a bitter irony in the fact that, as the original peoples of the land, First Nations were "citizens plus" and deserved better, not inferior, treatment from the state.[30] More irony was imminent. In 1969, the government of Pierre Elliott Trudeau attempted to terminate First Nations people as a separate category of citizens with its ill-advised White Paper on Indian policy. A revealing indicator of how attitudes and relationships had changed in Native-newcomer relations was the emergence, within a year, of a ferocious, united opposition to the White Paper from First Nations, which forced the federal government to recant and suspend the policy proposals it had championed.

The missionary churches inevitably were influenced by these ideological and political currents, as well as by concerns specific to their own mandates in the 1950s and 1960s. Winds of change were sweeping through the Roman Catholic Church both internationally and within Canada. The pontificate of John XXIII marked the beginning of the Second Vatican Council (Vatican II, 1962–5), which reformed many aspects of church ritual and theology. As well, in South and Central America the influence of the worldwide decolonization movement was reflected in the growing popularity among Catholic clergy of a strongly reformist set of doctrines that came to be known as liberation theology. Latin American clergy influenced by this movement emphasized that Jesus and the early church had found support among the poor and marginalized, the ordinary people, not the highly placed in society. The phrase that epitomized this part of liberation theology was "a preferential option for the poor," which meant that the church should give preference to the poor and marginalized, not the affluent and powerful. The decolonizing implications of such religious thinking in Latin America and elsewhere in the western hemisphere were obvious. Within Canada, specifically, the strongest gusts in the Catholic Church were felt in Quebec, where the 1960s brought a period of rapid institutional modernization and secularization known as the Quiet Revolution. Church attendance and the incidence of "vocations" to religious orders dramatically declined. To a lesser extent, reformist impulses were strengthened in the Catholic Church in the rest of Canada as well, though probably more as a consequence of Vatican II.

The influences that worked to move the Anglican Church of Canada towards a revised approach to Aboriginal peoples were more homegrown than was the case with the Roman Catholics. Those responsible for the Native missions and residential schools watched with growing unease the evolution of federal government policy in schooling for

Indigenous youth. A direct consequence of the increased government financial support that became noticeable by the latter 1950s was waning church influence in setting policy and administering the schools. By 1965, the process had gone so far that the Bishop of the Arctic noted that a "frustrated R.C. Principal" commented, "We have so little control any more that we might as well hand over our residential schools to the government to manage, since all we seem to be doing is providing cheap labour for them."[31] When the federal government announced in 1969 that it intended to phase out all the residential schools, replacing them with hostels for the children in remote regions where families lived away from the school sites, there was hardly a ripple of reaction from the Anglican Church. The single article on the subject that appeared in the Anglican national newspaper, the *Canadian Churchman*, reported simply that the church had transferred a dozen of its residential schools to the government and would withdraw from the operation of three others in the Mackenzie River region by the end of March 1970.[32]

Part of the reason for the Anglicans' low-key reaction to the government's decision on residential schools was that they were caught up in a radical re-evaluation of their approach to Aboriginal people in general. The Canadian experience in part reflected efforts within the worldwide Anglican Church to "affirm the unity of the human race," in line with an injunction the Archbishop of Canterbury had delivered during a sermon to the Anglican Congress in Toronto in 1963. The Canadian church's synod in 1965 confronted the Anglican role in colonialism in Canada and called for renewed effort to work with Indigenous peoples to improve the dismal conditions in which too many lived. Another synod in 1967 allocated money to carry out research to determine a more appropriate and effective policy towards Indigenous peoples. The result was *Beyond Traplines*, which became known as the Hendry Report, released in the spring of 1969.[33] Its author, Charles (Chick) Hendry, a professor of social work at the University of Toronto and active United Church layman, rather pointedly asked in his subtitle, "Does the Church Really Care?"[34] "The really crucial question," Hendry said bluntly, "is does the Church mean what it says about wanting to minister to Canada's native peoples? Or will it be content with token measures: In man-in-the-street language, the time has come for churches 'to put up or shut up.' The church must face the fact that – whatever have been its merits or deficiencies in the past – present social programs are having little effect on the massive poverty and alienation of the native people."[35] The report called on Anglicans to work with Indigenous people, as well as other churches, to build support for programs that would assist Native peoples to improve their living conditions and education. Hendry urged Anglicans to act, saying that the "Church dare not hesitate to act as a pressure group vis-à-vis governments, courts or industry whenever some Christian principle is involved in dealing with the Indians and Eskimos, particularly in efforts to improve the laws."[36]

Beyond Traplines provided a hard-hitting and challenging assessment of the Anglicans' work with Indigenous peoples. It bluntly recounted and criticized the pursuit of assimilation in which the church had been complicit for such a long time, warning that the usual authoritarian, top-down approaches had to be abandoned. It called on the Anglican Church to "engage native peoples in the administration of residential schools, giving them a voice also in the reform of the curriculum, particularly in regard to native languages."[37] In addition, Hendry argued, "top priority must be directed to changes in basic attitudes, especially attitudes toward native peoples, but also attitudes toward other churches working with native peoples and toward other agencies, including government." "The most fundamental need in this realignment of attitudes, which calls for an explicit reformulation of goals, is to find effective ways of respecting and releasing the resources of indigenous leadership."[38] As well, Beyond Traplines called for a modification of Anglican Church governance in order to create the institutions it would need to introduce, and operate within, a sort of partnership with Indigenous people and other churches that Hendry believed had to replace the old paternalistic approach.[39] Thanks to Beyond Traplines, Indigenous issues began to take a much more prominent place in discussions and decisionmaking within the Anglican communion. Hendry's report would lead to substantial changes in governance and expenditures, shifts that would over the next several decades create a more prominent and self-determining role for Native members of the church.

The United Church noticeably lagged behind the Anglicans in its response to Aboriginal issues. During the 1960s, the church underwent a shift in its evangelistic approach from a focus on matters of individual morality to concerns about social justice. But its engagement with Aboriginal peoples remained weak. "While missions with Aboriginal communities became more culturally sensitive, and 'Indian Rights' found their way to the pages of E&SS [Division of Evangelism and Social Service] reports, the church was far from seeking full participation of its Aboriginal members, or from articulating its collective shame in that colonizing relationship."[40] Into the 1970s, the church remained supportive of causes affecting Aboriginal peoples but largely unresponsive to the needs, desires, and criticisms of its own Aboriginal members.[41]

In the 1970s, another shift occurred in the missionary churches' approach to their relations with Indigenous people. This movement was characterized by a greater acceptance of more secular tactics and a tendency to enter into partnerships with Native people rather than proposing to act as leaders and tutors. Such a change was not restricted to the churches. The Indian-Eskimo Association of Canada (IEAC) was a similar example from the secular world. Founded in 1960s as a spinoff of the Canadian Association for Adult Education, the IEAC's purpose was "to study the problems of natives in communities when natives were off the reserve." In 1973 it moved its headquarters from Toronto to Ottawa and changed its name to the Canadian Association in Support of Native Peoples.[42] A similar process occurred with the missionary churches that had operated residential schools. In 1975 they joined five other churches to found Project North, a coalition dedicated to the support of Indigenous groups' rights and to campaigns to protect and advance those rights.[43] The transformation underpinning such moves was notable for at least three features: first, it represented a much more ecumenical approach to Native affairs, in line with what the Hendry Report had recommended; second, it took a far more secular approach than the churches had emphasized separately; and, third, it undertook an effort, at least as far as Project North was concerned, to work with Indigenous organizations as they pursued their own agenda.

Project North also reflected a new reality in Canada's economy. Many of the development projects that had a direct impact on Aboriginal groups were taking place in northern regions of the country, where population was sparse. As the Anglican Church's newspaper put it, Project North's goal was "to increase the capacity of the Church to deal with ethical issues raised by the northern development boom."[44] By the time Project North was founded, two of the most strenuously contested of these developments already had occurred. Between 1972 and 1975, the James Bay Cree and Inuit of Quebec battled the government of the province over the James Bay Hydro Project, a proposal to harness a large portion of the James Bay watershed that would, in the process, inundate lands traditionally used by Indigenous peoples. The resistance of the James Bay Cree had led to a settlement, the James

Bay and Northern Quebec Agreement in 1975, the first treaty negotiated between the Crown and First Nations since 1921.[45] The dynamics
underlying the Mackenzie Valley pipeline controversy were similar to
those in the James Bay Hydro case. Indigenous people in the North
opposed a proposal to bring natural gas from Alaska via the Mackenzie
River Delta to the Canadian south and the United States. Their opposition was based both on environmental concerns about the effect of the
pipeline on the game and fish on which they relied, and on the fact
that their Aboriginal title to the land had not been dealt with. Native
opposition led to the appointment of British Columbia Supreme Court
Justice Thomas Berger, formerly counsel for the Nisga'a in the *Calder*
case, which dealt with the question of Aboriginal title, to consider the
likely environmental, social, and economic impact of a pipeline. Berger's 1977 report, *Northern Frontier, Northern Homeland*, recommended
a ten-year pause on any energy project in the North until better planning and regulation could be set up and Native land claims could be
resolved. Project North and its individual member churches forcefully
supported northern First Nations on the Mackenzie Valley pipeline
issue.

Through the remainder of the 1970s and well into the 1980s, the
churches, through Project North, continued to stand in solidarity with
First Nations in opposition to resource corporations and the governments that enthusiastically supported their projects. Two of the most
heated confrontations involved First Nations in British Columbia. The
first, the Nisga'a of the Nass Valley of northern British Columbia, had a history, stretching back to the 1880s, of standing up for their rights in the
face of governments that ignored them. Indeed, they had taken Aboriginal title litigation to court, which had resulted in a breakthrough in the
1973 *Calder* case and subsequently the federal government's creation
of an Office of Native Claims to deal with Aboriginal claims. In the
early 1980s, the Nisga'a were opposing the Amax Mining Corporation,
which wanted to reopen a mine on Nisga'a land and dump effluent that
contained mercury, lead, arsenic, and radium into Alice Arm. In 1981,
Anglicans bought a handful of shares in Amax Mining and opposed
the project unsuccessfully at a meeting of shareholders of the mining
company. Success was mixed, however, as the mine continued to function until 1982, when the company closed it.[46] The churches and Project
North similarly offered support to a First Nation in northern Alberta
that was facing the deterioration of its traditional territory as gas and
oil exploration went on, with the enthusiastic support of the provincial

government. The Lubicon Lake Cree, who had never entered a treaty and therefore considered their Aboriginal title still to be intact, also had a lengthy history of wrangling with governments over their rights. The churches steadfastly supported the Lubicon in their campaign for recognition of their rights, though again without success.[47] In 1985, Project North entered into a partnership with the Haida nation located in Haida Gwaii, off northern British Columbia, to resist provincially approved logging on their traditional territory. Like the Mackenzie Valley, Amax Mining, and Lubicon cases, the Haida land claim combined environmental concerns with those about Aboriginal title. The struggle of the Haida and Project North would stretch into the 1990s and beyond.[48]

The churches' efforts to stand in solidarity with Aboriginal peoples entered a new phase in the 1980s as the churches adjusted both their organization and focus. In 1982, the members of Project North reorganized and renamed themselves the Aboriginal Rights Coalition (ARC), in recognition that the issues that confronted them and Aboriginal peoples also occurred in other parts of the country. Moreover, Aboriginal peoples were facing a new issue. Between the late 1970s and 1982, the federal government had sought to renew the country's constitution to respond to the emergence of a strong separatist movement in Quebec that culminated, in 1976, in the election of the province's first Parti Québécois government. Aboriginal leaders struggled to ensure that their rights and issues were recognized by the first ministers as the country stumbled towards the creation of a new constitution. When the new founding document was adopted in April 1982, ironically without the support of the Quebec provincial government, it contained a provision, section 35, that said that "The existing Aboriginal and treaty rights of the Aboriginal peoples of Canada are hereby recognized and affirmed." Yet, because the reformed constitution did not spell out what those "Aboriginal and treaty rights" were, government leaders agreed that four first ministers' conferences would be held between 1983 and 1987 to define what section 35 was protecting. Throughout this struggle, ARC supported Aboriginal political leaders' campaign, culminating in a united effort at the final conference on section 35 in 1987 to have self-government entrenched in the constitution as one of the rights protected.[49]

On the eve of the final first ministers' conference on the constitution, the churches in ARC issued what they called "A New Covenant." This name evoked historical understandings heavily freighted with religious significance: the ancient Israelites had had a covenant with Jehovah, and

Jesus Christ was often referred to as a new covenant between God and his people. Western Canadian First Nations believed that the treaties they concluded in the 1870s were also covenants – agreements in which the Great Spirit and the Christians' God took part.[50] For the churches, using the term "new covenant" indicated the seriousness with which they took the matter they were discussing:

> Indeed, the current road of constitutional talks may be the last opportunity for developing a new covenant between Aboriginal and non-Aboriginal peoples in this country. In retrospect, it has become all too clear that the old covenants, including many of the treaties, have not served the demands of justice. Initially believed by Aboriginal peoples to be instruments of friendship and peace, the treaties were often misused and broken, without consent, by the newcomers who wanted this land for their own.
>
> ... There are moral and spiritual dimensions to making and keeping covenants. These dimensions must be part of the task of creating a new covenant involving Aboriginal peoples in Canada today. A new covenant would recognize the rights and responsibilities of Indian, Inuit and Metis to be distinct peoples and cultures. A new covenant should affirm their rights and responsibilities as self-determining nations and societies within Canada. A new Covenant would also enhance Aboriginal peoplehood in this country. These are the major challenges at the heart of the current constitutional talks on Aboriginal rights.[51]

Clearly, the missionary churches had travelled a long way in the four decades since the hearings of the Special Joint Committee on the Indian Act.

A vital force pushing the churches to be more assertive partners and supporters of Aboriginal peoples were the Aboriginal members of the various denominations. Particularly in the case of the Anglican and United Churches, the role of Native adherents had been growing and increasingly influential in public policy matters. The Anglicans, although they had been, with the Hendry Report, the first of the missionary churches to tackle Aboriginal issues, were themselves slow to reflect a new attitude in their governance. A Sub-committee for Native Affairs, later renamed the Council on Native Affairs, was set up in 1973, but it did not adequately include and reflect Aboriginal members effectively. Matters began to change after a week-long Native Convocation in 1988 raised the issue of a more substantial Native voice in church decision-making.

The national governing body agreed that changes at all levels were required.[52] Once revelations of abuse at residential schools began to surface in the early 1990s, the Anglicans took more effective action. A Residential School Working Group was created, with equal representation by Indigenous and non-Indigenous members, a full-time member of staff, and half a million dollars to study the residential school issue. While the Anglican official responsible for Aboriginal matters remarked that these actions were appreciated, he added that "some members expressed concern that the Church move beyond mere study and the allocation of money. The key to the Church's response must be a change in attitude towards native people."[53]

The United Church went through a similar process of awakening to the presence and significance of its Aboriginal membership. By the early 1980s, the upper levels of the church bureaucracy were trying to figure out how to establish a more appropriate relationship with Aboriginal people.[54] A rising awareness of First Nations' dissatisfaction with the church was evident in the September 1980 issue of the *Observer*, the church's national news monthly. The Reverend Stan McKay, an Ojibwe minister in Manitoba and future moderator of the United Church, criticized his denomination for its relations with Native people, charging "there were plenty of people in the church 'who want to be my father, but few are interested in being my brother.'" He noted that, in the North, other denominations were taking over Native congregations that were frustrated by the unresponsiveness of the old churches. "Pentecostals are filling the gap because they allow the people some say in decisions. Our church doesn't."[55]

The United Church moved gradually towards making a place for Indigenous adherents in governance, starting with an all-Indigenous presbytery – the unit above individual local congregations – for three years in the early 1980s. In 1984, the church's General Council passed a lengthy resolution that addressed the background and task at hand. It noted, in part:

WHEREAS present church structures have been unable to facilitate the involvement of native members in decision making processes about their own future; and

WHEREAS the native church has different ways of approaching decision making and also has different priorities from the majority of the
members in the United Church; and
    WHEREAS the history of mission in Canada has included elements of
colonization, paternalism and racism; ...
    THEREFORE BE IT RESOLVED that the 30th General Council approve
in principle the continued development of native presbyteries and the formation of a Native United Church Conference which will be national in
nature.[56]

In 1986, a church official observed that Native delegates held a consultation and concluded that they wanted the all-Native presbytery
upgraded to a conference of the church: "the message to pass the power
on to the Native people was pretty compelling. I think we should take
it seriously," a church staffer noted.[57] In response to the increasing
requests of Native adherents that the church address their issues, the
General Council executive in November 1987 created the All Native
Circle Conference.[58]

    More fundamental demands were also at hand. In the spring of 1985,
Alberta Billy, a representative from Cape Mudge, British Columbia,
on the church's national executive, presented a report from the Native
Ministries (an advisory body within the church) that stated bluntly,
"The United Church of Canada owes the Native Peoples an apology
and make clear that our spiritualism was in fact, our natural sacredness
and not paganism as the missionaries implied." The General Council
executive quickly responded with a resolution that affirmed that "the
United Church of Canada owes the native peoples of Canada an apology and makes clear that native spirituality was in fact, their natural
sacredness and not paganism as the missionaries implied."[59] This resolution was followed by more than a year of preparation before the topic
was discussed at the General Council meeting of 1986 at Laurentian
University in Sudbury.

    The General Council at Sudbury was a dramatic affair. The Native
delegates reiterated their request for an apology and then withdrew
to await a decision. The ensuing debate was lengthy and sometimes
contentious. It was not so much that delegates opposed acknowledging
the injustices that had been done, including sometimes by the church
itself, to Native people. Rather, the concern of some was that admit-
ting that evangelization had been abusive of Native spirituality might
be misread as denying the validity of the Christian message, including

1.1 The United Church's Native Council addresses the General
Council, Sudbury, 1986. Reverend Stan McKay is at the podium;
Alberta Billy is directly behind McKay.

the importance of Jesus Christ, God's second covenant. Eventually, a
consensus was reached. About 500 delegates trooped out to the parking
lot, where their Native colleagues were gathered. Moderator Bob Smith
made the apology:

> Long before my people journeyed to this land your people were here, and
> you received from your elders an understanding of creation, and of the
> Mystery that surrounds us all that was deep, and rich and to be treas-
> ured. We did not hear you when you shared your vision. In our zeal to
> tell you the good news of Jesus Christ we were closed to the value of your
> spirituality.
>
> We confused western ways and culture with the depth and breadth and
> length and height of the gospel of Christ. We imposed our civilization as
> a condition of accepting the Gospel. We tried to make you like us and in
> doing so we helped to destroy the vision that made you what you were.

As a result, you, and we, are poorer and the image of the Creator in us is twisted, blurred and we are not what we are meant by God to be.

We ask you to forgive us and to walk together with us in the spirit of Christ so that our peoples may be blessed and God's creation healed.[60]

Clearly, the first United Church attempt at an apology addressed only part of the story from the past – it confronted evangelization in general, not the residential school legacy.

By the time the other churches involved in residential schooling apologized, the context had shifted sharply. In the wake of the Oka crisis that occurred in the summer of 1990, which raised the profile of Native issues in general, revelations started to come out about problems with the schools. In particular, a prime-time interview in October 1990 on the English CBC television network with Phil Fontaine, at the time chief of the Assembly of Manitoba Chiefs, focused attention on residential schooling as an especially egregious example of the ills that settler colonialism had created for Indigenous peoples.[61] And the seventy-seven-day confrontation at Oka, Quebec, between the Mohawk of Kanesatake and their supporters and the Quebec provincial police and Canadian army had aroused great interest in issues of Native-newcomer history in the country. Consequently, when other churches turned to express regret for the problems their work had caused for Indigenous people in the past, they concentrated on the residential schools in their remarks.

The Roman Catholics led off with two apologies. In the spring of 1991, a National Meeting on Indian Residential Schools, which was attended by some of the Canadian church's bishops, representatives of orders that had been involved in residential schooling, and a number of First Nations lay people, issued a "statement" that expressed regret at the pain and suffering that many Indigenous people had experienced and recognized that the "negative experiences" of residential schooling were part of "the indignities and injustices suffered by aboriginal peoples in our country." Further, the document pledged Catholic solidarity with Aboriginal peoples, reiterated the church's respect for "the dignity and value of their cultures and spiritualities" and promised to "support aboriginal peoples in pressing governments at all levels to respond to their legitimate aspirations."[62]

1.2 Oblate Doug Crosby apologizes for the order's role in residential schools, Lac Ste Anne, Alberta, July 1991.

That summer, at Lac Ste Anne, Alberta, a site of traditional First Nations spiritual observances and a place of pilgrimage for Roman Catholic Native people, the Reverend Douglas Crosby, president of the Oblate Conference of Canada, offered a homily and apology on behalf of the order. He said the Oblates had come to realize that they had failed to understand some of Aboriginal people's "cultural experiences and have thought to be bad what was strange in Aboriginal people's spiritual expressions," blaming this shortcoming on the assumptions of "superiority that the Europeans had when they arrived on Canadian shores." The order "apologize for the part we played in the cultural, ethnic, linguistic and religious imperialism that was part of the mentality with which the peoples of Europe first met the Aboriginal peoples and which consistently has lurked behind the way the native peoples of Canada have been treated by civil governments and the churches." The Oblates "apologize for the *existence of the schools themselves*, recognizing that the biggest abuse was not what happened in the schools, but that the schools themselves happened." And the missionaries "pledge ourselves to work with Native peoples in their efforts to recover their lands, their languages, their sacred traditions, and their rightful pride."[63] Although the Oblate apology was warmly received by those present at Lac Ste Anne, critics, both then and since, have pointed out that it fell short of recognizing the residential schools as a particular site of oppression and mistreatment, and minimized, in words like "for the part we played," the Oblates' role in causing the harm.[64]

The occasion of the Anglican apology, which was given in 1993, was the church's second Native Convocation or Sacred Circle. These gatherings of Indigenous and non-Indigenous Anglicans had developed as part of the church's efforts to recognize its Aboriginal adherents more fully. After several days of emotional discussion about residential schools, including a plea from a survivor that an apology for the schools be issued, the primate of the national church, Michael Peers, issued a "message" that contained an apology concerning the schools. The longer portion of the statement acknowledged the "pain and hurt experienced in the schools" and the fact that much of the "suffering [was] inflicted by my people." It also stated that the primate had heard and admired the stories of healing that survivors had delivered, and acknowledged that the church and its people were in need of healing too. "We failed you. We failed ourselves. We failed God." Peers continued, "I am sorry, more than I can say, that we were part of a system which took you and your children from home and family. I am sorry, more than I can say, that we tried to remake you in our image, taking from you your language and the signs of your identity. I am sorry, more than I can say, that in our schools so many were abused physically, sexually, culturally and emotionally. On behalf of the Anglican Church of Canada, I present our apology."[65] Although most Anglicans considered the primate's apology a major event, the restrained reaction of the Aboriginal delegates suggested that they did not view the apology as closing the book on residential

1.3 Primate Michael Peers delivers an apology for residential
schools on behalf of the Anglican Church, 1993.

schooling issues.[66] An Indigenous clergyman who was in attendance later recalled that the primate's apology came suddenly, and that he and his colleagues would have liked to have had time to consider it and frame their response. An Elder, however, "jumped the gun" and accepted the apology.[67]

The following year, the Presbyterian Church issued "Our Confession," a lengthy document that touched on many themes. It noted that it spoke "out of new understandings of our past, not out of any sense of being superior to those who have gone before us." After acknowledging that "we understand our mission and ministry in new ways, in part because of the testimony of Aboriginal peoples," it conceded that it had cooperated with the federal government's policy of assimilation and "encouraged the Government to ban some important spiritual practices through which Aboriginal peoples experienced the presence of the creator God." It admitted that "the Presbyterian Church in Canada presumed to know better than Aboriginal peoples what was needed for life," and "because of our insensitivity to Aboriginal cultures, we have demanded more of Aboriginal peoples than the gospel requires ... For the Church's presumption we ask forgiveness." Turning specifically to the residential school experience, the confession continued: "We confess that, with the encouragement and assistance of the Government of Canada, The Presbyterian Church in Canada agreed to take the children of Aboriginal peoples from their own homes and place them in Residential Schools." The schools deprived children "of their traditional ways, which were replaced with Euro-Canadian customs that were helpful in the process of assimilation." Moreover, "there was opportunity for sexual abuse, and some were so abused." The confession concluded, "For the Church's insensitivity we ask forgiveness."[68] The Presbyterian apology marked the end of an evolution in the statements that began in 1986 with the United Church. During the eight-year period, the apologies became ever more focused on the ills of the residential schools, a development that reflected both the increasing publicity being given to the schools issue in the early 1990s and the continued pressure of First Nations and Métis members of the individual churches.

When the United Church first apologized in 1986, the Native reaction had been instructive. First Nations delegates to the General Council at Sudbury that year responded that the moderator's "apology was not accepted," but it was nonetheless "joyfully received and acknowledged." They erected a stone cairn to mark the apology, but, "on the advice of the Elders who felt that time must be given to see how the church lives out the apology," it was left unfinished.[69] It was clear that Native people would wait to see if the United Church and the other denominations would act out – live – the apologies they articulated. In the 1990s, most of the churches did take steps to act on their expressions of remorse over the residential schools. Both the United and Anglican Churches created their own "healing funds," which provided money to survivors and their communities to carry out programs intended to facilitate dealing with and overcoming the trauma that the schools had left behind. The Roman Catholic Church had developed its own reconciliation program, *Returning to Spirit*, which some survivors found helpful. Given what was emerging in the 1990s about the residential schools and their problems, these were relatively modest initiatives, but they nevertheless were tokens of the churches' good intentions, and they were interpreted as such by the school survivors who had been watching and waiting since the General Council in Sudbury.

It was left to the United Church to round out the cycle of apologies and to show how far both the churches and their Aboriginal adherents had travelled since 1986. In 1998, Moderator Bill Phipps, who was trained both in law and theology, said, "I am here today as Moderator of The United Church of Canada to speak the words that many people have wanted to hear for a very long time." On behalf of his church, he apologized "for the pain and suffering that our church's involvement" in residential schooling caused, referring to "individuals who were physically, sexually and mentally abused as students at the Indian Residential Schools in which The United Church of Canada was involved. I offer you our most sincere apology. You did nothing wrong."[70] Later, Phipps recalled that the 1998 apology "was the result of hard negotiation with the church's lawyers, who wanted us to admit as little as possible ... The apology went through many drafts. The conditions in which it was drawn up explain why the 1998 apology was longer and 'less poetic' than the 1986 apology."[71] Seven years later, another moderator reiterated the apology from the church. This time, Native people who represented various divisions of the church "each placed a stone on the cairn and explained why they were adding their stone." Such actions reflected the decision of their Elders that the United Church had made meaningful efforts to promote reconciliation. The moderator later recalled that "several stones ('grandfathers') were mortared into place as a sign of significant steps that had been taken."[72]

The first efforts by Canadians to confront the legacy of residential schools were, appropriately, taken by the Christian denominations that had operated the institutions. With considerable difficulty, they faced up to their own role in the oppression that occurred in the schools. While also implicating the government of Canada in the sad history, they accepted their responsibility and expressed regret for it. For their part, Aboriginal people, as represented by Aboriginal members of the United Church of Canada, "received," acknowledged, and partially approved what the churches had done. The commemorative cairn at Laurentian University was started in 1986 but left incomplete. Stones were added to it in 2005 in recognition of the good intentions of, and efforts that had been made by, the churches, but the structure was still not quite complete. What would it take to lead Aboriginal people to say symbolically that the task of making amends was accomplished? Equally important, what would the federal government, the partner in administering the residential schools to which all the churches had pointed in their apologies, do about its role in the sorry story of the past?

2

The State Investigates:
The Royal Commission on
Aboriginal Peoples

Events in the summer of 1990 began to wake Canadians up to the negative aspects of Native-newcomer relations. An ancient dispute between a First Nation and a town in southwestern Quebec turned into a confrontation that lasted for two and a half months. The Oka Crisis, as the standoff was labelled, involved Canadian armed forces and galvanized Aboriginal people across the country in support of the First Nation at the centre of the conflict. Efforts by the prime minister of Canada to restore relations with Aboriginal peoples following the crisis included the creation of a royal commission with a mandate to examine the historical roots of the troubled relationship between Aboriginal peoples and government. This public inquiry, which sat from 1992 to 1996, publicized the record of Native-newcomer relations and injected that history into discussions about how to restore relations between Aboriginal and immigrant Canadians. Not only did its public consultations and research program emphasize history, but the commission's final report founded its analysis on a revision of the national narrative, which was new to most Canadians. In the course of carrying out its mandate, the royal commission also gave a platform to former residential school students to talk about their experiences at public sessions held across the country. Between the publicity given residential schooling through former students' testimony and the detailed account of the schools in its final report, the commission elevated residential schools to the status of a public policy issue and shone a spotlight on the federal government's role in both residential schools history and efforts to overcome the schools' legacy. Throughout the process, the history of Native-newcomer relations, including especially that related to residential schools, assumed enhanced prominence. The commission's contribution was important: until the problem of residential schools was exposed, Canadians could not deal with it.

Dramatic events in the 1990s concerning residential schools brought the federal government into the arena to pursue reconciliation. Often at the instigation of their Indigenous adherents, the Christian churches that had operated residential schools had raised reconciliation as an issue between 1986 and 1998. And, in the first half of the 1990s, residential school survivors seized the opportunity created by the work of the Royal Commission on Aboriginal Peoples (RCAP) to publicize the issue and engage a broad segment of the Indigenous population in reconciliation discussions. The federal government, the agency with the constitutional responsibility for "Indians and lands reserved for the Indians" and the authorizing power and principal funder of residential schools, had largely evaded engagement with either the history of residential schools or the challenge of reconciliation. In the 1990s, the government was brought into the discussion – belatedly, reluctantly, evasively – of what was to be done about the damage residential schools had wrought.

Between 11 July and 26 September 1990, the attention of many Canadians and others around the globe was riveted on Oka, Quebec. Early on the morning of 11 July, the Sûreté du Québec (SQ), Quebec's provincial police force, sent an armed detachment into the Pines, a forested area west of the town, to dislodge Mohawk protesters. A Native blockade of the area aimed to thwart a plan by the townsfolk to enlarge an adjacent nine-hole golf course to eighteen holes. The expansion of the golf course, which had been built in the 1960s over the opposition of local Mohawk, threatened both the Pines, a reforestation project carried out in the late nineteenth century, and a small burial ground that contained Mohawk graves. The confrontation in the Pines ended when the police withdrew following an outbreak of gunfire on 11 July that left SQ Corporal Marcel Lemay dead. The police established their own roadblock on a nearby highway, and an eleven-week standoff ensued. Before the crisis ended on 26 September, the federal government had sent in army personnel at the request of the provincial government; another Mohawk community, Kahnawake, on the south shore of the St Lawrence River opposite Montreal, had blockaded an important commuter bridge; and emotions had become inflamed throughout Quebec.

The Oka Crisis was rooted deep in Canada's past. The lands that were in dispute had originally been set aside by the French Crown as a seigneurie in the hands of Sulpician missionaries who ministered to a mixed community of Mohawk, Algonkin, and Nipissing First Nations. The victory of Great Britain over France in the Seven Years' War (1756–63) had prompted the First Nations in the mission to petition the new governing authorities for recognition of their ownership of the seigneurie, but for the first of many times the Crown rejected their petition.[1] Throughout the nineteenth century, the First Nations at Oka came under pressure from settlement in the area. As agricultural development of the region proceeded, the Algonkin and Nipissing in particular were hard pressed economically and moved north in search of lands that were still viable hunting-gathering territory. The more agriculturally inclined Mohawk who stayed behind in what was now called Kanesatake encountered problems of a different kind. Their efforts to harvest wood for sale brought them into conflict with their Sulpician landlords. The severity of the friction between priests and Mohawk increased when the First Nation abandoned the Roman Catholic faith and became Methodists. Litigation sponsored by Ottawa intended to settle the dispute over ownership of the lands was decided in favour of the Sulpicians by the Judicial Committee of the Privy Council in 1912, but the Mohawk did not accept the legitimacy of the judicial ruling.[2]

Through the twentieth century, relations between the Mohawk and non-Natives at Oka continued to deteriorate. In the early 1960s, the town of Oka set up a nine-hole golf course over Mohawk objections. In concert with other Mohawk communities in southwestern Quebec and Ontario, the people of Kanesatake tried to resolve the dispute by making use of a claims-resolution process that Canada established in 1973–74. Akwesasne, Kahnawake, and Kanesatake together lodged a comprehensive title claim to a large portion of southwestern Quebec with the Office of Native Claims in 1975. After this claim was quickly rejected, the Mohawk of Kanesatake regrouped and initiated a more limited specific claim to the lands in the immediate area of their settlement. Then they waited interminably – until 1986 – only to find out that their claim was rejected, with the finding that "the Oka band has not demonstrated any outstanding lawful obligation on the part of the Federal Crown." The minister of Indian Affairs offered to consider other means of redressing the grievance, but nothing came of that overture.[3] Thus, when the Oka golf course announced that it was going to expand to eighteen holes, its members faced a frustrated and determined Mohawk opposition that had been struggling for two centuries to establish ownership of the lands involved. As the dispute began to heat up in 1990, armed Mohawk Warriors established themselves in the Pines. The golf course obtained an injunction ordering the Mohawk to abandon their blockades in the wooded area, but the First Nation Warriors ignored the injunction and stood their ground. Thus, when the SQ moved into the Pines on the morning of 11 July, they blundered into a long-standing, heated dispute.

The events during the Oka Crisis itself only raised the temperature. Although no more lives were lost after the initial clash, there were many incidents of vigilante action by police and, later, the army. As well, violent acts against residents of another Mohawk reserve, Kahnawake, by non-Natives aroused sympathy for the embattled Mohawk across the country. By the time the Mohawk holdouts in Kanesatake gave up after seventy-seventy days, feelings were running high in many parts of Canada, especially in those regions referred to as "Indian Country." Although few noted it at the time, Canada was being forced to face up to a serious problem in Native-newcomer relations that was a product of a troubled history.

One of the positive outcomes of the Oka Crisis was the creation of a national inquiry into the state of Aboriginal peoples in Canada. During the confrontation, the government in Ottawa had been anything but helpful. Prime Minister Brian Mulroney had quickly sided with the province, and six weeks into the standoff he had dismissed Mohawk assertions of Aboriginal sovereignty as "bizarre." After the crisis ended in September 1990, the federal government declared that it would pursue a land assembly program to quiet Mohawk concerns about their title and bring peace to the area. Unfortunately, that program was never successfully carried out.[4] But the Mulroney government also made some positive moves in the wake of the crisis. As part of a program to conciliate First Nations, it modified the rules of the specific claims resolution program, the process that compensated First Nations for what the government termed "outstanding lawful obligations." In 1991, the government established the Indian Claims Commission (ICC), which was intended to give relief to claimants who had been rejected by Canada under the specific claims process. While the ICC would prove within a decade that it was not the solution for these claims, its creation was considered an advance by First Nations.[5]

More important in the short run, the federal government decided to establish the Royal Commission on Aboriginal Peoples.[6] The May 1991 Speech from the Throne announced the appointment of former Supreme Court Chief Justice Brian Dickson "to serve as a special representative of the Prime Minister in order to consult widely on the terms of reference and membership of the commission." Dickson moved expeditiously, consulting widely, and in August 1991 recommending the terms of reference and names of personnel for the inquiry.[7]

RCAP's mandate was wide ranging, but there was a surprising omission from its terms of reference:

The Commission of Inquiry should investigate the evolution of the relationship among aboriginal peoples (Indian, Inuit and Métis), the Canadian government, and Canadian society as a whole. It should propose specific solutions, rooted in domestic and international experience, to the problems which have plagued those relationships and which confront aboriginal peoples today. The Commission should examine all issues which it deems to be relevant to any or all of the aboriginal peoples of Canada, and in particular, should investigate and make concrete recommendations concerning:

1. The history of relations between aboriginal peoples, the Canadian government and Canadian society as a whole.

This investigation may include studies of historical patterns of aboriginal settlement and governance, the Royal Proclamation of 1763, the development and interpretation of pre- and post-confederation aboriginal treaties, the evolution of political arrangements in the North, and social tensions which had characterized the relationship between aboriginal and other Canadian communities...

The commission was to explore a wide range of other topics, including "education issues of concern to aboriginal peoples." It was striking that the RCAP's terms of reference contained no explicit mention of residential schools. Item 15 of the mandate – "Educational issues" – was framed to focus on contemporary and future issues.[8]

To carry out the ambitious inquiry suggested by RCAP's terms of reference, the federal government appointed seven people with impressive credentials and experience to oversee the work. The commission was co-chaired by Judge René Dussault, a justice of Quebec's Court of

Appeal, and Georges Erasmus of the Northwest Territories, the national chief of the Assembly of First Nations from 1985 until taking up his role with RCAP in 1991. Erasmus was one of Canada's most highly respected Aboriginal leaders. As a young man, he had been a field-worker and regional director for the Company of Young Canadians, an experiment in social animation and community organization launched by the government of Pierre Elliott Trudeau in its most innovative stage. Erasmus had also headed the Dene Nation, a political alliance of First Nations and Métis in the Northwest Territories from 1976 to 1983. His leadership occurred when the organization was at its most assertive, playing a major role in preventing the construction of a proposed pipeline through the Mackenzie River Valley.

Other notable commissioners included Allan Blakeney, the former New Democratic premier of Saskatchewan from 1971 to 1982. Blakeney did not complete his term on RCAP, though: he quit after two years and was replaced by an academic political scientist with long-standing involvement in provincial governmental affairs and university administration in Alberta, Peter Meekison. The Métis representative, Paul Chartrand, was also an academic, a lawyer in the Department of Native Studies at the University of Manitoba. The legal expertise on the commission – Dussault, Blakeney, and Chartrand – was bolstered by another commissioner, Bertha Wilson, a Scottish immigrant who had studied law in Canada and practised with a major Toronto firm prior to being appointed to the bench, rising eventually to the Supreme Court of Canada in 1982. Wilson had a reputation for being deeply concerned about human rights, discrimination, and women's issues. As well, she was scathingly critical about the hypocrisy of Prime Minister Brian Mulroney, who lectured other countries about the need to improve their human rights records while ignoring the scandalous conditions in which Aboriginal peoples lived in Canada.[9] The other two commissioners were Viola Robinson, a non-status Mi'kmaq from Nova Scotia with considerable experience in First Nations organizations, and Mary Sillett, a Labrador Inuk with a record of service among Inuit, especially Inuit women's organizations. None of the Indigenous commissioners – Erasmus, Chartrand, Robinson, or Sillett – had attended a residential school.[10]

The short, unhappy RCAP service of Allan Blakeney revealed where the commission was headed. As the former premier later explained, "I left the commission because of a difference with some of the other commissioners on what we should be about. Some of them felt that the commission should be documenting the conditions under which Aboriginal people live, should be examining the very real grievances that Aboriginal people have with non-Aboriginal society, and should make recommendations to governments on what they might do to deal with these living conditions and grievances." Blakeney "felt that much of that work had already been done. Rather, I wanted the commission to identify the specific next steps forward that Aboriginal leaders wished to take and to suggest what governments could do to assist the process." He wanted to work on practical solutions to specific problems in the hope that that approach would produce "a steady stream of small victories." He thought "small victories" could be important because, in "the words of an old hymn, 'each victory makes easier some other to win.' I felt that the time had come for Aboriginal groups to identify some small steps, forward steps which governments might be persuaded to accept and help along." He said he understood the importance and potential utility of "dwelling on grievances, ... practising the politics of victimhood," but overall his position was that "listing the grievances held by Aboriginal people against white society, however justified, is essentially a negative activity."[11] To Blakeney, "it is clear that we in white society must stand ready to assist our fellow Canadians of Aboriginal background as they improve their lot and make an even greater contribution to our common future. Our actions will be for their benefit and ours."[12] But he wanted to get on with the job, not explore all its dimensions and complexities. Other commissioners did not agree.

The royal commission moved fairly quickly to set a research agenda for itself and the individual researchers that it would commission. Early in 1992, sixty-five researchers in various fields dealing with Aboriginal peoples in Canada received a letter from Chief Justice Brian Dickson inviting them to submit papers outlining what investigations they thought the commission should undertake. Later that year, commission research staff convened two two-day symposia of specialists to discuss what sorts of research the commission ought to conduct.[13] The *Research Plan*, issued under the names of the commissioners but obviously the work principally of the co-directors of research, Marlene Brant Castellano and David C. Hawkes, signalled the priorities of the commissioners, which later would dominate their report. The topics, as listed in the research plan, were: governance, economics, treaties and lands, social and cultural matters, the North, women's perspectives, urban perspectives, historical perspectives, and youth perspectives. Residential schools were not yet top of mind for the commissioners.

Residential schools appeared under the heading "Social and Cultural Research Program" and were the subject of a "special study" in that category. The residential schools project was to be "a comprehensive examination of residential schools, including historical documentation of the schools and the social context in which the policy evolved and schools were established. It will also describe and analyze the consequences of residential schools for Aboriginal peoples today. The Residential School Study will examine options and strategies for redress and healing."[14] It was to be an example of "projects, like the in-depth study of residential school policy and its consequences in the lives of persons, families, communities and nations," that "will be historical studies that attempt to uncover the path to healing."[15]

The commission's approach to historical research was distinctive. As its final report put it, "the Commission believes it is vital that Canadians understand what happened and accept responsibility for the policies carried out in their names and at their behest over the past two centuries."[16] The commissioners received further support for this different approach to telling the story of the country's past from testimony of former residential school students at the early community hearings: "The versions of Canadian history that have dominated the popular imagination and educational texts, with few exceptions, have either completely ignored or repudiated the view that Aboriginal people have of themselves and their world." The *Research Plan* insisted that "historical perspectives" be "woven through almost all the work" of its research directorate." The commission's historical research would focus on communities and rely on the oral record.[17] According to the commission's research directors, the inspiration for this local, Indigenous focus came, in part, from what commissioners had been hearing during their initial consultations. "Again and again in public hearings in 1992 and 1993, Aboriginal people urged Commissioners to set the record straight, to see that their stories are accorded a place of dignity in the histories of Canada that will shape future attitudes and relationships." Because the commissioners and research directors were particularly keen on community studies, "the Commission proposes to develop a framework for a multi-volume general history of Aboriginal peoples and to produce the first volume as an example of new approaches to Aboriginal history."[18] Clearly, RCAP assumed that studies of the past affected the present and would shape the future of Native-newcomer relations.

Although, at its inception, the commission had not intended to focus on the impact of residential schools, that inclination was challenged by the content of the first round of public hearings. Between 21 April and 26 June 1992, "785 individuals and organizations" had the opportunity to express their views during forty-four days of hearings in thirty-six locations. All the commissioners were present at the opening session in Winnipeg, the closing one in Toronto, and at a National Round Table on Urban Issues that was held in Edmonton on 11 June.[19] As an official for the United Church summarized, "Of the problems identified in communities in the RCAP's first rounds of hearings, only the effect of Residential Schools was mentioned every time; only the issue of Residential Schools has prompted the RCAP to develop a specific strategy for research and possible recommendations at this point in their mandate."[20]

The report on the first round of hearings hinted that the commission's thinking about their task might be shifting a little. Whereas earlier documents, including the original terms of reference, had given priority to "history of relations," "aboriginal self-government," and the "land base for aboriginal peoples," the commission documents issued in late 1992 led off with a discussion of the social pathology afflicting many Aboriginal communities (poverty, unemployment, family breakdown, and so on), which was followed by a passage entitled "Aboriginal Traditions and Culture." Next came the lengthy section "Social Issues," in which the heading "The Residential School Tragedy" came first. Then briefer sections entitled "Governance and Aboriginal Rights," "Northern and Inuit Issues," "Métis Issues," "The Justice System," "Environment," and "Economic Development and Resources" appeared. It was clear that RCAP was focusing, as Blakeney had feared, on documenting problems.[21]

In the commission summary of the first round of hearings, discussions of residential schooling and its effects were numerous and devastating. It was clear that co-chair Georges Erasmus had received the message. At a 20 May 1992 public hearing at Port Alberni, BC, the site of some of the most egregious abuse in residential school history, he responded to a First Nations leader who had talked about the damage the schools had wrought and had called for compensation for survivors:

> You know, we have been getting – in the few short weeks that we have been holding hearings we keep hearing about residential schools. And it is really interesting, the similarities of what occurred and the impact it has had is amazing. We hear the same story, whether it is what happened to the Micmacs, or happening in Manitoba, or the prairies, or now on the west coast. It seemed there was a national program. The other similarity is, even though the passage of the years has gone by, decades, the fallout is still being felt today just as if it was only yesterday that they closed the doors, and how it is being passed down, generation by generation.

Erasmus was deeply struck by what commissioners had heard. "I do not think we have ever been able to understand in this country the full impact of the residential schools and how much a role it is still playing, how much a role it is playing in the way the language has been affected, the way in which parenting skills are lacking, the way the culture was affected. It is just amazing."[22] Years later, Erasmus would recall for the United Church General Council that the commissioners had heard far more about residential schools than they had anticipated.[23] For Erasmus, the first round of hearings was his "aha moment" about residential schooling.

The commission's summary of the first round of hearings concurred with Erasmus: "The impact that residential schools have had on generations of Aboriginal people, the poverty and social disruption that plagues many Aboriginal communities, and the reality that the majority of Canada's Aboriginal population now live in urban areas rather than on reserves – these were the themes that dominated the Commission's discussions on social issues." The schools' "repercussions have had devastating consequences in every aspect of Aboriginal life and society. People compared these schools to the Vietnamese re-education camps and to the policies of Nazi Germany." As the United Church noted, commissioners heard about residential schools repeatedly: "At almost every hearing intervenors raised the school issue and spoke of its impact on Aboriginal language and culture, and of the chain of abuse, violence, suicide and problems with the law that the experience of these schools had generated in Aboriginal communities."

Not for the last time, the commissioners were told that contact with Europeans had spoiled an idyllic Aboriginal Canada. "Aboriginal

2.1 The Royal Commission on Aboriginal Peoples National
Round Table on Education, 7 June 1993.

families were infected with family violence after contact, Ms. [Cath-
erine] Brooks maintained. From Europeans came the concepts of hierarchy in the family, with male dominance; of social punishment; and of
removing children from their homes. Aboriginal societies did not have
a tradition of violence; this was learned behaviour, part of a practice
of cultural genocide."[24] As for what should be done to respond to the
ills left behind, speakers emphasized the need for a state act of reconciliation and restitution. "Grand Chief Phil Fontaine of the Assembly
of Manitoba Chiefs, who himself had experienced abuse in residential school, emphasized the need for an apology related to residential
schools and a national inquiry." But several interveners questioned
whether an apology was enough. Said Will Basque of the Micmac
Grand Council in Nova Scotia, "The church has taught us that when
you commit a sin you have to do penance. Well the church committed
a sin ... against its own children. An apology is not good enough."
Compensation was demanded: "Some intervenors said that the survivors of residential schools should receive compensation for their treatment, in the same way as the government had compensated Japanese
Canadians."[25]

2.2 Phil Fontaine at Royal Commission on Aboriginal
Peoples hearings in Winnipeg.

The second round of public hearings consisted of seven weeks of consultations between 2 October and 10 December 1992. They again "covered
the length and breadth of Canada, from reserves on the Canada–United
States border to as far north as Rankin Inlet and Cambridge Bay ..., and
from Gander, Newfoundland, to as far west as Old Crow, Yukon." The
commissioners "heard from more than 600 individuals and organizations
during 49 days of hearings in 36 locations."[26]
Because these meetings began in the immediate aftermath of the
failure of the Charlottetown Accord on constitutional change, they initially paid a lot of attention to Aboriginal self-government. The failed
agreement had contained a rather confused commitment to enshrin-
ing the right of Aboriginal self-government in the constitution, and

had proposed the enhancement of Aboriginal participation in national institutions such as Parliament and the Supreme Court. Nonetheless, the accord had attracted much opposition from both Aboriginal and non-Aboriginal Canadians; at the end of the day, the former proved no more enthusiastic than the latter about the accord and its commitment to Aboriginal self-government. As the commission co-chairs subsequently noted, of comments on the results of the Charlottetown Accord vote that they heard in the second round, "Some people told us they regretted the outcome. But more said they welcomed it."[27]

According to an overview of the second round of public hearings,

> concern about the devastating effect of residential schools was again expressed during Round Two, but to a lesser extent than in Round One because the focus of the hearings had shifted to solutions ... In Rankin Inlet, Northwest Territories, for example, Marius Tungilik shared his traumatic experience of attending such a school in 1963. He spoke of not being able to speak his language, of rotten food, of sexual abuse and beatings, and gave other examples of physical and mental abuse.[28]

At a discussion featuring two Roman Catholic priests and First Nations people, "members of the panel called for a formal apology from the four denominations that had run residential schools and from the government of Canada. Steps should be taken to ensure that the residential school experience becomes a matter of public record." Former students "should receive financial compensation for their loss of culture, language, family, heritage, traditions and livelihood."[29] During the meeting in Timmins, Ontario, a chief reported on a 1992 inquiry carried out by Fort Albany First Nation that had "found that the system went horribly wrong for many children," and had included disclosures of "sexual abuse, use of an electrified chair as punishment, and the story of three boys who ran away from St. Anne's and were never seen again." The chief "recommended that the case of the three missing boys be investigated and that there should be a memorial service for them."[30]

Even before the second round of public hearings ended, the commissioners and research staff had adopted a "Residential School Strategy."[31] Research staff noted that, "without exception, the residential school system was a topic of presentation in every site of the first round of public hearings." The commissioners had determined that "the goals of our strategic effort are to become informed about healing in the Aboriginal community and public education for all Canadians." In the short term, and with additional rounds of public hearings in mind, the strategy made provision for both open and closed hearings to deal with residential schools evidence. Wherever there were support services in place, the preference was for closed hearings, because "this approach moves away from victim statements and focuses on solutions."

> [In] places like British Columbia, the hearing could be focused and open because people are already openly discussing the topic. Such open focused hearings would be a feature of the third and fourth round of public hearings. This type of open public forum lends itself more to victim statements than to solutions or recommendations. Some combination of open and closed public hearings could also be considered. These open hearings would take place only in communities which agree that these sessions could be also open to the press.[32]

Despite such statements, Erasmus was frustrated by the reluctance of interveners to go beyond describing problems; he wanted them to suggest possible solutions as well.[33] The commission appeared to be interested both in maximizing the potential for hearings to promote "healing" among residential school survivors and ensure that testimony about residential school experiences would educate the general public about the schools.

As originally conceived by the commission, research on residential schools would have both historical and contemporary approaches. "An analytical component examining the historical context will also be included and will address such questions as: Why were the schools established? What were their purposes? What was their relationship to the Indian Act and Canadian Indian policy in general? To educational policy in particular? How and why did abuses occur?" The study would examine "the impact of the schools on Aboriginal society" – what have "the consequences for individuals, families, groups and nations been"? The research directorate planned to hire three "principal investigators of Aboriginal origin, experienced in the field and available on a part-time basis" to conduct research and oversee the work of three research assistants, examine "various options" for "redress and compensation" for school survivors, and write "a definitive work on residential school history, consequences and policy imperatives."[34]

As RCAP's residential schools research eventually took shape, it contained a number of studies focused on different aspects of the schools. An investigation headed by psychologist Roland Chrisjohn of the University of Guelph that looked principally at the psychological impact of schools would eventually be published separately as *The Circle Game*. Denise G. Réaume and Patrick Macklem of the University of Toronto's Faculty of Law prepared a study, "Fiduciary Obligation and Residential School: A Case for Redress," coming to the conclusion that school survivors could claim redress from the government and churches by arguing that there had been a "breach of fiduciary obligation." Another study by Réaume and Macklem, "Education for Subordination: Redressing the Adverse Effects of Residential Schooling," concluded that legal solutions, though presenting difficulties, were a possible avenue to secure redress.[35] And Emily Faries, a consultant in Moose Factory, Ontario, provided a document entitled "Overview of First Nations Education."[36] While some of this research found its way into the commission's report, these were not the inquiries that had the greatest impact.

Historical research on the schools by Trent University historian John Milloy proved to be an important component of the commission's work. Milloy was a known scholar, with a well-regarded D.Phil. dissertation on early nineteenth-century imperial policy on First Nations in British North America and a published monograph, *The Plains Cree*, that was widely used in postsecondary institutions. As a colleague of one of the co-directors of research, Marlene Brant Castellano, he was also familiar to the people who decided research plans. Milloy worked with research assistants Shawn Heard, a Trent student, and Fred McEvoy, a former staff member of what was then the Department of External Affairs.[37] Heard did the research in Anglican, United Church, and Presbyterian archives, while McEvoy "scouted" for relevant documents in government records, which he then brought to Milloy's attention. Milloy had responsibility for work in the national archives and the offices of the Department of Indian Affairs and Northern Development (DIAND).[38] Very early in the consultations between researcher and research directors, Milloy expressed concern about the reliability of government records.[39] Before the research for the historical study was completed, Erasmus had to threaten to go to the prime minister if Milloy were not allowed unimpeded access to unredacted Indian Affairs records. When he was able to access the disputed records, Milloy had to review them in a room in DIAND headquarters, with a departmental employee in the room watching him. He could not make notes but could, and did, request photocopies of the items he expected to use in his writing.[40] All such vexations came on top of the reality that the team conducting the historical inquiry for RCAP had an enormous amount of research to do in a short time.

While the historical and other researchers pursued their projects on behalf of the commission, the commissioners continued with public hearings. During two concentrated rounds in 1993, they completed their consultations with "more than 2,200 groups and individuals in more than 112 communities."[41] The third round of hearings, which took place from April to June 1993, was bookended by two sessions in Ottawa. The first heard from representatives of seventeen Inuit families, "the High Arctic relocates," who had been transported from northern Quebec and Pond Inlet to Grise Fjord and Resolute Bay in the 1950s. The group hearing that ended the third round dealt with the Mohawk who had been caught up in the Oka Crisis of 1990 and "neighbouring non-Aboriginal communities."[42] The Mohawk took the commissioners up on their suggestions about making presentations, especially concerning self-government. "At Akwesasne, a Mohawk elder provided an outline of Iroquois history, of the wampum belts that symbolized the early Iroquois treaties with European settlers, and of the Great Law of Peace, on which the Iroquois Confederacy was founded and continues to be based. This presentation took up an entire day of hearings before the full Commission."[43] As had been the commission's standard procedure from the beginning, these rounds "normally began and ended with a prayer in an Aboriginal language, led by an elder." An innovation that was introduced in the third round was "a Commissioner of the Day drawn from the local community."[44]

The third round also was the occasion for RCAP to dig deeper into the problems that Aboriginal women in particular faced. As the commission explained, "Although 41 per cent of the interveners in Round Three were women, the Commission felt that some women and women's organizations were not coming forward at its hearings, whether because they feared community disapproval if they spoke out in public, or because they did not wish to talk about social dysfunction in their communities in a public forum." RCAP responded by holding a number of in camera sessions on top of its regular hearings. As a result of what they heard from the women, the commissioners decided after the third round to publish "a special interim report on violence and sexual abuse in Aboriginal communities." As well, in the public sessions, commissioners got an earful about the priorities they had presumed to set in their document, *Focusing the Dialogue*, which was intended to shape contributions to the final rounds of hearing. "In the public session in Round Three, women and women's groups were the strongest critics of the four touchstones put forward in *Focusing the Dialogue*." The women's contributions "concentrated on the need for healing in Aboriginal communities as a precondition for self-determination and self-government, rather than as a process that could be undertaken at the same time as self-government was being implemented."[45] The Quebec Native Women's Association was particularly pointed: "The Association asked that the Charter [of Rights and Freedoms] continue to apply to Aboriginal governments until such time as one or more Aboriginal charters provide women with equal or greater protection. In Quebec, it stated, no band council has yet adopted an anti-violence regulation or code of ethics – a measure of the immense work to be done."[46] Interveners continued to emphasize the troubled legacy of residential schooling: many presentations focused on "the devastating effects on language, culture and family life of having generations of Aboriginal children taken from their homes to attend residential schools."[47]

The royal commission's final round of public hearings concentrated on major organizations and on Native-newcomer issues in Quebec. In addition to all the major Aboriginal political organizations, including women's organizations, the commissioners heard from rights agencies such as the Aboriginal Rights Coalition and spent two days "in a special consultation with representatives of Canada's historic mission churches." All the denominations acknowledged that the schools they had run had contributed to the mistreatment of Aboriginal students and emphasized that they had begun to take countermeasures as individual churches to repair some of the damage. At the same time, the Roman Catholics sought to minimize the impact of the schools. A spokesman for the Canadian Conference of Catholic Bishops, Adam Exner, Archbishop of Vancouver, argued that "the schools were only part of an overall government strategy to assimilate or integrate Aboriginal peoples." During an exchange with the commissioners, Archbishop Exner "said historical research indicated that between one in six and one in ten Aboriginal children passed through the residential school system. He suggested the influence of the residential schools might be exaggerated, since Aboriginal people had the same problems even in areas where there were no residential schools, and that these problems might

2.3 Royal Commission on Aboriginal Peoples hearings at Kahnawake.

be looked at in a broader perspective." Exner also argued that, "to simply narrow down the problems of the native people as coming from the
residential schools seems to be denied by the facts."[48]

A special session devoted to Aboriginal peoples and Quebec took
place in an atmosphere dominated by memories of how relations had
been soured by the Oka Crisis only a few years earlier. As the commissioners put it, "Montreal was the only location where significant resistance was expressed to the implementation of Aboriginal rights during
Round 4. Many of the concerns expressed were put in the context of
the deterioration of relations between Aboriginal and non-Aboriginal
peoples in the province, resulting in part from the Oka crisis of 1990
and Aboriginal involvement with sales of untaxed goods."[49] The province's minister responsible for Aboriginal affairs refused to be drawn
out by the commissioners' question about whether his government was
"prepared to accept the inherent right of self-government rather than

insisting on its being determined by constitutional amendment or by the courts."[50] On the other side of the relationship, Grand Chief Matthew Coon Come of the Grand Council of the Crees was forthright in rejecting the claim of Quebec separatists that the province could secede from Canada "with its territory intact while vigorously denying the territorial rights of the Aboriginal peoples in Quebec." The Cree looked to the federal government to protect their interests but did not seem confident that Ottawa would back them up. "We are not discussing a Cree right to secede, but rather the situation where we are faced with the possibility of Quebec secession," the Grand Chief said. "The Cree people do not seek to oppose the exercise of self-determination by the people of Quebec with respect to their own territory. But if the entire Canadian constitutional landscape is to be unilaterally or bilaterally changed, the Cree people have the right to determine our own political status. Under these imminent circumstances, it is we who will determine our relationship with Canada, Quebec, or both."[51] At least the position of First Nations in northern Quebec was crystal clear.

The royal commission wrapped up its public hearings in December 1993. In the four rounds that had been held since April 1992, it had received representations from 674 individuals and 1393 organizations from every province and territory. Now the commissioners had to digest what they had been told, combining that input with the results of the research their staff had commissioned since 1992 to produce a final report.

The commissioners had, along the way, signalled where their thinking was taking them. As early as 1992, the commission had issued occasional reports and position papers. As was noted, it proposed to bring out a paper on violence following the third round of public hearings. Later, it would produce a report on suicide among Aboriginal people and another on treaty making.[52] The position paper on treaty making was an effort to tackle a particular irritant among Aboriginal groups that had never concluded treaties with the Crown. The federal government insisted that any group that settled a comprehensive claim had to agree to the extinguishment of their Aboriginal rights. In a world where section 35 of the 1982 Constitution loomed large and, at a time when the courts had been showing themselves more inclined to entertain arguments in favour of Aboriginal rights and title, many Aboriginal groups were understandably reluctant to sign off on the eradication of rights that might not have been recognized and defined by non-Aboriginal Canada. Such concerns had underlain the collapse of the agreement of a Dene-Métis claim settlement in the Northwest Territories in 1990.

The most pressing topic that the royal commission tackled was Aboriginal self-government. In the aftermath of constitutional renewal in 1982, governments and Aboriginal political organizations had made a concerted effort to define some of the "Aboriginal rights" that were "recognized and affirmed" by section 35 of the new pact. A strong push by the Aboriginal organizations for agreement on inclusion of the Aboriginal right of self-government had collapsed amid acrimony in 1987 at the fourth and final conference devoted to section 35. Then, with the renewal of constitutional discussions in the early 1990s, the issue was revived, taking a more specific – though still rather mushy – form in the Charlottetown Accord on constitutional change, which had included negotiations with Aboriginal leaders.

With a national referendum on the Charlottetown agreement scheduled for the autumn of 1992, RCAP had injected itself into the discussion on Aboriginal self-government. Although the terms of the accord were still being negotiated in early 1992, in February the commissioners released *The Right of Aboriginal Self-Government*. They explained, "We hope only to smooth the path to further exchanges between the parties, not to usurp their rightful place at the negotiating table."[53] The commissioners were concerned that the federal government's refusal to that point to recognize self-government as an inherent right would lead to an impasse. They sought to facilitate discussions by sketching the history of Aboriginal self-government, arguing that it was a viable and valid concept. The "right of Aboriginal self-government, exercised by Aboriginal peoples with diverse historical experiences, and acknowledged by the Crown in the Proclamation of 1763 and elsewhere, has never been relinquished." Things had gone wrong after Confederation: "After the enactment of the *Indian Act* and various laws of general application, the right to self-government was severely curtailed without Aboriginal consent, giving rise to many of the difficulties experienced in relations between Aboriginal nations and Canada."[54] The report canvassed a number of approaches to including Aboriginal self-government in a constitutional agreement and came down in favour of a treaty approach. As "a means of renewing the relationship between Aboriginal peoples and Canadians in general a National Treaty of Reconciliation has some appeal."[55] It favoured moving away from a government-Aboriginal relationship based on the paternalistic Indian Act in favour of the earlier treaty-based, nation-to-nation approach that had deep roots in Canadian history. "We urge all parties to seize this moment and recreate the spirit of co-existence and reciprocity that characterized early relations between Aboriginal peoples and incoming settlers."[56]

The commissioners returned to the topic of Aboriginal self-government in August 1993 with another position paper, entitled *Partners in Confederation: Aboriginal Peoples, Self-Government and the Constitution*, and a month later with an opinion piece signed by co-chair René Dussault in the *Globe and Mail*.[57] In the op-ed, Justice Dussault was explicit about the need for a better understanding of the history of relations between Indigenous and immigrant peoples in Canada: "Yes, we have succumbed to the unfashionable view that history matters. We even make so bold as to say that a greater familiarity with the history of relations between Aboriginal and non-Aboriginal peoples might promote greater understanding of the issues." More than half of *Partners in Confederation* was devoted to the history of Native-newcomer relations, emphasizing especially the Royal Proclamation of 1763 and the formal treaties that the Crown negotiated with western First Nations in the 1870s. Informed by their understanding of history, "we have called for a broader understanding of the sources of law and authority in this country and more inclusive ways of understanding the Constitution, so as to acknowledge the important role that treaties and Aboriginal rights have played in structuring Confederation. Central to this new understanding is the recognition that Aboriginal peoples have the inherent right of self-government within Canada."[58]

Given this background of increasing emphasis on the historical record, it was not surprising that the commission's final report, released in November 1996, was framed historically. The commissioners' tendency to stress the role of history in explaining and solving the problems bedevilling Native-newcomer relations had been strengthened by the views of some groups that appeared before them that had argued strongly about the importance of historical understanding. The United Church's brief to the commission, for example, stated, "Ignorance of the history and contribution of Aboriginal peoples in Canada lies at the root of many misunderstandings in mainstream society and the continuing blockages to the recognition of Aboriginal rights. The United Church is exploring strategies to ensure that Aboriginal history becomes an integral part of formal education systems across the country."[59] In the first of the RCAP report's five volumes, *Looking Forward, Looking Back*, Part 1 was entitled "The Relationship in Historical Perspective." Part 2 examined the impact of various historically rooted factors such as the Indian Act, residential schools, Arctic and other relocations of Aboriginal peoples, and the shabby treatment accorded Aboriginal people when they returned to the country after volunteering for service in Canada's wars abroad.[60] A final section, "Building the Foundations of a Renewed Relationship," concluded the volume.

What was striking was not just the prominence RCAP's final report gave to history, it was also the *version* of Canadian history contained in the report. RCAP embraced a radical reinterpretation of Indigenous peoples' role in Canadian history that had emerged in the two decades prior to the creation of the royal commission. Before the 1970s, historians writing both in French and English had tended not to focus on Aboriginal peoples as independent actors. When they were treated – for example, in histories of New France, studies of the fur trade, or chronicles of the "opening" of the Canadian West after Confederation – they were relegated to a status akin to that of the flora and fauna or were depicted only as people who were acted upon by the European newcomers. They were the recipients of missionaries' ministrations or helpless people drawn into a European-dominated fur trade that made them dependent on European goods and technology. Once agricultural settlement took centre stage, Indigenous people almost completely disappeared from the history books. Occasionally, the Métis could intrude on the national narrative by mounting the Red River Resistance or the Northwest Rebellion; or First Nations would be mentioned as entering into treaties that promoted reserve settlement and agricultural development under the tutelage of a wise and far-sighted federal government. In the nation's story, Aboriginal people were included only when they were problems to be solved or obstacles to be overcome as Canada expanded and incorporated their lands. As a survey of English-language general histories put it in 1970, the First Nation Canadian was "not often considered to be deserving of serious attention, or his society of scholarly analysis."[61]

Beginning in the 1970s, historians, particularly in English-speaking universities, began to devote more attention to Indigenous peoples. In part, this reorientation of the historiography was attributable to a shift in the historians' gaze to take in hitherto neglected groups – to "history from below," as it was termed. As well, though, academic researchers were reacting to a shift in their political environment, as Aboriginal Canada began to express itself more forcefully via the political organizations that had emerged with confident and effective leadership by the end of the 1960s. Historians were also indebted to the example of scholarly researchers in other disciplines. Anthropologists and historical geographers, particularly those looking anew at New France and at the fur trade, rewrote Canada's early history as a narrative of First Nations agents shaping historical change, contending with European fur traders and missionaries, and often forcing them to adjust their behaviour. The irrelevant or passive Indian was replaced by a more assertive and effective Indigenous agent of historical change. Obviously, the story of residential schools would require special attention in this changed interpretive environment.

Given RCAP's mandate, the work of scholars who in the 1980s began to re-examine the government's post-Confederation policies towards First Nations was of special relevance to the historical vision of the royal commission. Hitherto the few works that considered policy, as in the making of the numbered treaties and the early reserve period, for instance, portrayed First Nations as passive recipients of Ottawa's initiatives. For example, George Stanley, the dean of western Canadian historians, whose *The Birth of Western Canada* dominated the field for half a century after its publication in 1936, cast government policy in a profoundly Eurocentric fashion. According to Stanley,

> the European, conscious of his material superiority, is only too contemptuous of the savage, intolerant of his helplessness, ignorant of his mental processes and impatient at his slow assimilation of civilization. The savage, centuries behind in mental and economic development, cannot readily adapt himself to meet the new conditions. He is incapable of bridging the gap of centuries alone and unassisted. Although white penetration into native territories may be inspired by motives of self-interest, such as trade and settlement, once there, the responsibility of "the white man's burden" is inevitable.

The western treaties were an example of taking responsibility for "the white man's burden." In western treaty making, Canada followed a policy similar to that laid down by Britain in the latter half of the eighteenth century. "Western Indian history was merely the application of these well-founded principles to a new problem, the acknowledgment of the Indian title, and the formal negotiation for the surrender of the same."[62] Stanley's references in his section on Treaties 1 through 6 contained seven citations of an 1880 work by the federal negotiator of four

of the treaties, five of items in Parliamentary *Sessional Papers*, and one
of North West Mounted Police records as found in United Kingdom
Colonial Office papers. No evidence came from First Nations sources,
missionary records, or the Department of Indian Affairs.

The revisionist account of government–First Nations relations that
had emerged in the 1980s examined the government's own records and
found active and energetic First Nations communities combatting an
oppressive state. It was striking that the first analysis that signalled a
new approach came from a scholar, John Tobias, who had compiled
most of his evidence while working as a researcher for the Federation
of Saskatchewan Indians, one of the First Nations political organizations that were shaking up Canadian policy from the 1970s onward.
Tobias's re-examination of records of the Department of Indian Affairs
found that federal government policies about making treaties and settling western First Nations on reserves were anything but provident
and benevolent. Rather, his closely reasoned articles demonstrated that
Indian Affairs had had its hands full with restive First Nations after
treaty-making because of concerted efforts by leaders such as Piapot
and Mistahimusqua (Big Bear) to force a revision of the treaties that
were not working well for their peoples. Only the Northwest Rebellion
in 1885 provided Ottawa with the pretext to attack Plains Cree leadership judicially by misrepresenting the Métis insurrection as a joint
Indian-Métis campaign.[63] Tobias's insights were followed a few years
later by a devastating critique of the policies of Duncan Campbell Scott,
which showed both the malignancy of Indian Affairs' policies and the
widespread First Nations resistance to them.[64] Through the remainder
of the 1980s and well into the 1990s, a stream of revisionist works rolled
out that showed that Aboriginal peoples were active agents and that
the federal government was the antithesis of George Stanley's bearer of
"the white man's burden."

By the time the royal commission compiled its historically focused
final report, the historiographical revolution had been incorporated
into general works that surveyed the Native-newcomer relationship
from commercial contact in the seventeenth century to the late twentieth century.[65] These works, too, portrayed Indigenous peoples as energetic actors in their own lives, who, after 1867, often had to contend
with a central government that was at best uncomprehending and
indifferent, and at worst hostile to anyone in the Native community
who objected to its policies. Across the broad sweep of postcontact history, a picture emerged in these pages of a relationship that had begun

in relatively harmonious ways in the fisheries and fur trade, the first European industries in Canada, and then deteriorated when relations were framed by an emerging British society intent on building a settled agricultural country from the nineteenth century onward. The missionary and governmental policies, including residential schools, had emerged in this later period, when the non-Indigenous majority was not much engaged with and certainly not informed about Indigenous people. It was this new version of Canadian history to which the RCAP gave its imprimatur in the first volume of its final report.

The postcontact history of Canada that *Looking Forward, Looking Back* laid out was a story of decline. A chapter on precontact First Nations and Inuit, entitled "Separate Worlds," depicted the Indigenous peoples as communities with their own governance and means of maintaining social cohesion. The purpose of this approach was to refute the older view of the history of the western hemisphere that contended that Europeans came to *terra nullius*, lands devoid of people settled in organized communities. The next stage in the narrative, "contact and cooperation," emphasized Indigenous-immigrant partnership in the fur trade, military and diplomatic alliances, and formal treaties. Then came the sharp decline: stage three covered "displacement and assimilation" under the general heading "The Imposition of a Colonial Relationship." Although there were treaties in this period of European settler expansion, they were not honoured; the post-treaty record was one of "nonfulfilment of treaties." The fourth and final stage dealt with "negotiation and renewal," emphasizing government attempts to control Aboriginal peoples, the role of the courts in enforcing and then undoing the regime of governmental control, and, finally, the emergence of vibrant Aboriginal political organizations, including an international one in the form of the Inuit Circumpolar Conference, which was established in 1973.[66]

The Indian Act and a brief history of residential schools dominated the section of the first volume that dealt with specific instances of what the authors called "a failed relationship." The lengthy chapter on the Indian Act reflected the revisionist history that had emerged over the previous fifteen years, depicting government policy as misguided and authoritarian, and administrators of that policy as blind to Aboriginal culture in their single-minded campaign to control and change Aboriginal societies. The chapter on residential schools, also lengthy, was a hard-hitting overview of the history of the schools and their impact on the unfortunate children who spent formative periods within their walls. Prepared by John Milloy, who also produced a substantial history of the schools for the commission, the chapter basically convicted the federal government out of its own archives. Milloy's work typified much of the post-1983 scholarship on federal Indian policy; it relied on the records of the Department of Indian Affairs to expose the abuses that that department had meted out on behalf of successive governments of Canada. The most surprising thing about this excellent account was the recommendation with which it concluded: "The Commission recommends that Under part I of the *Public Inquiries Act*, the government of Canada establish a public inquiry instructed to (a) investigate and document the origins and effects of residential school policies and practices respecting all Aboriginal peoples." As well, Milloy's chapter recommended that the federal government "fund establishment of a national repository of records and video collections related to residential schools."[67] Given the vivid history of residential schooling presented in the volume, one might have expected more ambitious action than simply a recommendation for an additional inquiry.

Other recommendations in RCAP's final report were more substantive and sweeping. Probably those concerning governance were the most ambitious. "Canada's future development," the commission argued, "must be guided by the fact that there are three orders of government in this country: Aboriginal, provincial and federal."[68] Such a stance – that Aboriginal people were entitled to be considered a distinct level of government within Canada – was consistent with the commission's previously asserted position that Aboriginal self-government was already recognized in the Canadian constitution. The commission's version of this third order of Aboriginal government was what was radical: "The Commission considers the right of self-determination to be vested in Aboriginal nations rather than small local communities. By Aboriginal nation, we mean a sizeable body of Aboriginal people with a shared sense of national identity that constitutes the predominant population in a certain territory or group of territories. There are 60 to 80 historically based nations in Canada at present comprising a thousand or so Aboriginal communities."[69] The sixty to eighty "nations" would form governments that were "sovereign within their several spheres and hold their powers by virtue of their inherent status rather than by delegation. In other words, they share the sovereign powers of Canada, powers that represent a pooling of existing sovereignties."[70]

The proposed Aboriginal nation governments would have jurisdiction over "all matters relating to the good government and welfare of Aboriginal peoples and their territories." Each government's jurisdiction was to be made up of a core that "includes all matters that (1) are vital to the life and welfare of a particular Aboriginal people, its culture and identity; (2) do not have a major impact on adjacent jurisdictions; and (3) are not otherwise the object of transcendent federal or provincial concern." The periphery of jurisdiction was made up of "the remainder of the sphere of inherent Aboriginal jurisdiction." When an Aboriginal government law dealing with a matter within the core was in conflict with a federal law, one or the other might, on a case-by-case basis, take precedence, subject to one overriding consideration. A federal "law must serve a compelling and substantial federal objective and be consistent with the Crown's basic fiduciary responsibilities to Aboriginal peoples." Conflicts between an Aboriginal government law from the peripheral area of jurisdiction would be settled according to "a self-government treaty or agreement" that would be negotiated between the government of Canada and the Aboriginal nation government.[71]

The breathtaking constitutional vision of the Royal Commission on Aboriginal Peoples stood in sharp contrast to its views on residential schools. A thorough, well-documented history of the founding and evolution of residential schools led only to modest recommendations that the federal government hold an inquiry into the schools and fund an archive of records about them. Yet, the report's chapter on residential schools clearly provided sufficient evidence for the commissioners to draw conclusions about the motivation behind federal government policies and the impact of schooling on the students. It was not surprising, then, that Georges Erasmus in 2003 told the United Church's General Council that he and his fellow commissioners thought they had not done enough on residential schools.[72]

The bold and sweeping recommendations for creating a third order of government consisting of sixty to eighty Aboriginal nation governments rested on a less solid footing. The justification for the proposal to create this order of government was found in the commission's reading of the history of pre- and postcontact history in Canada. Precontact Aboriginal peoples had, of course, had rights of self-determination and self-government. According to the commission, many of their rights were recognized by the Royal Proclamation of 1763 and enshrined in Canada's written constitution in 1982, including the all-important section 35. If the commission's treatment of Aboriginal governance and residential schools appeared strikingly different, they were both based on the authority of history. That reading of Canadian history – whether in the specific case of a federal government policy such as residential schooling or in a general matter such as the persistent right of self-government – reflected the dramatic changes in historical interpretation that had emerged in academic writing on history and law since the 1980s. The commission both used and promoted a reading of Canadian history that would not have been familiar to the vast majority of Canadians raised on a historical pabulum that portrayed British and then Canadian Indian policy as beneficent and far-sighted. Like the standoff at Oka in 1990 that had been a major reason for the creation of RCAP, the commission itself and its final report brought to the foreground a new understanding of Canadian history. Oka and RCAP pushed Canadians, beginning with their national government, to confront their history. How would they respond?

3

The State Responds:
Gathering Strength and the Aboriginal
Healing Foundation

Response to the sweeping recommendations of the Royal Commission on Aboriginal Peoples (RCAP) disappointed those who had hoped the inquiry would be the first step on the road to improve the lives of Aboriginal Canadians. The commissioners pitched their proposals in terms that did not suit either the times or the government's approach. As a consequence, most of RCAP's central recommendations were simply ignored by the federal government when it got around to addressing the commission. One of the federal government's responses would prove in time to be beneficial, though: Ottawa created a national foundation to assist both individuals and communities to recover from the trauma and damage caused by the residential schooling experience. Until its demise, the Aboriginal Healing Foundation (AHF) did good work, both helping victims of residential schools and promoting a better understanding of the dark history of these institutions.

Before the commission wrapped up its hearings, the Liberal government of Jean Chrétien had signalled that it was not impressed with the direction in which Erasmus, Dussault, and the other commissioners were heading. Meeting in the spring of 1994 with representatives of the churches that had operated the residential schools, Indian Affairs minister Ron Irwin responded negatively when asked for his views on the royal commission. "Would you rather I build 1,000 houses in the south, 750 in the near north, or 500 in the far north, or write a report that tells me we've got problems?" he asked rhetorically. He said he was disappointed that RCAP was, in the words of one of the delegation he

met, "projecting a 60 volume final report. Irwin is not waiting for RCAP
to do what he perceives his job to be." The sentiments expressed were
no more encouraging when Irwin's assistant asked the church delegation "if the churches were waiting for the RCAP report to do something on Residential Schools." The delegation "asked in return if the
federal government would wait for the RCAP report to do something
on Residential Schools." A member of the delegation also reported that
Irwin was "preparing an options paper ... on responding to the legacy
of Residential Schools." The minister would not be drawn out on the
likely contents of that paper but indicated that issuing an apology "was
not his personal style. He was more comfortable getting on with solving problems and implementing self-government." As the delegation's
recorder concluded, "There is a challenge to the churches to articulate
for Irwin the benefits of an apology in terms of spiritual healing – a term
that probably isn't used frequently in government circles."[1] Irwin was
a tough-talking, no-nonsense Ontario lawyer who had served as mayor
of Sault Ste Marie, but the fate of RCAP's final report would show that
his attitude towards the commission was not unique within the federal
cabinet.

From the government's perspective – and it was a perception with
which Alan Blakeney would have agreed – RCAP's recommendations were untimely and politically unsellable. When the commission
reported in November 1996, the country was still licking its wounds
from a bruising referendum in Quebec over a proposal to declare sovereignty in the province. The referendum result had been a nail-biter, a
margin of about 60,000 votes preventing the winning decision for the
status quo from being a verdict for sovereignty. It had been revealed
after the referendum that Parti Québécois premier Jacques Parizeau
had been poised to declare sovereignty unilaterally if his forces had
prevailed. Among the political class federally and in central Canada,
nerves were shattered. Moreover, federal leaders recognized that they
had to deal cautiously with a separatist government in Quebec City in
the aftermath of the referendum.

What did RCAP propose that might provoke a reaction in Quebec?
The commission advocated the adoption of a new Royal Proclamation
affirming the relationship between Indigenous and immigrant peoples
in the country. It is doubtful that anyone in the inner circles of the commission understood how unpopular the Royal Proclamation of 1763
was in Quebec and why. That eighteenth-century imperial document
had truncated the territory in which French-speaking Roman Catholics

lived. The British-imposed Province of Quebec (1763–91) was a narrow parallelogram based on the St Lawrence River watershed that cut the settled area of the colony, anchored by Montreal and Quebec, off from its enormous hinterland that had stretched north, northwest, and southwest, even as far as the French colony of Louisiana. Worse still, the Royal Proclamation had proposed that the Province of Quebec would, like most British colonies of settlement, have an elective assembly. As Roman Catholics, *les canadiens* were not allowed to vote or hold office in the eighteenth-century British Empire.[2] Thus, any constitutional proposal to embrace a new "Royal Proclamation" was a political non-starter, particularly in the aftermath of the Quebec referendum.

A related complication from the federal government's point of view was RCAP's wide-ranging proposals for governance. When the commission reported in the mid-1990s, the tide of political opinion in western democracies was running heavily against "big government." Part of the reason for the anti-government sentiment was the lengthy reign of neo-liberal administrations in western democracies, which were influencing Canadian opinion. The impact of Margaret Thatcher's government in the United Kingdom (1979–90) and Ronald Reagan's in the United States (1981–89) tended to shift the political consensus dramatically to the right. In Canada, the pale counterpart of Thatcher and Reagan was Conservative prime minister Brian Mulroney (1984–93). Although Mulroney had won power in the general election of 1984 in large part because of growing antipathy to the interventionist, free-spending government of Liberal Pierre Elliott Trudeau, he proved in office not to be an aggressive opponent of government involvement in the economy. Apart from terminating the Liberals' National Energy Program, which was hated in the western provinces, and eliminating the Foreign Investment Review Act, Mulroney delivered little, compared to Thatcher and Reagan. In fact, he doubled the accumulated federal debt – an artefact of "big government" to those on the political Right – during his term in office.

Mulroney's failure to match the small-government style of Thatcher and Reagan was a factor in the emergence of the Reform Party, formed in 1987 and taking its first House of Commons seat in 1989. In the 1993 federal election, this protest party polled the second-largest number of votes after the Liberals, winning fifty-two seats, all but one of them in western Canada. Reform's focus on reducing government expenditure and attacking its accumulated debt augmented resistance to big government at the federal level. By the time RCAP reported, those who were concerned about the size of government were more frustrated and no less determined than they had been when Mulroney had been elected a decade earlier. And now they had a sizeable bloc of seats in Parliament from which to make their views known. This was no time for changes that would "grow government." RCAP's recommendation of sixty to eighty Aboriginal governments that would interact with other levels of government via a large number of agencies and institutions in an apparently endless regime of consultations and negotiations was simply not going to be acceptable politically.

More particularly, the primary goal of Jean Chrétien's Liberal government, which had taken office in 1993, ensured that Ottawa was not receptive to RCAP's ambitious vision. The Liberals were determined to get the annual federal deficit under control and to tackle the accumulated national debt. Both had reached unprecedented size under Trudeau and Mulroney. In fact, when RCAP reported in November 1996, the federal government was in the first phase of a fierce assault on spending. Finance Minister Paul Martin promised to reduce expenditure "come hell or high water," and the Liberals were busily trimming the civil service and off-loading the expense of cost-shared programs onto the provinces by reducing transfer payments. In a climate such as the Liberals had created with their budget in the spring of 1996, RCAP's proposal to increase expenditures on Aboriginal matters by all governments – estimated at $13 billion in 1996, and rising to $16 billion as a result of population growth alone – had no chance of being accepted. For reasons of cost alone RCAP's report was, in the words of a deputy minister, "dead on arrival."[3] Because of antipathy to the idea of a new Royal Proclamation, lingering opposition to the expansion of government, and widespread hostility to increased federal expenditures, the royal commission's recommendations were doomed.

RCAP's November 1996 *Report* was handed to a federal government that was singularly ill prepared to deal with it. Shawn Tupper, the official who would head Indian and Northern Affairs Canada's (INAC) handling of residential schools issues, was assigned to the task in November 1996, just as the *Report* arrived. He recalled that, when he joined the departmental group working on residential school issues, he was struck by how unsophisticated their approach was. The unit was using five-year-old "communication lines," the guidelines used to deal with media and prepare documents intended for the public. The government's position concerning the schools had evolved little over the previous half-decade, even though RCAP had brought increasing attention to the issue of abuse in the schools during that period. The department's decisions on how to respond to the rising chorus of demands about residential schools were driven, said the INAC unit head, by the ninety-six claims for damages for abuse from survivors that were on hand in 1996. In general, the schools unit was taking a legalistic stance, but RCAP's *Report* in November forced a rethink. The government might not be eager to implement RCAP's recommendations, but it was committed to responding substantively to its report, and INAC had to change its posture.[4]

In a step unprecedented in Ottawa's handling of Aboriginal issues, INAC staff working on the portion of the federal response that dealt with residential schools went into the field to talk to people who had been affected. Among the most influential survivors were those who had attended the Gordon school in southern Saskatchewan. Gordon, initially an Anglican institution, was taken over and run directly as a student residence by the federal government from 1969 until its closure in 1996. It had been the site of horrific abuse perpetrated by William Starr, the residence supervisor. The former administrator had been tried and convicted of assault in 1993, and more than 200 former students were compensated financially for their suffering, but the reverberations from Starr's actions lingered.[5] Among the important points that the Gordon survivors impressed on the INAC staff were that the government solution of compensating residential school abuse victims without any other measures did not work effectively for the community, and that INAC should involve the community affected by residential schooling in the development and implementation of policies intended to repair damage. For a bureaucracy with a long history of deciding things *for* rather than *with* First Nations people, these were difficult messages to "sell." Eventually, though, Tupper realized that survivors and their community already were involved in any process dealing with residential school damage.[6]

Indian Affairs found it challenging to formulate a response to RCAP that dealt effectively with its revelations about the impact of residential schooling. The Indian Affairs deputy minister from 1995 to 1999, Scott Serson, recalled that he "liked" the RCAP final report but found responding to it in a timely way challenging. He said, "It was so significant and has so many recommendations that we had to do triage … The first priority was those recommendations we could respond to soon within the fiscal limitations we had." Those "limitations" were significant: the federal government had recently instituted a 2 per cent cap on increases to departmental budgets, including for Indian Affairs, where annual rates of increase had been running much higher. The government's intention in formulating a response to RCAP "was to give immediate responses where we could, but then go carefully over the recommendations and do what we could with them." On one point the deputy minister and prominent First Nations leader Phil Fontaine agreed. "We spent a lot of time doing a broad response. Phil Fontaine wanted us to negotiate some things solely with First Nations. I wanted to give some attention to First Nations because there was a rising tide of (perceived) radicalism there."[7] Reaching agreement on the government response was made less difficult by the mutual trust that existed between Fontaine and Indian Affairs minister Jane Stewart.[8]

In January 1998, Stewart presented a "Statement of Reconciliation" on the government response to RCAP, which was televised nationally on the CBC's news channel. She began by embracing the revisionist history of Native-newcomer relations that the royal commission had championed in its final report. In the first section of her statement, "Statement of Reconciliation," Stewart began with comments related to "learning from the past." "It is essential," she said, "that we deal with the legacies of the past affecting the Aboriginal peoples of Canada, including the First Nations, Inuit and Métis. Our purpose is not to rewrite history but, rather, to learn from our past and to find ways to deal with the negative impacts that certain historical decisions continue to have in our society today." Among those lessons was that, "thousands of years before this country was founded," Aboriginal peoples "enjoyed their own forms of government. Diverse, vibrant Aboriginal nations had ways of life rooted in fundamental values concerning their relationships to the Creator, the environment, and each other." Aboriginal people "welcomed the newcomers to this continent," and over time there were "contributions made by all Aboriginal peoples to Canada's development." Indigenous peoples' contributions had not been properly recognized, but the "Government of Canada today, on behalf of all Canadians, acknowledges those contributions." She further noted that initial positive relations had, unfortunately, given way to a regime of "racial and cultural superiority [that] led to a suppression of Aboriginal culture and values." It was important to note the damage caused by such a system. "We must acknowledge that the result of these actions was the erosion of the political, economic and social systems of Aboriginal people and nations."[9]

The key portion of the government's Statement of Reconciliation was Stewart's apology for the damage done by residential schools. Said the minister, "The Government of Canada today formally expresses to all Aboriginal people in Canada our profound regret for past actions of the federal government which have contributed to these difficult pages in the history of our relationship together." An especially important part of those "past actions" were the residential schools. "This system separated many children from their families and communities and prevented them from speaking their own languages and from learning about their heritage and cultures. In the worst cases, it left legacies of personal pain and distress that continue to reverberate in Aboriginal communities to this day. Tragically, some children were the victims of physical and sexual abuse." The government "acknowledges the role it played in the development and administration of these schools. Particularly to those individuals who experienced the tragedy of sexual and physical abuse at residential schools, and who have carried this burden believing that in some way they must be responsible, we wish to emphasize that what you experienced was not your fault and should never have happened. *To those of you who suffered this tragedy at residential schools, we are deeply sorry.*"[10] The minister's statement then emphasized the need for a cooperative approach to "resolve the longstanding issues that must be addressed. We need to work on a healing strategy to assist individuals and communities in dealing with the consequences of this sad era of history." Then, in a departure that might have seemed strange to those unaware of the historical framing of the Statement of Reconciliation, the minister dealt with "the sad events culminating in the death of Métis leader Louis Riel. These events cannot be undone; however, we can and will continue to look for ways of affirming the contributions of Métis peoples in Canada and of reflecting Louis Riel's proper place in Canada's history."[11]

Stewart's statement was released as part of an "action plan" entitled *Gathering Strength*, the government's official response to the royal commission's many recommendations. The plan was as much of an anticlimax as the minister's statement on residential schools had been. *Gathering Strength* spoke in vague and general terms about the government's "commitment to Renewing the Partnerships" and stressed its willingness to work with Aboriginal peoples on governance, healing, a 'Treaty relationship,' "Language, Heritage, and Culture," "Public Education,"

"Urban Issues," and "International Partnerships." The section of the statement on governance, while agreeing that some form of Aboriginal self-government should be recognized, was vague and non-committal on specifics. Certainly, there was no embrace of RCAP's recommendations for refashioning Aboriginal governments into sixty to eighty national units or on restructuring federal institutions to make a house of Aboriginal peoples. The deputy minister who oversaw preparation of the government's statement recalled, "I hoped the recommendations concerning the creation of sixty-some Aboriginal governments would be implemented, but the sad fact is that First Nations leaders didn't go for it."[12] On the matter of treaties, an issue central to the concerns of prairie First Nations, *Gathering Strength* noted the model of Saskatchewan's Office of the Treaty Commissioner as a mechanism for resolving treaty issues. It had been "established with the agreement of the federal government, Treaty First Nations and the provincial government." Ottawa was "prepared to consider the creation of additional treaty commissions to contribute to treaty renewal and the development of self-government where its partners agree that such an approach would be useful."[13]

Gathering Strength was more specific about the damage residential schools had caused, but that portion of the minister's statement was not received any more warmly than the rest of the document. Phil Fontaine, national chief of the Assembly of First Nations (AFN), initially indicated approval, noting at the press conference that "this gathering celebrates the beginning of a new era in the relationships between the Government of Canada and the First Peoples of this land ... It took some courage on the part of the Minister and government to take this historic step, to break with the past, and to apologize for the historic wrongs and injustices committed against our peoples. It is therefore a great honour for me, on behalf of the first Nations, to accept the apology of the government and people of Canada." He then optimistically said, "Let this moment mark the end of paternalism in our relations and the beginning of the empowerment of First Peoples ... the end of assimilationist policies and the beginning of mutual respect and cooperation."[14] Fontaine's response was understandable in light of what he had said years earlier, when speaking to RCAP Commissioner Mary Sillett at a public session in Winnipeg in April 1992:

> It's not necessary for the Ministers to say to our people, "I apologize to you on behalf of the federal government." I mean, the apology can come

later. What would be very encouraging is if you were to tell us, "yes, I'm prepared to acknowledge that there is a serious problem there, and that it's hurting far too many people. And I'm prepared to assist you, to support you, to enable your people to begin to heal themselves. And I'm prepared to make available the necessary resources to allow this process to begin."[15]

Chief Fontaine's reaction to Stewart's apology was extremely important. Arguably, he had put the issue of abuse in the schools on the public agenda when he spoke out about his own experience at the Fort Alexander school in Manitoba in the autumn of 1990. Appearing on the CBC television public affairs show, *The Journal*, Fontaine had been grilled mercilessly by host Barbara Frum about what had happened to him at residential school. While he avoided responding directly to Frum's probing questions about his own physical and sexual abuse, Fontaine emphasized that the experience of abuse was widespread. He also made a point of calling for the creation of a public inquiry that would, he said, "document for posterity" what happened in residential schools and also create a healing process by means of which abused residential school survivors would be made whole again.[16] These two items – documenting the past and promoting healing – constituted the agenda that Fontaine would pursue for more than two decades. Ultimately, a broad phalanx of Aboriginal leaders and school survivors would succeed in pushing the federal government and churches into an agreement that would set up such mechanisms. In early January 1998, though, Fontaine found himself very much alone after the Stewart apology.

Leaders of all the other Aboriginal political organizations resoundingly condemned Stewart's Statement of Reconciliation as inadequate. They objected both to its form and content . First, they noted that it was not good enough to have a minister deliver a statement of regret, however heartfelt the delivery. For many leaders, the apology should have been delivered by the prime minister in the House of Commons and should have been accompanied with compensation for damage done. After all, as one leader had told RCAP at a community consultation, Prime Minister Mulroney had done no less in 1988 in the case of the Japanese Canadians who had been unjustifiably interned during the Second World War. As Chief Councillor Charlie Cootes of Uchucklesaht, BC, argued to RCAP co-chair Georges Erasmus in May 1992, an apology and compensation was provided "for the Japanese who were interned for a few years during World War II. It is only justice that compensation be paid for a hundred years of institutional abuse."[17] Another concern was whether survivors would actually see any compensation that was awarded. Willie Blackwater, a survivor of the United Church's Port Alberni school, predicted that most of the money set aside under the Statement of Reconciliation would go to bureaucrats rather than victims, affirming that, "This makes us more determined than ever to get our day in court." Viola Thomas, president of the United Native Nations, representing off-reserve First Nations, noted "It's less money than the government gave a company not to build helicopters." And Marilyn Buffalo of the Native Women's Association of Canada declared, "An apology to our people should be an admission of error and responsibility, no less than was given by the prime minister to the Japanese-Canadians in 1988 in the House of Commons."[18] Fontaine later recalled that Marilyn Buffalo and Métis leader Harry Daniels refused to accept their copies of *Gathering Strength* from the minister.[19]

An exasperated Jane Stewart reacted unhelpfully to the criticism her "Statement of Reconciliation" was receiving. "We said we're deeply sorry for the role we played and that it's not your fault what happened to you in residential schools, because that's what first-nations leaders, in B.C. in particular, were looking for. Do I now have to apologize for how we said 'We're sorry?'"[20] In a sense, the answer to the minister's rhetorical question was "yes." According to scholars who specialize in analysing apologies, there are definite criteria by which official apologies can be judged. They must be full and explicit about the damage that was inflicted. They must acknowledge that the group for which the speaker is apologizing was the perpetrator of the harm. They must express regret for causing the damage and apologize for it. And, finally, effective apologies must outline the steps that the speaker and group will take to ensure that such horrible acts do not occur again.[21] The other shortcoming that limited the effectiveness of the statement was the federal government's failure to mount a communications program to publicize the minister's statement. The government team charged with developing the official response to RCAP had debated whether to hold regional events associated with the minister's statement, but had finally decided not to do so. The consequence was that critical voices dominated the reaction to the apology and *Gathering Strength*, and the apology was soon dismissed as trivial.[22]

The cool reception accorded the minister's apology and the publication of *Gathering Strength* was only the beginning of the challenges that the government faced. The promise in the government's official response to establish an agency to promote the sort of healing among survivors about which Chief Phil Fontaine had spoken in October 1990 soon turned out to be one fraught with complications. The proposal to create an Aboriginal healing foundation had roots in the royal commission itself. At the end of RCAP's chapter on residential schools in the first historical volume of its final report, the commissioners had recommended that the government of Canada create a commission of inquiry to investigate the schools, one that could "recommend remedial action by governments and the responsible churches" to provide "compensation of communities to design and administer programs that help the healing process and rebuild community life."[23] Acting on this recommendation presented the Liberal government of Jean Chrétien with a major challenge. The government chose not to proceed with the public inquiry RCAP desired, but it did agree to provide $350 million for an agency that would back community initiatives to heal damage from residential schooling. Such a commitment was consistent with the content of Stewart's "Statement of Reconciliation." Just after the passage on residential schools and before the isolated paragraph concerning "Louis Riel's proper place in Canada's history," the minister had said, "In dealing with the legacies of the Residential School system, the Government of Canada proposes to work with First Nations, Inuit and Métis people, the churches and other interested parties to resolve the longstanding issues that must be addressed. We need to work together on a healing strategy to assist individuals and communities in dealing with the consequences of this sad era of our history."[24] This commitment by the government would lead to the creation of an important agency focused on healing.

It had not been easy to persuade the federal government to commit to this expenditure after the trauma its cutbacks in the 1996 budget had occasioned. Drastic reductions in transfer payments to the provinces had provoked a loud outcry, particularly from provinces that found themselves hard-pressed to "backfill" the funding gaps that Martin's cuts had left in their resources for health, postsecondary education, and social assistance. When, prior to the release of *Gathering Strength*, the finance minister met with Jane Stewart and Phil Fontaine to discuss support for a healing initiative, he had stressed the difficulty of allocating money for healing. "'Now, look,'" he recalled saying. "'This is $350 million at a time we're cutting spending elsewhere. Should we be spending this money here? Is this the right place to spend it?'" (In fact, the government was poised to begin reinvesting in policies as its revenues rebounded in 1997–8 thanks to exceptional growth in the economy. For example, in February 1997 it announced the creation of the Canada Foundation for Innovation, the first of what would turn out to be a series of programs to enhance research and scholarship in postsecondary institutions.[25]) As Martin recalled events, "Phil made the argument for healing as cogently as I've ever heard it. It was then that I really truly began to understand."[26] Once the cabinet was persuaded by the prime minister, finance minister, and minister of Indian Affairs, planning for a healing agency began. After Stewart met with a number of residential school survivors to hear their suggestions, her department announced the creation of the Aboriginal Healing Foundation (AHF) in early 1998.[27]

Securing approval for a foundation and a government commitment to funding it were only the first of many challenges the new agency faced in 1998. The publication of *Gathering Strength* on 8 January left those who would operate the AHF with little time to meet the government's deadline of the end of the fiscal year on 31 March 1998. A chair and interim board had to be assembled hastily, and terms of reference negotiated with a demanding team of government bureaucrats. The foundation did get lucky, though, with its initial appointment of a chair to head the interim board in the negotiations. The logical person to lead the AHF was Georges Erasmus, but, unfortunately, he was exhausted from his work as co-chair of the Royal Commission on Aboriginal Peoples. As he recalled, in early 1998 he was in hiding. "I decided to take time off. In the middle of the [late January 1998] ice storm [that hit western Quebec and eastern Ontario hard] I got a desperate call from Indian Affairs, saying 'You have to get involved in this.' I said 'I don't need to get involved in anything.'" He had barely put the telephone down when it rang with a call from AFN national chief Phil Fontaine: "Could you come on board and be our negotiator for this $350 million? It all has to be done in six weeks." Vainly, Erasmus pleaded that he wasn't "looking for a job." Fontaine persisted, saying that the money would disappear if they could not reach agreement with the government. Erasmus yielded. "I said, 'Okay, but only for six weeks.' That's how I got hooked. I really got interested in this work. Later, I had a chat with Phil and he just laughed, 'I knew it would happen.'"[28]

Once the leadership question was solved, the question turned to the key task of negotiating the form of the AHF with the federal government. This task was made all the more difficult because the five main Indigenous political organizations in Canada had not always gotten

3.1 Georges Erasmus.

along well in the past. In the world of government-Aboriginal relations, the Assembly of First Nations and Métis National Council had
perceived funding as a zero-sum game in which they were rivals: they
thought that what one organization received the other would not. Yet
they and the Congress of Aboriginal Peoples, which represented mainly
non-status First Nations, the Inuit Tapirisat of Canada (later renamed
Inuit Tapiriit Kanatami), and the Native Women's Association of Canada had to work together to secure the type of healing foundation they

believed would best serve their people. Not surprisingly, tensions often ran high among the groups, with the added pressure that somehow they had to unite in order to effectively haggle with bureaucrats. During the negotiations, the five organizations bargained among themselves in the morning and then faced government negotiators with as much unity as they could muster in afternoon sessions. It was a messy, contentious process made all the more perilous by the short timelines.[29]

The government side was comparatively unified and had the advantage of a clear set of objectives. The federal government was represented by a team composed of officials from the Intergovernmental Affairs Branch of the Privy Council Office (PCO) and the Treasury Board. The PCO was essentially "the brain" of government, with responsibility for the oversight of the bureaucracy; it was led by the clerk of the Privy Council, the most senior official in the Canadian civil service. Treasury Board, as the name suggests, was the organ of government responsible for prudent financial management. Sticking points in the negotiations were the mandate of the new foundation and the degree of freedom it would have in managing the principal amount government was providing. The leaders on the Aboriginal side believed the foundation should have an ambitious research agenda, arguing that it would be difficult to design healing programs without conducting research as to what was needed. Eventually, government officials yielded on the question of allowing the AHF to conduct a research program, but it refused to budge on the question of setting up healing programs aimed at language and culture, in addition to those aimed at victims of sexual and physical abuse. Likely, the officials' stance was based on the fact that Canadian law had not developed mechanisms and standards for measuring and compensating people or groups for loss of culture. In the tense negotiations of February–March 1998, the government would not yield on the point. Similarly, government negotiators were not prepared to loosen the strings on managing the AHF's endowment, although, when appealed to directly, the minister of Indian Affairs suggested that the matter might be revisited later. Recognizing the obduracy of government and conscious of the passing of time, the Aboriginal negotiators gave up the struggle for more fiscal flexibility. In a last-minute flurry, the final details were settled, and the agreement was signed one hour before midnight on 31 March 1998.[30]

Once the AHF was formally established, Mike DeGagné was recruited as its executive director. Born in northwestern Ontario, DeGagné grew up in an Ojibwe family that valued education. As he said later, his father

3.2 Dr Michael DeGagné is inducted into the Order of Canada, 2015.

started out as a farmer and subsequently became an educator after having completed "his degree one course at a time in a church basement in Fort Frances."[31] Michael had extensive schooling, including a BSc from the University of Toronto, a master's degree in administration from Central Michigan University, and a PhD in educational administration from Michigan State University. When DeGagné joined the foundation in 1998, he was in a management role at Indian Affairs, where he had watched the government's response to the RCAP final report with great interest. He noted that the department's initial inclination was to entitle its response to the commission "Charting a New Course," but that it changed the title to *Gathering Strength* because it feared that the other label might suggest the old course Indian Affairs had followed had been unsatisfactory.[32] Prior to joining Indian Affairs he had been on staff at Health Canada, where he had discovered fraud involving an assistant deputy minister and the leadership of an addictions counselling agency in Manitoba.[33] He would bring his detestation of financial malfeasance with him to the AHF.

Other key members of the foundation were assembled in 1998 and the early years of the body's operation. The intent was to have the organization run by Indigenous people for the benefit of survivors and other Indigenous people. The appointment of the staff who looked after the flow of funds – both revenue from the government grant and disbursements to applicants for grants under the AHF's various programs – was especially sensitive and important. In the words of Mike DeGagné, the person chosen as chief operating officer, Terry Goodtrack, was "as credible and honest a person as you could ever want in financial matters."[34] Another major consideration was the person who would oversee the research program for which Erasmus and the interim board had negotiated so urgently. Dr Gail Valaskakis, a former fine arts academic from Concordia University in Montreal who hailed originally from the Chippewa reservation in Lac du Flambeau, Wisconsin, played a vital role directing the foundation's research program until her premature death in 2007.

In addition to these principal staff, the members of the foundation board were critical to success or failure of the organization. The interim board had consisted of representatives of the main five Aboriginal organizations, with a few individuals who had been active in what would become identified as the reconciliation movement. When the interim board gave way to a regular body, those with strong political pedigrees fell away, and the board's centre of gravity shifted towards people with ties to healing and reconciliation. The first vice-president of the management committee was Richard Kistabish, a former grand chief of the Algonquin nation and a larger-than-life personality. The board's secretary, Garnet Angeconeb of Sioux Lookout, Ontario, was Kistabish's opposite in personality but an influential individual in his own right. He was a quiet presence, something of an inspirational force promoting reconciliation within the board. Similarly influential was Maggie Hodgson from Alberta, a long-time worker in the field of healing and a strong proponent of reconciliation. She had had a major role in recruiting Mike DeGagné as executive director, overcoming the young administrator's reluctance to become involved in what he told her was "just going to be another political aboriginal organization."[35] Members of the board of directors were all residential school survivors, save, ironically, for the chair, Erasmus.

Although the permanent board did not experience the same divisions that the interim board had had to overcome, it was still a challenge to get all the directors pulling in the same direction. DeGagné recalled that it took about a year to iron out the roles of board and staff. Some new appointees had unrealistic expectations. One, for example, said during a discussion of whether to eliminate or retain honoraria for meetings of the board that he had quit his job to accept board membership and expected his service at the board table to be a full-time job. It took some time for all board members to understand that they were to concern themselves with policy rather than administration. But, led by Erasmus, the board developed into the appropriate roles. Towards the end of the life of the foundation, DeGagné believed that the board chair and members were the strongest part of the organization. He noted that they all had learned to take off their representational hats before sitting down to discuss policy.[36]

A critically important item of business for the AHF was determining its objectives. The organization's terms of reference had been negotiated with the government, but deciding on goals was a matter that should, the board believed, be carried out by Aboriginal people. Indeed, Indigenous control of the organization was a top priority. For example, the "Frequently Asked Questions" section on the foundation's website began with "What is the Aboriginal Healing Foundation?" and responded with, "An Aboriginal-managed, national, Ottawa-based, not-for-profit private corporation established March 31, 1998 ..."[37] Under such an approach, it was essential that the fledgling board consult Indigenous people before drawing up the foundation's roadmap. This the directors did at a formative gathering in Squamish territory in North Vancouver in July 1998.

The Squamish meeting was stormy but productive. The delegates, who represented twenty-one different residential schools, were assertive with the fledgling board. They expressed considerable unhappiness that many individuals and groups were not represented, and those who were there did not always easily accept organizers' explanations that the start-up funding they had received from the federal government did not permit support for more people. There was more unhappiness to come for survivors. They greeted with great anger the news that the agreement by which the foundation had been set up excluded all but damage attributable to physical and sexual abuse experienced at the schools. Many representatives, understandably, considered cultural loss, especially loss of Indigenous languages, that resulted from schooling to be matters that needed healing. They felt that programs to address the consequences of cultural loss were needed to promote both healing and reconciliation. In spite of the emotional storms that the gathering experienced, the board was able to obtain guidance from the survivor representatives. The most strongly held views of former students were expressed in new guidelines, which the foundation's board members were to follow. Board members were expected to model the behaviour that survivors wanted to encourage: they should be engaged in their personal healing and not be dependent on substances such as alcohol or drugs. The board should be responsive to the survivor community, and should be open, transparent, and accountable to them and the communities of which they were a part. There was no question that, at the end of the gathering, AHF board members had a firm understanding of what a representative group of former students expected. It was crystal clear that survivors were not a passive client group that would accept board leadership unquestioningly. They would be vigilant, critical, and vociferous observers, and sometimes critics, of the foundation's work.[38]

The AHF also learned quickly that another source of scrutiny and criticism of its work was the media. The early media reception was unenthusiastic. When Georges Erasmus announced the creation of the new agency on 4 May 1998, there was no press interest in the story. The government team that oversaw the effort had arranged for a good deal of media access in order to publicize the story, but there was no take-up. When the head of the Indian Affairs team confronted some members of the press about ignoring the event, he was told that "good news stories don't sell."[39] To a great extent, the lack of interest at its birth would typify the treatment the AHF would receive throughout its existence. Because it worked quietly and effectively, and remained scandal free, it stayed largely below the radar of both the press and electronic media.

There were, though, spectacular exceptions, in which media interest tested the fortitude and good will of foundation personnel. Some of the harshest comments came from individual residential school survivors. Mike De Gagné was later to say that, at the outset, the foundation "got a lot of flak from our own community. Google 'Aboriginal people' and 'lots of money,' and you would not get a lot of positive sentiments."[40] Illustrative of this type of criticism was a blast from Gilbert Oskaboose, a survivor of the Jesuit boys' school at Spanish, Ontario, and frequent writer in online locations. His post "The Aboriginal Healing Foundation: A Nest of Maggots" blasted the staff of the AHF as "native fat cats," singling out the executive director and his $141,000 salary and asking, "How much did super Indian Georges Erasmus drag home?" Oskaboose thought the foundation was just another instance of trying to placate First Nations by throwing money at them for healing programs in their communities. "Who is bullshitting who with all this talk of 'healing?' Aboriginal Healing Foundation, my ass. We will never heal or recover from this experience. The best we can ever do is survive." He was particularly scathing about therapies that he thought healing programs would employ. "Band Offices and church-based groups can set up all the 'healing centers' they want. Born-again traditionals can dance about, buck-naked, muttering incantations and casting spells on decent folk until the cows come home. There is no 'healing' from this kind of shit. Indian Country will never recover from the time of residential schools, only survive." The writer denied he was "a disgruntled applicant" or "a truculent prospective employee" who was not hired. He was, Oskaboose said, "just a native citizen who does not like maggots or the way they go about profiting on the misfortune and pain of their betters."[41] It was impossible for foundation staff to respond to these kinds of attacks.

Other detractors were simpler to confront. Frances Widdowson, co-author of a critique of First Nations entitled *Disrobing the Aboriginal Industry*, criticized the AHF as a "boondoogle" in the pages of the *National Post*. Citing Oskaboose's "Nest of Maggots" piece, Widdowson pointed out that the foundation's head office and the programs in the field that it financed were responsible for 950 jobs. "But what do these 'jobs' consist of, and how effective have they been in addressing the psychological problems plaguing communities? As there has been no evaluation of the plethora of 'healing' initiatives, it is likely that these 'jobs' are actually sinecure positions aimed at buying off privileged members of the native population." She singled out Mike De Gagné and his record of work in Aboriginal-related organizations, including Indian and Northern Affairs Canada, as typical of the "Aboriginal industry" she deplored, and described the executive director as "the most significant non-aboriginal player" in the game of extracting public money for the support of the Aboriginal industry.[42]

The foundation responded to this attack in a letter to the editor over the signature of DeGagné. "It is false that 'the only "evaluation" of Aboriginal Healing Foundation (AHF) programs has come from the organization itself,'" he wrote. "The AHF and the programs it funds have been audited and evaluated by independent third parties in government and the private sector. These evaluations are available for public view on our website in their entirety. Only in this limited sense are they 'from' the organization." DeGagné was particularly touchy on this topic because he had insisted from the beginning that the foundation's conduct of business had to conform to the highest standards of transparency and accountability because it was an organization run almost entirely by Aboriginal people. He also rejected Widdowson's criticisms of the therapeutic approaches the foundation supported, and observed, "It is understandable that Ms. Widdowson denies the efficacy of aboriginal organizations; positive outcomes are inconsistent with the premise of her book. But the facts would reveal that the AHF is exactly what Ms. Widdowson espouses – a funder of high-quality services that are tailored to the special needs of the aboriginal population." And he rejected her denial of his Anicinabe roots: "If she had made a two-minute phone call to the AHF, she would not have described the AHF's executive director" as a "non-aboriginal player."[43] The foundation's response was especially robust in its insistence on the validity and efficacy of its healing programs.

In contrast to the charges of its critics, the AHF governance and fiscal accountability were rated very highly by external agencies. Fairly early in its life, the foundation received a positive review for its accountability from the auditor general of Canada, who praised its responsiveness to its funder and stakeholders.[44] The Institute on Governance (IOG), an Ottawa-based think tank specializing in governance that the AHF asked to evaluate its operations after the better part of a decade, was also enthusiastic about what it found. Using an eleven-category schema that probed a range of values and practices from accountability and ethics to long-term vision and rated them on a six-point scale, the IOG's analysts got "results [that] are nothing short of startling. No characteristic gets a rating of less than 5.5. Two characteristics – external relations and accountability – get an astounding average mark of 5.8. And the overall average of the 11 characteristics is well over 5.6, truly an impressive result, and one that we have not seen before in our work with boards."[45] The evaluation lauded both the results of the foundation's programs and the methods it used to achieve them. The study praised the AHF's ability to avoid conflicts of interest and nepotism. And it made a point of stressing that the foundation put a strong emphasis on Aboriginal culture in all its operations.[46]

It was clear that the AHF's success was the result both of sound personnel and good policies. The Institute on Governance evaluation paid particular attention to the leadership of the foundation, singling out its board, president, and executive director. It noted that the board, following a suggestion from an Elder, began each meeting "with an Aboriginal sharing circle. With a Board consisting of 17 members, the sharing circle is a substantial investment in time but it has proven to be an extraordinarily successful tool for creating Board cohesion. The practice is, in a sense, a realization of the notion of harmony, an important value shared by all Aboriginal groups." Each meeting began with an exercise: "Every member of the Board is asked to talk about something from their personal life, whether positive or negative. Topics can be as diverse as the joy of greeting a new grandchild to the feeling of grief over the death of a close friend."[47] The analysts also praised the board chair, Georges Erasmus, and the administrative ability of the executive director, Mike De Gagné, and said that the way in which the two men worked together contributed greatly to the foundation's efficiency, effectiveness, and credibility.[48]

The IOG report also evaluated another area dear to the hearts of foundation critics: the projects that the AHF funded. It noted that, right from its inception, the "Foundation has used explicit criteria to determine projects eligible for funding support." The approved projects had to deal with "the legacy of abuse suffered in residential schools, including the intergenerational affects [sic] of that legacy." They had to show that they "would build and support links with other health, social service or community programs." And accountability was a key requirement of all funded projects: "Accountability to all survivors, accountability to the community in which the project was running and accountability to the target group who the project was meant to serve." Foundation-funded projects had to be consistent "with the Canadian Charter of Rights and Freedoms as well as all other Canadian human rights laws." Under those guidelines, the foundation funded a total of 134 projects in its first six years, including some in every province and territory of the country. These projects were underwritten by the original $350 million, which was augmented by further grants of $40 million in 2005 and $215 million in 2007.[49] The AHF worked hard to ensure that all regions were involved: "When the AHF saw a lack of proposals for projects in communities or regions, the Foundation went out to those communities to engage with and support them in their efforts to establish healing programs. Inclusion of this nature speaks to the guiding principles of the organization, and its desire to ensure support for all Aboriginal peoples affected by the Legacy of Residential Schools."[50] The executive director later reflected that "there is no necessary correlation between the degree to which a community is isolated and its success. Some 'get it' and some don't."[51]

Throughout its existence, the Aboriginal Healing Foundation worked to ensure that the projects it supported would deliver assistance to communities in the short term and leave a legacy as well. It funded programs to provide counselling to people in need, suicide intervention, and workshops on violence and grief, and projects to help communities retrieve and deal with the history of residential schooling. Many of the projects and programs made use of both traditional Aboriginal healing methods and "western" medicine for both physical and mental health problems.[52] Throughout its existence, the AHF followed a philosophy that emphasized capacity building. Its board philosophy included the statement that the foundation "'does not fund need, it funds capacity.'" The executive director applied the same approach with AHF employees. He told his staff repeatedly "to be sure they do not end up leaving the organization with the same skill set they had when they joined it."[53] He provided a clear summary of how the foundation tried to ensure the success of its projects: "Whenever the full Board meets the group goes through projects closely and attempts to anticipate any problems which may arise. There is time set aside specifically to discuss programs and projects which are at risk or are having issues with their funds. Following such discussions the Board then establishes plans for possible scenarios and outcomes. The Board and senior staff have also used on-site reviews as a way of tracking project successes and ensuring ongoing risk mitigation."[54]

Throughout its existence, the Aboriginal Healing Foundation also relied on its publications program as a vehicle for the delivery of services. As a major agency administering public money designed to support healing programs for residential school survivors, the foundation was always eager to get word out on its activities. Naturally, a large number of its publications were annual reports and other updates on the nuts-and-bolts aspects of its operations.[55] A second important category of publications was a monograph series devoted to therapeutic and other aspects of the residential school story. For much of the foundation's existence, the ambitious publication program was led by Research Director Gail Valaskakis. Executive Director Mike DeGagné, who recruited Valaskakis after she retired from her position as dean of Fine Arts at Concordia University, described her as one of the three key people who made the foundation a success.[56] After her untimely death to cancer, the AHF named its library and resource centre after her. Her duties directing research were assumed by Jonathan Dewar.

Foundation publications on the therapeutic aspects of healing and reconciliation for residential school survivors were numerous. Titles included a 2003 volume, *Fetal Alcohol Syndrome among Aboriginal People in Canada: Review and Analysis of the Intergenerational Links of Residential Schools*, and the 2008 publication *Aboriginal Healing in Canada: Studies in Therapeutic Meaning and Practice* (2008).[57] A healing-oriented line of publications culminated in AHF's last release in 2014: *Origins of Lateral Violence in Aboriginal Communities*.[58] This volume, which dealt with the touchy subject of student-on-student abuse in the residential schools, had been suggested by a survivor who sat on the board: the executive director described Garnet Angeconeb of Sioux Lookout as "the driver of the project." Lateral violence was, De Gagné said at the book's launch, "a very difficult subject," and he noted that there would be critics who charged that the foundation was letting the churches and government "off the hook" by shifting the spotlight from perpetrators to residential school survivors.[59] But violence and abuse of students by other students was one of the prevalent, if little discussed, features of residential school history, and it was typical of the foundation's leadership not to shy away from discussing a potentially controversial and divisive topic.

The AHF books that did not deal directly with healing tended to fall into two categories. Particularly in the early years of the foundation's work, it released monographs that were intended to educate readers about the context of the Canadian residential schooling story. A 2003 volume, for example, was entitled *Where Are the Children? Healing the Legacy of Residential Schools*; three years later, the foundation published *Decolonization and Healing: Indigenous Experience in the United States, New Zealand, Australia and Greenland*. As time went on, the foundation began to produce volumes that aimed to connect readers with the experience of residential school survivors. A trio of titles – also made available as a boxed set of paperbacks – emerged in 2011: *From Truth to Reconciliation: Transforming the Legacy of Residential Schools*; *Response, Responsibility, and Renewal: Canada's Truth and Reconciliation Journey*; and *Cultivating Canada: Reconciliation through the Lens of Cultural Diversity.*[60] These handsome volumes, like all AHF publications, were available free of charge to anyone who asked.

The process of reaching out to Canadians with first-person accounts that the 2011 trilogy typified culminated in the foundation's most successful release. In 2012, it published a compilation of what those involved in the publications program considered its most effective essays – *Speaking My Truth: Reflections on Reconciliation and Residential School.*[61] Significantly, the lead essay in *Speaking My Truth* was a reminiscence by Garnet Angeconeb, "Speaking My Truth: The Journey to Reconciliation." The involvement of radio journalist Shelagh Rogers in the production of *Speaking My Truth* represented a more energetic effort to use celebrity and the media to spread the word. Rogers was the immensely popular host of a book show, *The Next Chapter*, on CBC radio and was well known to many in English-speaking Canada because of her earlier involvement in *Morningside* and *This Country in the Morning*, popular radio shows hosted by Peter Gzowski. Rogers acknowledged that she shamelessly used *The Next Chapter* to flog *Speaking My* Truth. She interviewed Mike DeGagné about the book and emphasized to listeners that they could get the book free from the AHF, adding that the foundation would supply sets of the volume to book clubs. The two, as well as fellow editor Glen Lowry, actually attended meetings of book clubs, as Rogers put it, from coast (Quadra Island, BC) to coast (Dartmouth, NS) to coast (Rankin Inlet, NU) and many places in between.[62] Not all the appearances at book clubs went well. DeGagné recalled that at one he was accosted by an immigrant from Serbia, who insisted that what went on at residential schools was nothing compared to what had happened to her people. "Do you think the Russians are going to apologize to us?" she asked scornfully. In reply, DeGagné asked "How would you react if the Russians did apologize to Serbian people?" and the Serbian Canadian replied, "I don't know."[63] Before the foundation wound up its work, it had distributed 35,000 copies of *Speaking My Truth.*[64] As the executive director mused at the AHF's last public event in 2014, "Ironically, an organization of Aboriginal people will be remembered mainly for our books."[65]

The foundation's final vehicle for spreading information about the schools was a spinoff organization known as the Legacy of Hope Foundation (LHF). Planned as a charitable organization to promote understanding of the schools and reconciliation, the LHF never succeeded in raising sufficient money from the general public to support the ambitious program that its founders had contemplated. In fact, it remained dependent principally on government grants.[66] Nonetheless, with a small, dedicated, staff, the LHF developed educational materials and promoted them in museums and at public events such as the national events that the Truth and Reconciliation Commission later convened as part of its mandate. Their approach, one of the leaders recalled, was based loosely on models of Holocaust education.[67] The LHF's work took the form of a travelling photographic exhibition on residential schooling titled *Where Are the Children? Healing the Legacy of Residential Schools* (2003) and another called *We Were So Far Away: The Inuit Experience of Residential Schools* (2011), as well as a set of curriculum materials for Grades 7–10, *100 Years of Loss* (2012).[68] The initial exhibition, *Where Are the Children?*, which was curated by Haudenosaunee photographic expert Jeff Thomas in cooperation with Library and Archives Canada in 2002, travelled widely and reached many people. Originally intended to be "a pop-up version" of *Where Are the Children?*, *100 Years of Loss* would prove influential. Endorsed by the Truth and Reconciliation Commission, it was adopted by the education ministries of Nunavut and the Northwest Territories. A more recent project of the LHF, an exhibit on the Métis, opened at the Canadian Museum for Human Rights in the autumn of 2015.[69]

The Legacy of Hope's exhibitions, books, and curricular materials continued the depiction of residential schooling that had dominated the final report of the Royal Commission on Aboriginal Peoples. The residential schools story was a story of abuse and mistreatment – full stop. Using poignant photographs of young students, the LHF's media implied that only bad things happened at residential schools. The fact that *Where Are the Children?* distorted historical reality by including many pictures of Aboriginal children attending day schools, rather than residential schools, seemed not to bother its creators. But there was a price to be paid for such a shaping of history. As Mike DeGagné noted about his experience at meetings of book clubs that discussed *Speaking My Truth*, a common response to the volume was that it was "not balanced." Where, people asked, were the stories of students who had good experiences? The exhibits and publications of the Legacy of

Hope Foundation had the same effect. The overall impact of its educational efforts, which were considerable, was somewhat diminished by its tight focus on the dark aspects of residential schooling. Did such a focus ultimately get in the way of promoting reconciliation, a mission to which both the Aboriginal Healing Foundation and Legacy of Hope Foundation were dedicated? Was history that was shaped a particular way beneficial or problematic?

The aftermath of the Royal Commission on Aboriginal Peoples produced mixed results for those who were interested in promoting healing and reconciliation. The federal government's response to RCAP's final report consisted of a message of reconciliation that included an apology delivered by the minister of Indian Affairs and a program, *Gathering Strength*, that largely avoided the main thrust in RCAP's conclusions. While the government refused to promote Aboriginal governance on the ambitious scale that RCAP desired, it did advance healing and reconciliation significantly by the creation and funding of the Aboriginal Healing Foundation. The AHF had many accomplishments from its creation in 1998 until the federal government terminated its funding in 2010. It enabled many communities to mount and operate healing programs that benefited thousands of survivors. It disseminated a great deal of information about residential schooling and its consequences through its publications and the work of its spinoff, the Legacy of Hope Foundation. And it could legitimately boast that, as an Aboriginal-run organization operating in the fishbowl of Ottawa, it carried out its work in an effective and accountable way that earned it glowing reviews. As Mike DeGagné said in answer to a questioner who asked what would happen when the AHF finally disappeared, the great tragedy of its experience was that there would be "a loss of institutional capacity" because the talented Aboriginal people he and his board had assembled would disperse. The sad thing was, he said, that "we lost an opportunity."[70]

PART TWO

Finding a Solution

4
The Bench Adjudicates: Litigation

As the twentieth century drew to a close, Christian churches and the federal Parliament were joined by a third Canadian institution as the venue for efforts to deal with the legacy of residential schools. Beginning in the 1980s, the churches that ran the schools apologized for their role. Then, in the 1990s, Parliament played an indirect role in the effort to grapple with the implications of residential schools by establishing the Royal Commission on Aboriginal Peoples (RCAP). RCAP produced an important report on the history and impact of the schools in 1996, but the cabinet, did not take engage effectively with its recommendations. Although the establishment of the Aboriginal Healing Foundation was a fruitful response to RCAP, the rest of the Chrétien government's January 1998 reply, including the minister's apology for residential schools, left survivors and Aboriginal political leaders unsatisfied. Unsurprisingly, it was the third branch of government, the judiciary, that was next called on to deal with the issue. Through the early years of the twenty-first century, the courts were the forum in which survivors attempted to resolve their grievances. Along the way, the churches that had operated the schools would get dragged into the adversarial legal processes, to their great cost. Eventually, the search for a solution would bring survivors, government, and the churches together to create a new mechanism for considering claims.

Although there was no necessary connection between disappointment at the government's response to RCAP and survivors' initiation of litigation, the emergence of lawsuits in 1998 seemed more than a coincidence.

It is likely that survivors on their own would not have turned to legal
action first, because what they usually sought was something the courts
could not deliver. Survivors looked for respect and regret from government and the churches. They desired the opportunity to talk about
their experiences with authority figures from the institutions that had
created and operated the schools. And they wanted representatives of
those agencies to acknowledge what had been done to them, admit that
their institutions were responsible for the damage, and express regret
for what had transpired. As one survivor put it:

> I want to make peace with myself and the federal government and grow
> gracefully and peacefully; at a young age, I did not ask to be abused in any
> way. [I was] born into a happy family; enjoyed [the] company of brothers
> and sisters until taken away to school; there was a time when my life was
> not worth anything; abused, mad[e] to learn English; [I] felt dirty, used,
> no solution for my life; only solution [was] to commit suicide; only reason
> I didn't was someone said "I love you"; heavy burden – heavy load on
> back – pain so unbearable; three simple words would lighten the load: "I
> am sorry."[1]

In 1998, negotiations to settle a claim by twelve men for abuse at the
Oblates' Williams Lake school in British Columbia proved the truth of
that comment. Following lawyers' wrangling just days before the trial,
a young Department of Justice lawyer and Indian Affairs official had
second thoughts about their courtroom tactics. The next morning, the
government lawyer began the proceedings with an apology for the way
the survivors had been treated and a request to hear their stories. The
mood changed and negotiations proceeded well the second day. The
men's final request – a healing ceremony to mark the agreement – was
beyond the on-site official's authority. A hurried telephone call to Indian
Affairs in Ottawa secured a promise to cover the cost of a ceremony, and
negotiations wrapped up the next day.[2]
   A respectful hearing and appropriate response from church and government officials were the most important things for most former students. Many survivors thought that, prior to 1998, the churches had not
apologized in a meaningful way.[3] As a group of survivors said in a consultation with government and church officials in the autumn of that
year, they "just want to have their experience validated and recognized
by both churches and government. Although there have been some
important apologies, there is still bickering about respective degrees of

liability." But the adversarial processes of Canadian justice could not deliver respect and expressions of contrition. As survivors observed, "Going to court is too painful – [the] story has to be told too many times, flashbacks, etc. Court process goes on and on – civil process can be more painful than criminal," and "Going to court is not healing."[4] Moreover, a matter that greatly troubled many survivors was the loss of their language as a result of residential school. Judicial processes were not likely to be effective in dealing with such loss because, in the 1990s, Canadian civil jurisprudence did not recognize language and cultural loss as wrongs that were compensable, and the federal government adamantly opposed any such claims.

Although compensation was important to many survivors, most recognized that money would not heal them. Indeed, survivors and their communities knew from experience with compensation following convictions of perpetrators in British Columbia and Saskatchewan that payouts to individuals usually caused both the recipients and their families intense grief. Following the conviction of William Starr, the former administrator of the Gordon school in Saskatchewan, for sexual abuse of students, for example, a number of survivors received large financial payouts from government. The sudden influx of money devastated many of the individuals and their communities, as the recipients succumbed to temptations of alcohol and drugs.[5] A group of former students at a meeting in Toronto in the spring of 1999 testified that being paid for being abused made them "feel ugly, dirty, used by what happened to us – paying cash can reinforce this." Compensation was usually spent quickly, and it affected the whole community adversely. It incited people who had been abused by a compensated abuser to demand their "share." The result often was community division.[6]

Still, through 1998 the number of civil actions on behalf of survivors continued to increase. One factor behind the growth was undoubtedly the entrepreneurial action of some law firms, as some lawyers began to promote litigation to survivors, usually on a contingency fee basis. Under this arrangement, the advocates would not be paid unless the action succeeded. But contingency fees also meant that the survivors who did succeed would find a large proportion of the award taken by their legal representative. George Thomson, a former deputy minister of justice, was appalled at these tactics and wrote to a number of provincial bar associations to urge them to rein the litigators in. His efforts produced no results.[7] The number of actions increased steadily. As Thomson recalled, the number of cases kept growing, and First Nations did

not seem reconciled by the government's 1998 Statement of Reconciliation. When he first dealt with residential school issues in the mid-1990s,
about three hundred legal actions were pending; by the spring of 1999,
the number had climbed almost eighteen-fold to 5300.[8]

The swelling number of legal actions led the government to seek a
different way to resolve litigation. Thomson, a special adviser to the
Minister of Justice, sat down to dinner with Phil Fontaine of the Assembly of First Nations and a facilitator, Glenn Sigurdson, to discuss the
situation. Survivors objected to the treatment they usually received in
court, as defence counsel rigorously cross-examined them about their
school history. Thomson wondered if there were not a better way than
civil litigation. But he also knew that the Department of Justice opposed
the use of non-traditional methods of dealing with abuse claims, such
as alternative dispute resolution (ADR) processes. The group at dinner
agreed that there were valid claims arising from the residential schools,
that the loss of language and culture was in the air as a potentially successful cause of action, and that there was a need for a process that
focused on healing and was more attuned to Aboriginal values. They
decided to hold a series of "exploratory dialogues" jointly sponsored by
the Assembly of First Nations (AFN) and the government of Canada to
consult residential schools survivors, church representatives, government officials, and lawyers who represented residential school clients.
It took some persuading to get all the churches to participate, but in
due course eight dialogues took place, in Kamloops, southern Alberta,
Regina, Winnipeg, Toronto, Rankin Inlet, NWT, Whitehorse, and Montreal between September 1998 and May 1999, with a final wrap-up dialogue in Toronto in late June 1999.[9] Between thirty and forty people participated in each of the first seven dialogues, with a larger attendance
at the wrap up.

The exploratory dialogues consistently incorporated Aboriginal practice and gave pride of place to Aboriginal leaders. Facilitator Glenn Sigurdson was assisted by Chief Mark Wedge of Yukon.[10] Two of the most
influential First Nations participants were Chief Robert Joseph of British
Columbia and Maggie Hodgson of Alberta, both long-time advocates of
healing and reconciliation.[11] Each dialogue began with opening cere mo-
nies and prayers conducted by Elders, and the final wrap-up dialogue
also featured the leadership of Elder Willy Hodgson, who smudged the
room with sweetgrass smoke at the beginning of each morning's deliberations. Opening rituals were followed by individual introductions,
with each person being introduced by the person next to them. One by

4.1a Maggie Hodgson.

4.1b Chief Robert Joseph.

one the participants offered their comments before any other discussions were held, and interruptions or speaking out of turn were not permitted. At the Winnipeg dialogue, it took two and one-half days of a three-day gathering to hear contributions from everyone in the circle. Only then were officials able to present their views.[12] Throughout, a respectful atmosphere prevailed as the groups discussed often sensitive and contentious issues.

Although the dialogues began with some testiness and suspicion, the process as a whole proved productive. The first session, at the former Kamloops residential school, began in a strained manner. Some of the survivors had participated in a criminal trial that had lasted twenty-six weeks and "were battle worn by the court process."[13] Facilitator Glenn Sigurdson recalled that there were some positive recollections of school days but that "there was no shortage of stories of abuse of every possible kind, including the widespread horror of sexual exploitation at the hands of pedophiles who migrated to those institutions like bees to honey."[14] Maggie Hodgson, who had heard many accounts of abuse in her work with alcohol addicts, recalled being moved by one participant whose suffering was extraordinary.[15] Chief Joseph, someone who had also heard many sorrowful tales from former students, acknowledged that the first dialogue was tense and angry in tone. But, he recalled, as the dialogues proceeded, the tone began to change as people listened to one another. "I saw people change right before my eyes – forgiving ..., hugging each other. I thought, 'Holy smokes! This really does make change.'"[16]

At a number of locations, participants questioned the motives of the agencies that had put the dialogues together. Some indicated that their suspicions were aroused by the fact that the AFN and government of Canada had started the process; others were put off by the participation of church representatives; and many people from the denominations were hesitant to participate, fearing that the churches would be demonized. At Regina, a survivor expressed "some concerns about the timing – is it in good faith?" The churches and government had known of abuse in the residential schools "for a long time. Why the government interest now?" The doubter suspected it was probably "because of the number of suits. Where were the AFN and FSIN [Federation of Saskatchewan Indian Nations] on this issue five years ago?"[17] At the Toronto wrap-up, the churches were criticized: "While church leaders come to the dialogues and talk about forgiveness and compassion, they then file motions that urge that the survivors' legal claims be struck out because of limitation periods. This leads to cynicism and mistrust and it is a great leap of faith for us to be here."[18] Not surprisingly, a number of the former students were angry, still bearing painful memories of their school experience. At the Alberta dialogue, two of the survivors of the Oblate-run Grollier Hall in the Northwest Territories just listed the numbers they had as students on their name tags.[19]

In spite of the tension and suspicion that understandably accompanied the exploratory dialogues, considerable progress was made. Among the reasons for this progress were the consistent use of Aboriginal protocol and influence of trusted Elders such as Chief Bobby Joseph and Maggie Hodgson. As well, the fact that the government representatives steadfastly denied they had a hidden agenda and insisted on hearing the views of survivors and church people helped to allay suspicions. A common theme at the dialogues was that litigating over residential school abuse was not only hurtful but often counterproductive. For their part, the churches indicated that their survival might be at risk because of the expense of litigation. And there was, understandably, distress at the tactics that some law firms used in recruiting survivors and prosecuting their cases. At the Alberta dialogue, speakers complained about lawyers "approaching people on reserve"; one had heard of lawyers charging contingency fees of 40 per cent and more: "There is a feeding frenzy going on in the community as lawyers sign people up without there being supports in place. Some sign forms and then commit suicide – some are as vulnerable as they were at the schools." At the Regina dialogue, a speaker expressed concern "about levels of contingency fees – heard up to 47 percent." Some lawyers, allegedly, "have come to communities and lined people up like at residential schools."[20] Such concerns, along with those about the tendency of civil litigation to compel survivors to relive their school experience, made many survivors who attended the dialogues unhappy and suspicious.

While testimony about the shortcomings of litigation was frequent, an alternative took some time to emerge. It was a notable breakthrough that the first dialogue in British Columbia, begun amid suspicion, at least agreed on a general statement of what participants wanted. The objective should be, as one federal representative put it, "to get to a good place in a good way."[21] This statement became a mantra, repeated frequently at subsequent dialogues. Another point that came through clearly was that any alternative to court processes had to be directed by the survivors. The "ADR process must be developed and controlled by the survivors," was how it was expressed at the first Toronto dialogue.

The proceedings had to be "sensitive to cultural differences and decisions must be binding." Survivors from Grollier Hall, from whose ranks two militants had appeared at the Alberta dialogue, were almost elder statesmen of the consultation by the time of the wrap-up gathering in Toronto. Not only had they made presentations to other dialogues, but they had returned to Yellowknife and set up their own alternative dispute resolution process. At the final meeting, their advice to others "was to give ADR a try but keep control. 'Some of our guys can finally see the light at the end of the tunnel,' they said. 'We feel confident in this process. We're going to move ahead.'"[22]

Other themes that emerged from the exploratory dialogues included the importance of Aboriginal healing methods, the mixed history that residential schools represented to survivors, and the need to memorialize the experience. Participants at the Alberta gathering agreed that "healing must be based in traditional practices. The traditional forms of healing are still there. Language, culture and spirituality are critical elements in healing."[23] At the Regina dialogue, speakers emphasized the necessity "to get back language" and complained that First Nations "Elders [are] not recognized as healers" – that recognition was extended "only [to] people with degrees." Participants also noted that "government needs to recognize that healing is a process, not a deliverable with a specific time frame."[24]

In spite of some survivors' anger, the dialogues were often surprisingly balanced in their assessment. The predominant recollections about their school days that First Nations participants shared were very negative. Besides frequent stories of abuse and subsequent psychological damage, some speakers emphasized the tyrannical nature of the schools: "Residential school was just like a cult," a survivor remembered in Whitehorse.[25] The tone conformed so closely to the negative history of residential schooling that had emerged from the Royal Commission on Aboriginal Peoples and the press in the 1990s that, when ending the final circle, Elder Willy Hodgson went out of his way to thank the "representatives of the institutions that we have called abusers and perpetrators of cultural genocide." "We thank the Creator for their presence," he continued, suggesting that they must have felt "like a dartboard during the course of these dialogues."[26] He was not alone in acknowledging the difficult situation of these representatives. Speakers at the Alberta and Regina conclaves noted that "some good things happened" at the schools and that some people "got good educations" in spite of the travails of school life. They acknowledged that "many staff ... were not perpetrators" and, moreover, that not all the perpetrators were staff: there "was a lot of abuse by older boys."[27] In light of survivors' balanced views, it was not surprising that some demanded memorialization. "The deep need to tell the story, and have it memorialized in a public way must be respected – including finding a means to commemorate those who have died." The schooling experience had to become part of the historical record: "who attended, the memorabilia, the trophies – must be recorded and told and remembered. If we do not hear from the past we are doomed to repeat the mistakes of history."[28]

As early as the third dialogue, a consensus began to form that included using memorialization of the past to instruct. "The discussion evolved," noted the recorders at Regina, "to the point that there appeared to be broadly based support – four interconnecting building blocks needed to be in place within any process of resolution: disclosure, with safety; validation, with sensitivity; reparation, with flexibility; and commemorations, with respect."[29] These precepts remained prominent in the remaining discussions. Fifty of those who had participated in earlier dialogues attended the final gathering in Toronto and held "quite detailed discussions around the design of dispute resolution models."[30] One of the items they listed under "immediate doables" concerned commemoration: "It is necessary to tell the story. Build a memorialization into each of the [ADR] pilots, with the agreement of all the participants, which is accessible to all the participants." Those involved should "create a public 'truth and reconciliation' process consistent with the Royal Commission [on Aboriginal Peoples'] recommendation."[31]

The Toronto finale endorsed the key points that had been made at earlier dialogues, including a survivors-centred process. "While the government and churches can deal with compensation, only the survivors can heal themselves[;] that part is none of the government's business. I sometimes think the attitude is that they buggered us up[;] now they'll fix us up. We can fix ourselves." Again participants noted, "Many survivors are seeking compensation for more than physical and sexual abuse (e.g., cultural genocide, loss of identification, pride, language, culture and family)."[32] And the theme of tolerance was prominent. "All parties," according to the record "expressed a commitment to the continued existence of the other institutions. 'Reconciliation shouldn't wipe any of us out,'" said a government official, and one survivor added, "we have to help the churches survive – It's not a good history, but it's our history."[33]

The Toronto wrap-up dialogue endorsed the idea of developing an alternative dispute resolution process for survivors who did not wish to pursue their case in the courts. Indeed, an experiment in ADR was already underway. As noted above, the survivors from Grollier Hall who had such an impact on the Alberta dialogue had set up their own ADR program. It became the first of two such experiments that were running by March 1999, and the government had indicated a willing-ness to create more to give the alternative to litigation a thorough test.[34] The wrap-up dialogue endorsed ADR pilot projects: "Go forward with the pilot projects as the only way to build trust is by doing." And the first of a series of "possible next steps" was to "complete the rest of the ADR pilots. Perhaps the most important immediate action is to move quickly to identify and proceed with the other 10 pilot projects in accordance with the objectives set out in the [dialogue] principles docu-ment. Nothing could demonstrate more the value of those principles than to complete ADR projects in each region of the country success-fully."[35] Eventually, ten pilot projects were conducted, although only two were successfully completed.[36] The "Guiding Principles for Work-ing Together to Build Restoration and Reconciliation" that the represen-tatives adopted at the final meeting emphasized respectful dealing with other participants, a role for survivors in developing a process, holistic and spiritual methods, and voluntary participation.[37] When those who had been involved with the dialogues from the beginning saw the dis-tance survivors, churches, and government had travelled from the tense gathering at Kamloops to the consensual conclusion in Toronto, they had to be impressed.

No one would have been more astonished with the progress than church leaders. They had heard someone say that they should not be wiped out by litigation and that the churches' record, even with all its flaws, was the survivors' history, too. Nonetheless, the churches viewed the pro-posed ADR pilot projects with misgivings. "There is a real fear that this process, under the prevailing assumptions, will mean the elimination of many of our church organizations and that, as a result, we won't be able to care for our people." They found it difficult "to trust others in this context, including governments."[38] If they had known what senior government officials thought about them, they would have been even more alarmed. Three of the most senior bureaucrats who dealt with residential school issues, from the Departments of Indian Affairs and Justice, expressed little sympathy for the churches.[39]

The reality was that, by 1999, the churches that had operated the residential schools were facing an existential threat. All four of the denominations involved – the Roman Catholic, Anglican, United, and Presbyterian Churches – had to deal with serious financial problems, and one of them, in addition, was wrestling with a moral challenge. Even though the government and the churches had agreed, following the dialogues, to examine non-adversarial ways of dealing with survivors' lawsuits, the litigation process continued to unfold while pilot projects were launched. Lawyers for aggrieved survivors always recommended that a suit name the federal government as the respondent because the government of Canada had deep pockets and the churches did not. But Ottawa immediately responded by cross-suing or "third-partying" the denomination involved. This strategy made sense legally, because Canadian jurisprudence was not clear where liability for damage inflicted by the schools resided or, more appropriately, how legal and financial liability should be apportioned between government and church. The schools had been authorized and largely funded by the government, but they were operated day to day and partially financed by the denominations. Accordingly, there was a legal argument for having the courts apportion liability by bringing the churches into the litigation.

For the churches, though, the practice made no sense at all, especially from a financial perspective. As the number of lawsuits swelled, the denominations found that they were facing not just mounting legal bills from their own lawyers but sometimes also for court awards in favour of the plaintiff. Very quickly the financial toll increased, and the denominations believed they were facing financial exactions that threatened their very existence. The Oblate "province," or administrative unit, in Manitoba and Saskatchewan approached insolvency by 2001. Similarly, the Anglican diocese of Caledonia in northern British Columbia chose to wind up its affairs late in 2001 in the interest of having an orderly shutdown rather than a bankruptcy,[40] while the primate of the Anglican Church warned his flock in a pastoral letter that the costs associated with the "1,600 claims" the church faced could "exhaust all the assets of the General Synod and of some dioceses involved."[41] The United Church was watching its financial reserves shrink steadily as lawyers' bills mounted. The denomination was saved by what must have seemed divine intervention. Out of the blue, the church got word that a former minister, who was also a medical doctor and later a land developer in California, had left the church $20 million. "It's clear that if that money wasn't there," said Rev David Iverson, one of the United Church's key people on residential school matters, "we would be looking through a different set of lenses."[42]

By 2000, the government and the churches found themselves at loggerheads. The churches lobbied the government for some relief from litigation expenses, and the government in turn sought a way out of the political crossfire it faced as church leaders and parishioners complained about the its tactic of offloading legal liability onto the churches. Over the increasingly troubled relationship, two factors loomed. First, and the issue that most motivated the government, was a determination to avoid any agreement that contemplated awards for loss of language and culture. Second, both the churches and the government were perplexed as to how to divide liability. By 2000, federal officials who were looking after the residential school file, including the ADR pilot projects, faced an impasse with the churches. One sign of the government's political concern was the fact that the prime minister's trusted chief of staff, Jean Pelletier, met with representatives of the churches in April and "expressed a sincere desire to find a solution to this crisis that church organizations are facing, saying that it was not in the public interest for denominations or congregations to disappear, to go bankrupt."[43] When government officials asked cabinet to appoint a federal negotiator to deal with the churches, the executive surprisingly named Deputy Prime Minister Herb Gray. After dealing with the issue for several months, Gray decided he wanted responsibility for "the whole file" – that is, all aspects of the residential schools abuse issue. Granting the senior Liberal his wish meant creating a separate department, Indian Residential Schools Resolution Canada (IRSRC), complete with its own staff, which was eventually headed by Dr Jack Stagg, a bureaucrat with historical training.[44]

Gray's action accelerated the government's talks with the churches, but it did not make them any easier. Federal officials still refused to budge on the issue of liability for loss of language and culture, even though survivors clamoured for compensation and at least some of the churches felt sympathy for their position. By late 2001, even federal officials conceded that "exclusion of language and culture" was contributing to problems that the ADR pilot projects were experiencing, but there was no change in the government stance.[45] On the issue of dividing financial liability the courts had provided varied answers. A case in the interior of British Columbia had produced a split of liability of 60 per cent church and 40 per cent government. The government had wanted a 70:30 split, while the churches had favoured Ottawa shouldering all liability but knew that this was unlikely. A high-profile case that arose subsequent to the criminal conviction of Arthur Plint, a boys' dormitory supervisor at the United Church's Alberni Indian Residential School in British Columbia, was trundling its way through the courts. The suit by twenty-two survivors against Plint and the church resulted in an excruciating trial – 13 days in 1998, 30 in 1999, and 49 in 2000 – before the Supreme Court of British Columbia ruled in 2001 that liability belonged 75 per cent to government and 25 per cent to the church.[46]

The churches found themselves in the government's bad books in 2001. Relations between Ottawa and the Anglican church were strained by the Anglicans' public relations efforts to promote their point of view in the press. Apparently in frustration at the slow pace of talks with the churches, government officials lashed out. In the autumn, Minister Gray responded to suggestions in an *Anglican Journal* editorial that the government was forcing the churches into insolvency. After denying that Ottawa was pushing the Diocese of Cariboo into bankruptcy, Gray reminded the editor that a court had agreed on a 60:40 split favouring the government, and he suggested the church was using a legal dodge to minimize financial damage: "The Anglican church has relied on its corporate structure to insist that only those dioceses, parishes, or orders where abuse occurred are liable." He also hinted that the government believed the public agreed with his views regarding liability. "I believe that Canadians expect that other organizations of the church contribute to the financial burden when some of its smaller parishes cannot pay their share of the compensation for abuses that took place."[47] That Gray's perspective was now the government's "talking point" on the issue was suggested by the fact that an Ottawa-area Liberal MP, Marlene Catterall, reproved a clergyman in her riding in almost exactly the same words Gray had used with the *Anglican Journal*. "I believe that Canadians expect that other organizations of a church contribute to the financial burden when some of its smaller parishes cannot pay their share of the compensation for abuses that took place," she wrote the cleric.[48]

The executive assistant to Deputy Prime Minister John Manley told a group of church representatives, "We will solve this with or without the churches." The bureaucrat "assured us that it is not the intention of the govt. to cause any of the churches to go bankrupt. But he said realistically that is not going to happen. He suggested that some parts of some churches might cease to function, but that is not bankruptcy." When confronted with the case of the Oblates on the prairies, "he seemed surprised to learn that what was precipitating the financial crisis was not compensation payments, there have to this point not been any, but the cost of legal fees."[49] If government officials did not know how litigation was affecting the churches financially, what was the likelihood that they would sympathize with their predicament?

It emerged in September 2001 that Indian Residential Schools Resolution Canada had commissioned a public opinion survey on residential schools. Particularly alarming for the churches was that Ottawa chose to release the poll just before a scheduled negotiation session. Primate Michael Peers angrily wrote to Herb Gray about this action. He reminded the minister that, at a meeting with Anglican prelates in the spring, Gray had spoken "strongly" and "at length" about his "view that the Anglican Church was being irresponsible in its public campaign regarding the residential schools litigation and our pending financial crises" and had "admonished us to avoid negotiating through the media." Now, "on the eve of the fourth meeting of church and government representatives, your government released polling information that is enormously prejudicial to the churches' negotiating position."[50]

If the churches were offended by the government's hypocrisy, they were disturbed by what the public opinion survey revealed.[51] The Pollara/Earnscliffe pollsters had found that the residential school problem "is a high profile issue with which most Canadians are familiar" and is one that "most Canadians are interested in, including coming to a resolution." "Almost all Canadians (85%) think there is validity to some of the claims," and, while they "do not believe financial compensation is the only means to help the victims," almost "all, including frequent churchgoers, see government and churches as both legally and morally responsible, and as such, believe the ideal resolution would be a 50/50 share of responsibility." Polling "evidence suggests that there will be significant opposition, even anger, if churches evade their share of responsibility and as a result taxpayers pick up the shortfall. A major cleavage exists between churchgoers and the rest of Canadians" on this point. Most respondents were content to see the churches experience any financial pain short of actual bankruptcy to pay their share. "Most people are quite untroubled by the churches having to divest assets to meet their obligations ... Even frequent churchgoers do not find divesting assets to be unacceptable." If there was a silver lining in the poll results for the churches, it was that "most people see the government as having responsibility, believe it should accept that responsibility and want it to deal fairly and generously with victims of a very serious crime." Not surprisingly, representatives of the various churches were disillusioned and disappointed with the poll results and particularly with the way the government handled their publication. They felt that had been "played" and coopted by officials. Nonetheless, they concluded they should resist the temptation to give the IRSRC deputy minister, Jack Stagg, "personally a hard time – keep the good manners. Let's sit down ecumenically and figure out the right thing to do for aboriginal people and white people."[52]

The urgency about the Anglican Church's financial situation that had been discernible in the primate's pastoral letter in May 2000 led the denomination to seek its own deal with the government. In addition to being told by accountants Ernst and Young that their finances were precarious, the Anglicans had been held 60 per cent liable for damages to be paid out in an abuse case that arose from their school in Lytton, BC. The church approached the deputy minister of finance, Scott Clark, who seemed amenable to finding a solution to their problem. Then they worked with Stagg on a bilateral deal, which was concluded in the autumn of 2002. Under that agreement, government and church would split all residential school costs 70:30, respectively, but, equally important for the Anglicans, the church's liability was capped at a maximum of $25 million. As part of the agreement, the church had to raise $25 million in December–February 2003 and persuade all of its thirty dioceses to sign on to the arrangement, and the dioceses would then have five years to honour their pledges. Another clause said that, if the government struck a better deal with one or more of the other three churches involved in abuse claims, the Anglicans would benefit from it, too. After the dioceses agreed and the specified funds were pledged, the deal with the government was ratified in the spring of 2003.[53]

Peremptory action by the federal government resolved the finance issue with the other three churches, in the process ruffling feathers among the church leaders. Frustrated by the way the talks with the churches had bogged down in 2001, and recognizing that sharing liability continued to be a problem, Ottawa announced unilaterally that, henceforth, it would pay 70 per cent of any court award, leaving the remaining 30 per cent to be picked up by the religious organizations. Some churches' refusal to pay awards unless ordered to do so by a court had cast a pall over the dispute resolution pilot projects. Understandably, claimants were reluctant to settle without some assurance that the church would pay its share.[54] As well, some survivors were unhappy with the pilot projects because they couldn't easily form a group to participate, as survivors from Grollier Hall had done and recommended all along. In other words, the differences between government and the churches not only complicated relations between these two institutions, they also interfered with the efforts of survivors, lawyers, and officials to find a better process. All in all, it was a severely troubled relationship. The moderator of the United Church in this period later recalled, "I was ashamed of my own government." He would have liked, he said, to have church and government put their heads together with survivors and lawyers to solve the problem, but Ottawa was not interested in doing so.[55]

In these years, the United Church (UCC), the largest Protestant denomination in Canada, faced another problem. The church was finding litigation extremely divisive and unsettling, marked by friction between head office and local adherents. The UCC was composed of individual congregations, which were grouped into regional presbyteries, and then geographically larger conferences. Above the conferences was the nation-wide General Conference. Congregations sent delegates to the General Conference every two years to discuss and decide both social policies, such as the church's stand on the question of the ordination of homosexuals, and spiritual matters, such as adoption of a new Sunday School curriculum. Theoretically, General Conference had the authority to bind conferences, presbyteries, and congregations. The reality was always much messier than the organization charts and would be especially tested in the troubling residential school abuse litigation known as the Blackwater case.

Following the criminal conviction in 1995 of Arthur Plint of the UCC's Port Alberni residential school, Willie Blackwater and twenty-one other survivors sued for compensation. During the three years it took to hear the case, sittings of increasing length were held in, first, Nanaimo, then Prince Rupert, and finally Vancouver. The church was represented by lawyers from headquarters, who were under instructions to make their case while inflicting as little damage on survivor witnesses as possible. David Iverson, a United Church minister who was often "the face of the church" at the civil trial, recalled that the church instructed its lawyers not to use an individual claimant's employment report from British Columbia that would have worked against claimant's arguments for damages.[56]

The United Church congregation in Port Alberni did not view their church's conduct positively. The people of St Andrew's Church had responded to Plint's conviction with shock and a desire to uncover the church's complicity in the abuse at Alberni Indian Residential School (AIRS) in order to make amends.[57] After a period of studying residential school history on their own, they initiated contact with local survivors, a few of whom were members of their congregation, to pursue reconciliation. As their movement began to make headway and it looked as though the congregation would make a public apology to survivors, national officials intervened. Headquarters personnel were persuaded by their legal advisers that an apology would jeopardize, or at least weaken, the church's defence in the civil action. Bob Smith, the former moderator of the United Church who had delivered the denomination's first apology in 1986 and was a resident of British Columbia, described the situation as a dilemma. He and Brian Thorpe, he recalled, "spent our time in Toronto arguing that the church had no choice but to apologize – regardless of the cost, and our time here in BC reminding the eager-beavers here that there were sound reasons not to jeopardize the institution."[58] Despite the Toronto office's arguments, the St Andrew's congregation in May 1997 held a feast with local Nuu-chah-nulth groups at which they issued a fervent apology. While not all AIRS survivors accepted the gesture, the Nuu-chah-nulth Tribal Council did. The same was true of local United Church people: while most approved of the gesture, a few did not.[59]

The feast and apology did not end the strains that the Blackwater civil trial created. The St Andrew's congregation asked the national church to make a similar apology, and it succeeded in getting support from its presbytery and the British Columbia Conference. But to their intense disappointment, when the General Council met in Camrose, Alberta, in August, the national leadership persuaded delegates not to approve an apology but rather to issue a statement of repentance. For some in British Columbia, including clergy, such caution was offensive. Two lay people wrote to a Vancouver Island newspaper "that the General Council's decision was certainly made with the best of intentions. But if there is anything that we have learned from our experience with the Residential School system it is this: good intentions and fine motives are not enough."[60]

The onset of another phase of the Blackwater trial in 1998 kept relations strained. In an effort to inform themselves and smooth relations
with the Nuu-chah-nulth and St Andrew's congregation, a delegation
from the executive of the General Council met with the local church
and was profoundly moved by the stories of survivors who were present. That experience, according to Bill Phipps, the moderator at the
time, changed a lot of minds at headquarters and made possible the
apology he offered late in 1998 on behalf of the national church for its
role in residential schooling.[61] One measure of the apology's impact
on Port Alberni and the Nuu-chah-nulth survivors was the response
of Ron Hamilton, one of the most outspoken and critical of the former
students. He wrote the moderator "to thank you, as much as one can
do this in writing, for the apology you issued," which he described
as "clear, concise, honest, moving, and not cowardly." Referring to BC
United Church personnel such as Brian Thorpe and former moderator
Bob Smith, he said, "They have all helped clear a path for us to meet on,
finally, as friends. I am deeply moved by their action."[62]

As beneficial as the 1998 apology was, it did not eliminate the problems the United Church had in dealing with the Alberni legacy. Phipps
described the conundrum simply: how do we give plaintiffs their due
legally and morally, while trying to walk a new path together? Matters
were exacerbated by differences within the UCC team. One fault line
arose over the degree of responsibility the church thought it had. The
national leadership by 1998 recognized that it had a large share of the
blame, but one of its paid staff, John Siebert, believed – and said loudly –
that his research demonstrated that the federal government was the
legal operator of the schools and consequently was solely responsible.
At one point, a UCC official located in Vancouver and one of its lawyers
published a letter in the *National Post* dissociating the UCC from the
individual staff member's opinion.[63] Siebert recalled that, while he was
never pressured to recant by national leaders or their lawyers, his views
did cause some United Church people unhappiness. They thought the
position he took was an attempt to have the UCC shirk its responsibility.[64] Another fault line within the church emerged in relations between
national staff and their counsel. As Brian Thorpe said to one of the lawyers, "It must be challenging to have a client who doesn't want to win."[65]
Siebert recalled that the church's national leadership instructed its lawyers to avoid use of certain standard tactics in defending the Blackwater
case. When interviewing plaintiffs in the out-of-court examination for
discovery, they were not to use humiliating questions, in order to avoid

revictimizing them. In doing so, Siebert thought that the church lawyers were working with one hand tied behind their backs.[66] Despite such restraint, courtroom proceedings brought to the fore all the tensions among staff and between the local and national church. Moderator Bill Phipps recalled walking into the courtroom in Nanaimo in 1998 and being stopped in his tracks by the sight before him. The audience contained a large number of First Nations people, but at the front of the chamber was an all-white group of lawyers, judges, and court officials. To Phipps, the layout in the courtroom symbolized the colonial situation that had produced the case.[67] The UCC point man in BC, Brian Thorpe, recalled the tensions between the local people, including non-Native church members, and the United Church team from Toronto. People, he said, came out of the courtroom saying they felt ashamed of being members of the United Church:

Coming to terms with the legacy of the residential school system has for some in our denomination been akin to a loss of innocence. When your self image as a church is that of an activist church in solidarity with the poor and the marginalized, the realization that for generations you were involved in a system which separated children from communities and which aided in the destruction of languages and cultures and which contributed to a colonizing process resulting in increasing power and marginalization among aboriginal peoples can be quite devastating.

For United Church clergy like him, who thought of themselves as being "on the said of the angels," it was painful to discover that now they were on the other side. It was, he concluded, "a kind of loss of institutional innocence."[68] There were also moments when healing and harmony seemed more evident than stress and strife. Phipps noted that, at the Nanaimo hearings, the local United Church people provided lunch for everyone, including First Nations people who were supporting the plaintiffs.[69] And in spite of the pain that was caused by having to testify at the Blackwater trial, Jessie Oliver, who had worked at the school and knew, but loathed, Plint, was given flowers by a number of the claimants.[70] Oliver and Blackwater were subsequently elected commissioners to the next General Council.[71] On the other hand, the national church's decision in July 1998 to appeal an initial ruling on liability caused another eruption of local anger. A member of the St Andrew's congregation objected to the moderator about the way the church's lawyer, despite instructions from Toronto, had cross-examined survivors. "At the end of the day, we ... came across as 'weasels,' squirming to get off the hook and trying to 'pass the buck' onto the Federal Government. Good lawyering? – maybe – but a human relations disaster. We came across as just another corporate client concerned about the legality, rather than the morality of the case."[72] The Blackwater trial was a revelation. United Church leaders learned lessons from it – including the court's finding that liability belonged 75 per cent to government and 25 per cent to the church[73] – that it would use more effectively in later relations with First Nations members.

The churches soon were also involved in another quasi-judicial area, dispute resolution pilot projects. These projects, which grew out of the exploratory dialogues held across the country in 1998 and 1999, were designed to find less adversarial ways of resolving former students' claims for damages than through the courts. Because they were experimental, federal justice and Indian and Northern Affairs Canada (INAC) officials such as lawyer Doug Ewart and Indian Affairs official Shawn Tupper had much more latitude than normally would have been the case when overseeing them. Prior to 1998, the federal government had opposed settling schools abuse litigation by arbitration. Ewart recalled that cabinet only grudgingly agreed to the pilot projects.[74] At the Alberta exploratory dialogue, a delegation from Grollier Hall had told other participants that they had developed their own group dispute resolution process. "We're ready to go. Come up to Yellowknife." In such processes, Ewart and Tupper had considerable flexibility to fashion procedures with the survivors, provided that two conditions were met. Any process would compensate only legally recognized causes of complaint; in other words, complainants could be compensated for abuse, but not for loss of language and culture. As well, any validation method that the dispute resolution process used had to be robust enough to withstand scrutiny. Ever present in the minds of federal officials was the debacle associated with an alternative dispute resolution process for former inmates of a correctional school in Shelburne, NS.[75] It was notorious in governmental and legal circles for a lax verification process that led to a number of claimants with dubious cases being compensated.

In December 1998, Ewart and Tupper travelled to Yellowknife to meet with the Grollier survivors. The first meeting, with about twenty men, was stormy. The group refused to permit the bureaucrats to make notes, destroying in the middle of the circle the notes the two had thus far taken. The officials' return to Ottawa was delayed because the survivors insisted that they not leave. In spite of the difficult beginnings, discussions eventually settled on an inquisitorial method for presenting and verifying the claims. To this and some other groups of survivors, the possibility of handling former students' claims collectively was an attractive feature.[76]

The rich potential of these pilot projects to overcome the shortcomings of traditional court procedure and address the desire for reconciliation was demonstrated in another pilot project in British Columbia. In the early spring of 2004, the government of Canada and the United Church served as co-hosts of a feast in the Gitxsan feast hall in Hazelton.[77] The extraordinary event, a modified version of a traditional First Nations ceremony for recording and validating important events in the life of the community, was the culmination of a pilot project focused on a group of about two dozen Gitxsan who had attended the United Church's Edmonton Indian Residential School (EIRS). As guests in the hall would learn, these individuals had suffered the full range of abuses that were becoming familiar to those Canadians who followed the continuing residential school story. Once the issue of compensation had been settled by discussion among survivors, United Church representatives, and government officials, the focus shifted to commemoration. What the Edmonton survivors were proposing was more properly viewed as a mechanism for reintegrating them into the community from which they had been removed. One of their greatest fears was that their families and neighbours would not accept them fully because of their estrangement and loss of cultural knowledge. They wanted a feast to reintroduce them to the Gitxsan and welcome them back.

The proposal to use a Gitxsan ceremony to complete dispute resolution was welcome to United Church leaders in British Columbia, who had been working hard since the Plint and Blackwater cases to advance reconciliation. For the government officials directly involved, too, the proposal was acceptable; they had, after all, approached the pilot projects with the intention of finding new ways to resolve issues and restore relations. But "selling" the idea of a feast co-hosted by Canada, with all that entailed financially and politically, was a higher hill to climb for senior bureaucrats back in Ottawa. The government and church would divide the cost, estimated at $50,000; part of the traditional ceremony involved the hosts – government and church – giving cash payments to those in attendance. This presented something of a problem, as such gifts would not be recorded in the ways that auditors like to see. Nonetheless, the people from the Department of Justice, a group that had tutored Indian Affairs personnel on alternative dispute resolution processes, strongly supported adopting Indigenous methods. Government personnel who were involved with the pilot projects pushed for Ottawa to allocate money for community solutions to address issues like language and cultural retention. (The pilot projects had been a constant learning process for bureaucrats. For example, though they were authorized to try out different approaches, they generally ended up with similar methods: alternative dispute resolution for a group of about fifty former students from the same institution seemed to work well.) With some difficulty, Tupper and the other officials involved with the EIRS pilot project got authorization, and money, to participate in the ceremony that the Gitxsan survivors desired.

For the non-Aboriginal hosts of the proposed feast, learning how to discharge their duties involved putting themselves into the hands of knowledgeable and patient Gitxsan. In effect, they found history being rolled back and the colonizers being tutored by the colonized. Because what was being proposed – a Gitxsan traditional feast hosted by non-Gitxsan – was alien to First Nation practice, the church and government representatives had to ask the Gitxsan for permission to attend and apologize for not observing the usual forms. Two and a half weeks prior to the feast day, the government and church representatives, accompanied by two Gitxsan chiefs, a survivor from the Hazelton pilot project, and the Gitxsan-appointed coordinator for the feast (really, the teacher for the non-Indigenous participants), visited six Gitxsan villages to carry out "Tets," or invitations to the chiefs. As Brian Thorpe recalled:

> First, we invited the chiefs to the feast. Second, we stressed the fact that we were aware that we were not part of the feast system and apologized in advance for any lapses in protocol resulting from this fact. We apologized as well for the fact that, due to space limitations in the hall, we were able only to invite the chiefs and not their household as would be the custom. Finally, we apologized for the fact that, once again, because of the unique nature of this feast, we could not guarantee that each chief could be seated in their accustomed place ... Each chief, in turn, responded to the invitation. All of the chiefs we met accepted the invitation.[78]

The emissaries were also introduced to other aspects of Gitxsan culture. In a process known as "knock-knock," the chiefs all made their own statements. "The most powerful," noted Thorpe, "came when one of the chiefs took off his belt and bound my chest to the chair in which I was sitting. In a symbolic way the church through me was being bound just as children at residential school had been put in bondage." Thorpe did not think that mere words could "convey the profound and mysterious emotion of that moment."[79]

On 20 March 2004, close to five hundred people made their way to the feast hall in Hazelton for the ceremony. Government and church officials had been active since early that morning making sure everything was in place. There had been a rehearsal the previous day, but the co-hosts were on tenterhooks because they wished to avoid any errors that would shame them – and the government of Canada or the church – and embarrass the Gitxsan who had been so kind in instructing them about the rituals. Chiefs and other dignitaries were formally announced by name and escorted to their places in the hall. The most powerful moments in the day's events were those associated with what a representative of the federal government, Paulette Regan, referred to as "the real work of reconciliation." As the speaker announced their names and struck the talking stick on the floor, the EIRS survivors came forward one by one to be greeted by the men and women who were the leaders of their house and clans. These leaders "wrapped them in the commemorative button vests emblazoned with symbolic crests that were made especially for this occasion. They were welcomed home with traditional ceremonies and songs of lament and joy so poignant that, as the sound of voices soared upward and in the sacred silence that followed, the pain of deep loss and the evocative feeling of belonging – of coming home – hung tangible in the air."[80]

Speeches by representatives of the government and the United Church were also important in accomplishing the reconciliation goals of the Hazelton feast. The significance of the occasion was clear, and Ottawa's spokesman, Shawn Tupper, recalled, "I was nervous as hell." He employed a railway metaphor in his remarks to the gathering: "The train that took these individuals away so many years ago when they were just starting their lives has been slow to return them home. Today the train has returned. But not with the same people that left." His presence represented "many who are trying hard to understand what happened to you, to your families and your communities. People who want so much for you to know that we are sorry for what happened to you."

Tupper said that he was present "to offer, on behalf of the government of Canada, a long overdue apology. An apology that is clear, unambiguous and unrestrained. We are truly sorry for what happened to you. The suffering you endured as a result of your experience at Edmonton Indian Residential School was wrong, it was our fault, and we accept that responsibility." The government officials were grateful for this opportunity: "We know the resolution process we are completing today has not been easy. We also know that this train has not stopped; we must continue in our journey to make things right again." He acknowledged that "our work is not done, but the job will be easier with all of us joining forces and moving forward together. In closing, for those of you who are able to find it within your hearts, either now or in the future, we ask your forgiveness." Former moderator Marion Best delivered the United Church's apology. "The removal of children from families and communities, the punishment exacted for speaking Gitxsanimax in residential schools and the disruption of Gitxsan spirituality and tradition are wrongs which cannot be excused," she said. "For our role we offer our profound apology."[81]

In keeping with Gixsan custom, little was said directly to the representatives of the church and the government to indicate that the feast and homecoming resolved the differences with the First Nation. Of course, monetary compensation for abuses suffered had been negotiated and paid as part of the pilot project discussions, but the feast in many ways was more important than cash. If there was any doubt about that fact, it was removed a few months later when the Edmonton survivors asked the two government of Canada case workers who had been involved with their pilot project and Brian Thorpe of the United Church to join them at a survivors' gathering at the site of the former Edmonton institution. The school grounds were occupied by Poundmaker's Lodge Treatment Centre and the Nechi Institute, which hosted the gathering. The 2004 meeting was in fact the fourth such annual event, but the first to which government and church representative had been invited. The non-Natives were fully involved, including Thorpe's reluctant joining in a sweat lodge ceremony. As he reported, "The Gitxsan survivors made it quite clear at this [giveaway] and, indeed, at every other point in the two days" that they wanted the case workers and the church and government representatives "to stand with them." The claims had been settled, but the work was not done. "Much of the process of the Hazelton ADR, while much better than litigation, was frustrating and, at times, painful for the survivors involved. Yet, it is so clear that one of the goals of that process was to insure that this was just a starting point in the development of right relations. The participants last weekend in Edmonton, through their graciousness and inclusion, made it clear to us that we are in the midst of a process which goes far beyond settling legal claims."[82]

The outcome of the pilot projects was mixed. The experiments in some cases had shown the potential for non-judicial processes not only to avoid harm to claimants, but also to make progress towards a type of reconciliation. They also produced an instance of legal creativity that would become an enduring part of the government's dispute resolution process. The pilot projects adopted a "plausible link standard" rather than the more cumbersome and difficult existing civil law criteria for determining if there was a cause-and-effect relationship between an event, such as an abusive act at school, and difficulties the abused person had in later life.[83] Survivors (or their lawyers), churches, and government built on the positive aspects of the projects by developing what was usually termed a dispute resolution (DR) alternative to litigation for compensation for abuse suffered at residential schools, but they did so in a manner that cut out some of the most creative and potentially beneficial innovations that had been tried. The federal government was advised by an Aboriginal Working Caucus of about a dozen residential school survivors from all regions of the country. Government thought that representative survivors, rather than Aboriginal political organizations, should play a consultative role and should have input on personal matters such as abuse, although Aboriginal organizations were consulted on a couple of occasions. The caucus, whose animating spirit was Maggie Hodgson, had a profound influence on deliberations in Ottawa.[84] The United Church representative on the caucus argued unsuccessfully for a more holistic approach that would include Indigenous ceremony in the dispute resolution proceedings.[85]

The new DR process that was developed in late December 2002 and fully implemented by the autumn of 2003 adopted the inquisitorial method of inquiry by an adjudicator. There were two streams of individual claims, one for serious physical (causing a lasting injury) or sexual abuse, and the other for less serious abuse. There was also provision for group claims. Approximately ninety adjudicators worked under the supervision of Chief Adjudicator Ted Hughes, a retired judge originally from Saskatoon who lived in Victoria.[86] Each decision was reviewed by the chief adjudicator, and, if necessary, discussed with the individual adjudicator to ensure overall consistency and fairness. The objective of the process was to hear the claimant's case and to validate the claims on a "balance of probabilities" standard of proof. Adjudicators were told that their role was inquisitorial but not investigative: they were to help the survivor bring the story out, assess the claimant's credibility, determine which allegations were proven, and assess damages according to a grid provided by the program.[87]

In many respects, the DR process was innovative. For one thing, Ottawa kept its hands off at the beginning. "We were pretty much left on our own to structure the program," the chief adjudicator recalled.[88] And DR introduced automatic payment of plaintiffs' counsel. Any award the adjudicator declared would be augmented by 15 per cent as a payment to the lawyer.[89] More important, perhaps, the selection, review, and renewal of adjudicators were unusual. The government had only one vote in the process, but all four parties – survivors, churches, government, lawyers – could veto individual candidates. During implementation planning, the Aboriginal Working Caucus decided that it could not support the program without two more changes. It wanted the claimants not to be bound by the adjudicator's decision: a dissatisfied claimant could go to court, though the other parties were barred from doing so. As well, the caucus insisted that any release that was signed at the end of the adjudication process not prevent the clamant from participating in future language and culture claims that might be lodged if Canadian courts ever recognized these as wrongs that could be compensated. After considerable discussion, cabinet approved. That government would be bound by a decision maker that it did not appoint and over whose decisions it had only a very light review – while survivors could walk away from the decision and litigate their claims in court – was remarkable.[90] Less formal steps were taken to make the process friendly to survivors. Adjudicators were told, "Let the survivor control the room." They were trained to ask claimants, "Where do you want me and the others to sit?" As well claimants could be accompanied by a counsellor as well as their lawyer, and health support workers were also available to assist in the event of distress.

Not everyone shared government officials' positive view of this approach to DR. Jamie Scott, a United Church representative, later said that he regretted that Aboriginal ceremonies, something that had frequently been part of the pilot projects, were dropped from DR.[91]

4.2 Phil Fontaine at apology, 11 June 2008.

Completing the lengthy and complex application form was made only a bit less onerous by the introduction of paid form fillers, an innovation for which Maggie Hodgson pressed for many months.[92] It quickly emerged that survivors who underwent the process and the lawyers who assisted them also accumulated objections to the way the system operated. Moreover, the principal Aboriginal political organization, the Assembly of First Nations, and its national chief, Phil Fontaine, had even more emphatic objections. He regularly complained to the deputy minister of Indian Residential Schools Resolution Canada that DR was seriously flawed.

The flaws in DR, actual and/or perceived, would lead to its replacement by a similar process as part of a larger settlement of school claims. One symptom of the troubles that put an end to DR was the fact that fewer survivors than expected applied for it. In its first year of operation, only 120 applications were forwarded to the adjudication secretariat. Noted the deputy minister, "This is considerably below our expectations, and well below the number needed to resolve all the claims within a 7-year period."[93] On the whole, though, legal practitioners thought DR was successful and was doing good work when it ended. One of its architects, Doug Ewart, noted that the rate of settlement under the process was accelerating by 2005; and he thought that the accumulated cases could be cleared in a few years. Another senior official, a former deputy minister of justice, also viewed it as a useful process but thought its creators had miscalculated when they had not pushed to complete more hearings in its first year or two. When opposition to it began to mount because of its lack of achievements, DR could not point to any settled cases. The former deputy minister thought it was "an opportunity missed"; with the demise of DR, those who were grappling with the legacy of residential schools were back at the Gordon school settlement approach that had attracted harsh criticism in 1997.[94] DR was far from the most creative processes that had been discussed in the dialogues or that had been given a trial in some of the pilot projects.

Between 1998 and 2005, Canada turned to the judiciary to resolve claims from survivors of abuse at residential schools. Litigation was bruising to survivors, and costly and morally harrowing for the churches. As suits mounted in number, survivors were frustrated, while the churches believed they were being dragged towards the financial brink. Exploratory dialogues among survivors, lawyers, churches, and government in 1998–9 opened up the possibility of using different methods. The pilot projects that grew out of these dialogues, though few were successful, did illustrate that non-adversarial methods were preferable. And the events of the remarkable homecoming feast at Hazelton, in which history was reversed and a First Nations leader took a church representative captive, demonstrated the potential for a process that promoted reconciliation with survivors as well as compensated them financially. One of the continuing gifts of the new thinking was the fact that the government of Canada offered a "Statement of Reconciliation – Learning from the Past" to claimants after the conclusion of their case.[95] Clearly, the non-Indigenous parties were learning as they went along. But, by 2004 or 2005, a consensus was developing that the experiments to date were not effective responses to the problems of litigation.

5

The Parties Negotiate

When the national chief of the Assembly of First Nations (AFN) and the AFN's legal counsel unexpectedly turned up at a meeting of high-powered lawyers and federal government officials in 2005 to partici-pate in negotiations to settle all aspects of the residential school issue, they came with a surprise for the other attendees. As introductions were being made, they requested that they go last. Looking around the room, they saw dozens of senior bureaucrats, church representatives, and only one other survivor gathered for the critical discussions. With the exception of the two litigant-survivors, the only people who were officially invited to the meeting were government litigants, lawyers, and church representatives. When the national chief's turn arrived during introductions, he said, "My name is Phil Fontaine and I'm the litigant in a class action we just filed for forty million dollars."[1] It was only as a litigant that Fontaine, arguably the former student who had done more than any other to push the issue of schools abuse forward since the early 1990s, and his counsel could be part of the most impor-tant negotiations over the legacy of residential schools that had yet taken place.

The negotiations that Fontaine and his lawyer and partner Kathleen Mahoney "crashed" were necessitated by relentless criticism of the set-tlement processes that had been employed to that point. Litigation by survivors, which had begun to swell in numbers in 1998, had produced minimal satisfaction and maximum discomfort for both former students and the churches that the government of Canada had regularly drawn into the cases by cross-suing the denominations. An alternative known as dispute resolution (DR), had been launched in the latter part of 2003, but had never enjoyed widespread support. Changed conditions at the federal government level had also opened the way by 2004 to replacing DR with a negotiated general settlement of residential school issues. A significant component in changing the government's thinking was the emergence of several class actions over residential school abuse that had recently emerged. The result of the convergence of these factors was the Indian Residential Schools Settlement Agreement (IRSSA), a wide-ranging package of measures that sought to address all aspects of the issue, including ones at which the government hitherto had balked, and that would begin to be put into operation in 2006–7. Today, the country is living with the results of the IRSSA more than a decade after the fateful meeting to which Mahoney and Fontaine had invited themselves on behalf of residential school survivors.

One reason for the negotiations for a comprehensive settlement of abuse litigation was a widespread perception that DR was gravely flawed. Some of the problems were inherent in its design. For example, the application form was thirty-seven pages long at a minimum count, a daunting instrument to older survivors whose language skills might not be equal to the task of submitting the information. In defence of the elaborate form, one official pointed out that the detail it provided reduced the inquiries that an adjudicator had to make at the hearing.[2] In addition, Indian Residential Schools Resolution Canada (IRSRC) had adopted a suggestion from survivors' advocate Maggie Hodgson to develop a kit to help claimants fill out the application and provide funding for Aboriginal form-fillers to assist those in need. Still, as a senior IRSRC official conceded, the application form "was not their finest hour."[3] Bud Whiteye, from Walpole Island First Nation, expressed the frustration of many in an essay entitled "Residential School Survivors Face Bureaucratic Babble." "The application is 51 pages including cover," he wrote, "the instruction guide is 67 pages, and there are 20 pages of inserts, which provide more instruction. A total of 138 pages of madness or nonsense." The form was "ridiculously huge … I don't know of any person in their 70s or 80s who would try to get through it. Those age 75 and above and the terminally ill are the first in line for compensation. Are they going to try to get through this application? Are they well enough? Can they see? Can they read?"[4]

Other problems that DR encountered had less to do with inherent flaws than with others' perceptions and with some participants' failure to embrace the intent of the mechanism. One target was the grid for determining the amount of compensation of claimants whose allegations were validated. The system of setting compensation was sometimes dismissed as "a meat chart," but it was an attempt to bring precision to the task. The grid, which came from an Irish inquiry into abuse at industrial schools, used points to assess abuse, as well as for psychological impact, aggravating factors such as racism, consequential loss of opportunity, and even provision for future care. It permitted the adjudicator to fine tune compensation and even allowed a claimant who had suffered abuse rated as relatively minor under the "acts proven" heading to nonetheless get a larger amount if the victim had suffered what the adjudicator evaluated as serious damage in the "consequential harm" category.[5] An experienced adjudicator argued that, even without a prescribed grid, something similar would have emerged from review and appeals of awards.[6] Another problem with the compensation scheme was that the same harm, of the same intensity, might result in differing amounts of compensation in different provinces because the grid followed the varied compensation levels of the provinces and territories. National Chief Phil Fontaine observed that "no distinction in compensation can be justified between British Columbia, the Yukon and Ontario and the rest of the country. The Indian Residential School system was a national system, involving national wrongs to national victims and there should be no discrimination among the regions."[7] It was not surprising, perhaps, that compensation under DR never escaped the "meat chart" opprobrium. Another problem that would resurface was the unaddressed issue of language and culture loss in the schools.[8]

Government actions sometimes made matters worse for DR. Perhaps the most egregious example was Ottawa's decision to appeal the award of a small amount on narrow grounds. Flora Merrick, an eighty-eight-year-old survivor of the Portage la Prairie residential school and her sister had been prevented by staff from accompanying their father to their mother's funeral. When the school's principal told the children's father, "We don't allow that," the bereaved father left and the girls "cried so much, we were taken away and put in a room away from the rest of the school."[9] Flora Merrick was awarded $1500, even though what she had experienced did not fit the categories of DR. She appeared before the House of Commons Standing Committee on Aboriginal Affairs and Northern Development in 2005 after the award, and elicited considerable sympathy from members. The Anglican observer at the committee meeting thought that Merrick's "presentation and that of other survivors moved and convinced the majority of the committee that the current federal government approach is wasting enormous amounts of money and substantially delaying settling outstanding claims with ill and aged survivors."[10] The episode was distasteful and, according to the deputy minister of IRSRC, embarrassing.[11] The general secretary of the United Church was appalled and saw to it that a church representative quickly delivered the church's share of the award personally to Flora Merrick.[12]

Some adjudicators found that DR, in spite of the intent to make hearings respectful of claimants, sometimes was too similar to the courts. Few of the adjudicators were Aboriginal, and there was not sufficient understanding of Indigenous values and practices among government officials, church representatives, and some adjudicators. One adjudicator recalled an incident that occurred during the orientation provided to new adjudicators in Saskatoon. Maggie Hodgson had arranged for a smudging ceremony as part of the training, something for which the Aboriginal participants were appreciative. But when this trainee was at dinner that evening, she overheard some judges who were also in the adjudicator-training group talk dismissively about the smudging ceremony and express disbelief in what a survivor had told the group earlier that day. She and another adjudicator recounted that they had been pushed by the government of Canada representative at the scheduled intermissions after the survivor's evidence had been heard to go back over ground already covered, some of it highly personal. (Another adjudicator recalled a hearing in which the federal government representative had asked at the break for more questioning of the claimant, who had seemed shy about going into detail with several women present, only to have the claimant say that nothing more had happened to him than he had already recounted.) One of these adjudicators said that it was maddening that they could not take the claimant's statements from the lengthy application but had to lead the survivor through a statement of the abuser's acts, which often were very personal and invasive, before they could be considered evidence. It was, this arbiter said, degrading for elderly claimants to have to answer questions about where the priest put his finger or penis, how many times, how they felt, and so on. In one case, a hearing in Alberta failed to proceed when the church representatives, a group of Roman Catholic female religious, turned up in full religious habits. Such a display upset the claimant, and the hearing was rescheduled. In general, these adjudicators considered the DR process insufficiently sensitive to survivors and too closely aligned with traditional courtrooms.[13]

The problems with the dispute resolution process could be summarized as the failure of DR in operation to live up to the principles that the exploratory dialogues had agreed upon in 1998–9. The dialogues had concluded that resolution processes should be inclusive, fair, accessible, and transparent; offer a holistic and comprehensive response to the harms left by residential schools; respect human dignity and equality, including racial and gender equality; contribute to reconciliation and healing; and do no harm to survivors and their families.[14] They had also emphasized the importance of incorporating Aboriginal culture and practices, and paying attention to the wishes of survivors. Perhaps the best example of implementing the principles enunciated in the exploratory dialogues had been the pilot project that the Gitxsan survivors of the Edmonton Indian Residential School had participated in with representatives of the government of Canada and the United Church of Canada (UCC). Not only did the agreement they reached provide financial compensation to the victims of abuse, but it advanced the cause of reconciliation significantly by including a Gitxsan ceremony in the feast hall at Hazelton, BC, to welcome back and reintegrate the former students into their community and families.

As it operated from late 2003 until it was succeeded by a new agreement in 2006, the dispute resolution system was excessively legalistic and mechanical. Access to DR was only by means of the lengthy, complex application form. No matter how skilful and empathetic the Aboriginal form-fillers that the government supported were, there was no way around the daunting length of the form. And even though adjudicators were asked to lead claimants through their case, avoiding adversarial tactics, the reality was that at the hearing the claimants still had to testify before a number of people, some of whom might be strangers, about events that were already covered in their applications. Part of the problem was that the DR system was staffed, top to bottom, by lawyers, who could not help bringing their experience and attitudes developed in adversarial settings into the deliberations. It might be unfair to highlight, but the pettifogging nature of much of the DR proceedings – in spite of efforts that all parties made to avoid

replicating courtroom procedure – was revealed in one of the instructions that adjudicators received from the adjudication secretariat: when
expressing the value of an award, the adjudicator was to round *down*
the sum to the nearest dollar.[15] Such an approach, in combination with
the absence of ceremonies such as the Hazelton feast in the pilot project,
spoke eloquently to the nature of DR. As a legal specialist has evaluated
it, DR was colonial in character: created and controlled by government,
it did not allow claims for cultural loss.[16]

Even from a lawyer's point of view, there were numerous other
shortcomings in the dispute resolution program that would offend
some claimants. Similar instances of abuse, for example, were not
always compensated at the same level. The lawyers who designed the
operational plan of DR quite understandably paid close attention to
the existing standards for compensation. Unfortunately, compensation
levels varied among provinces; compensation rates for mistreatment
were considerably higher in British Columbia, Yukon, and Ontario than
in the rest of the country. Accordingly, successful claimants from those
jurisdictions would be compensated more generously for the same
wrongs, as much as $50,000 more according to one expert's estimate.[17]
There were also glaring gender differences in the system's treatment of
harms, too. Harms that were specific to female students, such as preg-
nancy and forced abortion or adoption, were not included. Such discrepancies were not in keeping with the spirit of the principles that had
been adopted by consensus during the exploratory dialogues.

Unfortunately, the federal government could be pigheaded in its
response to legal professionals who pointed out shortcomings in DR.
The adjudicator who awarded Flora Merrick a modest amount for
being prevented from attending the funeral of a close family member
was criticized implicitly by having Ottawa appeal the award to the
court. A professor of law who attempted to point out the shortcomings
of DR found the effort ending in frustration. After analysing DR and
finding it wanting, Kathleen Mahoney of the University of Calgary
wrote a long letter to the senior bureaucrat responsible for operating
DR. She was optimistic when, in response, she was invited to join
in a conference call to discuss her letter. During the call, she listed
her objections to aspects of DR to a number of government officials
on the line, making sure to include her objection to rounding down
awards to the nearest dollar. At the end of the discussion, officials
thanked her but said that they would not be making major changes to
DR, although the instruction to adjudicators on rounding the value of

awards down to the nearest dollar would be changed to round up to the nearest dollar. As she put it, "So for all my efforts, I succeeded in gaining some loose change!"[18]

The Assembly of First Nations soon became involved in efforts to modify the way Dispute Resolution operated. With funding from IRSRC, the AFN and the University of Calgary law school held an influential conference in March 2004 focused on the question, will dispute resolution bring about reconciliation? In a sense, the question was misguided: as its design and operations showed, DR was not intended principally to promote reconciliation, but rather to deal with survivors' claims for compensation for damages experienced at residential school. As it turned out, the misleading question did not matter to conference participants. Those who spoke at the gathering overwhelmingly argued that the system would not advance the cause of reconciliation. Mario Dion, the deputy minister of IRSRC who was responsible for DR, was in attendance. He had re-established communications with AFN and Phil Fontaine, the national chief, after a period of coolness. Fontaine, he recalled, said to him regularly "the system is flawed." For his part, Dion thought DR could not deliver even on its minimal goals. His office estimated in 2003 that DR and litigation together would take fifty-three years to clear all the cases that had accumulated to that point. Dion agreed in a conversation with Fontaine during the conference to a proposal that Kathleen Mahoney would assemble a blue-ribbon group to develop a solution to the problems with dispute resolution.[19]

The result of this collaboration emerged in the autumn of 2004 as a report of the Assembly of First Nations. The deputy minister of IRSRC recalled it as a good job that paved the way for a comprehensive settlement over the next two years.[20] Mahoney, the report's principal author, said that it was the work of "an expert team ... comprised of national and international experts, who rapidly conducted research, [and] convened in workshops and study sessions for an intensive three-month period in the summer of 2004."[21] The AFN report reiterated many of the complaints with DR that had become familiar by 2004, repeating familiar objections to the application form, regional variation in compensation maxima, gender discrimination, a lack of consideration of Aboriginal culture and traditions, high administration costs relative to the amount paid to claimants, and the meagre scope for actions that aimed at commemoration and reconciliation. The existing approach was simply too limited to do what needed to be done: "Canada has acknowledged responsibility in the current dispute resolution model, but only for a narrow band of personal injuries caused by physical and sexual abuse and wrongful confinement." The AFN would work with Canada to fashion a system that would ensure "that proper acknowledgement of the magnitude of the injuries for First Nations occurs and appropriate remedies are provided."[22]

The AFN report grounded its recommendations in an existing consensus and sketched a broad program of measures that went well beyond what DR could do and even further than the government of Canada had in the past been willing to consider. Its "guiding principles," it said, were the points that the exploratory dialogues had agreed upon in 1998–9. It was to be "inclusive, fair, accessible and transparent"; "offer a holistic and comprehensive response"; "respect human dignity and racial and gender equality"; "contribute towards reconciliation and healing"; and "do no harm to survivors and their families."[23] A significant breakthrough was the report's recommendation of a lump sum award that survivors would qualify for simply by virtue of having been residential school students and for which they would not have to endure a hearing before an adjudicator. The report argued that the negative experience of being a residential school inmate was so pervasive and enduring that "a lump sum award [should] be granted to any person who attended an Indian Residential School, irrespective of whether they suffered separate harms generated by acts of sexual, physical or severe emotional abuse." This award would have two components: $10,000 for attendance at a school, and an additional $3,000 per year of attendance. This payment was intended to compensate for the loss of language and culture.[24] As well, the AFN report recommended an arbitrated program to compensate for serious physical and sexual abuse, but by means that avoided the shortcomings of the DR program.

The AFN's emphasis on "a holistic and comprehensive response," in keeping with the approach of the exploratory dialogues, led to more ambitious recommendations. To accomplish truth sharing, healing, and reconciliation, it recommended measures to promote survivor and community healing, and reconciliation between residential school victims and the rest of society. The AFN report began with the final act of the proposed revised procedure for adjudicating major abuse claims, with the labelling of the release that a claimant signed once the process was concluded as "an 'Agreement towards Reconciliation.'" The report also urged adoption of a "truth-sharing and reconciliation process" that would benefit communities as well as individual survivors and would be accessible widely. While it considered the definition of such a process to be beyond the scope of its work, it argued that such a mechanism should provide "a space for the survivors to tell their stories" and "create public awareness and a public record of what happened and the consequences."[25] It was little wonder that the deputy minister of Indian Residential Schools Resolution Canada later noted that the report's recommendations were similar to what became the elements of the Indian Residential Schools Settlement Agreement.[26]

Fairly quickly, federal officials approached the Assembly of First Nations to inquire if it was interested in entering discussions intended to produce a better way of dealing with claims. Six months later, the two signed a political pact that amounted to an agreement in principle for a comprehensive approach to resolving residential schools issues. The final phase of negotiating the political agreement occurred over a weekend during part of which National Chief Phil Fontaine was running a half-marathon. Dion, Mahoney, and AFN adviser Bob Watts talked intermittently by telephone with Fontaine, while Dion relayed developments to Ann McLellan, the minister of IRSRC, who was in Edmonton, by telephone. Finally, it all came together.[27] Among the innovations in the two-page agreement that was signed 30 May 2005 were "an improved system of reparations for abuse, a common experience payment for each resident of a residential school, healing funds, a truth commission, a fund for commemoration, a fund for legal fees, an early payment for the elderly, an apology and the appointment of [former Supreme Court of Canada] Justice Frank Iacobucci to bring all of the parties together to hammer out the details of a formal settlement agreement."[28]

Meanwhile, other developments in the legal world were pushing the federal government towards the radically different approach to solving the residential schools abuse litigation challenge that the May political accord represented. In addition to the thousands of individual suits or claims under the dispute resolution process, a series of class actions by former residential school students was making its way towards hearings in the courts. A class action, as the term implies, is a lawsuit on behalf of a group of people who share features or experiences that justify treating them as a unit for the purpose of litigation. They have been similarly affected by actions of the person or entity at whom the suit is directed. A class of people might be purchasers of a defective model of automobile, or patients of a medical practitioner who had provided useless, and possibly harmful, treatment. Obviously, a group of former residential school students, whether of a particular school or group of schools, or even the entire class of former students who were still alive, were potential participants in such an action.

Under Canadian law, getting a class action to a trial on its merits was not a simple matter. Lawyers for a particular class action had to demonstrate to a judge in a separate legal process that the people they represented were an appropriate "class" of litigants, that they had experienced something that was actionable in Canadian civil law, and that the defendant of the action had a similar relationship to them all. Only when a judge was satisfied that the criteria for a class action had been met could such a suit be certified to proceed to trial. And even then, there were provisions that individual potential claimants could opt out of the action.[29] Among the residential school class actions that were being considered on their merits were one launched by Nora Bernard, a Mi'kmaq woman; one in the name of Baxter; and, most relevant, the Cloud class action. The Cloud class action was the first to achieve certification. After two lower levels of court had found against the application, the Ontario Court of Appeal approved it as a superior method for a group of 1,400 students who attended the Mohawk Institute between 1922 and 1969 to put their case forward. When the Supreme Court of Canada early in May 2005 refused the federal government leave to appeal the Ontario appeal court's decision, a significant new element was injected into the campaign to resolve grievances over residential schools.[30]

Stars in the Ottawa firmament were aligning themselves in favour of a more comprehensive approach to residential school problems than dispute resolution in other ways, too. In a fashion reminiscent of the propitious conditions that made the emergence of the Aboriginal Healing Foundation possible in 1997–8, a booming continental economy was overfilling federal government coffers with taxation revenue each fiscal year. In the recent past, Jean Chrétien's Liberal government had devoted such surpluses to a concerted program of investment in research and higher education. It provided funds for programs such as the Canada Foundation for Innovation, Millennium Scholarships, and Canada Research Chairs, and support for research institutions' overhead costs of research. The advent of Liberal Paul Martin, Jr to the prime ministry late in 2003 practically guaranteed a change of direction on the part of Ottawa. For one thing, government thought that it had done quite handsomely by the universities and research hospitals of the country. As well, Martin himself was interested in taking on problems that beset Aboriginal Canada. His preoccupation with tackling such woes would result in 2006 in the finalization of the Kelowna Accord with

Aboriginal leaders, which committed large sums to dealing with problems of Aboriginal education and housing. Contrary to the flippant dismissal by the Stephen Harper Conservatives, who killed the accord soon after they took office later that year, the financing of the Kelowna Accord was not scratched on the back of a restaurant napkin. The plan, which was negotiated with Aboriginal leaders over more than a year, had twice been presented to cabinet and approved, and the Department of Finance had "booked" funds for it before the Liberals lost power.[31]

The key personnel in the Martin cabinet who would have the most to say about how they should approach the residential school file were coincidentally all sympathetic to a generous approach to the troubled policy area. The minister of Indian and northern affairs, Andy Scott from New Brunswick, was eager for an aggressive approach to the challenges of First Nations social policy. When he assumed his portfolio, the department was considering how to handle both the Kelowna Accord process and residential schools issues. The Aboriginal community, he recalled, were struggling to decide which should receive priority if government could tackle only one, but Scott favoured a two-track approach that would reduce pressure on the community to choose.[32] In addition to a sympathetic prime minister and minister of Indian and northern affairs, other key ministers were from regions where the residential school issue was considered important. The minister of finance, Ralph Goodale, was from Regina, and the president of the Treasury Board, Reg Alcock, hailed from Winnipeg. In addition, the new minister of justice, Irwin Cotler, was a strong and respected advocate of human rights. The group made a front bench that was primed for an adventurous approach on the residential school file. Even Edmonton's Ann McLellan, minister for Indian Residential Schools Resolution Canada, who had a reputation within government as "a tough cookie," was now onside. Her deputy minister had used both financial and policy arguments to persuade her that DR could not deliver the respect, recognition, and fair treatment that residential school survivors wanted of any compensation program. Moreover, the existing DR procedures were expensive and, the deputy minister contended, paid three dollars to government lawyers for every dollar that went to claimants.[33]

A major factor propelling the government towards making an agreement to settle abuse suits arose in the spring of 2005, when Pope John Paul II died. Prime Minister Martin invited, among others, Phil Fontaine to be part of the official party that attended the funeral in Rome. Early in the delegation's visit, Martin invited Fontaine to join him, his wife, and some others for dinner. During the meal, Martin grilled Fontaine about aspects of a possible new approach to residential school issues, as front-bench Conservative stalwarts Stephen Harper, Jason Kenney, and Rob Nicholson carried on a separate conversation at the table. The prime minister challenged Fontaine, asking if an expensive comprehensive settlement would "solve the problem." The chief responded that it would not solve all the residential school problems, "but it will recognize and accept that harm had been done." After a bit, Martin looked at Fontaine said, "'Look. Okay, Phil. We'll get this done.'"[34]

Persuading the bureaucracy that dispute resolution needed to be replaced was not a simple matter. There were strong proponents of the system, particularly within the Departments of Justice and Indian and Northern Affairs. The principal architect of the procedure, Doug Ewart, thought that the model had run well. He and his colleagues found that they got reassuringly positive feedback, including from survivors who felt that they had been well treated and were pleased that they had been able recount their narrative in their own way without being questioned. By the time the search began for another system, between 1,500 and 2,000 of the 3,000 claims on hand had been settled, although the refusal of some church groups to contribute their 30 per cent to awards was slowing the pace.[35] The man who recruited Ewart, former deputy minister of justice George Thomson, complained that the consultant the government had retained to look at DR had done a poor job. This review focused on the high costs of DR, but Thomson pointed out that these included start-up costs, which would not have been sustained had DR continued. Moreover, Thomson noted, the consultant did not consider what the cost of any alternative process was likely to be.[36] Shawn Tupper of Indian Affairs also argued that the DR process was not accurately evaluated. One of the criticisms that had been levelled by the consultant was that, at the pace DR was disposing of claims, it would take fifty-three years to get through them all – a point also made by the AFN task force report and the deputy minister of IRSRC. Yet, as Tupper observed, when the consultant examined DR, the pace of settlements was picking up, and output was doubling each year. He and his colleagues thought DR would clear the cases in five to seven years. What he and colleagues had no effective response to, Tupper conceded, was that a comprehensive settlement of a class action would solve everything at once. A settlement of a class action would take years to implement but would relieve the pressure on the government in the short term.[37]

A final factor of undetermined weight in the decision for a comprehensive settlement was the individual who would be a key figure in the negotiation of a general resolution. Frank Iacobucci, the Supreme

5.1 Frank Iacobucci, 2005.

Court of Canada justice, had retired from the bench and joined the Toronto firm Torys in November 2004.[38] In addition to being a former jurist, Iacobucci was a former deputy minister of justice. As a senior bureaucrat, he had had a reputation as "a very human person" and someone with both skill and sympathy in dealing with disadvantaged groups. Equally important, he enjoyed a stellar reputation with members of the legal community. Given that a negotiated settlement would involve many lawyers – between sixty-five and eighty, it was estimated – the credibility of the chair with lawyers could be important.[39] The fact that he might be available to facilitate a settlement was encouraging. As Mario Dion of IRSRC said of the situation in 2004–5, "the stars were aligned."[40] On the other hand, Chief Robert Joseph, a veteran campaigner for reconciliation, recalled that many survivors were dubious about the prospects for reaching an effective comprehensive settlement, given the large number of issues to be addressed.[41]

After Iacobucci had been retained by the federal government to represent it in talks with lawyers, churches, and survivors, and after he had taken some preliminary soundings of the views of various parties, negotiations began in earnest in June 2005 for a comprehensive settlement that would resolve the looming Cloud class action and almost all other litigation. The negotiations were bookended by dramatic events in the House of Commons. Just prior to the commencement of talks, the Martin government survived a vote on the budget, which was, of course, a confidence motion, with the vote of BC Conservative MP Chuck Cadman. Cadman, who was suffering from terminal cancer, had made the trip to Ottawa with difficulty to cast his vote, which produced a tie. The speaker then broke the tie by voting with the government. (Cadman's widow would later allege that senior Conservative Party officials had offered her husband a bribe in the form of a $1 million life insurance policy not to support the government.) The circumstances around the conclusion of negotiations were equally dramatic. In November 2005, the Martin government was facing another confidence motion in the House of Commons, this time one that they expected to lose. The government advised Frank Iacobucci that it wanted to conclude negotiations and settle quickly, before it lost power. Consensus was reached on a settlement agreement just before midnight on a Sunday, and shortly thereafter Martin was defeated in the Commons and resigned. In between, during the autumn phase of the talks, there was a climactic week of long days of bargaining in a boardroom at the law firm Torys. As one participant recalled, every day they saw the rising sun reflected in the building on the west side, and much later saw the setting sun reflected in the Royal Bank Tower to the east.[42]

The structure of the negotiations was interesting in itself. Frank Iacobucci was both Canada's representative and the titular chairman of the talks. Only someone with his sterling reputation could have managed to maintain such a dual role effectively. Several times a day he was on the telephone to Mario Dion, the deputy minister of IRSRC, in Ottawa to discuss details of proposals that the parties were making.[43] While it would not be accurate to say he was on a short leash, there were definite limits to what he could commit his principal, the government of Canada, to do. For example, the Aboriginal Healing Fund wanted $600 million to carry on its work, but Iacobucci said that the "envelope" he had from the government was not sufficient for such a commitment.[44]

Others fared better in the negotiations. The numerous lawyers in the negotiations got agreement to $100 million to compensate them for their work to that point. Moreover, under the dispute resolution process that was part of the settlement agreement, they stood to eventually earn as much as $1 billion in fees. The agreement included a commitment by government to pay an additional 15 per cent of any award in future dispute resolution hearings towards lawyers' fees, with the expectation that lawyers would charge their clients a further amount, perhaps equal to another 15 per cent of the award.[45] (One-time deputy minister of justice George Thomson described the expected windfall for lawyers as something Canadians should be ashamed of.[46])

The overall agenda for the deliberations was set by the terms of the 30 May 2005 political agreement that the AFN had signed with the government, but there were many other groups involved. Survivors were the most obvious interest group, but they were grievously underrepresented at the Toronto talks. The two survivors who were deeply involved were Phil Fontaine of the Assembly of First Nations and Charlene Belleau of Alkali Lake in British Columbia. The three relevant Protestant denominations were represented; the Roman Catholics stood aloof.[47] The United Church lead, Jamie Scott, who had assumed leadership on the residential school file for his church in 2003, believed that his denomination was better prepared than most because of preparatory work they had been doing long before the talks for a comprehensive settlement were on the horizon. Georges Erasmus, formerly co-chair of the Royal Commission on Aboriginal People and at that time head of the Aboriginal Healing Foundation (AHF), had addressed the UCC's General Council and urged the delegates to press the government for a major inquiry into residential schools. The United Church leadership did call on Ottawa for such an investigation, but the church itself also began examining the legacy of schooling and the problems facing proponents of reconciliation in 2004 through a body it termed the Truth and Reconciliation Roundtable. Consequently, when UCC representatives took a place at what was known as the second table of talks chaired by Iacobucci, Scott was prepared to deal with topics such as a truth commission, commemoration, and the AHF. Phil Fontaine and Kathleen Mahoney also sat at the second table, likely reflecting Fontaine's long-standing desire for an inquiry into the schools, and they managed to have some other survivors invited to the talks as well. The first table, which was dominated by lawyers, dealt with compensation and lawyers' fees. The split into two separate negotiations reflected what the chair, Iacobucci, desired.[48]

Some of the most interesting discussions at the second table concerned the proposal for a truth commission. Two visions competed for acceptance. The Assembly of First Nations, which was still led by Phil Fontaine, pushed hard for mechanisms to get the history of residential schools on the public record and kept available for all time through a national research centre that would collect, store, and make available as complete a record as could be gathered. The churches and survivor groups brought to the table the importance of community-based and national events, at which their advocates would help educate the Canadian public. This group saw community events as being initiated by the grass roots, with the commissioners being invited to attend. They saw subpoena powers for the commission as inconsistent with restorative justice and a healing process.[49] Kathleen Mahoney also considered subpoena powers a bad idea. Based on advice she and her colleagues had received in 2004 from survivors and people experienced in an inquiry into abuse at industrial schools in Ireland, as well as her own observation of the Irish tribunal at work, she believed that subpoena powers would stultify the work of any truth commission. The Irish precedent suggested that likely perpetrators of abuse who appeared under subpoena would simply "lawyer up," and the commission's proceedings would degenerate into legal wrangling and a version of adversarial court proceedings.[50] As everyone involved in events going back to the exploratory dialogues and moving through to talks at the second table in Toronto in 2005 knew, such an adversarial process dominated by lawyers was not conducive to healing and reconciliation.

Thanks to the commitment of many of those involved in the talks, not to mention the pressure created by political events in Ottawa as the Martin government slid towards defeat, a comprehensive agreement was reached in an impressively short time. United Church representative Jamie Scott recalled that Iacobucci manifested a sense of urgency and pushed the parties to make decisions expeditiously.[51] The deputy minister of Indian Residential Schools Resolution Canada had thought that it would take twelve to eighteen months to conclude an agreement, but the task was accomplished in five.[52] Iacobucci later emphasized "the importance of collaboration. The negotiations were kept strictly confidential, in spite of the number of people involved. 'Not one person breached the confidentiality agreement, to my knowledge, although there were temptations. No one played games,'" he recalled.[53]

Yet, Iacobucci did weigh in heavily in the negotiations on occasion. Phil Fontaine recalled that, near the end of the talks, he was having a private conversation with lawyer Tony Merchant when the former justice charged into the room. "Judge," Merchant began, but Iacaobucci cut him off. He tore into Merchant verbally concerning some position he was taking against the draft settlement agreement. The lawyer signed the pact after that storm.[54] Despite such episodes, the process by which an agreement was reached was impressive, and the agreement itself was a major achievement.

Although the negotiators of the settlement agreement deservedly had a sense of accomplishment in the autumn of 2005, the deal still faced two more obstacles before it could be implemented. The first was the discontent of the Roman Catholic "entities" who were to be party to the agreement. The fact that the Catholics took the position that there was no single Roman Catholic Church in Canada that could participate in talks was always an impediment to relations with government and survivors. In the Catholics' view, there were seventeen dioceses in which there had been residential schools and thirty-five religious organizations – to be known as the "Catholic entities" – but no single Catholic Church. The government, at least, saw this stance as a "dodge" designed to shield most of the components of the church from legal liability, but the denomination's leaders hewed to that position vigorously. Compounding the Catholics' apprehension with the 2005 settlement agreement talks was their feeling that they had been "burned" by the negotiations that had gone on with the churches in 2001–3, but which at the end of the day had benefited the Protestant denominations. They were not keen to be involved again. The fact that Frank Iacobucci in June 2005 took the position that he did not have a mandate to negotiate with dozens of Catholic bodies ensured that they were not party to the November 2005 agreement, and a separate negotiation would have to take place. Talks over several months led to a revised agreement that included the Catholics.[55] All these developments stalled implementation of the IRSSA.

A further delay was caused by the procedure needed to make the settlement agreement enforceable throughout the country. As a negotiated settlement of class actions, it required approval by courts across Canada. Two judges – Donald Brenner, Chief Justice of the Supreme Court

of British Columbia, and Warren Winkler of the Ontario Supreme Court
(and later chief justice of Ontario) – were involved in overseeing its
implementation. Winkler later recounted that he scheduled hearings
in the various courts across the country so as to enhance the likelihood of acceptance, and that he had persuaded lawyers for the federal government to accept conditions on Ottawa administration of the
settlement.[56] Compounding the difficulty of getting court approvals in
the various provinces was the fact that the Roman Catholics did not
wish to participate in the process before the courts. Their chief counsel
explained that participation would just lead "to moments of bashing
the Catholics again." The fact that there was no place in the approval
process for church people to express themselves would mean that
they would participate "only for window dressing ... for bashing."[57]
The Catholic refusal and the federal government's insistence that they
participate caused another delay of six months. The Roman Catholics'
tough negotiating stance benefited the other churches as well. Lawyers for the Catholic entities secured a government commitment to pay
their fees for the period when they were negotiating separately "in full
and unconditionally." The government also offered the non-Catholic
churches, which, of course, had not been involved in the negotiations
between government and the Catholics, "a substantial percentage of
the fees and expenses incurred" in the period from the conclusion of
the Catholics' negotiations and the formal signature of the IRSSA, as
well as payment in full for their earlier work towards the settlement
agreement.[58]

It was almost anticlimactic that the settlement agreement contained
an opt-out clause: if 5,000 survivors who had been involved in litigation that led to the agreement negotiations did not wish to participate in
the mechanisms prescribed by the agreement, the whole pact would be
null.[59] As it turned out, only about 1,080 survivors took such a position
in the opt-out period, which lasted to August 2007.[60] By the latter part of
2006, the Indian Residential Schools Settlement Agreement was, finally,
a real plan. Courts in all the required jurisdictions had approved the
settlement after conducting hearings, and it was clear that not enough
survivors would choose to opt out to nullify the agreement.

Not surprisingly, the agreement was a mammoth, complex document. But its simple thrust was that the various class actions that had
been mounted in different regions of the country would be considered
settled by implementation of the numerous provisions of the IRSSA.[61]
Court approval and signature by the parties to the agreement meant

that the several class actions that had been lodged, including the one that had been certified to proceed by the Ontario court, were settled. "The Parties, subject to the Approval Orders, have agreed to amend and merge all of the existing proposed class action statements of claim to assert a common series of Class Actions for the purposes of settlement." And the survivors, government, churches, and lawyers involved, when "the expiration of the Opt Out Periods without the Opt Out Threshold being met, have agreed to settle the Class Actions upon the terms contained in this Agreement." Of course, individual suits by survivors who chose to opt out of the settlement could proceed to trial irrespective of the settlement agreement.[62]

Significantly, following technical provisions, the first article in the agreement dealt with funding. Although it was not the only, or even the principal, goal, securing compensation for survivors of residential schools, especially those who had been subject to abuse, had always been a major objective of survivors, the Assembly of First Nations, and lawyers. But the IRSSA's provisions on funding went far beyond covering individual compensation, churches' financial liability, and lawyers' fees. They also committed the federal government to provide $125 million to the Aboriginal Healing Foundation over five years, $60 million for a truth and reconciliation commission, and $20 million for commemoration projects to memorialize schools history. The commitment to the AHF was far less than the foundation had sought and the negotiators had contemplated at one point. According to David MacDonald, a United Church representative, the AHF was vague about how much money it was seeking. By the time the foundation settled on an "ask" of half a billion dollars, negotiators had allocated most of the money elsewhere, and it had to settle for $125 million.[63] Since the government had not been keen on keeping the foundation going financially, it likely was not broken-hearted at the outcome. It was noteworthy that financial commitments to the AHF, a truth and reconciliation commission, and commemoration were consistent with imperatives that the exploratory dialogues had established in 1998–9.

The government of Canada also agreed to a revised alternative dispute resolution process, the Independent Assessment Process (IAP), to deal with abuse: "Canada will fund the IAP to the extent sufficient to ensure the full and timely implementation of the provisions set out in Article Six (6) [i.e., the IAP provisions] of this Agreement." And the federal government promised to "make its best efforts" to obtain agreement from the provinces and territories that payments received

pursuant to the IRSSA would "not affect the quantity, nature or duration of any social benefits or social assistance benefits payable to" any
survivor covered by the agreement. Similarly, the government would
"make its best efforts to obtain the agreement of the necessary Federal
Government Departments that the receipt of any payments pursuant
to this Agreement will not affect the quantity, nature or duration of any
social benefits or social assistance benefits" from Ottawa "such as old
age security and Canada Pension Plan."[64] The deputy minister of Indian
Residential Schools Resolution Canada at the time of the agreement,
Mario Dion, said that a steering committee of deputy ministers had
been established "to pacify the system" and get input. Presumably that
committee would deal with any intragovernmental frictions.[65]

The first substantive article of the settlement agreement introduced
an item over which survivors and the government had contended since
the onset of litigation in the mid-1990s. As the exploratory dialogues
had revealed, survivors were greatly pained by the adverse impact their
time in residential schools had had on the retention of their Aboriginal languages and culture. And as the government's behaviour from
the late 1990s onward had shown, Ottawa was determined to avoid
expanding the range of compensable injuries to include language and
culture. Nonetheless, the settlement agreement introduced a "Common
Experience Payment" (CEP) for anyone who had attended one of the
residential schools that the agreement recognized, who applied by the
deadline for the program, and whose claims in the application were
"validated in accordance with the provisions of this Agreement." An
applicant who satisfied the criteria for the CEP would receive $10,000
for the first year of attendance at a residential school and $3000 for
each subsequent year of validated attendance.[66] An applicant who was
denied compensation could appeal to a national advisory committee
set up under the agreement, and ultimately to a court if the committee
turned the applicant down as well.[67] Conspicuous by its absence from
the settlement agreement was any statement of the purpose or ratio-
nale for the Common Experience Payment. But AFN national chief Phil
Fontaine stated publicly and repeatedly that the CEP was established to
compensate for language and culture loss.[68]

Another critically important compensation program that formed part
of the settlement agreement was the Independent Assessment Process
for cases of severe physical and sexual abuse. The IAP was the successor
to the much pilloried dispute resolution process that had been implemented in 2003, following the discussions at the exploratory dialogues

FINAL: MAY, 2006

II: COMPENSATION RULES

	Acts Proven	Compensation Points
SL5	• Repeated, persistent incidents of anal or vaginal intercourse. • Repeated, persistent incidents of anal/vaginal penetration with an object.	45-60
SL4	• One or more incidents of anal or vaginal intercourse. • Repeated, persistent incidents of oral intercourse. • One or more incidents of anal/vaginal penetration with an object.	36-44
SL3	• One or more incidents of oral intercourse. • One or more incidents of digital anal/vaginal penetration. • One or more incidents of attempted anal/vaginal penetration (excluding attempted digital penetration). • Repeated, persistent incidents of masturbation.	26-35
PL	• One or more physical assaults causing a physical injury that led to or should have led to hospitalization or serious medical treatment by a physician; permanent or demonstrated long-term physical injury, impairment or disfigurement; loss of consciousness; broken bones; or a serious but temporary incapacitation such that bed rest or infirmary care of several days duration was required. Examples include severe beating, whipping and second-degree burning.	11-25
SL2	• One or more incidents of simulated intercourse. • One or more incidents of masturbation. • Repeated, persistent fondling under clothing.	11-25
SL1	• One or more incidents of fondling or kissing. • Nude photographs taken of the Claimant. • The act of an adult employee or other adult lawfully on the premises exposing themselves. • Any touching of a student, including touching with an object, by an adult employee or other adult lawfully on the premises which exceeds recognized parental contact and violates the sexual integrity of the student.	5-10
OWA	• Being singled out for physical abuse by an adult employee or other adult lawfully on the premises which was grossly excessive in duration and frequency and which caused psychological consequential harms at the H3 level or higher. • Any other wrongful act committed by an adult employee or other adult lawfully on the premises which is proven to have caused psychological consequential harms at the H4 or H5 level.	5-25

5.2 Independent Assessment Process "Compensation Rules" (excerpt).

and the pilot project experiments. Although DR had been much criticized by Aboriginal people and officials within government, it was striking that, as the government lawyer who had been "the scientist" who designed the technical details of DR put it, during the talks over which Frank Iacobucci presided, most people, including survivors, church representatives, and lawyers, spoke in favour of a process modelled on DR.[69] Indeed, the new Independent Assessment Process did bear striking similarities to the former dispute resolution process.[70] A long-term adjudicator who had served in both DR and IAP recalled that, for her, "nothing changed" when the new scheme of adjudication was introduced.[71] The IAP used an inquisitorial approach, rather than the adversarial system of the courts, and it distinguished between "a standard track" and "a complex issues track," the latter for claims that included a request for "an assessment of compensation for proven actual income losses." But a detailed application form was still part of the adjudication process, as was a complicated chart designed to assist adjudicators in determining the amount of compensation for severe abuse.

The chart that IAP adjudicators were to use had several components. One section, entitled "Acts Proven," dealt with allegations the adjudicator found proven; another ("Consequential Harm") considered degrees of dysfunction stemming from the proven harms. Then the adjudicator had to consider "aggravating factors," such as "verbal abuse," "racist acts," or "threats." A range of points was established for each of the preceding categories (see chapter 6 for specifics about points and corresponding monetary compensation). In addition, the adjudicator had discretion to award additional points for proven acts and harm. The adjudicator added up the claimant's points and then chose an amount from a wide range of compensation.[72]

If the Independent Assessment Process was largely a refinement of its DR predecessor, the same could not be said of the Truth and Reconciliation Commission (TRC) that the parties agreed would be established. Here, again, it is noteworthy that participants in the exploratory dialogues had pushed for such a body, although such demands had not been a major component of those dialogues. And there were other precedents for calling for such an inquiry: The final report of the Royal Commission on Aboriginal Peoples had concluded its authoritative chapter on residential schools with a recommendation that the government set up an inquiry into residential schools history. Moreover, it was well known that Phil Fontaine had been calling for such a commission for many years. In his view, such an inquiry or commission on residential schools would have two objectives: enabling former students to put their experiences on the record for the information of all Canadians and creating a repository of documents and other sources on the history of the schools.

The settlement agreement provided for the creation of a truth and reconciliation commission whose goals included the two that were dear to the heart of National Chief Fontaine. The TRC was to "acknowledge Residential School experiences, impacts and consequences"; "provide a holistic, culturally appropriate and safe setting for former students, their families and communities as they come forward to the Commission"; "promote awareness and public education of Canadians about the IRS [Indian residential school] system and its impacts"; and "identify sources and create as complete an historical record as possible of the IRS system and legacy. The record shall be preserved and made accessible to the public for future study and use."[73] The architects of the TRC had the gift of second sight, or at least had a lively sense of what could go wrong, when they made detailed provision for resolving disputes. The IRSSA provided that the TRC "may refer to the NAC [National Administration Committee] for determination of disputes involving document production, document disposal and archiving, contents of the Commission's Report and Recommendations and Commission decisions regarding the scope of its research and issues to be examined," but allowed "either or both the Church Organization and Canada" to appeal any such decision.[74] Finally, the TRC was to prepare and submit to the parties to the IRSSA a report that would include "the history, purpose, cooperation and supervision of the IRS system, the effect and consequences of IRS (including systemic harms, intergenerational consequences and the impact on human dignity) and the ongoing legacy of the residential schools."

The question of legal fees, which the settlement agreement also tackled, would turn out to be almost as controversial as some parts of the TRC's mandate. In addition to committing the government to pay various legal firms for their participation in the negotiation of the settlement agreement, the government also agreed to compensate a "National Consortium" of firms $40 million for their work to date. As well, the agreement provided that government would pay the Merchant Law Group, the Saskatchewan firm headed by Tony Merchant that had been notably active and aggressive in signing up clients, a sum to be determined following the principles negotiated earlier between the firm and government during the settlement agreement negotiations. Should the

Merchant Law Group and the government not be able to reach agreement, the sum would be fixed by the Saskatchewan Court of Queen's Bench.[75] There were more provisions for remunerating lawyers in the setting up of arrangements for the Independent Assessment Process. All of these payments for work prior to, during, and subsequent to negotiation of the settlement agreement would prove controversial.

Another section of the IRSSA that would prove contentious contained the lists of officially recognized residential schools. Inclusion on the list meant that, if a person had attended one of the institutions, he or she would be eligible to apply for compensation under the Common Experience Payment and/or Independent Assessment Process. Similarly, it was a fair presumption that if an institution were not on the lists in Schedule E (Residential Schools) or Schedule F (Additional Residential Schools), it might be difficult to qualify for participation in compensation programs, the commemoration support program, or the activities of the Truth and Reconciliation Commission. Negotiations led by Frank Iacobucci had resulted in 107 former residential schools in Schedule E, and another 24, most of which were federal hostels rather than schools, in Schedule F. The hostels were former schools, mostly in northern Canada, that were turned into dormitories after 1969, when the federal government announced that it was winding down the residential school system. Students in the hostels attended nearby day schools before returning to their residence, which was operated by either the Anglican Church or by the Oblates on behalf of the Roman Catholics.[76] The difficulty was, as was inevitable when negotiations were so compressed, some institutions that former students or residents considered to be like residential schools were overlooked. Part of the reason for the oversight was the personnel at the negotiating table. Only First Nations representatives were present, and there were few enough of them, but there were no official representatives of the Métis or Inuit. Understandably, the latter two groups would later complain about their exclusion from compensation and an official role in commemorative activities and the public observances of the Truth and Reconciliation Commission.

Both the process by which the Indian Residential Schools Settlement Agreement was produced and its outcome were highly fraught. The agreement was not a finely crafted document, but it was a near miracle that it existed at all. The odds had been long against the parties involved in the aftermath of residential schooling ever coming to an agreement, even when the pilot projects and dispute resolution mechanism had laid the groundwork for the agreement. A major impediment to reaching a general settlement of residential schools claims was the issue of language and culture loss. As had been evident for a long time, at least since the exploratory dialogues in 1998–9, many survivors considered cultural loss a harm for which they should receive an official apology and compensation. Canadian common law at the turn of the century did not recognize language and culture as things whose loss were compensable, but there were signs in the early twenty-first century that the courts might be willing to revisit the issue.

Other legal issues had also influenced negotiations for a comprehensive settlement. Discontent with the dispute resolution process implemented in 2003 was certainly one, especially after a government review of DR indicated that it would take more than half a century to resolve all the claims through this process. Another legal phenomenon – class actions – began to emerge and multiply. By 2004, the legal balance was shifting towards trying to settle all outstanding claims with one measure. Such a negotiated settlement could resolve the individual actions, settle the class actions, and, perhaps, quiet the restiveness of the churches that had been involved in operating the schools. In Ottawa, a number of personnel changes brought into positions of influence people who were dissatisfied with DR and favoured a general settlement. The prime minister, the ministers of justice, finance, and Indian Affairs, the president of the Treasury Board, and the Indian Residential Schools Resolution Canada minister and deputy minister all favoured such a solution. And, by 2004, the federal treasury was flush with cash thanks to a steadily expanding economy.

The negotiations that produced the Indian Residential Schools Settlement Agreement in 2004–5 had some peculiarities. They were "chaired" by a retired jurist whose actual assignment was to represent the federal government. Apparently, no one complained about Frank Iacobucci's dual role, such was the respect he enjoyed as a former deputy minister of justice and Supreme Court justice. Representation among survivors of residential schools was sparse; one survivor, Phil Fontaine, had to resort to legal finesse to ensure his place at the table. The Protestant churches were present, although they had little at stake, given the existence of the deal that the government had proclaimed earlier to take on the lion's share of abuse litigation awards and to cap the churches' financial liability overall. The Roman Catholic agencies were not satisfied with the agreement that had been fashioned by November 2005 and they were accommodated by means of additional negotiations that delayed signature of the IRSSA until May 2006. The best-represented interest at the negotiating table was the legal profession: indeed, dozens of lawyers participated in the negotiations for an IRSSA.

The content of the agreement illustrated how important it was to have been a negotiator. The lawyers made a killing in the settlement. Their time for participating in the negotiations was expressly covered, and they stood to make more in future if they continued to act for survivors in adjudication of claims of serious physical and sexual abuse under the Independent Assessment Process. The churches held on to what they had. As far as survivors from the various Aboriginal peoples – First Nations, Métis, and Inuit – were concerned, First Nations were the most successful, as the schools they had attended were covered by the IRSSA. Phil Fontaine, national chief of the Assembly of First Nations, was a notable winner, too. Since at least the time of the Royal Commission on Aboriginal Peoples, he had been pushing for a national inquiry into residential schooling that would provide a platform on which survivors could talk about their experience and ensure that a permanent historical record of this failed experiment in social engineering would be made. Having finally secured a commitment to establish such a platform, it remained to be seen how the elements of the settlement agreement that dealt with collective memory, such as commemoration and the ambitious Truth and Reconciliation Commission, could fulfil the goal of solidifying the rewriting of Native-newcomer history that had been going on since the 1980s. It remained to be seen, as well, if individual survivors and Aboriginal political organizations other than the AFN would be satisfied with what had been accomplished in the settlement agreement. And would the complex conclusion to the negotiations advance the cause of reconciliation?

6

Implementing the Indian Residential Schools Settlement Agreement

Putting the Indian Residential Schools Settlement Agreement (IRSSA) into operation was fraught with difficulties. For one thing, there were many organizations involved in implementing its various parts. In addition to the official "parties" to the agreement – the survivors, government, churches, and lawyers – existing agencies would have a role, and a number of new organizations would be created to carry out specific tasks. The Aboriginal Healing Foundation (AHF), for example, would continue to operate, but with enhanced funding. But the Independent Assessment Process (IAP) created by the agreement would require the development of an adjudication secretariat to oversee claims for serious physical and sexual abuse. As well, agencies new and old would continue to interact with the federal government, principally Aboriginal Affairs and Northern Development Canada (formerly Indian and Northern Affairs Canada), but also with departments that oversaw accounting for the expenditure of taxpayers' money. Thus, it was not surprising that implementation of the settlement agreement, which began in September 2007, would not be completed until 2009. In part, the lengthy process was explained by the large scope of the agreement's provisions. In addition, some elements of the package encountered obstacles peculiar to themselves. Getting the IRSSA functioning efficiently was a complex process.

In some ways, the Aboriginal Healing Foundation was a relatively simple component to make work in the post-agreement era. It had been set up, not without difficulty, in 1998 pursuant to the federal government's statement of reconciliation, *Gathering Strength,* and had functioned effectively since its inception. The Liberal government was sufficiently impressed by it to add $50 million to the original grant of $350 million from the surplus the government enjoyed at the end of the 2004–5 fiscal year. The IRSSA added another $125 million to its coffers.[1] But the more interesting – and, as it would turn out, more complex – aspect of the settlement agreement's provisions for the AHF were the sections that dealt with the churches and their financial obligations.

The schedule of the agreement that covered the arrangement the "Catholic entities" had negotiated after the agreement in principle was concluded in November 2005 was a lengthy document. Whereas matters involving the "Anglican church entities" were covered in fifty-three pages, those with the United Church in twenty-four, and the Presbyterians in nineteen, the Catholic entities' deal with the federal government required seventy-five pages. Undoubtedly, the length (including for the signatures of fifty-four entities) and complexity of Schedule 0-3, which covered financial arrangement with the Catholics, reflected the defensiveness that had come to characterize the that church's approach to schools abuse litigation and the government.

Part III: Healing and Reconciliation and Financial Commitments of the settlement agreement required the United Church and the Anglican Church each to contribute $25 million. While the two largest Protestant churches raised the required amounts, the effort sometimes created strains within a denomination. An Anglican survivor who was also an ordained clergyman recalled that harsh words were sometimes spoken by non-Native congregants to people like him. "It wasn't a good time to be an Aboriginal Anglican," he remembered.[2] This clause also required the Catholic entities to provide $29 million as a cash contribution and commit to provide $25 million in in-kind services. In addition, over seven years the Catholic entities would "use their best efforts ... to raise $25,000,000 through a Canada-Wide campaign." The latter funds were to be disbursed "on an annual basis and awarded as grants in accordance with Schedule B."[3] The Catholics' non-profit corporation for healing and reconciliation was to set up a seven-person evaluation committee, including three representatives from the Assembly of First Nations (AFN) and one from Indian Residential Schools Resolution Canada (a government department), to make grants to Aboriginal people "regardless of denomination" in order to promote reconciliation.

Problems beset these provisions even prior to the beginning of implementation of the settlement agreement. While they were in negotiations with the government about the details of their separate financial agreement, representatives of the Catholic entities approached the Aboriginal Healing Foundation about the possibility of the foundation distributing the reconciliation funds that the Catholic entities were committed to pay. Although some preliminary discussions took place, no agreement was reached, and the Catholics subsequently approached the Assembly of First Nations about distributing the funds. Outgoing national chief Phil Fontaine was open to discussions, but his successor, Shawn Atleo, wanted no part of such an arrangement. Still, Mike DeGagné, executive director of the AHF, was stunned to discover before the settlement agreement was concluded that the Catholic entities had named the foundation as the agency through which money from the entities would flow to grant recipients. Recalled DeGagné, "The fact was, I found out quite late in the game that the Catholic Entities were negotiating with the feds to route their settlement money through the AHF. Of course, we had had some discussions with their lawyers, but we had never received a formal sign from them to go to our board for approval of a definite plan."[4] The foundation found itself bound by the settlement agreement to participate in distributing funds whose arrival was uncertain and according to mechanisms which it had not agreed to with the donors.

Further problems stemmed from the fact that the promised money did not arrive in full or in a timely way. After several years had passed, Georges Erasmus, chair of the AHF board, wrote to the Indian Affairs minister to explain "the many efforts the Foundation had made – including meetings, phone calls and correspondence – to bring the Corporation of Catholic Entities into compliance with their obligations, but to no avail." Erasmus copied the letter to the Corporation of Catholic Entities (CCE), and soon afterwards the foundation received its first remittance from the CCE, $3 million. In total, the corporation transferred three payments of $3 million each, a far cry from the amount committed to in the IRSSA.[5] Matters were not helped by the fate of the Catholics' fund-raising campaign. Four years into the seven-year life of the Canada-wide fundraising project, the organizers had a loss of over a million dollars.[6] The uncertainty about funding from the CCE, combined with continuing friction with their lawyers over procedures to evaluate proposals and make grants, meant that the provisions of the settlement agreement to augment the

AHF's funds for reconciliation efforts were more bother than they were worth. As the foundation's historian put it, "The CCE lawyers were creating headaches for the Aboriginal Healing Foundation, as well as uncertainty."[7] People associated with the foundation would not have been broken-hearted early in 2014 when the federal government took the Corporation of Catholic Entities to court over its non-performance.[8]

Evidence came to light in 2016 of a development that incensed many former students of the Roman Catholic residential schools. For reasons that have not been made clear, a lawyer for the government of Canada accepted a proposition from a lawyer for the Catholic entities that Ottawa agree to consider the Catholic commitments cancelled for a payment of $1.2 million. Those obligations included most of the $25 million the Catholics had pledged to fund raise under the settlement agreement. The Catholic campaign, in spite of what one of their lawyers claimed was "our best effort," turned into "a fiasco."[9] Ottawa attempted to "walk the deal back," but a justice of the Court of Queen's Bench in Saskatchewan ruled that there was a meeting of minds between the two lawyers, and that Canada was bound by the agreement.[10] During the ensuing flurry of press comment, anger was not reduced when it was revealed that lawyers for the federal Department of Justice had initiated an appeal of the Queen's Bench decision but then dropped it six days before the new government headed by Justin Trudeau took office.[11] In another bout of press comment, the other churches who were party to the settlement agreement were accused of benefiting from the arrangement the Catholic entities had secured, leading to stiff rejoinders by representatives of the Anglican and United Churches to the effect that they had paid all they were committed to by the settlement agreement.[12] Clearly, nothing in the episode could be considered conducive to the cause of reconciliation.

Catholics' non-cooperation stemmed largely from unhappiness with the settlement agreement. They had felt ignored and then pressured as the IRSSA had been put together. As the Independent Assessment Process for dealing with abuse claims took shape, they feared that the standard for accepting evidence had been lowered. They believed that someone named by a claimant in an IAP adjudication was automatically regarded as guilty. As a result of this growing fear, many Catholics who had earlier supported IAP became opponents who counselled others not to participate in the process. As a

Catholic representative summarized his denomination's opposition to IAP, "the veneer of adjudication is far worse than the absence of adjudication."[13]

By comparison, implementing the provisions for commemoration was a relatively non-controversial exercise, although one that occurred after much delay. Memorializing the story of residential schooling, especially the experiences of the students, had been central to various stages of the movement that culminated in the IRSSA. Former students who attended the exploratory dialogues in 1998–9 had often insisted that steps be taken to ensure that what had happened in the schools would not be forgotten. As the summary of the second dialogue, held in Alberta, noted, "The deep need to tell the story, and have it memorialized in a public way must be respected – including finding a means to commemorate those who have died." Many details should be recorded: "who attended, the memorabilia, the trophies – must be recorded and told and remembered. If we do not hear from the past we are doomed to repeat the mistakes of history."[14] The next dialogue, in Regina, included memorialization as one of the "four interconnecting building blocks needed to be in place within any process of resolution: ... commemorations, with respect."[15] Not surprisingly, then, the need to remember the past figured among the principal conclusions of the wrap-up dialogue in Toronto. Participants in the concluding dialogue said, "It is necessary to tell the story. Build a memorialization feature into each of the [alternative dispute resolution] pilots, with the agreement of all the participants, which is accessible to all the participants."[16] The support of Phil Fontaine, twice the national chief of the Assembly of First Nations, was also important in ensuring that processes for memorializing the school experience were in the settlement agreement. Fontaine believed strongly that a concerted educational program about the residential schools and their impact was needed to engage Canadians in a process of reparations for the economic setbacks First Nations had experienced and to promote reconciliation. Because memorialization was integral to his overall approach to schools policy, Fontaine strongly supported the inclusion of memorialization in the settlement agreement.[17]

The IRSSA's provisions for commemoration were brief and simple. The $20 million that the agreement provided for memorialization was to be supplied by the federal government and disbursed according to procedures set out in a separate schedule of the agreemeent. The two pages that made up the "Commemoration Policy Directive" defined commemoration as "honouring, educating, remembering, memorializing and/or paying tribute to residential school former students, their families and their communities, and acknowledging their experience and the broad and systemic impacts of the residential school system." The objectives of the policy included "honouring and validating the healing and reconciliation of former students and their families" and providing support for "efforts to improve and enhance Aboriginal relationships and [relationships] between Aboriginal and non-Aboriginal people." As well, commemoration was to "promote Aboriginal languages, cultures, and traditional and spiritual values" and to "memorialize in a tangible and permanent way the Residential school experience." The agreement contemplated both large-scale projects and more modest observances related to an individual school or community. Proposals for funding were to "be submitted to the Truth and Reconciliation Commission for evaluation," which would "make recommendations" to government. The IRSSA expected a number of annual calls for proposals and awards, and Schedule J noted that "proposals that are not approved in any given year may be re-submitted in subsequent years."[18]

As events transpired, support for commemoration was slow in developing. When it did reach fruition, it was inconveniently concentrated in a couple of years. In large part because the Truth and Reconciliation Commission was slow to become operational, it was not until the 2011–12 year that the government distributed financial support, which was extended to 68 projects.[19] In the following year, a further 75 applications received funding, and the program then ceased because the $20 million allocated had been completely spent. The funded projects were heavily weighted to groups in the western provinces, with 83 of the 143 projects going to the four western provinces over the two years. Forty-three successful projects came from British Columbia alone, reflecting the large number of schools there and also likely the high degree of organization among that province's survivors. Ontario had 22 projects, Quebec 12, and the Atlantic provinces, which had only had one school, Shubenacadie, 9. The northern territories were similarly lightly represented: the Northwest Territories had 4, and Nunavut and Yukon 3 each. The remainder were from "national" organizations such as the Inuit women's organization, Nipiqartugut Sanaugatigut, and the Assembly of First Nations, which received $1,609,068 "to develop a framework that established commemorative plaques and monuments at the site of each of the Indian Residential Schools recognized under the Settlement Agreement." Some successful applications were for commemorative events at individual schools, such as the former United Church Mount Elgin School in southwestern Ontario. Other projects focused on communities.[20] About half of the approved projects had a healing component to them.[21]

A number of the commemorative initiatives were highly imaginative and captured public attention. For example, the Royal Winnipeg Ballet received $50,000 to help develop a new ballet that was based on the stories that had been recounted by survivors at the various meetings of the Truth and Reconciliation Commission. The production, *Going Home Star – Truth and Reconciliation*, enjoyed a short run in early October 2014 and more performances in several western centres in 2016.[22] Another artistic creation designed by British Columbia artist Carey Newman, with the sponsorship of the Victoria Native Friendship Centre, used $942,350 to collect documents, artefacts, photographs, and audio in a lengthy memory wall that highlighted residential school history. "Canadians of all faiths, backgrounds and ethnicities were invited to participate in the reconciliatory process. A commemorative plaque was installed at each spot across the country from where pieces are collected."[23] The project culminated in an exhibition, "Witness Blanket," which opened in Victoria in September 2014 and then had a cross-country tour to exhibit the 600 artefacts that were arranged like a wall.[24] It had a considerable impact on those, especially students, who saw it.[25]

Some individual awards led to simple but effective programs that engaged large numbers of Canadians, especially school children. Sylvia Smith, a high school history teacher in Ottawa and recipient of the Governor General's Award for Excellence in Teaching History, received $586,290 in the second competition for commemoration funding for "Project of Heart – Commemorating the Children for Future Generations." The idea was simplicity itself. Teachers had students colour with indelible pens on small (approx. 2 cm x 2cm) ceramic tiles some aspect of residential school history that resonated with them. Each tile was to represent a child who died in a residential school. The completed squares were then assembled into a type of mosaic. An Elder or residential school survivor would be invited to speak to the student artists about residential schools.[26] Developed by Smith to engage her own students about residential schooling, the

project caught the imagination of many teachers who wrestled with
the knotty problem of how to present the residential school story to
elementary school children. With commemoration funding the initiative spread across the country, capturing the attention and engagement of many thousands of young people.

Government-sponsored commemorations could be evocative, too.
Such was the case with an installation in the national capital. In
October 2011, Aboriginal Affairs and Northern Development Minister John Duncan announced that, "as a gesture of reconciliation,"
Canada would commission a piece of stained glass commemorating the legacy of residential schools and install it permanently in
the Centre Block of the Parliament Buildings on Parliament Hill. In
announcing the project, the minister revealed a woeful grasp of history, as he went out of his way to laud the then prime minister, Stephen Harper, claiming that his apology on 11 June 2008 "led to the
creation of the Truth and Reconciliation Commission." (In fact, of
course, the TRC was a product of the settlement agreement, which,
as was discussed in chapter 5, predated Harper's government.) A
selection committee of five "leading Aboriginal art experts and former Indian Residential School students with First Nations, Métis and
Inuit representation" unanimously selected a design by Métis artist
Christi Belcourt. When rendered into twin stained glass panels commemorating various events related to the Indian residential school
experience, the artwork was installed above the western entrance
to the Centre Block. To date there has been no confirmation that the
window fulfilled the minister's prediction, that it would "encourage
all Parliamentarians and visitors for generations to come to learn
about the history of the Indian residential schools and Canada's reconciliation efforts."[27]

Although comparatively modest in cost, the commemoration provision stimulated a great deal of creativity and positive activity. The
funded projects supported a number of existing organizations, such as
the Assembly of First Nations, in their ongoing work of healing and reconciliation, while simultaneously providing an outlet for local survivor
societies and communities, which had often had painful relationships
with a particular residential school, to honour and remember those who
had suffered there. As well, as the initiatives of the Royal Winnipeg
Ballet and Project of Heart showed, the commemoration program also
provided an opportunity for individuals and groups, notably including
artists, to turn the emotional reactions they often had to learning of the

6.1 Christi Belcourt's commemorative window, Centre Block, Parliament.

schools into wide-ranging creations that frequently had public impact. Finally, the installation of a memorial window in the Centre Block in Ottawa was an eloquent symbol of the state's recognition of the significance of the history of the schools.

Other portions of the settlement agreement were intended to compensate individuals for the specific harm they had suffered during their schooling. While survivors were eager to continue to access healing services and desirous of finding ways to honour and remember their fellow students, a large number of them also wanted compensation of a material sort for the mistreatment they endured. As the summary of discussions at the first exploratory dialogue held at the former Kamloops school at the end of September 1998 noted, "Violence, substance abuse and poverty flow from the residential schools experience. Some want healing, others compensation, in part because they are poor. Whatever is done, needs to be individually driven – directed at those who went through the residential schools system."[28] The Winnipeg dialogue a few months later concluded, "Financial compensation is key. The [1998 ministerial] apology was not enough. Maybe compensation would make it easier."[29] To be true to survivors' wishes, whatever the settlement agreement made available as compensation for harm experienced at a residential school would have to benefit individual survivors.

The compensation element of the Indian Residential Schools Settlement Agreement that had the widest application was the Common Experience Payment (CEP).[30] Unlike some other parts of the IRSSA that had been discussed in earlier consultations among survivors, churches, and government, the CEP was completely novel. As its name implied, the Common Experience Payment aimed to compensate all eligible survivors for attendance at residential schools or hostels. AFN national chief Phil Fontaine also maintained that the CEP provided some limited compensation for – or, more accurately, recognition of – loss of language and culture, although, not surprisingly, the written text of the CEP section of the IRSSA did not allude to language and culture loss as abuse to be compensated.

Claiming compensation under the Common Experience Payment program was intended to be simple, but its administration would reveal innumerable complications. A trust fund of $1.9 billion supplied by the federal government would pay survivors $10,000 for the first year of attendance at a residential school, and $3,000 for each additional year. Elderly survivors would get a small, interim payment immediately: "In all stages of the CEP process, the elderly (65+) and seriously-ill applicants receive priority."[31] "All CEP applications will be subject to verification," which would be carried out by Indian Residential Schools Resolution Canada (IRSRC). The application period would run for four years from the IRSSA's implementation date, 19 September 2007. Applicants who were denied could appeal to the National Administration Committee and, if turned down there, had a right of appeal to the courts. The federal government would pay administrative expenses. In the event that the funds for the CEP were underspent, the first claim on the excess would be a "pro rata" apportionment to all those who received a CEP, in the form of a personal educational credit of up to $3,000 per person. Other unclaimed amounts would go to First Nation and Inuit organizations to be made available to all former students – First Nations, Métis, and Inuit – equally.[32]

Judging by the number of applicants, the Common Experience Payment program was wildly popular, at least at first. Government planners had expected 110,000 applications and, in fact, received 105,530. The 79,309 successful applicants received an average payout of $20,457, representing an average verified attendance of only 4.5 years. The amount was well below the $28,000 that was anticipated when the program was designed.[33] Presumably the assumption was based on average attendance of seven years. There were many possible reasons for the surprisingly low average payout. First, documentation might have been lost or misplaced. As late as the first part of 2015, Aboriginal Affairs and Northern Development Canada was turning up hitherto unknown quarterly reports of residential schools.[34] These documents contained invaluable information on students' names, ages, health, academic performance, behaviour, and eventual dates of leaving the schools. Apart from such losses, administrative changes in the schools could lead to undercounting attendance. In the case of students who were in residential schools when they shut down, there were many opportunities to fall out of the official net. If they attended day schools while staying in accommodations that were not official hostels under the IRSSA, their time after the residential schools' closure would not count for the CEP.[35] Among the total applicants were 27,798 initially unsuccessful applicants who asked the administrators to reconsider their case. Of these, 9,771 were successful. Another 5,259 unsuccessful applicants appealed to the National Administration Committee, with about one-fifth of them (1,164) succeeding. And, of the 741 survivors who resorted to the courts, the third avenue of appeal, only thirteen had succeeded as of March 2016, while 723 had been turned down yet again, and five were still under judicial consideration. In all, $1,622,422,106 was paid out under the CEP.[36]

Behind those bald statistics lay stories of miscalculation, frustration, and disappointment. The government's own evaluation of CEP revealed some of the problems, especially those that had occurred at the outset. Service Canada, the department that processed applications before passing them on to the people who verified the information, had seriously underestimated the numbers that would rush to apply: the initial "volume was much greater than expected and greatly exceeded planned processing capacity," observed the evaluation. Such was the initial rush when the program began in September 2007 that Service Canada's telephone lines were simply overwhelmed. Calls peaked at more than 100,000 in November of that year "and remained elevated even as application intake started to decline." By the end of 2007, Service Canada had handled over 83,000 applications, almost 80 per cent of all that would be received during the four-year application period. And the high number of applications in the opening months of the program was, as the government evaluators put it, "compounded by missing information and the complexity and type of claim."[37]

The application form was mercifully short by government standards, four pages, but the fact that it was available online in pdf format, which required the use of a computer and printer for completion, made it intimidating for many former students, especially older ones. Applicants were encouraged to call a 1–800 help line for assistance. Other aspects of the application could create snags, too. For proof of identity, applicants could submit an original birth certificate or substitute other documents from an approved list as long as one of the alternative documents had the applicant's photo. In the absence of the approved verifying submissions, a four-page "Guarantor Declaration" had to be completed. If the applicant using alternative proof of identity was not taking the application to a Service Canada office, it was possible to mail the two supporting documents to a central office. In the case of an application that did not have a birth certificate or verifying documents with photograph, a guarantor had to write "I certify that this is a true copy of the original." All identifying documents had to "include their printed name, position, signature, contact information and the date they certified the document."[38] For elderly survivors or those with limited education, applying for CEP was daunting.

For applicants with poor memories, the CEP application was challenging in other ways. In accordance with the language of the settlement agreement, claims about attendance were subject to verification. Indian Residential Schools Resolution Canada, which provided the verification service in the early years of the CEP program, had made many advances in data storage and methods. By 2007, IRSRC had assembled its massive National Research and Analysis database of residential school information, which could be tapped. Moreover, IRSRC was prepared to be flexible. If its database showed that an applicant attended a school in, for example, 1957–8, 1958–9, and 1962–3, but records for the 1959–62 period were missing, IRSRC would assume that the applicant had also attended in 1959–62. It would also examine school year books or student publications in search of confirming information.[39] The cases that would cause survivors the most anguish were those in which written records were insufficient and IRSRC had to ask applicants for further information. The agency's validation process provided that, "When a request for additional information, due to insufficient student records is made, four (or more) questions will be asked of applicants to assist in the validation of their application." These questions required a good deal of recollection on the part of the survivor. "What can you tell us about the buildings and/or property at [insert school] where you lived during [insert years]? What can you tell us about the people at [school] where you lived during [years]? What can you tell us about special events at [school] ...? What else can you tell us about [school] that may help us confirm that you lived there during [years]?" There were also follow-up questions that could be used if necessary. Concerning buildings, an IRSRC verifier could ask, "Were there any major renovations during your time there? Where did you sleep? Where was the bathroom? Can you describe the set-up of your classroom and/or residence? How many grades were taught in the same classroom? What grade were you in at the time?" There were similar groups of follow-up questions for the other interrogations about people, special events, and other areas the student might recall.[40]

The recollections of survivors who went through the Common Experience Payment process confirmed that the program's design was problematic. They reported problems in several areas – learning about CEP, applying, dealing with government agencies as their application worked its way through the bureaucratic mill, verification, and, of course, the results they received once the often-lengthy process reached a conclusion. That did not mean that none of the applicants had a positive experience. For example, an eighty-three-year-old First Nation woman had nothing but good things to say about CEP. A Service Canada worker helped her with her application, and the money arrived sooner than she expected. "To her CEP was 'a double treat': she was 'paid' for having attended a good school." She was comfortably off and just added her compensation money to the "treasury bill that I had before ... It was all positive."[41] An elderly Métis man whose claim had benefited from the expedited handling those over sixty-five received did not find the process too difficult or lengthy. He felt "really good" after he received his compensation and paid some bills.[42] And a sixty-year-old British Columbia woman had an easy time with the application and then found the compensation money arrived sooner than she expected: "I went to the bank one day and all of the sudden I had some money in there that I was not expecting. It was sooner than I thought."[43]

While a fortunate minority had a positive or mixed experience with CEP, negative memories were far more common. Commenting on applying, a fifty-two-year-old First Nation man objected to the lack of assistance provided to applicants. He charged that "there was no support ... for your emotions ... no financial, no counseling, no nothing."[44] A sixty-three-year-old First Nation woman was unimpressed by the information she received: "When the process started I thought it was about getting individual help. I did not think it was about compensation. Communication is lacking." And she resented the fact that the onus to prove attendance fell on the applicants. "It was them who came [to] get me to go to Residential school, and now it was up to me to prove it."[45] Another applicant, a sixty-two-year-old First Nation woman, reacted strongly to receiving less compensation than she thought she deserved: "I was expecting more than what I got, it was really a disappointment. They're calling me a liar because they say I wasn't at that school. My family knows I was, I know I was, that kind of hurt that I was a liar."[46] A fifty-eight-year-old First Nation woman thought claimants "were getting paid to stop any further recourse. I hate to declare that I am defeated. I felt powerless. I thought we were getting paid and that was it. I was enraged and powerless, that is how I felt."[47]

Once applications were filed, survivors found the most distressing aspects of the CEP process were the mixed signals they sometimes received, or the complete absence of signals. Métis in particular were often frustrated by the way the system had been designed. A seventy-two-year-old Métis man who had attended a residential school as a day student ("they called us 'externs,' whatever that meant") was angry at being rejected. "We're not getting recognized and we'd like to. We suffered, if not more then the same as the people who lived in the Missions. In them days there was no bus, no nothing, we had to walk through the bush 3 or 4 miles to go to school and when we did get there we had to have our lunch outside, you won't get in, in the morning, before too early." A clerk at a 1-800 number informed him that he, like many others, was rejected "cause a lot of them are Métis and a lot of Métis are getting left out, never mind being a day student." He agreed with the Aboriginal Healing Foundation's interviewer that Métis day students had been kept out in the cold when they were students and were still out in the cold when trying to access compensation.[48]

Many who went through the CEP process were frustrated by Service Canada, as well as with the telephone lines that were set up to help people cope with the stress that the process often engendered. A First Nation woman who had attended Shingwauk school in Sault Ste Marie organized a group of survivors on Walpole Island in southwestern Ontario to help other former students deal with bureaucracy. When a Service Canada team came to her community to help applicants, it was unprepared for the number who wanted assistance. All the same, the government personnel were condescending when local survivors offered to assist with filling out the forms.[49] A fifty-six-year-old First Nation woman initially thought the process was all right but found the waiting for a decision stressful. "It was just like going through Residential School again. It brought up the memories for one thing. When they said that it was finalized and they were going to admit that it happened … I had a panic attack. I ended up in the hospital … I thought I was having a heart attack." She also recalled having difficulty with the telephone help line. "You know, you phone there and you ask, and then somebody will say this, and then you phone again and somebody will say that."[50] A fifty-two-year-old First Nation woman chose, out of frustration, not to ask for reconsideration of her diminished compensation:

They did ask me to appeal and provide proof of the other two years but I haven't done that. I just shied away from the whole thing. It is just really unpleasant, it is like begging for payments for the horror that I went through. So I just never pursued it … Well, who can I talk to? I can't go into Service Canada ... It is a faceless bureaucracy and you can't face-to-face talk to someone and make your case. Like everything with the Government of Canada, you talk to them through the computer and there is no person there.[51]

A few claimants had acrimonious experiences with the counsellors who were available by telephone as part of the CEP application process. A fifty-year-old First Nation woman who had had a turbulent childhood and adolescence because of family breakdown and alcohol abuse had a dim view of counsellors. She intended to get help if she could find a Native counsellor. Her daughter had seen a counsellor who told her that if she "got off her butt," she wouldn't be so depressed. That counsellor

> had that lazy Indian stereotype and was non-native. And that is the other thing – you can't really see native people (counsellors) as there aren't that many around. And it is really difficult trying to educate non-native people about what happened. That is what I found in my previous counselling, I have gone through a lot of counselling and have a lot of sobriety now but invariably I end up teaching them about the colonial experience and residential schools and child welfare system and all the huge barriers that we face as Aboriginal people. They are sitting there getting professional development experience out of my sessions.[52]

Complaints about the telephone assistance from Service Canada and the help line were frequent. A sixty-five-year-old First Nation woman reported that when she called the toll-free number, the person who answered wanted to know where she got the number, even though "it was on the CEP application form."[53] A fifty-eight-year-old First Nation woman in British Columbia had an altercation with staff on the Health Canada line that was available to applicants. "I did call them up, and they were not very helpful. This one lady, she was quite nasty with me on the phone, she says I don't have time to talk about Jesus, if you need a counselor, I'll give you a counselor right now. I said, 'You know what? Fuck you!' That's what I said."[54] Another man, a sixty-four-year-old First Nation former student in British Columbia, had a mixed experience with the help line. When he learned what his compensation was going to be, "I swore at the person on the line, and then somewhere along the line I got my humor back when they said a little joke. I spoke to this dude for like 2 hours, whoever he was."[55] Most typical of reactions to the phone lines

> was that of a former First Nation chief in the North West Territories who said that they were not of much use. He called and was told he would have to wait four hours because they were busy. When he got to the reconsideration stage he called the 1-800 number he had been given but did not understand the explanation he received. "But I still do not understand who makes the decisions. It is not my fault my records was [sic] gone. It is not my responsibility to find them, it is theirs."[56]

And for another survivor, a fifty-eight-year-old First Nation man, dealing with Service Canada's 1-800 number led him into a catch-22. When he called the help line to check on his application and was told they were looking for a document, he lost patience and hired a lawyer. Then he found that IRSRC would not deal with him directly because he had legal representation.[57]

What most annoyed applicants were the delays they often encountered at various stages of the process. A sixty-one-year-old First Nation man who received only partial compensation and applied for reconsideration complained about how time-consuming the process was: "I have been waiting a whole year or something. It's taken a while. There are so many applications."[58] A man who had attended residential school for twelve years recalled, "It's a time consuming thing, it will take another 9 months, it's frustrating. It can take 3 to 9 months. I think it's still psychologically abusing the people who lived in residential school, the people who witnessed the abuse."[59] Although some applicants found help, many more ended up angry and frustrated.

Results, like the process, produced a mixture of critical and favourable responses, with the former predominating. Particularly striking were the harsh terms survivors had for the cash involved. A fifty-three-year-old First Nation man who attended a Quebec residential school for ten years viewed compensation darkly: "I felt like a prostitute, like I sold my body."[60] A thirty-three-year-old First Nation woman compared the CEP to "handing candy to a kid so that they go away and leave you alone."[61] A forty-five-year-old First Nation woman called compensation "'off money' because it has killed so many people already."[62] Another woman had a less negative response: "I didn't think of it like blood money like a lot of my peers have. They say it's their blood money. I feel that, because I didn't go out and have fun in my twenties, thirties, and forties – this is my time. I'm going to go treat myself ... I already treated all of my kids already, so this is my money. I spent the last $10,000 in late June or early July, so I saved that for 5 months."[63]

Regardless of their view of the money's significance, CEP recipients often considered the quantity inadequate. A forty-eight-year-old First Nation man who attended residential school for one year reflected:

> To be honest 10000 isn't enough. 10000 is a little drop in the bucket, look at Mount Cashel orphanage, I mean for the atrocities Native people went through you can compare it to the genocide in WWII, there were children who died here and buried at these schools, taking away their language, their culture, telling them their culture is wrong changing their way of life ... what I'd like to see ... in every community is a language retention program, qualified language instruction, that's what I'd like to see. 10000 is nothing, I spent that in a week.[64]

A sixty-four-year-old First Nation woman recalled, "I felt belittled – $31,000, what is that? For eight years of misery?"[65] The words of a fifty-three-year-old First Nation man belied his claim that he felt positive about the compensation he received for three years' attendance:

> It wasn't enough money 10000 is not enough in this world. Not when they're giving out millions to other countries, they don't look to natives in their own country. Every house on our reserve is over filled, we can't drink the water. Not enough money to build new houses. They don't realize they keep all the money in Ottawa to INAC, by the time the reserve gets money they're always in the hole. There's not enough money to build a house or run a band office. These governments, Canadian governments have to honour the treaties, the medicine chest, education, that's all we're asking for. (pause – while crying) We're not bums. This was our country. (pause for crying).[66]

A fifty-three-year-old First Nation man said, "A lot of people [are] at the poverty level. The government, if you starve a dog for a long time if he finally gets a meal, of course, he'll take it. You can't say no. It brought a lot of negativity. A lot of strife between family members that had never been there before."[67] Clearly, survivors often felt compensation undervalued their experience.

Whatever they thought of the compensation, recipients found a variety of ways to put it to use. Not all used the money wisely, a problem that some observers had anticipated. Prior to implementation of the agreement, when some anonymous critics had advocated measures to restrict survivors' use of the money, National Chief Phil Fontaine countered that it was money paid as compensation for suffering. "It's not a handout," he said.[68] And, indeed, there were cases where survivors used the funds to finance unhealthy behaviours. For a forty-four-year-old First Nation man, the money simply enabled his self-destructive habits:

I just stayed drunk [until] it was all gone. When I started dealing with these boarding school issues I got drunk. I've been sober for 4 days now that's the longest I've been sober in 15 years. If I wasn't incarcerated I was drunk ... When I get sober, I get depressed and hear voices in my head, I just go to the bottle ... it's better that way then [sic] to sober up and deal with it. I've been very suicidal. The only thing that keeps me alive is staying drunk.[69]

A forty-six-year-old First Nation woman tried to give her children her money but they refused "because they told me that they were just trying to tell me to shut up. I told them to just help me spend it." She went ahead and "just spent it. Drank it, and went to the casino. I said, 'What the heck, this is on the government.'" She knew of friends who were beaten up and robbed, and some older people were victimized by their own children after receiving their CEP payment.[70]

On the other hand, many survivors used the funds they received in positive and creative ways. Likely the most common use of compensation was to help the recipient's family. A forty-three-year-old First Nation woman who was compensated for only one-third of the time she had spent in residential school was nonetheless positive about CEP. "I felt I had nothing to worry about, I paid my bills and I did things for my kids. I was able to give them things they wouldn't normally receive ... I felt a lot better after I received the money. I was less stressed. No stress."[71] For at least one survivor, a fifty-three-year-old First Nation woman, compensation was a tool to reconcile with her children. She got "an auntie" to contact the children she had not raised herself, because they had been taken from her, and arrange for them to come and see her. Meeting her children and giving them the money made the CEP a positive experience for her.[72] A seventy-five-year-old First Nation woman "divided up the money to all my [thirteen] children and grandchildren that I brought up ... I gave all my children money. I kept just, you know, a couple of hundred dollars for myself but the rest went out. I didn't want, you know, to remind me ... if I kept it it would always be on my mind ... It made me feel good doing that, to give it all away," but "it reminded me of what I went through, eh?"[73]

Other uses ranged from the mundane to the imaginative. A sixty-year-old First Nation woman bought household items. When "I got that money, I said that's pots and pans the first thing I'm going to buy. I've never ever got myself pots and pans. Nothing. And I said, I've never had that [sic] new pots and pans. I've never had a really nice bed, I've never had a good TV [upset], I've never had a lot of stuff that I wanted. An Indian couldn't have it. Or I didn't ... I look at my place now and I'm just so proud."[74] Some funds were used with particular sensitivity. One claimant considered using some of his compensation to host a ceremony at which money would be given away. He had given a poor woman a thousand dollars before Christmas, and then won three thousand at the casino a short time later. "My elders say that if you give a lot, you get returns. I did give a lot of money away, and I did get returns on it. I was planning on having my final give away. I had one when I was an adult, and it took about a year or two before I can gather all of [the] gifts that I can give away."[75] A sixty-four-year-old First Nation woman said that her award enabled her to take "my husband's ashes up North because he wanted to have his ashes there."[76]

However recipients used their money, and whatever their attitude towards the process, they recognized that compensation was not a solution to the problems residential school had caused. A sixty-four-year-old woman who had attended the Shubenacadie school in Nova Scotia for eight years, and been part of a long struggle to have a class action certified, reflected that, "we went through hell on the CEP ... after 12 years, we're drained. I know some people that didn't get their money yet, because of records. It's like opening up old wounds. They put the children through a lot, it brings out the child in you. Why would the government keep victimizing us over and over?"[77] A fifty-nine-year-old First Nation man who had attended two schools in Quebec for thirteen years thought that the CEP "did not help me, the lump I have in my throat is still there. It is like some cement has been poured on that lump and made it even harder, it made it worse. I have some anger inside me and it is like by giving us money they wanted to calm me and shut me up."[78] Another woman in her sixties who had attended Shubenacadie for five years but been compensated only for two said she cried when she received her money. When the interviewer asked her why, she responded: "Release and hurt about it. All the things we went through for $13000. What is that going to bring us? The hurt will stay with us till we drop dead."[79] In spite of the positive objectives underlying the CEP, for too many recipients this woman's lament rang true.

In addition to the CEP, the settlement agreement included the Independent Assessment Process (IAP) to deal with serious physical and sexual abuse. Its predecessor, the dispute resolution (DR) program, had been created to replace individual litigation after the exploratory dialogues and pilot projects. It had been designed to avoid putting claimants through an adversarial process, specifically cross-examination about the abuse they had suffered, which would have been required in a court procedure. But critics of DR, including a good number of claimants, had contended that they suffered revictimization as a result of the arbiter's questioning in a DR hearing. A government study of dispute resolution had emphasized the adverse impact the process often had on survivors, as well as the slow pace at which claims were settled. Another examination by the Assembly of First Nations that was funded by the federal government also produced an indictment of dispute resolution. These critiques were the public justification for the push by the AFN and the government for what became the settlement agreement. And certainly the IRSSA included a lengthy Schedule D on IAP. One section of that schedule was intended to reflect the claimant-centred nature of the new program as well as aid commemoration. It said, if "a claimant requests a copy of their own evidence for memorialization," the survivor "will also be given the option of having the transcript deposited in an archive developed for the purpose."[80]

Given the contested nature of DR and other procedures that had preceded the IAP, one might have expected it to differ sharply from its predecessors. And yet the striking thing about IAP was its similarity to the apparently discredited dispute resolution. Indeed, lawyer Doug Ewart, who had designed DR, recalled that Frank Iacobucci had drawn him into the talks leading to the settlement agreement. The former Supreme Court justice had asked Ewart to accompany him to Edmonton for a meeting of the parties to the talks, at which Iacobucci asked representatives of survivors, churches, government, and law firms if they should design a new adjudication model or continue with DR. The Department of Justice did not take a position, but most of the plaintiffs' lawyers said they wanted to keep DR, with some improvements, because it was working for their clients. The AFN was content to go along with the latter approach.[81] And that was largely what happened. The chief adjudicator under DR, Ted Hughes, was succeeded by Deputy Chief Adjudicator Dan Ish, a Saskatoon law professor, to head the Independent Assessment Process, and his office and staff in Regina continued to function, though named the Indian Residential Schools Adjudication Secretariat (IRSAS). Yet, there were some differences. Compensation would no longer vary according to the region from which the claimant came, and it was possible to be compensated for loss of income. In addition, IAP adjudicators would review and could re-assess fees that a claimant's lawyer charged: according to the settlement agreement, "Adjudicators may resolve disputes about the disbursements to be paid." The government would pay an additional 15 per cent of the compensation to the claimant's lawyer, who could charge up to another 15 per cent to the claimant, subject to review by the adjudicator.[82]

According to Schedule D, IAP "consists of a standard track, a complex issues track, and a provision for access to the courts" in limited circumstances. The complex track differed from the standard in that "the Claimant seeks an assessment of compensation for proven actual income losses resulting from" the abuse suffered. Claimants could access the courts, with the chief adjudicator's permission, when "there is sufficient evidence that the claim is one where the actual income loss or consequential loss of opportunity may exceed the maximum permitted by this IAP" and there was a prospect that the courts might award greater damages. Under IAP, the adjudicator's "role is inquisitorial, not investigative. This means that while the adjudicator must bring out and test the evidence of witnesses, only the parties may call witnesses or produce evidence, other than expert evidence." The adjudicator "must both draw out the full story from witnesses (leading questions are permitted where required to do this), and test the evidence that is given (questioning in the form of cross examination is permitted where required to do this.)"

As well as hearing procedures that would have been familiar to parties who experienced DR, the IAP continued the use of a series of charts to quantify damages experienced by a claimant. "Acts Proven," the first chart, once more assigned categories and points for abuse ranging from "severe," such as "repeated, persistent incidents of anal or vaginal intercourse" or "penetration with an object" (45–60 points) to the relatively minor, such as "one or more incidents of fondling or kissing" (5–10 points). Once proven acts were established, the adjudicator next assessed the "Consequential Harm" of the acts. The categories here ranged from "serious dysfunction" (20–5 points) down to "modest detrimental impact" (1–5 points). The adjudicator was also to assess "aggravating factors," which included "verbal abuse," "racial acts," and "being abused by an adult who had built a particular relationship of trust and caring with the victim." If these factors were present, the adjudicator could add another 5 to 10 per cent of the previous points total "rounded up to nearest whole number." Adjudicators could also award up to $10,000 for future medical care or counselling, as well as an additional $15,000 if psychiatric treatment were required. Finally, compensation points for "Consequential Loss of Opportunity" could range from 21 to 25 for "chronic inability to obtain employment" down to 1–5 points for "diminished work capacity – physical strength, attention span." When points had been established under the various categories, the adjudicator would determine an appropriate compensation level: one to ten points received $5,000–$10,000; 111–120 points brought $211,000–$245,000; and a claimant with a point total of 121 or more could receive "up to $275,000."[83] The absolute maximum, available only "in narrow circumstances," was $445,000.[84]

IAP rules attempted to ease the burden on survivors. Claimants could bring "support persons" to the hearing at the expense of the IRSAS, counselling services would be provided, and "cultural ceremonies such as an opening prayer or smudge will be incorporated at the request of the Claimant to the extent possible." Claimants and witnesses would give evidence under oath "by affirmation or another way that binds their conscience." And efforts were made to ease the strain on a claimant: "Hearings will take place in a relaxed and comfortable setting. Claimants will have a choice of location, subject to hearings being scheduled to promote economy."[85] The IAP also employed a lower standard of proof, something that had been developed in some of the pilot projects. An adjudicator, having established that wrongful acts took place, needed only to discern a "plausible link" between the actions and harms suffered, a test that was less stringent than "the more complex principle of causation utilized in civil litigation."[86] As had been the case with dispute resolution, the IAP set up an oversight committee: "The Chief Adjudicator Reference Group shall be reconstituted as the IAP Oversight Committee," which had representation from government,

survivors, and the churches. The Oversight Committee recruited adjudicators, and could, on "the advice of the Chief Adjudicator, renew or
terminate the contract of an adjudicator." The committee could consider matters referred to it by the chief adjudicator, and "monitor the
implementation of the IAP and make recommendations to the National
Administration Committee on changes to the IAP as are necessary to
ensure its effectiveness over time."[87]

Beginning in 2010, the Department of Justice began using a tactic
that effectively deprived some claimants of restitution they otherwise
would have been awarded. At that time, departmental lawyers began
to argue at IAP adjudication hearings that some of the institutions listed
in the settlement agreement, principally in the North, had ceased to be
residential schools when the government and churches switched from
custodial schools to a combination of hostels run by the denominations
and government-supported day schools. Government lawyers managed to persuade IAP adjudicators that anyone who was abused in a
school rather than a hostel after such a change was not eligible for compensation for serious physical or sexual abuse under IAP. Not surprisingly, when the use of this tactic became widely known in early 2016,
there was a loud outcry.[88]

If the Independent Assessment Process were judged solely on the basis
of how many survivors applied for compensation, it would have to be
pronounced a roaring success. The program's designers expected that
the IAP would receive 12,500 applications, but the adjudication secretariat was looking at that number by September 2009, a full three years
before the deadline for applications. As the deadline approached, the
rate of applications accelerated – 8,000 were received in the last year – and
at the deadline 38,087 applications and cases transferred from dispute
resolution were in hand.[89] In the first year of operation, the IAP program held 1,700 hearings with claimants, and the number of hearings
per year steadily increased as the secretariat struggled to cope with the
unexpected deluge of claims. By the end of March 2016, the IAP had
resolved 91 per cent (34,571) of the total number of claims, and had
paid compensation of $3.004 billion. The average compensation award
was $97,538 (plus 15 per cent contribution to lawyer's fees, for a total
of approximately $112,169).[90] The statistics were impressive, but they
masked several disquieting features of the IAP in operation. Almost

one-tenth of claims (3,516) had not been completed by March 2016, and the 34,571 that were resolved included applications that the secretariat had not admitted to the process or that had been withdrawn. Perhaps the most dramatic figure, though, was not a number, but a date: 2017. Some of the applications that had been received by the September 2012 deadline would not be resolved until sometime in 2017. Moreover, although the designers of the IAP had expected a claim would take a year to process, even when the adjudication secretariat was operating at its highest rate the average claim took twenty-one months. And although the settlement agreement had specified that adjudicators were to render their decision on a claim in the simple track in 30 days and the complex track in 45, the reality was that adjudicators' reports usually took 160 days.[91]

Why the IAP results fell so far short of expectations was simply explained: the system was overwhelmed and unable to cope with a caseload more than triple what had been anticipated. Working within the constraints of federal government regulations, which were usually stifling, the secretariat scrambled to ramp up. The staff in the first year of operation increased from 33 to 150, by the end of the second year to 200, and by 2013 to 270.[92] Dispute resolution had been led by a chief adjudicator, the experienced Ted Hughes, but the IAP secretariat expanded to include several deputy chief adjudicators, eventually five by 2011. Ish and his deputies were concerned to ensure that the adjudicators followed the rules laid down in Schedule D and produced consistent awards. In 2013, a deputy chief adjudicator was added specifically to protect claimants' interests in a system that had grown quite large.[93] Every adjudicator's report was reviewed by either the chief adjudicator or one of his deputies. In many ways, the adjudicators were the key to the successful operation of the IAP.

Adjudicators were both the good news and the bad news of the IAP system. They were carefully selected by the Oversight Committee. This committee had to agree unanimously to proposed names, and it had the power to renew or drop adjudicators when their terms were completed. New adjudicators were subjected to a week of intensive training.[94] During the orientation week, trainees heard from experts in a variety of fields, including survivor and church representatives, as well as the chief adjudicator and his deputies, about how to carry out their duties fairly, empathetically, and efficiently. Still, there were problems associated with the adjudicators, not necessarily of their making. The men and women, almost all lawyers and some former judges, who held hearings, recommended awards, and reviewed counsel's fees, were federal government "contractors." As such, they were subject to all the rules that the federal Treasury Board applied to contractors, and the result of complying with the governmental recommendations was that it took a year before someone nominated to be an adjudicator could deal with claims. The federal government also applied its rules about security to contractor-adjudicators; moreover, if they had office staff who helped them with IAP files, they had to get those people security clearance, too. The additional staff vetting would usually take another four months.[95]

An especially troubling problem with adjudication was that the IAP secretariat had a difficult time attracting and retaining Aboriginal adjudicators. The paucity of Indigenous arbiters was especially problematic because IAP procedures permitted claimants to request an Aboriginal person to conduct the hearing. Besides making it difficult to allow claimants to feel at ease, the shortage of Indigenous adjudicators made scheduling the hearings more complicated and time consuming. The Oversight Committee used what was known as the "set-aside" provision of the federal government's Request for Proposals process that permitted contracts to be designated for Aboriginal suppliers. The committee also advertised opportunities through the Indigenous Bar Association, but the number of Aboriginal adjudicators "remained relatively low." According to a former executive director of the IAP, the disappointing results were likely attributable to the fact that many Aboriginal lawyers were connected personally or through family with the residential school experience and therefore might find hearings too challenging. "As well, many Aboriginal counsel do not come from conventional law practices or highly-supported legal environments, and may as a result not have had as much experience in dealing with the degree of administrative requirements of contracting with the IAP."[96] It was not surprising, then, that, as a First Nation Elder remarked during the opening session of adjudicator training in 2011, "I don't see no brown faces here today."[97]

A problem graver than the shortage of adjudicators was the lawyers who served as counsel for claimants, or at least a minority of them. Chief Adjudicator Dan Shapiro once noted that almost every clause of the compensation grid "had been litigated."[98] An area that agitated some counsel more than the "grid" was the IAP's limitations on fees and the requirement that adjudicators review fees for fairness and reasonableness and, if necessary, revise the fees that claimants' counsel proposed. When the court-ordered cap of 30 per cent on fees was implemented, there were "some spectacular" protests from lawyers, including a refusal to provide the secretariat with claimant's address or logs of time worked, supposedly on grounds of "solicitor-client privilege." That protest collapsed when the secretariat told the rebels that they could not be paid without the information. The chief adjudicator and others also had to be vigilant that some counsel did not supplement their earnings improperly by inflating charges for disbursements and expenses, which Canada paid under the terms of the IAP. And, finally, deputy chief adjudicators in at least two cases awarded counsel less than 15 per cent of the award on fees because lawyers in these cases had not provided adequate representation. The chief adjudicator anticipated that going below 15 per cent in such cases would be their "next frontier" on fees, but the counsel in these cases did not appeal the reduced awards. On the other hand, lawyers representing claimants in Quebec agreed to limit their fees to the 15 per cent that the government paid, and in the rest of the country there was a group of lawyers – known informally to the IRSAS as "the 15% club" – who did the same.[99] Even so, counsel did not suffer financially. On average they charged 22 per cent of the amount awarded, and the average billing to the IRSAS for a standard-track hearing was $4,200, including time for preparation and writing the report.[100]

A few lawyers gave their profession a black eye. The Merchant Law Group of Regina got into a dispute with the federal government over its fee entitlement for work done down to the conclusion of the settlement agreement, which ended up in litigation in 2015.[101] A sixty-year-old First Nation man claimed that, after going through an examination for discovery process without any positive result, he demanded that lawyer Tony Merchant give him his file for the case. "Tony Merchant, I said I want my file and I want someone else to look at it, but he wouldn't give up my file cause I owe him money for what he did so he won't give up my file to me."[102] Dan Ish, who served as chief adjudicator after Ted Hughes and prior to Dan Shapiro, noted when he retired that three firms had been particularly notorious. Ish complained to the Law Society of Manitoba about the conduct of Winnipeg lawyer Howard Tennenhouse, who was eventually disbarred. As well, the IRSAS raised the behaviour of Vancouver lawyer Stephen Bronstein with the British Columbia oversight society and settled for a "review" of his practice and his alleged connection with a paroled murderer who was said to be doing intake work for Bronstein's firm.[103]

In some ways, the most problematic law firm IRSAS encountered was that of David Blott of Calgary.[104] When Blott was finally hauled before the court in British Columbia in 2012, his firm had represented 1,500 claimants in IAP hearings, "was the lawyer on record for approximately 2,900 other claimants awaiting hearings, and had more than 1,200 additional IAP applications that it had not yet submitted." There had been allegations that he had provided, or cooperated with a firm that provided, advances to claimants at high interest rates. Following complaints to the Law Society of Alberta, IAP adjudicators began to file information about "the inaccuracy of some Blott & Company IAP application forms and discrepancies between the information contained on those forms and that provided by the claimants during their hearings." An inquiry by the court monitor who oversaw the settlement agreement turned up

> client signatures being added to documents that they had not signed; of inaccurate information on applications; of lawyers meeting their clients for the first time at the actual IAP hearing; of an inability of clients to contact their counsel; of more than 380 loans being made to Blott & Company clients – some of them by family members of Mr. Blott – with interest rates and fees as high as 60% per annum; and of widespread dissatisfaction among claimants about the quality of representation by Blott & Company.

The British Columbia Supreme Court dealt with Blott & Company firmly in 2012. It noted the firm's earlier brushes with the Law Society of Alberta (LSA), and commented in particular that "the LSA also recognizes IAP claimants as a vulnerable class in regard to which special care must be taken by counsel." Blott had been instructed by the LSA to improve the firm's handling of IAP claimants, but had failed to do so. The court noted,

> That Mr. Blott has not reformed his practices despite LSA intervention or the concerns imparted repeatedly by the IAP administration and adjudicators, indicates that direct and persistent supervision would be required to ensure that his clients were protected. Mr. Blott has shown no capacity for rehabilitation, a conclusion reinforced by the fact that Mr. Blott, in the weeks before this application was heard, attempted to summarily terminate his solicitor-client relationship with 2,238 IAP claimants.

The justice noted that the Law Society of Alberta had concluded "that Mr. Blott does not appear to understand what it means to be a lawyer." He "does not recognize that his primary role is as a fiduciary and everything else is secondary." The justice said "I share the LSA's concern that Mr. Blott does not understand what it means to be a lawyer." He ordered the company be stripped of its IAP clients, and that they be reassigned to other lawyers.[105]

The Blott case illustrated the truth of a statement by a former executive director of the adjudication secretariat: "Although the number of counsel who have been implicated in these problems is relatively small, their impact has been broadened both by the large number of claimants that they represented and by the attendant media attention that they garnered."[106] The woman who had administered the program for many years estimated "maybe 35–40 percent" of counsel were bad apples.[107] When Dr Dan Ish retired as chief adjudicator of the IAP early in 2013, he remarked that the program should have had a process for screening potential participants as claimants' solicitors. He thought that lawyers should have had to qualify to represent claimants by applying to the court, go through a training program, and sign an agreement to abide by IAP regulations.[108] Lawyers were essential to the setting up, operation, and monitoring of the IAP, but some of them created a poor image for their profession.

Delinquent and unsympathetic counsel constituted only one of many complaints that survivors had with respect to IAP. The chart that helped adjudicators calculate points to award for abuses proven continued to attract negative media comment.[109] The chart deterred a thirty-five-year-old First Nation woman. "It is stupid to put in a chart, you get so many points for having something put up you, and being forced to have anal sex. It just gives me the shivers thinking about it." Nor did she like the application, which was twenty-one pages long and had a forty-four-page guide for applicants: "And one of the things it says is to, please write in black ink ... [laughs] ... I don't get it."[110] The prospect of dealing with the IAP administration frightened some survivors, such as a fifty-two-year-old First Nation woman who said, "I think I need counseling before I get there because I just ... ohh ... I just get the heebie jeebies trying to go up against that bureaucracy ... It is so impersonal and I have to go to this personal thing and tell my story? ... I went with my uncle. He went through it and yeah, it was really harsh and difficult to hear what happened to him."[111] A forty-four-year-old First Nation man was hesitant to apply to IAP because he heard stories about applicants being victimized by their lawyers.[112] A fifty-year-old First Nation man also was not inclined to apply: "I don't know if I want to. It sounds like you have to stand up to a lot of people, just like to get through it. It's like post-traumatic stress disorder, peeling an onion to get to the core of it."[113] A seventy-four-year-old First Nation woman said that she would "like to file for it, but I hate to bring back memories."[114] In rare cases, such as that of a sixty-one-year-old First Nation man, survivors did not apply because their residential school experience had been mostly positive.[115]

For most survivors, the hearing process was traumatic. A sixty-six-year-old First Nation woman recoiled from her exposure to an IAP hearing: "The first one, I went to it killed me for the day and I was shaking and wanting to cry and scream … it's not easy especially when it comes to sexual abuse. It's like being victimized all over again. If there are some men and women who can't handle IAP I don't blame them … Cause I suppressed a lot of things. It doesn't come that easy to get your childhood out."[116] A sixty-five-year-old First Nation woman recalled, "I had to be very explicit about things. That brought up a lot stuff for me. [upset]. How long did it last? How often did it happen? [crying]" Following "my hearing [strained voice] I went into a deep depression for a long time." She became "very suicidal," thinking on her way to work, "What it would it be like if I just stepped in front of the bus?" Her brother had accompanied her at the hearing and was very upset by it. The hearing "really impacted him. He ended up drinking after that you know, I think it's really hard for him to talk about things. That's what he's told me."[117] Likewise, a First Nation man of sixty-eight found that being asked questions at the hearing made him "relive it all over. I started crying. I couldn't help it. It was like I was back there again and I had buried it."[118] A seventy-six-year-old First Nation woman who received compensation of only $3,500 for being slapped at school nonetheless found preparing for her hearing stressful: "A lot of things I've hidden away. I had to dig it up and think of it and remembering and that was horrible."[119] There were rare exceptions. A sixty-eight-year-old First Nation woman who had her hearing the day she was interviewed by the Aboriginal Healing Foundation said that she now felt "a little bit lighter" and less stressed.[120] For most survivors who went through the IAP process, though, the experience was trying, and for some traumatic.

No portion of the settlement agreement was free from implementation difficulties. The lack of cooperation and commitment by the Roman Catholic entities spelled problems for the Aboriginal Healing Foundation. That the differences between the Catholic entities and the AHF ended in litigation was as surprising as it was disheartening. By comparison, the settlement agreement's modest program to commemorate residential schooling avoided litigation, even if its implementation was slow. Nonetheless, many of the activities and artistic creations that the commemoration section funded were imaginative and were effective in spreading knowledge of the residential school experience among at least a small minority of Canadians. The large compensation programs, the Common Experience Payment and Independent Assessment Process, encountered the greatest difficulties. In both cases, a major part of the explanation for problems and survivor dissatisfaction was the scope of the programs. The CEP dealt with more than 100,000 applications, scrambling all the while to assemble the documentation that was needed to validate survivors' claims of school attendance. The fact that the CEP expended less money than anticipated – $1.66 of an anticipated $1.9 billion – was a reflection of the problems that led to awards that left many survivors dissatisfied. The Independent Assessment Process was, to a great extent, a victim of its own success. Try as the adjudication secretariat might, it never succeeded in coming to grips with the reality that more than three times as many former students applied for compensation for serious physical and sexual abuse than had been anticipated. That it would not be able to wrap up its work until a decade after the start of the implementation of the settlement agreement is clear evidence of how overwhelming the challenge was.

PART THREE

Redress and Reconciliation

7
Truth and Reconciliation

Standing in the House of Commons on 11 June 2008, Prime Minister Stephen Harper ended his apology for the government's role in residential schools with a reference to the near future. Alluding to the Indian Residential Schools Settlement Agreement (IRSSA), he observed, "A cornerstone of the settlement agreement is the Indian residential schools truth and reconciliation commission." The commission, he said, was "a unique opportunity to educate all Canadians on the Indian residential schools system." And he concluded his remarks with a prediction: the Truth and Reconciliation Commission (TRC) "will be a positive step in forging a new relationship between aboriginal peoples and other Canadians, a relationship based on the knowledge of our shared history, a respect for each other and a desire to move forward together with a renewed understanding that strong families, strong communities and vibrant cultures and traditions will contribute to a stronger Canada for all of us."[1] Closing with an upbeat reference to the TRC, which was to begin its work a few weeks later, was, perhaps, the most improbable element of an unlikely event. Harper's speech represented an effort to move from searching for a solution to problems residential schools had created to taking action aimed at redress and reconciliation. Few observers would have predicted that the prime minister would usher in a new era with a historic apology in Parliament. Nor would many have been as optimistic about the TRC as he was on that June afternoon. Getting to the apology was an adventure; so, too, would be the operation of the Truth and Reconciliation Commission that Harper hailed so positively.

Although often criticized as shallow and cynical exercises, official apologies in fact serve several important purposes. As Canadian examples
have illustrated, expressions of regret and responsibility for state actions
against specific groups can serve to quiet, if not eliminate completely,
long-running agitation for redress of a historic wrong. In 1988, Prime
Minister Brian Mulroney delivered an apology for the Canadian government's internment in 1942 of Japanese and Japanese-Canadian residents on the west coast following the attack on Pearl Harbor. In addition to words of contrition, the state apology on that occasion included
provision of funds to commemorate events important to the Japanese-
Canadian community. The drastic action against Japanese Canadians
had been overwhelmingly popular at the time, when internment began,
because the community was widely regarded as a potential fifth column
for Imperial Japan. Over the ensuing decades, opinion shifted, thanks
in no small part to the work of historians who probed the events. Forty
years after internment, it was clear that the people incarcerated had
not constituted any form of subversion or even dissension. Moreover,
it was understood that a large majority of those interned – likely as
many as three-quarters – were Canadians either by birth or naturaliza-
tion. Mulroney's apology served to quiet criticism and lobbying, much
as other apologies in later years would appease opinion concerning
untoward state actions, such as internment of so-called enemy aliens
from countries with which Canada was at war in 1914–18 and Chinese
immigrants subjected to a racist "head tax" intended to discourage
immigration from the Middle Kingdom. In all these cases, the political motive of the apologies was clear, and the statement had a positive
political effect.

But there is much more to official or state apologies than responding
to a political problem with a political gesture. The Truth and Reconciliation Commission would later point out that "apologies are important
to victims of violence and abuse." They "have the potential to restore
human dignity and empower victims to decide whether they will accept
an apology or forgive a perpetrator."[2] A study of public apologies by a
political scientist has argued that "apologies are desired, offered, and
given in order to change the terms and meanings of membership in
a political community," with the citizenry's interpretation of the history behind the apology being the key to understanding how apologies
come about and what they accomplish.[3] Apologies "perform three tasks,

with national histories and their reinterpretations necessarily at their center," Melissa Nobles argues: they "validate reinterpretations of history by formally acknowledging past actions and judging them unjust"; they "may strengthen history-centered explanations of minority disadvantage"; and they "advance reconsideration of the obligations and boundaries of membership in the national community."[4] The relevance of Nobles' analysis to the treatment of residential schools in Canada is obvious. During the many decades in which the unquestioning interpretation of Native-newcomer relations had been rose-coloured, these schools had been below the radar of historians and citizens in general. Beginning in the 1980s, however, historians began to reinterpret the history of policy directed at First Nations and the victims' response to these forays, bringing about a revision that resulted in the depiction of state Indian policy as malignant.

This revisionist interpretation of Canadian Indian policy was embraced and promoted energetically by the Royal Commission on Aboriginal Peoples (RCAP) in the first half of the 1990s, most notably in its final report, issued in 1996. There the depiction of Canadian history emphasized an early period of relatively harmonious relations based on commercial cooperation between indigenous and immigrant Canadians. It gave way to a longer period in which the two groups, with the immigrants greatly outnumbering the original peoples, were at loggerheads over coercive state policies and was followed after 1945 by a growing movement of resistance and protest by an increasingly well-organized and assertive Aboriginal political movement.[5] The reinterpretation of the historic treatment of Native peoples by the Canadian government had been affirmed briefly in other state actions, the 1998 Statement of Reconciliation and the 2006 Indian Residential Schools Settlement Agreement, most notably. According to the typology of apologies that Nobles outlined, what remained to be done after RCAP took up the revisionist interpretation of Native-newcomer history that had developed in the previous twenty years was for the Canadian state to endorse the historical revision by means of an apology.

What happened in Canada between the 1980s and 2008 was a muted echo of a much more clamorous process that took place in Australia in the same period. There, the reinterpretation of the history of relations between Aborigines and European immigrants was hotly contested in what was termed "the history wars."[6] As in Canada, Australian historians' reconsideration of the country's history led to revision of the dominant narrative of relations between Aborigines and newcomers. The revisionists soon came under criticism, first by the eminent historian Geoffrey Blainey and later by Liberal prime minister John Howard after his coalition formed the government in 1996, for promoting what was decried as "black armband history." Howard began by musing in 1996 that "one of the more insidious developments in Australian political life over the past decade or so has been the attempt to rewrite Australian history in the service of a partisan political cause," and before long he stated, "I do not take the black armband view of Australian history ... I believe that the balance sheet of Australian history is overwhelmingly a positive one."[7] For their part, the minority of Australian historians and commentators who agreed with Blainey and Howard were derided for clinging to a "three cheers" version of the history of the country and of relations between Indigenous and immigrant peoples. The intensity of the clash of interpretations in Australia far outstripped the discussion of Native-newcomer history in Canada. One conservative columnist in Australia, for example, referred to revisionist historians as "part of ... the 'moral mafia,'" and another writer described them as "white maggots."[8] Unlike in Canada, debates over the history of state-Aborigine relations roiled not only academic halls but national political debate and newspapers, particularly of the political right in Australia. In Canada, the closest parallel was an earlier debate over official bilingualism and Quebec-Canada relations that made its way into the pages of national newspapers and magazines in the 1960s.[9]

In Australia, a national reconciliation movement had been advancing steadily prior to the election of Howard's Liberal-National government in 1996, and it had seemed likely that the government soon would have made a gesture of reconciliation, perhaps an official apology or perhaps even a treaty with Aborigines, to provide the foundation of a renewed relationship. With Howard's election, all such movement ceased, and he spent the next decade avoiding pressure for reconciliation. When the Labor Party returned to power in 2007, the political landscape again changed. In February 2008, Prime Minister Kevin Rudd offered an official apology to "the Stolen Generation" for the coercive assimilative policies directed at Australia's Aborigines for many decades.

Stephen Harper had initially shown a similar pattern of resistance, but he came to a different conclusion. Residential schools had been below his personal radar until 2007 or 2008. University of Calgary political scientist Tom Flanagan, who worked closely with Harper between 2001 and 2006, said that he did not remember a single conversation with the leader or in the Canadian Alliance caucus about the residential schools issue while he was heavily involved in Ottawa.[10] There had been no reference to an apology for the residential schools in the Indian Residential Schools Settlement Agreement (IRSSA), but a commitment that the prime minister would apologize had been part of the "political accord" that the Assembly of First Nations (AFN) had concluded with Prime Minister Paul Martin in May 2004 and that led to negotiation of the IRSSA.[11] When, in the aftermath of concluding the settlement agreement, commentators asked government leaders about an apology, the response initially was that there would not be one. Indian Affairs minister Jim Prentice angered many Aboriginal people in March 2007 when he said that, although the Harper government had apologized to Maher Arar for the government's role in his detention and torture in Syria and to Chinese Canadians for the head tax, it would not apologize for residential schools because that was a different sort of issue. He denied that an apology was part of the settlement agreement and played down the significance of the earlier political accord.[12] Six weeks later, however, Conservatives surprised the Commons when they supported a Liberal motion for an apology for residential schools. Prentice, however, was still saying that it would be better to wait until the Truth and Reconciliation Commission had completed its work before issuing a government apology.[13] Evidence that pressure for an apology was working on the minority government came in the autumn of 2007. The mid-October Speech from the Throne contained the promise that the prime minister would use the launching of the TRC "to make a statement of apology to close this sad chapter in our history."[14]

Lobbying for an apology had involved a number of members of Parliament, including a number of Conservatives. Former Indian Affairs minister Chuck Strahl thought there should be one, as did Jim Prentice, in spite of his public pronouncement. Conservative Senator Gerry St Germain, a Métis who had influence with the prime minister because he had helped bring about the merger of Progressive Conservatives and the Canadian Alliance that brought Harper to power, strongly supported an apology. Federal New Democratic leader Jack Layton energetically advocated a conciliatory gesture. He told Harper that, in the case of the apology to the Chinese – a cause for which MP Olivia Chow, Layton's wife, had been a leading advocate – the gesture came so late that many of those who had been affected died before they could hear it.[15] And it was well known that former Liberal prime minister Paul Martin, who had signed the political accord with the AFN in May 2004, was a proponent of a government apology.

7.1 Prime Minister Harper apologizes for residential schools, 11 June 2008.

The principal Aboriginal political organization was left out of the loop during this campaign for an apology. As Phil Fontaine recalled, "The government did not come to us": no one in the government consulted the AFN about what, if anything, would be done. Fontaine noted that, at one point, the federal government let it be known that it would have a cabinet minister issue a statement of apology. In response, the AFN organized a press conference at which Fontaine said, "If that's what they'll do, we'll sit on our hands. The apology will be rejected." Back-room discussions between the AFN and government and official opposition leaders began at that point and went on for months, right up to the evening before the event. "Inch by inch we advanced. We got more elements that would make the apology a major event," Fontaine recalled.[16]

The setting of the apology was lavish and certainly not something the Assembly of First Nations had any reason to boycott. Leaders of all the national Aboriginal organizations – the Assembly of First Nations, the Métis National Council, the Congress of Aboriginal People, the Native Women's Association of Canada, and Inuit Tapiriit Kanatami – entered the Commons chamber in traditional garb and took their places together in the centre of the room between the government and opposition benches. Although, on rare occasions in the past, a prominent individual had been seated on the floor of the Commons, it was unprecedented for such a large group of external political leaders to be featured so prominently in the House. The galleries were full, many of the observers Aboriginal people, including a good number of former residential school students. Other survivors and family watched events from the remote viewing facilities that were set up in an adjacent room. The stage was set for a solemn and memorable statement.

Although Harper started awkwardly, with a partisan dig, he delivered an emotionally powerful speech of apology. As he began, the Internet was buzzing with controversy about residential school compensation stirred up by one of his MPs. On a local radio show the day before, Pierre Poilievre, a young Ottawa-area MP, had questioned the wisdom of compensating residential school survivors. "Now," argued Poilievre, "along with this apology, comes another $4 billion in compensation for those who partook in the residential schools ... My view is that we need to engender the values of hard work and independence and self-reliance. That's the solution in the long run – more money will not solve it."[17] In the Commons, the Conservative leader engaged in his own partisanship, going out of his way to single out NDP leader Jack Layton as an important contributor to the day's events, in the process snubbing Liberal Paul Martin. Martin, of course, had been the author of the Kelowna Accord that Harper had trashed and was well known as a strong supporter of measures and programs to assist Aboriginal people. Such petty behaviour aside, the prime minister spoke well.[18]

More than half the official apology was devoted to what had by now become the historical consensus on residential schooling. Harper began by describing the "treatment of children in Indian residential schools" as "a sad chapter in our history." The "primary objectives of the residential schools system," he said, "were to remove and isolate children from the influence of their homes, families, traditions and cultures, and to assimilate them into the dominant culture. Those objectives were based on the assumption aboriginal cultures and spiritual beliefs were inferior and unequal." He then reached for a phrase that, though it was becoming a commonplace description of the purpose of residential schools, in fact came from American, not Canadian, Indian policy history. "Indeed, some sought, as it was infamously said, 'to kill the Indian in the child.'"[19] The prime minister then moved to a recitation of a familiar litany of wrongs inflicted on residential school students:

> The government of Canada built an educational system in which very young children were often forcibly removed from their homes, often taken far from their communities. Many were inadequately fed, clothed and housed. All were deprived of the care and nurturing of their parents, grandparents and communities. First Nations, Inuit and Métis languages and cultural practices were prohibited in these schools. Tragically, some of these children died while attending residential schools and others never returned home.

The apology then moved to the present and the government's response to the schools' legacy. "The government now recognizes that the consequences of the Indian residential schools policy were profoundly negative and that this policy has had a lasting and damaging impact on aboriginal culture, heritage and language." Harper noted that "some former students have spoken positively about their experiences at residential schools," but said that the positive memories "are far overshadowed by tragic accounts of the emotional, physical and sexual abuse and neglect of helpless children, and their separation from powerless families and communities." Broadening its explanation of the impact of the schools in contemporary Canada, the apology noted that the "legacy of Indian residential schools has contributed to social problems that continue to exist in many communities today." Praising individual survivors' "resilience" and "the strength of their cultures," Harper observed that, "It has taken extraordinary courage for the thousands of survivors that have come forward to speak publicly about the abuse they suffered." He acknowledged that "many former students are not with us today and died never having received a full apology from the government of Canada," and said that the "government recognizes that the absence of an apology has been an impediment to healing and reconciliation."

> Therefore, on behalf of the government of Canada and all Canadians, I stand before you, in this chamber so central to our life as a country, to

apologize to aboriginal peoples for Canada's role in the Indian residential schools system. To the approximately 80,000 living former students, and all family members and communities, the government of Canada now recognizes that it was wrong to forcibly remove children from their homes and we apologize for having done this.

We now recognize that it was wrong to separate children from rich and vibrant cultures and traditions, that it created a void in many lives and communities, and we apologize for having done this.

We now recognize that, in separating children from their families, we undermined the ability of many to adequately parent their own children and sowed the seeds for generations to follow, and we apologize for having done this.

We now recognize that, far too often, these institutions gave rise to abuse and neglect and were inadequately controlled, and we apologize for failing to protect you. Not only did you suffer these abuses as children, but as you became parents, you were powerless to protect your own children from suffering the same experience, and for this we are sorry.

The burden of this experience has been on your shoulders for far too long. There is no place in Canada for the attitudes that inspired the Indian residential schools system to ever again prevail.

You have been working on recovering from this experience for a long time and in a very real sense, we are now joining you on this journey.

The government of Canada sincerely apologizes and asks the forgiveness of the aboriginal peoples of this country for failing them so profoundly.

...

We are sorry.

The final expression of sorrow was repeated in French, Ojibwe, Cree, and Inuktitut.

In concluding his statement, the prime minister permitted himself cautious optimism about the future. "In moving towards healing, reconciliation and resolution of the sad legacy of Indian residential schools, implementation of the Indian residential schools settlement agreement began on September 19, 2007," he noted. The IRSSA "gives us a new beginning and an opportunity to move forward together in partnership." The Truth and Reconciliation Commission, which Harper described as a "cornerstone of the settlement agreement," was "a unique opportunity to educate all Canadians on the Indian residential schools system." The TRC, he concluded, "will be a positive step in forging a new relationship between aboriginal peoples and other Canadians, a relationship based on the knowledge of our shared history, a respect for each other and a desire to move forward together with a renewed understanding that strong families, strong communities and vibrant cultures and traditions will contribute to a stronger Canada for all of us."[20]

The responses from the leaders of the five Aboriginal organizations that were seated directly in front of the prime minister were impressive and moving, too. Before they spoke, however, the heads of the other political parties represented in the House of Commons had a brief say. Liberal leader Stéphane Dion acknowledged what the prime minister had not pointed out: that the Liberals had formed the government during much of the period when the residential schools were operating. "I acknowledge and accept our shared responsibility in this tragedy. I am deeply sorry. I apologize." Bloc Québécois leader Gilles Duceppe and New Democratic Party head Jack Layton took the occasion to criticize the government for not signing on to the United Nations Declaration on the Rights of Indigenous Peoples, to considerable applause from some quarters of the chamber.[21]

In contrast, the representatives of the Aboriginal organizations avoided all partisanship and even recriminations to focus on the usefulness of the prime ministerial apology and to express hope for the future. AFN national chief Phil Fontaine claimed that residential school "survivors, through the telling of their painful stories, have stripped white supremacy of its authority and legitimacy." He chose to emphasize the positive. "What happened today signals a new dawn in the relationship between us and the rest of Canada. We are and always have been an indispensable part of the Canadian identity." There still would be struggles, "but now we are in this together." Mary Simon of the Inuit Tapiriit thanked the prime minister in Inuktitut for apologizing. While it had been a long struggle to get an apology, "I am filled with hope … I am also filled with optimism." Beverley Jacobs of the National Aboriginal Women's Association asked pointedly, "What is it that this government is going to do in the future to help our people?" Clem Chartier of the Métis National Council, and Patrick Brazeau of the Congress of Aboriginal Peoples also spoke positively, but with less impact.[22]

Response to the prime minister's apology was, understandably, mixed. Most Aboriginal people who heard or watched the events in the Commons appeared to appreciate Harper's words, although, not surprisingly, some were negative or cynical about the gesture. Mi'kmaq Grand Chief Ben Sylliboy probably spoke for many when he reacted by saying, "I really feel emotional here. What took them so long to apologize?"[23] Seventy-one-year-old Geronimo Henry, who had attended the Mohawk Institute in Brantford, wondered, "Is that apology going to bring back my culture and my ceremonies? No, it's not going to do nothing. It's just a bunch of words."[24] Mike Cachagee, one of the founders of the residential school alumni association at the Shingwauk School in Sault Ste Marie and a long-time advocate for reconciliation, agreed that the apology was a moving experience, but noted it would not please everyone. Still, survivors who had been waiting for an official apology "will rest a little better tonight."[25] Perhaps most poignant of all were the words of Willie Blackwater, who had been at the centre of the trials that arose from the horrific abuse Arthur Plint had inflicted on students at Alberni Indian Residential School. Blackwater, who was one of the survivors invited to sit on the floor of the House of Commons to hear Harper's speech, said before the event: "This apology is going to affect every survivor right across our great nation. It will trigger a lot of emotions."[26] For Anglican cleric and survivor Andrew Wesley, the apology certainly evoked strong emotion. Present in the House for the ceremony, Wesley felt the apology as an intense, sacred experience.[27]

Although comprehensive data on reactions to the apology are not available, a variety of indicators can be used to assess them. So far as the general Canadian population was concerned, an Innovative Research Group poll conducted between 11 and 13 June revealed that 83 per cent of respondents were aware of the apology, and, among those who knew of it, 71 per cent agreed or strongly agreed that the government should apologize.[28] According to a large sample of opinions collected by the Aboriginal Healing Foundation, survivors' reactions varied. They were positive or negative, short and simple or more complex, and in some cases thoughtful and reflective. Opinions clashed: some survivors expressed pleasure with it and others were harshly critical. Among the survivors who experienced the apology positively was a fifty-four-year-old Inuk man who had been in a room near the Commons. "It was good. It was a lot more than I expected. I think that they said everything – almost everything that had to be said and it was really good. And also the other – like the NDP, Liberals and [Parti] Quebecois, what they said after the apology – I liked it and it was good for me."[29] For an elderly First Nation woman, the experience was "really emotional. For him, to personally apologize for things they did in the 1920's–1970's, I was crying and crying. We were there. We were in the building … I was so happy and so sad at the same time, when I was listening to him. It was awesome, I'm glad I went."[30] And a sixty-four-year-old First Nation man said, "It made me forgive the government and churches. Without forgiveness I would still be in bondage, now I am free."[31]

Among those with a largely positive response was a fifty-two-year-old Saulteaux (Western Ojibwe) man who listened to the ceremony on the radio. He said Harper's words "didn't mean nothing to me until the PM used Ojibway, I broke down and cried … when he said it in my language." He "thought he was sincere."[32] Recalled a sixty-year-old status Indian woman, "When the Prime Minister made an apology, that's the time when it struck home, it really, really had a strong effect on me."[33] A seventy-six-year-old male status Indian watched the broadcast with his father: "I really liked it and I really … like [that] my Dad was sitting there and was just mesmerized to the TV like listening to each speaker and whatnot. But he doesn't like Harper so he was just swearing around, saying lying bastard and whatnot … but when he listened to the other speakers and all the groups that were there, the Inuit and all that he was really mesmerized watching it. It made me feel good, actually."[34]

Some, including a thirty-nine-year-old male former student, seemed to think the prime minister had a credibility problem in making the apology: "For one, he never set foot in a residential school, he never looked in their eyes, he just sent them over the airwaves, it will take years to apologize, shake hands and say sorry to everyone."[35] A male status Indian was harsher: "The apology from Harper, it sounded sincere, but he's a bullshit man." He thought "he looked sincere, talked sincere, but he's not going to help Natives. He's a man with 2 tongues. White politicians are finding that out now."[36] This sentiment was shared to some extent by a trio of status Indian women in their sixties. One, who had gone to residential school for eleven years, said, "I don't think it came from the heart, he was just reading it off the paper."[37] A second refused to accept the apology: "It was just words, blank words, I put a blank ear to it."[38] Equally mistrustful, a third assumed the prime minister had been forced to apologize and noted that, "It would have been better if the pope had something to say."[39] A fifty-eight-year-old status woman who had attended a Quebec residential school for six years was left cold by the event: "Even when the Prime Minister offered his apology to Aboriginal people (on TV)

I didn't feel anything special. I thought if it brings him satisfaction then good for him."[40] Those who reacted negatively were conditioned to do so in part by Harper's record of acting contrary to the views of Aboriginal leaders.

Some, like a fifty-five-year-old status Indian man, had a mixed reaction. He was not impressed with the prime minister's statement, saying "Harper when he said that apology, there was no remorse, it was cold, someone must have scratched it down a few seconds before he went up. He had no remorse." However, he noted that, "In our tradition, we still have room for forgiveness, with all my strength in my body, that apology, did mean something."[41] A fifty-eight-year-old status Indian woman who was in the Commons said, "I cried. I felt angry ... Why wait a hundred years? Even my sister who went to residential school for two years it has affected her the rest of her life. Imagine me ten years? It has affected me so much. I was so mad I was ready to punch all the time. But sometimes I get back into this more and I think I have to let it go."[42]

Others were more thoroughly negative in their assessment. For a forty-year-old status woman, Harper was cold: "The way he stood, and there was no emotion. He was like an iceberg standing up there."[43] A sixty-four-year-old First Nation woman was likewise unimpressed: "It didn't do any good. Knowing he's apologizing didn't do anything for me anyway."[44] Another woman, a sixty-six-year-old status Indian, "wasn't convinced ... because politicians are liars. It was big words coming from a big fancy building. He is not here to see the suffering, the true meaning of the suffering that has happened to us."[45]

A good number thought that the apology had been a long time coming, too long for many survivors who had passed away. A sixty-nine-year-old status woman was reluctant to give Stephen Harper much credit: "I think it was long coming. It was very good, even though the PM before did most of the work on it. It was well spoken I guess ... I think it was well said. It was a big step for the government to realize what a big mistake this was."[46] Echoing some of these sentiments, a status Indian man in his forties commented that "it's been a long time coming, the sad thing about that, some of the people who went to residential school who passed on never got to hear that. My parents, some of my family members, never got that opportunity to hear that apology."[47] "It came too late," agreed a seventy-seven-year-old status Indian woman. "He wasn't there so he didn't know what he was talking about that is what I felt."[48] Said another, "I was thinking of all the ones who passed away, like my parents and grandparents and friends who died, who never got a chance to hear and realize what was happening, dying without parenting skills and shame and have no chance to release it. They never had a chance."[49] A younger woman thought "it helped a bit. It was tough hearing it though ... For me, personally I accepted it. The only way to move on is to accept it. I accepted the apology. It was a long time coming though."[50]

Some witnesses offered particularly reflective comments. As one Inuk woman who had attended the Commons session observed, "It was a special kind of event. And it was funny, like, afterwards, I asked ... myself, like, why is he apologizing? But then the loss is never going to come back, you know the loss we felt towards our families. Specially the teachings, the counseling that we might have had from our family. Events we might have missed. Changing lives, changing events we might [have] missed. (tears) And, cultural pride, family pride we have had. It's not there."[51] As a fifty-two-year-old status Indian woman who was sceptical about the apology reflected:

What may come afterwards is important and we will see how they navigate this. I get so annoyed when I hear they are going to shut down the AHF at a time like this, when we are supposed to be going into the Truth and Reconciliation Commission. It is ludicrous that they would say such a thing. But they keep threatening it ... In personal relationships, when you vocalize an apology, it doesn't mean this is a way for me to be responsible for my behaviour. But it is a way of taking responsibility for your behaviour and then changing that behaviour. And so changing the behaviour of this country means ending the neo-colonial practices. So if we are going to end neo-colonial practices, they need to hear this out ... and that comes from the TRC. We need to be heard for what we went through and if they don't create the programs and the avenues and policies to allow us to do that, then there is no sincerity in the apology.[52]

Mi'kmaq leader Ben Sylliboy was similarly unconvinced. "Call me in a year's time," he responded when asked what he thought of the apology. "They make it sound good, but they don't follow up on what they're saying."[53]

Further reflections came from a sixty-two-year-old First Nation man had attended the event in Ottawa only because his wife, who was going, thought he should go so they could share the experience. "When the words 'I'm sorry' came out," he recalled, "I finally felt

free. I talked to my mother, my brothers, and my cousins who died
before – I told them that they were free at last." As soon as the ceremony was concluded, he left Parliament Hill and went to the railway station "because I didn't want to share with anyone. I wanted to
keep that moment for my wife and for my children." He "accepted
the apology, but as I listen to our nation, especially the ministers that
made negative remarks about Aboriginal peoples ... when is it going
to stop? When are they going to start to understand our history?"[54] A
thoughtful status Indian man who had attended a residential school
for thirteen years concluded that the apology "seemed empty to me,
cause the policies are still there, the Indian act is still there, the legislation is still there, we're still not equals in our own land, we're still the
poorest of the poor." Yet he still welcomed the apology. He knew that
survivors would "start our healing, but our partners to treaty, if they
don't heal themselves what good is it to us, cause they'll still treat us
the same, they need to heal too ... they have to step up to the plate."[55]
A sixty-six-year-old woman who had attended the Lytton school in
British Columbia expected little would result from the apology: it
came from the government, and "they have never followed through
with anything."[56]

By the time Stephen Harper apologized for the residential schools,
there was a well-developed body of scholarly literature that could be
used to evaluate the various apologies that proliferated in the 1990s
and early twenty-first century. Indeed, a volume of scholarly writing
on the subject that appeared in the same year as Harper's apology
was entitled *The Age of Apology*.[57] While academics argued – as academics do – over the necessary constituents of a sound and effective
apology, they concurred that an official apology needed four elements
to qualify as valid. First, the wrongs for which the apology is being
delivered must be spelled out clearly and unequivocally. Second, the
person making the apology on behalf of an organization or institution must explicitly acknowledge that agent's responsibility for the
wrongs. Next, there should be a commitment that such offences will
not be repeated in future. And, finally, the representative must explain
what steps will be taken to ensure that the objectionable events will
not recur.

Judged by these criteria, the Harper apology was good but not complete. It spelled out the coercion, the poor care, the lack of nurturing, the
language suppression, and the physical and sexual abuse that occurred
in residential schools, thus satisfying the first criterion. Second, the

7.2 The "end" of residential schools?

prime minister admitted "Canada's role in the Indian residential schools system." Moreover, a series of statements ending "and we apologize" or "for this we are sorry" indicated acceptance of government responsibility for the harms perpetrated. Third, the official apology indicated that abuse in future would not be tolerated: "There is no place in Canada for the attitudes that inspired the Indian residential schools system to ever again prevail." Where the apology fell short was in not spelling out what the admitted perpetrator, the federal government, would do to ensure such horrors were not repeated. Nor, unlike Australian prime minister Kevin Rudd's apology a few months earlier, did it describe the actions the government would take to make reparations by improving Aboriginal peoples' social conditions. Rather, the Harper apology referred to the work that the prime minister anticipated the Truth and Reconciliation Commission and other agencies that were part of the Indian Residential Schools Settlement Agreement would undertake. Thus, while impressive as a performance, the 2008 apology fell short of satisfying an objective measure of what constitutes an effective apology and, at the same time, failed to impress many of the Aboriginal people who witnessed it.

In the weeks and months after June 2008, Canadians would have good reason to wonder about the sincerity of Stephen Harper's apology. The bumptious Conservative MP Pierre Poilievre was made to apologize for his ill-considered words uttered the day before the apology. In the Commons he said, "Yesterday, on a day when the House and all Canadians were celebrating a new beginning, I made remarks that were hurtful and wrong ... I accept responsibility for them and I apologize."[58] In other respects, though, the Harper government's later actions were notable for not being in accord with the apology. Indian Residential Schools Resolution Canada, the government unit set up to deal with litigation and survivors' claims, first under dispute resolution and then under the Independent Assessment Process (IAP), was closed down and its operations transferred into the Department of Indian and Northern Affairs (renamed Aboriginal Affairs and Northern Development Canada by the Conservative government).[59] In 2010, the federal budget announced that there would be no more funding for the Aboriginal Healing Foundation, sealing the fate of an agency that, since 1998, had done a great deal of work with healing programs. The government's announcement that, in future, support for such activities would come from Health Canada was not at all reassuring to survivors and those working with them.

Perhaps the most striking evidence that the Harper government's approach to residential school issues was not altered by the prime ministerial apology came late in 2010. As noted earlier, Department of Justice lawyers began to enter a technical argument in Independent Assessment Process cases to disqualify some claimants for consideration: Ottawa argued that, in the northern institutions that were transformed from residential schools into church-run residences in the 1960s and 1970s in what was known as the administrative split, the federal government was not liable for damages incurred in the schools to which the residence students went daily for instruction. They were, the government contended, no longer residential schools. When, in April 2015, a judge of the Alberta Court of Queen's Bench upheld the federal government position, the IAP directorate instructed adjudicators to rule accordingly on claims that were affected by the administrative split. (Subsequently, in February 2016, Carolyn Bennett, Indigenous Affairs minister in the new Liberal government, ordered that the restrictive policy be reviewed after it was disseminated by a national newspaper.)[60] This episode, combined with the 2014 deal that exempted the Catholic entities from paying a sizeable amount of compensation it had committed to under the IRSSA (see chapter 6), bore out an observation that Justice (later Senator) Murray Sinclair made in June 2015: "the apology was never messaged down to the bureaucracy in a way that meant they had to act on it."[61]

Even a belated decision in November 2010 to adhere to the United Nations Convention on the Rights of Indigenous Peoples was hedged with unnecessary qualifications. The declaration, said the Harper government, was "an aspirational document" and "a non-legally binding document that does not reflect customary international law nor change Canada's laws." The government reiterated concerns expressed earlier, especially in relation to the declaration's impact on lands, territories, and resources. The greatest concern appeared to be that the declaration's reference to the need for "free, prior and informed consent" was unacceptable when the requirement was "used as a veto" by Indigenous peoples.[62] The government's behaviour was consistent with what the May 2008 Speech from the Throne had implied: it saw the apology as closing a sad chapter of Canadian history rather than beginning a new one on reconciliation. As an editorial cartoonist acidly illustrated, the prime minister regarded his apology as closing a file rather than recognizing that it had to be the first of many steps towards a better relationship. In a cartoon that appeared two days after the apology, Harper walked beside a downcast First Nation man, his arm around the man's shoulders. "… Glad that's finally behind us," the prime minister observed. The First Nations man was dragging a ball and chain labelled "residential schools."[63]

The Truth and Reconciliation Commission, described by the prime minister as a "cornerstone of the settlement agreement" and "a positive step in forging a new relationship between aboriginal peoples and other Canadians," began work at the end of June 2008. While the commissioners and observers were conscious that Canada's TRC was the latest in a long line of truth commissions and reconciliation agencies around the world, there were distinctive, even unique, elements in the Canadian TRC. Most bodies assigned to investigate the causes of social cleavages and recommend ways to combat them had been the result of civil wars or horrific regimes of repression and persecution. The South African Truth and Reconciliation Commission, which had been appointed by the Nelson Mandela government in 1995 and began hearings the next year under the leadership of Anglican archbishop Desmond Tutu, came out of the usual conditions for such bodies – a period of destructive war or, in the South African case, a half-century of oppression under apartheid. The Canadian TRC, in contrast, was part of the negotiated out-of-court settlement of thousands of individual lawsuits and class actions by and on behalf of former residential school students. It was the result of elite accommodation among leaders rather than the response to a groundswell of public opinion.[64] The commission's make-up, powers, and purposes were determined by negotiation among the survivors, churches, federal government, and lawyers who represented claimants. Moreover, the Canadian TRC was unique in being devoted principally to an investigation of what had happened to children.[65] Some of the features of the TRC that later people complained about resulted from the process and people that created it.

Although the Indian Residential Schools Settlement Agreement of May 2006 dealt with many topics, uncovering what had happened in the schools and finding ways to recover from the damage they had created were prominent among its goals. The United Church representative at the talks leading to the settlement agreement said that the TRC was the issue that took the most time. As well, he pointed out, the necessity to set the mandate of the TRC in a short space of time – from August to November 2006 – ensured that Schedule N, which established that mandate, would be a vision statement rather than a detailed work plan.[66] After noting that the government and churches had operated the schools, the IRSSA stated that "the Parties desire a fair, comprehensive and lasting resolution of the legacy of Indian Residential Schools" and "the Parties further desire the promotion of healing, education, truth and reconciliation and commemoration."[67] Anticipating that the commission might encounter controversy among the parties, the settlement agreement said the "Commission may refer to the NAC [National Administration Committee] for determination of disputes involving document production, document disposal and archiving, contents of the Commission's Report and Recommendations and Commission decisions regarding the scope of its research and issues to be examined."[68]

Schedule N, which gave more detail on the intended operation of the TRC, emphasized a series of principles that were to govern the commission's work. The commission's "truth telling and reconciliation process" was identified as "a sincere indication and acknowledgement of the injustices and harms experienced by Aboriginal people and the need for continued healing." It represented "a profound commitment to establishing new relationships embedded in mutual recognition and respect that will forge a brighter future. The truth of our common experiences will help set our spirits free and pave the way to reconciliation." The TRC's antecedents were acknowledged: the commission "will build on" the 1998 federal government apology and the principles developed by "the Exploratory Dialogues (1998–1999)." The dialogues' principles of accessibility, victim centredness, confidentiality, respect, flexibility, and looking to the future were to be embraced in pursuit "of rebuilding and renewing Aboriginal relationships and the relationship between Aboriginal and non-Aboriginal Canadians." Schedule N defined reconciliation as "an ongoing individual and collective process [that] will require commitment from all those affected including First Nations, Inuit and Métis former Indian Residential School (IRS) students, their families, communities, religious entities, former school employees, government and the people of Canada."[69] Yet, as legal scholar Jennifer Llewellyn has pointed out, Schedule N is much more forthcoming on how the TRC is to pursue truth seeking than it is regarding how reconciliation might be achieved.[70]

The goals of the TRC that were laid out in Schedule N were many and challenging. The commission was to "acknowledge Residential School experiences, impacts and consequences." To that end, it would "provide a holistic, culturally appropriate and safe setting for former students, their families and communities as they come forward to the Commission," hold national and community events to promote its goals, and work to enhance "awareness and public education of Canadians about the IRS system and its impacts." It was also to create a legacy of its own. It was to "identify sources and create as complete an historical record as possible of the IRS system and legacy," which would be "preserved and made accessible to the public for future study and use." It would issue "a report including recommendations to the Government of Canada" for the parties to the settlement agreement that would deal with "the history, purpose, operation and supervision of the IRS system, the effect and consequences of IRS (including systemic harms, intergenerational consequences and the impact on human dignity) and the ongoing legacy of the residential schools." And it was to "support commemoration of former Indian Residential School students and their families."[71] And all of this was to be done in five years.

Besides its ambitious scope, what was striking about the goals of the commission was the way they largely ignored the people who had worked in the schools. These people, some of them federal government employees but most religiously committed enthusiasts who worked for the churches, were arguably an important part of the schools' "experiences, impacts and consequences." Yet, although Schedule N noted that the goal of reconciliation "will require commitment from all those affected" and mentioned explicitly "religious entities, former school employees, government and the people of Canada," the church workers who had staffed the schools and their superiors at the churches' head offices were not included in the list of people for whom the commission was to "provide a holistic, culturally appropriate and safe setting" to recount their experiences. There was no reference to the need to make the commission's work hospitable to school staff. Similarly, apart from their role as parties to the settlement agreement, there was no consideration of what the headquarters of the churches and the Catholic entities might contribute or how they might benefit from the everyday work of the commission. It was, perhaps, an unconscious ignoring of the Christian groups that the passage that laid out the need to "witness, support, promote and facilitate truth and reconciliation events" had a footnote that said "This [witness] refers to the Aboriginal principle of 'witnessing,'" as though Christianity did not also have a lengthy and important tradition of bearing witness to important events. All in all, the goals of the commission that were established in Schedule N were tightly focused on survivors, their families, and their communities, even though these important groups could not promote reconciliation by themselves. They would have to work with others who had been involved in the schools as well as with Canadians in general.

Schedule N made it clear what the parties to the IRSSA expected the Truth and Reconciliation Commission to be, and even more so what they did not want it to be. The first item mentioned in the schedule's section on powers and duties said that the commissioners "are authorized to receive statements and documents from former students, their families, community and all other interested participants, and ... to archive all such documents, materials, and transcripts or recordings."[72] This statement was part of an emphasis on statement taking and record preservation that permeated the schedule. But even more space was given to functions that the TRC was not to perform. It "shall not hold formal hearings, nor act as a public inquiry, nor conduct a formal legal process." The commissioners "shall not possess subpoena powers, and do not have powers to compel attendance or participation in any of its activities or events. Participation in all Commission events and activities is entirely voluntary." In conducting meetings, taking statements, and issuing their report and recommendations, the commissioners were to carry out their duties "without making any findings or expressing any conclusion or recommendation, regarding the misconduct of any person." Commissioners "shall not name names in their events, activities, public statements, report or recommendations."[73]

These requirements sharply distinguished the TRC from the South African Truth and Reconciliation Commission, which had had subpoena powers and which had operated an amnesty program under which individuals who had committed gross human rights abuses could receive amnesty if they testified fully to the commission about what they had done. As Kathleen Mahoney, legal adviser to the Assembly of First Nations and an influential figure in the negotiation of the settlement agreement, explained, the Canadian TRC was set up in such a way to avoid such processes. Its designers feared that if the commission had subpoena powers, individuals called before it would simply invoke the right not to testify, thus involving the commission in a legal morass. Moreover, they wanted the emphasis of the Canadian commission to be on reconciliation rather than bringing miscreants to justice.[74]

Another feature of the commission that was emphasized strongly in Schedule N was its role in collecting and preserving records on the history of residential schools. A separate article of the schedule was devoted to research. It stated that "the Commission shall conduct such research, receive and take such statements and consider such documents as it deems necessary for the purpose of achieving its goals."[75] Among the "responsibilities" of the commission, which were listed in section 3 of the schedule, were the need "to employ interdisciplinary, social sciences, historical, oral traditional and archival methodologies for statement-taking, historical fact-finding and analysis, report-writing, knowledge management and archiving" and "to establish a research centre and ensure the preservation of its archives."[76] Essential to compiling a historical record were both the oral histories that people would provide to the commission and accumulated documents in various archives. The schedule stressed that the commission was to pay attention to "the significance of Aboriginal oral and legal traditions in its activities," but also that it be guaranteed access to church and government archives: "Canada and the churches will provide all relevant documents in their possession or control to and for the use of the Truth and Reconciliation Commission." The duty, though, was "subject to the privacy interests of an individual as provided by applicable privacy legislation."[77] With conditions, Schedule N also contemplated collecting documents from some legal processes: "Insofar as agreed to by the individuals affected and as permitted by process requirements, information from the Independent Assessment Process (IAP), existing litigation and Dispute Resolution processes may be transferred to the Commission for research and archiving purposes."[78] The settlement agreement clearly proposed that the commission cast a wide net for information on the history of residential schooling.

The eventual destination of the oral accounts and the documents that the TRC was authorized to collect was a "National Research Centre." Such a repository was to be created "in a manner and to the extent that the Commission's budget makes possible," and it "shall be accessible to former students, their families and communities, the general public, researchers and educators who wish to include this historic material in curricula." The commission was to ensure that "all materials created or received pursuant to this mandate" were "preserved and archived with a purpose and tradition in keeping with the objectives and spirit of the Commission's work." To the extent the law allowed, "all materials collected through this process should be accessible to the public."[79] Although the point was not spelled out explicitly in Schedule N, all the documents that the commission was empowered to collect from the federal government and the churches – the mammoth volume of which the negotiators of the agreement obviously did not appreciate – were destined to go to the national research centre.

To carry out the commission's daunting responsibilities, the settlement agreement provided the TRC with specific staff and advisory bodies. Even before the commission began to function at the end of June 2008, it had a small office in Ottawa in which acting executive director Bobby Watts, historian Helen Harrison, and a few other key personnel worked to get things ready for the commissioners. Watts, a First Nations man, was experienced in governmental and First Nations affairs, and Harrison held a doctoral degree in history. They would be joined for a time by an experienced archivist, Marianne McLean, on loan from Library and Archives Canada.[80] A group of "Regional Liaisons" were to be appointed by the executive director and commissioners after consultation with an "Indian Residential School Survivor Committee" to act as conduits with communities and "provide a link between the national body and communities for the purpose of coordinating national and community events."[81] The survivor committee was to be made up of ten "representatives drawn from various Aboriginal organizations and survivor groups" on a regional basis. These ten were to be appointed by the federal government "in consultation with the AFN, from a pool of eligible candidates developed by the stakeholders." The members of the committee would advise the commissioners on "community and national processes" and commemoration.[82] All staff and advisers would be paid from a budget that the commission was to prepare "within the first three months of its mandate" and that was to be approved by the minister in charge of Indian Residential Schools Resolution Canada following "Treasury Board policies." The costs of "copying, scanning, digitalizing" archival documents "will be borne by the Commission."[83] The budget for the commission's work was set at $60 million.

Obviously, the most important personnel associated with the TRC would be the commissioners themselves. Schedule N specified that the commission "shall consist of an appointed Chairperson and two Commissioners, who shall be persons of recognized integrity, stature and respect," and that "consideration should be given to at least one of the three members being an Aboriginal person." Former students, Aboriginal organizations, churches, and government were to nominate candidates, and the "Assembly of First Nations (AFN) shall be consulted in making the final decision as to the appointment of the Commissioners."[84] Schedule N was surprisingly mute about who would actually make the appointments, but the necessity to have the commission established by order-in-council implied that the federal government would at least formally make the selection.

The appointments that officially took effect 1 June 2008 more than satisfied the criteria in the settlement agreement. The selection committee, which was chaired by lawyer Thomas Berger, picked Justice Harry S. LaForme of the Ontario Court of Appeal, a Mississauga of New Credit (Ojibwe) from southern Ontario, to be chairperson. LaForme had been the first First Nation person to be appointed to a Canadian appeal court. He had had considerable experience as commissioner of the Indian Commission of Ontario and as the chair of Ontario's Royal Commission on Aboriginal Land Claims prior to his appointment to the TRC. The other commissioners were also highly qualified. Claudette Dumont-Smith, an Algonquin from Kitigan Zibi near Maniwaki, Quebec, had trained as a nurse, had a master's degree in public administration, had served as a consultant for fifteen years, had worked with a federal Panel

on Violence against Women in 1991–3, and then was the health director of the Native Women's Association of Canada. Jane Brewin Morley,
a member of an Ontario family with strong democratic socialist roots,
was a lawyer in private practice in British Columbia for many years
until she shifted the emphasis of her work to mediation and dispute
resolution. Her experience relevant to the work she would do as a commissioner was significant. Between 1996 and 2001, she had chaired the
Jericho Individual Compensation Panel that had been set up to adjudi-
cate claims of sexual abuse at the Jericho Hill School for the Deaf and
Blind in British Columbia. From 2003 to 2006, she had been the Child
and Youth Officer for British Columbia, where she had encountered a
good deal of evidence about the intergenerational effects of residential
schooling. And immediately prior to her appointment, she had joined
the ranks of adjudicators in the Independent Assessment Process. The
new commissioners brought impressive credentials and experience to
the work of the TRC.

Unfortunately, the skilled team also had flaws that undermined it
and soon did it in completely. Justice LaForme, an experienced jurist,
was used to giving directions and having them obeyed. In addition, he
came under enormous pressure during the summer of 2008 because
a controversial staffing decision he made caused an uproar in First
Nation circles in Ontario. He appointed Owen Young, a First Nation
lawyer, to be commission counsel, an office not mentioned in Schedule N, even though Young had made himself unpopular because of his
role in a case involving a First Nation, Kitchenuhmaykoosib Inninu-
wug, and a mining company in northwestern Ontario. Acting for the
province of Ontario, Young had asked a judge to levy heavy financial
penalties on a group of First Nation protesters whose defiance of a court
order had brought them convictions for contempt of court. This stance,
which was contrary to First Nations' traditions of respecting Elders,
caused widespread anger. At a meeting of Assembly of First Nations
chiefs in Quebec City in July 2008, some chiefs questioned LaForme
about his selection of Young, and the group passed a resolution asking
the commission to reconsider the appointment.[85] As well as contending
with this controversy, LaForme soon found that he was serving with
two independent-minded commissioners who thought TRC decisions
should be arrived at collegially, not made by the chairperson.

The stress mounted for LaForme, and on 20 October 2008 he
informed Chuck Strahl, the minister of Indian Affairs, that he was step-
ping down because of "an incurable problem" facing the TRC: "The

two Commissioners are unprepared to accept that the structure of the Commission requires that the TRC's course be charted and its objectives are to be shaped ultimately through the authority and leadership of its Chair." The other two commissioners, he said, "repeatedly and openly" disagreed with this approach. "Challenging the reality that they were appointed as providers of advice and assistance to the Chair, the two have chosen to compete for control of the Commission by insisting that it is to be run on the basis of simple majority rule ... Efforts on my part and on the part of others to move the Commission away from their position toward one that would restore functionality and respect have been futile." This clash of views about how the commissioners should operate put the TRC "on the verge of paralysis," but, LaForme continued, it was not the full story. Morley and Dumont-Smith, he contended, "see the TRC as primarily a truth commission," whereas he saw the task of uncovering and recording the history of the schools "as but a part, however important, of the greater whole of reconciliation." And he hinted that the "majority rule" that he said the others favoured "would not be grounded in Commission independence but would be shaped by the influence by some of the parties and their political representatives."[86] The last statement was a none-too-subtle reference to lobbying by the Assembly of First Nations.

The statement by the chairperson of the commission was at best opaque. Although he insisted that he was to chart the course and shape the objectives of the TRC, there was nothing in the commission's mandate to justify his contention. Schedule N said that the commission was to operate with one commissioner as chairperson and two others as commissioners, but there was nothing in the mandate that specified that the chair was anything more than *primus inter pares*, first among equals. Nothing in Schedule N supported the notion that one commissioner was to chart the commission's course and shape its objectives while the other commissioners were simply to advise and assist the chair. In addition, LaForme's veiled allusion to some of the parties to the settlement agreement and their political representatives influencing Morley and Dumont-Smith suggested strongly that there was more to the justice's disgruntlement than a dispute over governance of the commission.

Although LaForme's abrupt resignation was a devastating blow to the Truth and Reconciliation Commission, it actually slowed but did not stop the commission's work. Dumont-Smith and Morley soldiered on with the work for another few months, giving notice in January 2009

of their intention to leave the commission in June. One of the key projects on which the two worked was a study of missing Aboriginal children. Identifying students who had died or gone missing at residential
schools and, if possible, determining their resting places had emerged
as an emotionally charged topic even before the commissioners were
appointed in June 2008. A working group was formed that developed
a mature research plan approved by Commissioner Dumont-Smith by
the autumn of 2008.[87] A spokeswoman for the TRC described the project
as archival research to determine "the number and cause of deaths, ill-
ness and disappearances of children at the residential schools as well
as the location of burial sites." This research resonated with survivors,
who often carried traumatic memories of classmates dying at residential school. Mike Cachagee, chair of the National Residential School
Survivors' Society, recalled burying a classmate at the Anglican school
in Chapleau when he was eight years old. "We can't just have our people planted in the ground and forgotten about. That's basically what
they did."[88] As well, before they resigned, Morley and Dumont-Smith
spent many months preparing briefing papers for the new commissioners they knew would succeed them. Later, the new chief commissioner,
Murray Sinclair, would acknowledge that the briefs that the first commission had bequeathed his group proved "really useful."[89] In spite of
this good work after the TRC was disrupted by LaForme's resignation,
there was no doubt that the events of 2008 had dealt a severe blow to
the commission. At a minimum, it had lost most of its momentum; at
worst, it might have been fatally wounded.

The developments of 2008 had constituted a good news, bad news story
for redress and reconciliation. Both the prime ministerial apology and
the commencement of the Truth and Reconciliation Commission had
occurred in a productive atmosphere that gave advocates of efforts
to repair relations between Indigenous peoples and other Canadians
hope and enthusiasm. Both the occasion and the speeches on 11 June
2008 were heartening for many. The solemnity of the ceremony in the
House of Commons and the prime minister's eloquent address about
the history of residential schooling created a measure of optimism. A
positive outlook seemed all the more justified, as the prime minister
emphasized, because the long-awaited Truth and Reconciliation Commission had been appointed and would soon begin full-time work. But

in both cases, the encouraging beginnings were soon undermined. The government's failure to follow through on the apology – to walk the walk, as a current cliché had it – aroused grave doubts. Government actions in relation to Indian Residential Schools Resolution Canada, the United Nations Convention on the Rights of Indigenous Peoples, and the Aboriginal Healing Foundation seemed to confirm the suspicion that Harper regarded his apology as the conclusion of a process rather than an important beginning of one. Similarly, the TRC was launched in June amid high expectations and great hopes for both laying bare the truth of the residential school history and creating support and momentum for a reconciliation movement. The question in many minds by 2009 was, could the good will, optimism, and momentum that were so much in evidence in early June 2008 be resuscitated?

8

The Truth and Reconciliation Commission

Speaking to the Assembly of First Nations (AFN) three weeks after he took office in June 2009, the new chief commissioner of the Truth and Reconciliation Commission (TRC) began on a humble note: "What I have to apologize to you about is relatively simple. To this point in time, the Truth and Reconciliation Commission of Canada which was created by the Indian Residential Schools Settlement has failed you."[1] Humility was certainly appropriate for the TRC, though the new commissioners bore no responsibility for the debacle that had overtaken their predecessors in 2008. Still, it was clear that the new commission had a huge task before it to reassure doubters about the TRC process and re-establish the momentum that had been lost.

The country was fortunate in the new personnel who led the organization. The three commissioners worked very hard to overcome the setback they faced at the outset, conduct an inquiry into the history of residential schools, and initiate a movement towards reconciliation between Aboriginal peoples and the rest of Canadians. Over the next six years, the commissioners and their staff would labour devotedly. They met with stakeholders of all sorts – survivors, church people, and groups of the general public – to spread their message and solicit support. They held seven national events, two regional events, and hundreds of local assemblies to spread the word and collect the recollections of former students and other people connected with the schools. At the end of their mandate in June 2015, the chief commissioner, who had begun his tenure with an apology, and his two colleagues could look back on their many years of effort in pursuit of truth and reconciliation with confidence that they had discharged an impossible mandate exceptionally well.

Individually, the new commissioners were impressive; and collectively, unlike the first trio, they worked well together. The position of chair became that of chief commissioner. It was ably filled by Manitoba judge Murray Sinclair, who had been called to the Manitoba bar in 1980 and had been appointed to the Provincial Court in 1988 and the Court of Queen's Bench in 2001. The first Aboriginal judge in Manitoba, he had co-chaired the historic Aboriginal Justice Inquiry and later conducted another investigation into the deaths of twelve children in the pediatric cardiac surgery program at Winnipeg's Health Sciences Centre.[2] Sinclair had been asked to chair the first TRC but had begged off in 2008 for personal reasons. As a father of four children, he had found that the inquiry he had conducted into the deaths of children too draining, and he realized that anyone taking on the work of the Truth and Reconciliation Commission could anticipate hearing many accounts of mistreatment of young children.[3]

After he accepted his appointment, Justice Sinclair was provided with a list or "four or five" nominees who had been shortlisted by the search committee for the role of commissioner. From the list, he chose Marie Wilson and Chief Wilton Littlechild, conveying his choices to Indian Affairs minister Chuck Strahl. Wilson had had lengthy experience in journalism and public service in the Northwest Territories, culminating in her appointment as the CBC's senior manager for northern Quebec and the three territories. She had received an honorary doctor of laws degree from St Thomas University in Fredericton, NB. She was married to Stephen Kakfwi, a First Nations leader and former premier of the NWT.[4] Wilton Littlechild of Alberta was the first treaty First Nation person to earn an LLB from the University of Alberta. He later received an honorary doctorate from the same institution, and the leaders of the four reserves in his home area near Wetaskiwin, Alberta, named him honorary chief of the Maskwacis Crees, while the chiefs of the Treaty 6 First Nations in Alberta made him international chief for the Treaty 6 Confederacy. These honours gave him a handy icebreaker for meetings: with some audiences, after summarizing his credentials, Littlechild would joke, "You can see I'm a doctor, a lawyer, and an Indian chief."[5] In addition, he was an enthusiastic all-round athlete, maintaining a regular exercise program through the travel and meetings on the TRC. Together, the three made an impressive and productive team. Sinclair was particularly effective with large audiences, usually beginning any presentation with a joke, often at his own expense, while the other two, though not without a sense of humour, would play their parts "straight." Most people who participated in commission events found the trio engaging and likable.

A gift for humour was all very well, but there was not much to laugh about in the situation the commissioners inherited in July 2009. Their biggest obstacle, as they saw it, was that the TRC's credibility with residential school survivors and other Aboriginal groups had been severely damaged. Sinclair would say later that it took him and his colleagues six months to a year to re-establish trust. In those early days, he recalled, he told his fellow commissioners that they all needed to talk with people about what they were doing to rebuild credibility and trust.[6] The commissioners' desire to repair that damage was on display in Sinclair's address to the AFN general assembly shortly after the new TRC began work. At the outset, he noted that the assembly was the first group he had spoken to since taking office. Before talking in detail about the TRC's plans, Sinclair said, "After you hear what I have to say, I also invite you to hold me to what I tell you we're going to do." He praised the small commission staff in Ottawa, who "have worked to keep afloat a leaky boat," and asked the assembled chiefs "for your forgiveness for this flawed start." The commissioners could not just "ignore what has happened and ... simply say 'Oops, sorry about that, we're going to try again,' such an approach would fail to do justice to the lives of those many of our relatives who have died in the last year." He explained that the commissioners had "spent the last several weeks engaged in team-building, a form of commission speed-dating in a sense." To get to know each other they spent a good deal of time "discussing two major questions: who are you and why are you doing this? Our discussion around those two questions has allowed us to form a strong, united and respectful approach to each other and to this work."[7]

The commissioners were united in a commitment to "seek out the stories of all those connected to the schools who are still alive, from the students and the teachers to the managers and the janitors as well as the officials who planned and carried out the whole thing." In pursuit of that goal, "we will go to as many communities as we humanly can manage and where we can't go ourselves we will send our delegates armed with our authority to record the stories of all those who wish to tell them." The commissioners, he said, "Hope to leave you with a most important legacy, the one that we wish to attain: knowledge about the pathways to reconciliation." It was striking that, while the

TRC promised to make great efforts – to "go to as many communities as we humanly can manage" – it was modest in what it committed itself to accomplish. Rather than undertaking to bring about reconciliation, or even to launch a movement to promote reconciliation during their term, the commissioners promised only to provide information "about the pathways to reconciliation."[8] During their first six months, the commissioners met with survivors on many occasions. In late August, for example, Sinclair joined former students of Shingwauk Hall in Sault Ste Marie and paid his respects to the deceased in the cemetery near the school. Commissioner Littlechild visited with former students on Walpole Island, Ontario, and had a group picture taken in front of a monument survivors in the community had erected to all the children from Walpole Island who had attended residential schools. Commissioner Wilson met with a number of different groups of survivors and said that one of the most powerful experiences she had was listening to former students in sharing circles.[9]

While strengthening relations with survivors and Aboriginal political leaders, the commissioners also addressed another important interest group in its first six months. The issue of the TRC's relations with the federal government and the potential for interference by Ottawa had lurked in the background with the first trio of commissioners. Both sets of commissioners correctly said that they were responsible to "the parties" to the Indian Residential Schools Settlement Agreement (IRSSA): survivors, churches, government, and some lawyers. The second set of commissioners, especially Chief Commissioner Murray Sinclair, placed former residential school students far ahead of the other stakeholders. At a public lecture at the University of Toronto Law Faculty in December 2009, for example, he described the commission's $60 million budget as "survivors' money."[10] When disputes about interpreting the settlement agreement, and Schedule N in particular, arose, "the parties" could refer the issue to the National Administration Committee, and, if that recourse were unavailing, to the two judges who remained "seized" (that is, had continuing oversight) of the settlement. But the reality was that the government was the paymaster, the source of funds that the commission spent, and Schedule N specified that financial matters were to be administered according to Treasury Board rules. Moreover, it was a brute fact of Canadian politics that government bureaucracies inexorably sought to extend their control over arm's-length agencies that they funded. For example, the three "independent" agencies that supported advanced research in postsecondary institutions and research hospitals – the Canadian Institutes of Health Research, the Natural Sciences and Engineering Research Council, and the Social Sciences and Humanities Research Council – all found both their priorities and their procedures being recast from time to time to accommodate government wishes.[11] It would be no different with the Truth and Reconciliation Commission. Awareness that there were problems with relations with the federal government had surfaced during the short life of the first TRC. More important, if less measurable, was a perception among Aboriginal leaders, especially First Nations, that the commission might be too close to the government. Finally, many survivors in particular were uneasy about the apparently close relationship between the TRC and the federal government, especially one headed by Stephen Harper.

The new commission's solution to this perception problem was dramatic. It moved its headquarters to Winnipeg between July 2009 and early 2010, retaining only a small operation in Ottawa. According to a TRC press release, the chief commissioner "said the move to Winnipeg brings the TRC closer to the majority of residential school survivors who live [in] western and northern Canada." Furthermore, most of the schools themselves were located in the west and the north. Finally, "by locating in Winnipeg Sinclair said the Commission is underscoring its independence from the Government of Canada."[12] Yet, as Sinclair recognized fairly quickly, the relocation to Winnipeg "was a lot more challenging than I thought it would be," and it added a significant financial burden as well.[13] The move was slow and vexatious, partly, as Sinclair noted publicly, as a result of the many concerns and issues raised by the Department of Public Works. That department and the Public Service Commission not only complicated the move to Winnipeg but also affected the appointment of personnel. Sinclair complained publicly that, for example, the commission waited three months for the appointment of the executive director that he and his colleagues had selected. Nonetheless, by early January 2010, the relocation to Winnipeg was completed, at least officially. In addition, the commission's had a new executive director in lawyer Tom McMahon of Winnipeg, who had served in the same role with the Aboriginal Justice Inquiry that Sinclair had co-chaired.[14]

The relocated commission team had no time to waste because the first of seven national events the settlement agreement required was approaching. According to Schedule N of the IRSSA, these major occasions were to be "a mechanism through which the truth and reconciliation process will engage the Canadian public and provide education about the IRS [Indian residential school] system, the experience of former students and their families, and the ongoing legacies of the institutions." The events were to be an opportunity "for a sample number of former students and families to share their experiences," "for some communities in the regions to share their experiences as they relate to the impacts on communities," and "for participation and sharing of information and knowledge among former students, their families, communities, experts, church and government officials, institutions and the Canadian public." The parties expected "participation of high level government and church officials," as well as the presence of "health supports and trauma experts during and after the ceremony for all participants." Schedule N also required that, in conducting the national events, the "Commission shall recognize that ownership over IRS experiences rests with those affected by the Indian Residential School legacy."[15]

For a fledgling organization still finding its feet in a new location, the first national event at The Forks in Winnipeg in June 2010 was a tall order. As the commission's second executive director explained, everything was new to the TRC team. In part because they were still finding their way and in part because of the shortness of time, the commission did not hold community and regional hearings in advance of the Winnipeg gathering, something it would do routinely before the other national events. The result was that there was huge pressure on the statement-gathering process, a major component of each national event, because former students and staff in the region feared that if they did not make their statement in Winnipeg, they would not get to make one. In addition, not all of the health support workers (HSW) that Health Canada had trained were well prepared for what they encountered. During the Winnipeg event, a group of support workers talked loudly in a corridor in the area where statements were taken about their shock at what they were hearing; another HSW who was also a former student did not know what to do and wanted to give a statement himself; and yet another HSW, a professional psychiatrist, had to be prevented from sending an informant to the psychiatric ward of a local hospital. On the first day of the event, a group of Midewiwin, Anicinabe medicine women, turned up and wanted to perform ceremonies in the statement-gathering area. Accommodating them required rearranging part of the area where witnesses gave statements, throwing proceedings behind schedule. More witnesses than expected wanted their statements video-recorded, creating more backlog. One survivor took five hours to provide her statement, backing things up still more.[16] To add to the headaches, the first three days of the event, which was held at the junction of the Red and Assiniboine River, a location that had great significance for Métis and First Nations, occurred in a heavy rain. The weather literally soaked attendees and figuratively dampened spirits.[17]

The national events, like all TRC gatherings, prominently featured Aboriginal ceremony and symbolism. The ceremonial element that continued through all seven national events and tied these showpieces together was the Seven Sacred Teachings – sometimes referred to as the Seven Grandfather Teachings – which were part of the culture of most First Nations. The seven teachings, which the commission drew on "in the work of truth-gathering, truth-telling, and reconciliation," were symbolically represented in the logo of the TRC, which featured a circle composed of seven flames. Each of the seven national events highlighted the theme of a different teaching.[18] The first event, in Winnipeg, bore the slogan "It's about Respect," and the event program and other literature carried that tag line. Subsequent events reflected the other six virtues: courage (the second national event, in Inuvik, NWT, in June 2011); love (Halifax, October 2011); truth (Saskatoon, June 2012); humility (Montreal, April 2013); honesty (Vancouver, September 2013); and wisdom (Edmonton, March 2014). The slogan of the closing event in Ottawa in June 2015 was "It's Time for Reconciliation."

As well, in keeping with Aboriginal practice, each national event had a sacred fire that was lit ceremonially with prayer, song, and smudging at daybreak on the first morning of the event and was kept burning by fire keepers throughout the event. A ceremony was held each morning at the fire as well. When people left the fire and entered the site of the event, they were surrounded by Aboriginal symbols and ceremony. An ornate bentwood box was usually in a central location at the front of the stage. "Carved by Coast Salish artist Luke Marston, the TRC Bentwood Box is a lasting tribute to all Indian Residential School survivors," said the commission's website. "Steamed and bent from a single piece of red cedar, the carved panels represent the unique cultures of former First Nations, Inuit and Métis students."[19] The box also held paper tissues that had collected people's tears during the day's proceedings. From the ceremonial box, the tissues were taken at intervals to the sacred fire and incinerated. From Halifax until Ottawa, after prayer, an Inuit Elder lit a *kidluk*, a seal oil lamp, as part of the opening ceremonies.

A day's formal events began with a ceremonial entrance of the commissioners and other dignitaries, after which statements and prayers by Elders were offered before one of the commissioners, usually Chief Commissioner Sinclair, officially opened proceedings. The last formal event of the day, scheduled for the dinner hour but sometimes delayed by schedule slippage, was a call to gather, at which invited individuals and groups made a statement and deposited some artefact symbolic of residential schooling in the bentwood box. On one of the evenings of each event, the atmosphere was lightened by popular entertainment: for example, Plains Cree performer Buffy Sainte Marie performed at both the fourth national event in Saskatoon in 2012 and at the Ottawa closing event in June 2015. Although the daily lineup varied as the national events rolled out, all the gatherings featured a number of key elements. What was known as the Commissioners Sharing Panel (a sharing circle) usually ran several times during an event, with one or more of the commissioners present to hear statements from former students, government representatives, church leaders, and occasionally members of the public. The TRC's literature for an event stressed that sharing circles did not exist to expose wrongdoers or identify alleged perpetrators of violence, and the commission also made this position clear in announcements before and during the sharing circles. Nonetheless, especially at the first event, a few survivors referred by name to people they said had abused them when they were students.

Another permanent feature at the national events focused on the honorary witnesses. These were prominent Canadians, usually non-Native, who served as champions of the commission's work. Honorary witnesses were inducted with great formality at each national event and spoke about their own commitment to reconciliation, usually in another session of the event. It was striking how moved some witnesses were by their role and how earnest they were. Andy Scott of Fredericton, a former minister of Indian and northern affairs, said that, after he was inducted as an honorary witness at the Atlantic event, he dedicated himself to the promotion of reconciliation. He also testified to the fact that promoting better relations could sometimes be daunting. When, after the Halifax event, he spoke to a club in Fredericton composed of "professionals," he thought he was doing well, carrying his audience with him, until someone asked about allegations of nepotism and corruption in First Nation bands. After that, he recalled, he "lost" his audience – they became distracted by the corruption charges, which Scott lacked the information to refute. As a result of that experience, he urged the commission to appoint people with a reputation in financial matters, such as the former auditor general of Canada, Sheila Fraser.[20]

Indeed, Fraser was inducted as an honorary witness at the next national event, in Saskatoon. Other prominent witnesses included former prime minister Joe Clark and broadcaster Shelagh Rogers. Rogers, who hosted a popular weekly CBC radio show focused on Canadian literature, became a workhorse at the national events. Her warm and genial manner was accompanied by a sometimes sly sense of humour. At Edmonton in March 2014, she mentioned while facilitating a panel of honorary witnesses that she had been dyslexic all her life, and appreciated that "listen" could also be read as "silent." Then she added that "dyslexia" can also be read as "daily sex."[21] Rogers effectively chaired panels and sessions at which reconciliation was discussed.[22]

Other set pieces at the national events dealt both with private storytelling and public expressions. Every event had several occasions for what the commission termed "Private Statement Gathering," the opportunity for former students and others associated with the schools to record their recollections for the commission. In contrast to sharing circles, which were chaired by the commissioners or members of the commission's Survivors Committee, the private statement gathering took place in a separate location that was not accessible to the public. Prospective statement-givers registered and were briefed about what would transpire. Then they went into a small, curtained-off area and delivered their accounts to a videographer. Health support workers were on hand as people gave their statements. Videographers also often found that they needed counselling at the end of a day of recording statements.[23] Ruth Cameron, a Cree survivor who had attended the Lebret school, noted that she greatly appreciated the fact that the health support worker who had attended her statement, which lasted for five hours, telephoned her several times during the weeks after the Saskatoon national event to make sure she was doing well.[24]

Much more public than the private sharing sessions were the opportunities for learning about the history of the schools and the presence of representatives of the churches who had operated them. From the Winnipeg event onward, the TRC included a Learning Place run by TRC staff. (At Winnipeg, research director John Milloy and TRC historian Helen Harrison laboured late into the evening before the first day to get the learning place ready.) As well, representatives of the various churches' archives were present with photographs from the schools their denomination or organization had operated. These quickly became one of the "hits" of the national events, as former students and their families looked through the picture files, finding images that related to their own attendance. Archives staff made photocopies of any pictures that a visitor to their area wanted. In addition, senior church representatives made themselves available to survivors in what were termed "Listening Areas," places in which anyone could speak with church people about their experiences and feelings about school experience. Although this practice began somewhat awkwardly in the early events, over time the encounters of church officials and survivors settled down into an apparently warm and useful dialogue.[25]

As the national events unfolded, the emphasis on various features shifted. One example was the scholarly element. Initially a one-day symposium organized by university faculty at the Winnipeg event in 2010, this component was meant to be part of the national gatherings. However, organizing for the third national event, in Halifax in 2011, was accompanied by friction between TRC staff and the Aboriginal Policy Congress, a Mi'kmaq organization, which spilled over into the planning for a scholarly component. As a result, the vestigial remnant of a scholarly component was an afternoon session that bore little resemblance to the ambitious symposium at Winnipeg.[26] There was no evidence of scholarly contributions at the Saskatoon event in June 2012, save for posters on each of the residential schools in the province, which had been prepared by students of a fourth-year Native Studies class at the University of Saskatchewan. The next event, in Montreal in April 2013, also lacked scholarly exchange. Rather, the program featured brief sessions (entitled "Two-Row Wampum and Reconciliation" and "The Treaty of Montreal and Reconciliation") that seemed to have as much to do with appeasing local First Nation political leaders as advancing either reconciliation or truth. Scholarly symposia or conferences were not part of any of the remaining national events.

Perhaps a more significant learning opportunity was the participation of school students. There was usually a "Learning Day" at a national event; the occasion at the Vancouver national event in September 2013 was wildly successful. Thousands of area school children were bused to the Pacific National Exhibition grounds for the occasion, and local media coverage leaned heavily on the reactions of engaged students. The Edmonton national event the next year featured another hugely successful Learning Day that also helped to garner press coverage. As well, the Edmonton event featured Project of Heart, the program developed by Ottawa teacher Sylvia Smith with commemoration funds from the IRSSA (see the discussion in chapter 6), and Smith was honoured for her contribution by being made an honorary witness at the Ottawa closing event in June 2015.

Between 2010 and 2014, the national events evolved as commission staff and others became more familiar with the dynamics associated with them. In a sense, the weather at the first national event in Winnipeg was emblematic of the national event experience as a whole. For most of the Winnipeg meeting, the weather was unfavourable, but conditions, and auguries, turned auspicious on the final day, when, coincidentally, the governor general was to visit the national event. As Michaëlle Jean led the grand entry, the ceremonial beginning to many First Nations events, an eagle was spotted over the powwow area of The Forks. The appearance of a bird with great symbolic importance for Plains First Nations, something that had not been observed in recent memory, seemed to augur better things.[27] In a sense, the weather at the Winnipeg event was representative of the national events as a whole: they started unpromisingly and struggled on several occasions, but rallied at the end to suggest more encouraging times were ahead.

The last two events revealed growing support for the commission and its mandate of reconciliation. The Vancouver national event in September 2013 seemed to have more "energy" than earlier gatherings. Perhaps it was the large number of young people who attended. In addition to the thousands who appeared on Education Day, the University of British Columbia cancelled classes for the first day of the gathering and urged its students to attend the TRC. Obviously, many of them did. The mayor of Vancouver, Gregor Robertson, whose council had declared 2013 a Year of Reconciliation, spoke movingly about the need for repairing relations between Native and non-Native peoples. The day after the national event, a Sunday, several thousand supporters of reconciliation participated in a Walk for Reconciliation organized principally by Reconciliation Canada, an organization inspired by the work of Chief Bobby Joseph, a long-time proponent of reconciliation. In spite of a steady rain, the large throng walked four kilometres through downtown Vancouver.[28] At Edmonton in March 2014, further evidence of support came from the political level. The provincial government representatives pledged to revise Alberta's curriculum to incorporate material on residential schools and on treaties, and the mayors of both Edmonton and Calgary announced that their cities would be observing

8.1 The Walk for Reconciliation, Vancouver, 22 September 2013.

a Year of Reconciliation. Even Chief Commissioner Sinclair seemed more upbeat than usual at the Alberta event: he acknowledged at the opening session that reconciliation would not take place in the lifetimes of most of those present, but he expressed the hope that it would in the lifetimes of the many young people who attended.[29]

The closing event in Ottawa in June 2015 undoubtedly ended the commission's public labours on a high note. Reminiscent of Winnipeg in 2010, the pre-dawn fire-lighting ceremony in Ottawa took place in a cold drizzle but with a large number of people in attendance. Later that morning, a Walk for Reconciliation, which had begun in Gatineau across the Ottawa River and had proceeded past the Supreme Court of Canada and Parliament Hill before ending up in the square in front of city hall, attracted a large, enthusiastic throng. Chief Commissioner Sinclair said the next day that the walk had involved "10,000 of our closest friends." Estimates of the size of the walk varied, from the 3,000 reported by the *Ottawa Citizen* to up to 12,000 by Ottawa police.[30] For a crowd that stretched, six or eight abreast, all the way across the Portage Bridge and part way up Wellington Street, the estimate of 6,000 provided by an observer at St Andrew's Presbyterian Church on the parade route seemed most accurate. This observer, who was St Andrew's administrator, was on hand, along with a custodian, to ring the church's bell as the parade passed. When the crowd reached their site, they began ringing the bell and shouting to the parade, "We're ringing the bell for you, brothers!" First Nations people on the route responded warmly. "'Here,' a woman wearing a red survivor t-shirt handed me a small pouch of tobacco. 'Thank you so much for doing this. I want you to have this.'" A pair of young men "bounded up the steps with their cameras. 'We must record this! This means so much to us! Keep pulling!'" A chief in full eagle feather Plains headdress paused and saluted the bell ringers. And an elderly Inuit woman supported by two younger women made her way slowly up the church steps and said, "'I am a survivor ... May I ring the bell with you?'" After pulling the rope seven or eight times, she handed it back and said, "'That was wonderful ... Thank you for doing this for us.'" After half an hour, when the walk had passed their vantage point, the people at the church stopped, tired, hoarse, and very happy.[31]

Another evolution that was observable over the course of the national events concerned the relative emphasis that "truth" and "reconciliation" received. There was a heavy stress on the "truth" element of the TRC's mandate from 2009 until 2015, but the way in which "reconciliation" was discussed and the attention it received changed over time. Perhaps reflecting the political stresses commissioners had experienced – there was considerable criticism before and during the Atlantic event on a couple of fronts. Chief Commissioner Sinclair was subdued about the potential for achieving reconciliation in Halifax. At the opening session in that city, he made it clear that the TRC would not accomplish reconciliation, speaking about the goal in terms of future generations. "Reconciliation is about love," he said, echoing the theme of the Atlantic National Event. "If you love your children, if you love your grandchildren ..." he observed, perhaps hinting at the modest hopes commissioners had about reconciliation.[32] Similarly, at the national event in Saskatoon in June 2012, he talked about truth, the theme of the event there, in his opening remarks and said that the TRC gave priority to survivors "reconciling with themselves and with their families." On the other hand, with the active cooperation of honorary witnesses such as Shelagh Rogers, sessions on reconciliation assumed a more prominent place in the national events. A session entitled "It Matters to Me: A Town Hall on Reconciliation," an "open mic session for the public," appeared on the program in Saskatoon in June 2012. In subsequent national events in Montreal, Vancouver, Edmonton, and Ottawa, similar sessions to discuss how to promote reconciliation assumed greater prominence. They were also better attended as time went on. While the room had been filled mainly with non-Indigenous people for "It Matters to Me" in Saskatoon, it was noticeable that there was a better balance in similar sessions at later events. By the Ottawa gathering in 2015, it appeared that substantial momentum in support of reconciliation had been built up.[33]

The vicissitudes that the cause of reconciliation had to contend with between 2009 and 2015 were mirrored by difficulties that the commission experienced in its operations. In the early years, as noted, a major problem concerned personnel and organizational structure. The commission followed up the delays it had experienced with time-consuming adjustments concerning staffing, finances, and relations with the federal government. Even before the national event in Winnipeg in June 2010, it was obvious that friction at the top was impeding the work. In particular, the commission's research director, Dr John Milloy of Trent University, found the close supervision by the commission's executive director, Tom McMahon, insupportable.[34] Other members of the TRC staff described McMahon as "a micromanager" and difficult to work with.[35] Milloy himself had embarrassed the commission in the spring of 2010 by expressing his frustration over problems with access to archival documents, suggesting that the Catholic entities were reluctant to surrender documents that might show some clergy in a bad light. Flippantly, he repeated a comment he had heard from a lawyer to the effect that archivists did not want to hand over diaries that might reveal that a priest was "'buggering boys in the basement.'" Chief Commissioner Sinclair sent a letter of apology to the church entities, and Milloy apologized to them in person after his comment hit the press.[36] Although Milloy had been talked out of resigning once before by Sinclair, he did bow out after Winnipeg.[37]

Initially, oversight of research was handed to Dr Paulette Regan, a lawyer theoretically "on loan" from Aboriginal and Northern Affairs Canada. But she found that the new supervisory work was uncongenial and that it interfered with her work on reconciliation. Eventually, oversight of commission research was handled by a new executive director.

In July 2010, Kim Murray, formerly of Aboriginal Legal Services in Toronto, became executive director, and McMahon, whose skills, experience, energy, and dedication made him valuable, took up the role of general counsel for the commission.[38] Symptomatic of the unsettled nature of the TRC's organizational structure was the fact that Murray had originally joined the organization in a subordinate position, working under Ry Moran, who was in charge of statement gathering. With the reshuffle, she moved from reporting to Moran to having him and others report to her. Other organizational changes that occurred in the first two years included getting rid of a subcommission on Inuit matters and offloading the organization of national and other major events. After the Inuvik national gathering, the position of director of national events was eliminated and the work was done by event planners hired on contract.[39] All these adjustments proved at least temporarily distracting and time consuming.

Also problematic was a continuing dispute over which schools were eligible for compensation. The IRSSA specified the schools that could be considered and provided a limited appeal mechanism. The Métis in particular were aggrieved that a number of schools their children had attended were not on the approved list. They and others, a total of 9,471 people in all, requested that some 1,531 institutions be added to the list, but the Aboriginal affairs department approved only 7 of them, and appeal to the courts led to the addition of another 2. The total of 139 residential schools and hostels whose students were eligible to apply for a Common Experience Payment and consideration under the Independent Assessment Process was significantly smaller than many people would have liked.[40] The shortfall constituted a source of grievance throughout the existence of the Truth and Reconciliation Commission. At the Halifax national event, for example, protests were made by Labrador Inuit whose custodial schools had not been included in the settlement agreement and who were, therefore, not eligible for compensation under settlement agreement programs.

Also vexing throughout the commission's existence were finances. The original allocation of $60 million in the settlement agreement had never been enough to fund all the operations within the TRC's mandate. The financial problem was aggravated by the position of the federal government. Aboriginal Affairs initially told the new commissioners who took over in 2009 that it was deducting the $2 million it had spent setting up initial operations from their overall funding. When the commissioners objected to the reduction, the department backed off, in a fashion. Later, when the commission successfully negotiated a one-year extension to compensate for its late start in 2009, the federal government agreed to provide an additional $8 million (which then covered the initial set up plus $6 million extra). Thus, the total funding for the TRC amounted to $66 million ($60 – 2 + 8 million). At the end of the commission's mandate, the federal government agreed to a further six-month extension with limited operations after June 2015 and provided an additional $1.3 million to cover the costs of producing the final report.[41] As vexatious and time-consuming as disputes about funding could be, they were minor compared to another issue over which the commission locked horns with government.

Schedule N of the Indian Residential Schools Settlement Agreement seemed to be clear about the commission's right to receive documents from the parties. To fill the "research centre" that the agreement required the commission to create, "Canada and the churches will provide all relevant documents in their possession or control to and for the use of the Truth and Reconciliation Commission, subject to the privacy interests of an individual as provided by applicable privacy legislation."[42] There were several problems with this provision. Quite apart from issues arising with the institutions that had documents in their possession, the wording itself created headaches: as Murray Sinclair remarked, there are millions of court cases about the meaning of "relevant." Beyond the question of relevance was the issue of privacy. Specifically, the privacy exceptions could cause archival repositories, particularly religious archives whose staff were sensitive to the interests of members of their communion, to hesitate about releasing documents that concerned some individuals.[43] Chief Commissioner Sinclair complained publicly more than once about the denominations' reservations, and commission staff seemed to take the stance that the religious institutions were using "privacy" as a dodge to avoid making embarrassing material public.[44] Eventually, however, the problem with denominational archives was thrashed out, more or less satisfactorily.

Less easily resolved was conflict with Ottawa over access to documents in the government's possession. Library and Archives Canada, as well as the RCMP and government departments such as justice, health, and others, housed millions of documents that were "relevant" to the history of residential schools. According to Sinclair, there were three aspects to this part of the documents problem. First, some "elements" within government regarded the commission as just another department of government, and they tended to view the Commission as a rogue unit when it told departments what they had to do. Second, said Sinclair, some within government thought they could just outwait the commissioners. The bureaucracy would be around long after the TRC's mandate had expired. Third, senior officials in Aboriginal Affairs simply had no idea of the enormity and expense involved in providing the "relevant documents" that they held. (For that matter, in the opinion of an experienced archivist who briefly worked for the TRC, the commissioners and executive director did not understand the nature of archival documents or the vastness of the trove that were "relevant," either.[45]) Initially, the commission attempted to work with the government on the documents issue. Since Ottawa, said the chief commissioner, thought that the commissioners should ask all the units of government that were involved for permission to access their records, they did so. But not all units were forthcoming.[46] Eventually, in December 2012, operating in the name of a group of survivors, the TRC took the federal government and the many church entities that were party to the settlement agreement to Justice Warren Winkler, one of the two judges who supervised the IRSSA.

Justice Winkler referred the matter to the Ontario Court of Justice, where Justice Stephen Goudge ruled in the commission's favour in January 2013. The court did not buy the government's arguments, including the contention that the TRC was just another unit of government, and ordered the federal government to comply with the commission's requests. According to a press account of the hearing, a Department of Justice lawyer told Justice Goudge that "the commission was clearly overstepping its mandate by taking the government to court" and also that "there are so many documents held in Library of Canada Archives [sic] that the parties to the settlement agreement could not possibly have expected the government to collect and digitize them all."[47] The court's decision was that government did have to do so. The judge did not, however, agree that Ottawa had to provide documents concerning governmental responses to "the impacts of the Indian Residential Schools experience" or materials concerning the prime ministerial apology of 2008.[48] At first, the government said that it was the commission's responsibility to fund collection of the documents, but it soon relented and provided not just cooperation but also funding for the task.[49]

Complications, though less severe than those associated with finances and relations with the churches and federal government, also arose over having people testify about their experiences in and with residential schools. Personal testimony about the schools was a key part of the settlement agreement. The commission's goals, as laid out in Schedule N, were to "acknowledge Residential School experiences, impacts and consequences" and to "provide a holistic, culturally appropriate and safe setting for former students, their families and communities as they come forward to the Commission."[50] What commissioners referred to as "story-telling" was the strongest emphasis of the TRC throughout its existence. Not just at the national events, but also at regional gatherings and in community events that were usually held as part of the preparation for a national event, opportunities for people to talk about the schools were always present. At the national events there were both public occasions – as in the Commissioners' Sharing Circle or Survivor Committee Sharing Circle – and private opportunities for people to come forward and speak. Following the Winnipeg national event, TRC staff tweaked the commissioners' circle to give it more prominence in an effort to attract more statements.[51] By 2015, about 6,750 individual (or, in some cases, family) statements had been collected for what had become known as the National Centre for Truth and Reconciliation.[52]

Although the commissioners frequently said they wanted to hear from school staff and other non-Native peoples as well as former students, the oral record that the commission collected was composed overwhelmingly of survivors' statements. Indeed, the professional historian on the TRC staff said that commissioners' actions were not consistent with its claims to wish to include non-Aboriginal voices on the record. Her budget for the project on school staff was cut from $100,000 to $10,000, and she was told that the commission would not transcribe the interviews she had conducted.[53] Nonetheless, there were notable exceptions to the absence of staff input. One occurred at the Atlantic National Event in Halifax in October 2011, when an Anglican layman, Mark DeWolfe, spoke at length. He had spent six years attending the Blood Anglican residential school in southern Alberta while his father was principal there. He described the positive, honourable way he had observed his father treat First Nation people, while emphasizing that he was talking about only "what I saw in that place at that time" and his recollections were not meant to invalidate what others had said about their unfavourable experience in residential school. Although he spoke at considerable length, only a few people drifted out while he talked, and the larger number who remained listened attentively and applauded warmly when he was finished.[54] This man's contribution was remarkable both for its content and for its exceptionalism. Very few former staff members came forward to speak publicly, despite the commissioners' sincere efforts to encourage them. The commission's final report said that it had usually been able to "create a space for respectful dialogue between former residential school students and staff," but "in other instances, Survivors and their family members found it very difficult to listen to former staff, particularly if they perceived the speaker to be an apologist for the schools." The report then provided an example of an Oblate brother speaking as an apologist to the displeasure of many.[55]

Long before the TRC began its work, many former church workers were already "gun-shy" about speaking in public about their role. The lawyer who represented all the Catholic entities except the Jesuits in the IRSSA negotiations in 2005–6 expressed reluctance to have Catholic leaders participate in court hearings on the agreement because their participation would lead "to moments of bashing the Catholics again."[56] Similarly, non-Catholics who had worked in the schools often reacted to the bad publicity that the churches received in the media between 1990 and the time of the TRC by hunkering down and staying silent. A woman who was not a former student, though her mother and grandmother both had attended residential school with positive results, explained that many Protestant former church workers were chastened by negative reactions and did not wish to appear before the commission. She gave her own statement to a representative of the TRC privately in her home.[57] The environment that had developed before the commission began its work was usually a deterrent for former missionaries, discouraging them from speaking at TRC events. The course of public gatherings at which there were open sessions when former students spoke, which were usually well reported in the media, only intensified the fears of former workers. The commission tried to compensate for the absence of workers' voices by having researcher Helen Harrison make a concerted effort to locate and interview some of the former residential school staff.[58]

Thus, the overwhelming number of personal accounts provided at the public sessions of the TRC came from survivors and were mostly negative. A volume of excerpts of such recollections published by the commission as part of its final report in June 2015 devoted 184 pages to topics such as "forced departure," "bedwetting," "strange food," "separating siblings," "despair," "abuse," and "student victimization of students" before turning to twelve relatively positive pages of "warm memories" and accounts of "sports and recreation."[59] One academic critic of the commission suggests that its processes and materials encouraged an emphasis on grim experiences and memories.[60] Certainly, the media that reported on the major TRC events reinforced the negative image and intensified any inclination informants might have had to frame school history as solely a story of abuse.[61]

The emotional testimony that former students gave at the sharing circles covered every imaginable facet of the residential school experience. Charlene Belleau, the highly respected former chief from Alkali Lake in the British Columbia interior who had been instrumental in the conclusion of the IRSSA, explained at the Vancouver national event how she had been "Number One," referring to the identifying number that she was given. Ted Quewezance, a prominent First Nations leader in Saskatchewan, brought a number of his family members on stage in Saskatoon while he recounted some of the horrific abuse to which he had been subjected. Pointedly, he referred to the residential schools as "genocide." At the Atlantic National Event in Halifax in 2011, a man who had attended the Anglican school in Sioux Lookout, Ontario, spoke movingly about the "shame" he felt as a survivor, even later when he was working with other survivors to help them deal with trauma. He had never even told his wife and children about his school days until he decided to apply for compensation.

As early as the Halifax event, it was apparent that most of the statements followed a similar arc: roundup, separation, initial reception, emotional deprivation, cultural disrespect, abuse, poor living conditions, troubles after leaving school, and, often, how the speaker found a way out of shame and anger and onto a "healing journey." In a minority of cases, the speakers explicitly forgave the perpetrators because, they usually explained, forgiveness was essential to their own healing.[62] It was the norm that speakers would be hugged, amid tears and laughter, by family and friends after speaking. It was clear that the act of recounting their experience was, as many claimants reported testifying before an Independent Assessment Process arbitrator to be, a liberating and lightening experience. Ruth Cameron, a Cree woman who had attended an Oblate school in Saskatchewan, said that she had cried and had "dug out some guilt." After speaking, "those knots were all gone … I feel lighter." Speaking about painful events "messes you up a bit, but it's okay now." She concluded that "the TRC made me a prouder woman than I was before."[63]

One of the most striking features of survivors' testimony was their concern about setting history straight. During an orientation session at the Atlantic National Event at which potential speakers were briefed on their options – public or private statements – it was clear that those present were conscious of the importance of the historical record. Many who spoke alluded to getting the record straight and/or leaving a cautionary historical record for future generations.[64] At the same time, the similarities among statements and the rarity of any sort of positive recollection suggested that there may have been some psychological pressure to cast statements in a unfavourable frame. Political leaders, the media, and usually the TRC itself portrayed residential schooling that way. As the TRC events went on, there was accumulating suasion to state one's recollections as others did. To do otherwise would be to let one's fellow survivors down. This is not to say that former students were misrepresenting their experience, or that they were deliberately shaping their recollections a particular way. It was just that everything in the TRC process and media coverage encouraged the perpetuation of an existing tendency to interpret residential schools in negative ways.[65] Thus, the oral history that TRC events left behind, as its publications *What We Have Learned* and *The Survivors Speak* attest, perpetuated the trope that the Royal Commission on Aboriginal Peoples, the Aboriginal Healing Foundation, and Independent Assessment Process had established: the residential school story was only dark, negative, bad.

The commission's culminating task was to issue reports on its work and findings. Schedule N specified "completion of all national events, and research and production of the report on historic findings and recommendations, within two years of the launch of the commission, with the possibility of a six-month extension, which shall be at the discretion of the Commissioners." As well, Schedule N said that the TRC was "to prepare a report" and "to have the report translated in the two official languages of Canada and all or parts of the report in such Aboriginal languages as determined by the Commissioners."[66] By the time they were finished, the commissioners had produced three reports. The first was an interim report titled *The Came for the Children*, released at the end of 2011. It was followed in June 2015 at the Ottawa closing event by an "executive summary" entitled *Final Report of the Truth and Reconciliation Commission of Canada. Volume One: Summary: Honouring the Truth, Reconciling for the Future* (hereafter *Summary Final Report*). And, once the task of translating the final report fully into both official languages and five Indigenous languages was finished, on 15 December 2015 the commission released a six-volume final report that totalled over 3,200 pages.[67]

The three reports combined continuity and change over the period 2011–15. The most persistent feature of the successive documents was that they continued to depict the residential school experience as principally one of abuse and pain. Such a depiction continued the practice – which had surfaced in the final report of the Royal Commission on Aboriginal Peoples in 1996 and been maintained in the prime ministerial apology of June 2008 – of painting the history of the schools in an unfavourable light. While the overall depiction was negative, there were variations among the reports. *They Came for the Children*, which was based on documentary evidence, provided a fairly balanced assessment of the school experience for students, but the *Summary Final Report*, which relied mainly on oral evidence provided by survivors at TRC sessions, was much harsher in its portrayal. Although the commission acknowledged in that volume that many good people had worked in the schools and that a small minority of students had had a positive experience at school, its coverage of school history was overwhelmingly dark.[68]

It was, therefore, surprising that the detailed *Final Report* reverted to a more balanced account of the schools' impact on the students. Certainly, large sections of the volumes subtitled *The History* (volume 1), *The Inuit and Northern Experience* (volume 2), *The Métis Experience* (volume 3), and *The Legacy* (volume 5) dwelt on neglect, mistreatment, and abuse.[69] Especially in the two-part *History*, there was, understandably, considerable attention paid to neglect, poor diet, inadequate health care, and abuse, as well as many instances of student resistance that took the form of arson and running away from the schools.[70] But there was also a consistent effort to place the grave inadequacies of staff treatment of students into historical context, as well as to point out that there were many staff who tried hard to provide good, supportive care.[71]

One thing that did not change throughout the evolution of the commission's reports was a strong insistence on the importance of history in both understanding and recovering from the harmful legacy of these institutions. *They Came for the Children*, for example, concluded that a major problem in the Native-newcomer relationship was faulty history. "Canadians generally have been led to believe – what has been taught and not taught in schools – that Aboriginal people were and are uncivilized, primitive, and inferior, and continue to need to be civilized."[72]

The *Summary Final Report* said, "Too many Canadians know little or nothing about the deep historical roots of these conflicts. This lack of historical knowledge has serious consequences to First Nations, Inuit, and Métis peoples, and for Canada as a whole." The past, said the commissioners, "plays an important role in reconciliation; to build for the future, Canadians must look to, and learn from, the past."[73] The volumes of the final report, which were issued in December 2015, placed even more emphasis on history than the earlier volumes had. If the 1,775-page *History* is combined with *The Inuit and Northern Experience* and the brief *The Métis Experience*, fully 2,277 of the report's 3,232 pages (or about 70 per cent) were historical in orientation.

The implications of the commission's focus on history emerged in the report's volumes *The Legacy* and *Reconciliation* (volume 6). Not surprisingly, volume 5, *The Legacy*, drew a direct line between the problems revealed in the volumes that preceded it and the consequences for Aboriginal people in a number of areas, which were enumerated in that volume's chapter titles: "Child Welfare: A System in Crisis," "The Failure to Educate," "The Erosion of Language and Culture," "An Attack on Aboriginal Health," and "A Denial of Justice."[74] The commission pulled no punches about what residential schools represented in the history of government policies towards Aboriginal peoples. "For over a century," volume 1 of the *Final Report* said, the "central goals of Canada's Aboriginal policy were to eliminate Aboriginal governments; ignore Aboriginal rights; terminate the Treaties; and, through a process of assimilation, cause Aboriginal peoples to cease to exist as distinct legal, social, cultural, religious and racial entities in Canada." Residential schools "were a central element of this policy, which can best be described as 'cultural genocide'."[75]

The characterization of residential schooling as cultural genocide was interesting in at least two ways. First, it suggested that the commission had retreated from Chief Commissioner Sinclair's earlier use of the term "genocide" to describe the schools. Speaking at the University of Manitoba in February 2012, Sinclair had acknowledged that the schools did not appear to satisfy the United Nations criteria for genocide, which had allowed the Canadian government to reject the charge that they were an act of genocide. "But," he continued, "The reality is that to take children away and to place them with another group in society for the purpose of racial indoctrination was – and is – an act of genocide and it occurs all around the world."[76] Second, the impact of the use of the term "cultural genocide" in the *Final Report* was enhanced by its echoing a

statement in a controversial speech given only a short time earlier by
Beverley McLachlin, the Chief Justice of the Supreme Court of Canada,
in which she described the history of Canadian policy towards Indigenous peoples as a record of attempted "cultural genocide."[77]

The *Final Report* dwelt at length on the role of history in shaping
Canadians' understanding of residential schools and their impact
and on the link between history and reconciliation, which it defined
as "as an ongoing process of establishing and maintaining respectful
relationships."[78] To achieve such relationships, "Schools must teach
history in ways that foster mutual respect, empathy, and engagement. All Canadian children and youth deserve to know Canada's
honest history, including what happened in the residential schools."[79]
Of a range of issues, including the schools and the "Sixties Scoop,"
it lamented:

> Too many Canadians know little or nothing about the deep historical
> roots of these conflicts. This lack of historical knowledge has serious con-
> sequences for First Nations, Inuit, and Métis peoples, and for Canada as
> a whole. In government circles, it makes for poor public policy decisions.
> In the public realm, it reinforces racist attitudes and fuels civic distrust
> between Aboriginal peoples and other Canadians. Too many Canadians
> still do not know the history of Aboriginal peoples' contributions to Can-
> ada, or understand that by virtue of the historical and modern Treaties
> negotiated by our government, we are all Treaty people. History plays an
> important role in reconciliation; to build for the future, Canadians must
> look to, and learn from the past.[80]

The first section of volume 6 of the *Final Report*, entitled "The Challenge
of Reconciliation," again returned to the theme of history and its importance to reconciliation. "Canada," it began, "Has a long history of colonialism in relation to Aboriginal peoples. This history and its policies
of cultural genocide and assimilation have left deep scars on the lives
of many Aboriginal people, on Aboriginal communities, as well as on
Canadian society, and have deeply damaged the relationship between
Aboriginal and non-Aboriginal peoples."[81]

Given the commission's belief in the centrality of history to improving relations, it is not surprising that the report had a lot to say about
how an updated, accurate history could contribute to reconciliation.
The Commissioners took it as a matter of faith – certainly, the point
was not something their reports argued or proved – that there was a

necessary connection between accurate history and respectful attitudes towards Aboriginal peoples. Such attitudes would, in turn, help to generate reconciliation: "As Commissioners, we believe that reconciliation is about respect. That includes both self-respect for Aboriginal people and mutual respect among all Canadians."[82] And a fuller understanding of Aboriginal history was a necessary element in developing such respect: "In the Commission's view, all students – Aboriginal and non-Aboriginal – need to learn that the history of this country did not begin with the arrival of Jacques Cartier on the banks of the St. Lawrence River. They need to learn about the Indigenous nations that Europeans met, about their rich linguistic and cultural heritage, about what they felt and thought as they dealt with early explorers." As well, "Canadians need to learn why Indigenous nations negotiated the Treaties and to understand that they negotiated with integrity and in good faith."[83] Accordingly, the commission had a number of recommendations – or calls to action, as it termed them – concerning steps to improve Canadians' understanding of their history. So, for example, call to action 62:

We call upon the federal, provincial, and territorial governments, in consultation and collaboration with Survivors, Aboriginal peoples, and educators, to:

i. Make age-appropriate curriculum on residential schools, Treaties, and Aboriginal peoples' historical and contemporary contributions to Canada a mandatory education requirement for Kindergarten to Grade Twelve students.

Similarly, there were recommendations to modify curricula and teacher training to ensure that such subjects were taught appropriately in future.[84]

The commissioners also recommended that Canada's public institutions correct the historical record. Museums, particularly the Canadian Museum for Human Rights (CMHR), came in for considerable comment. The *Final Report* noted that museums in general and the Canadian Museum of History (formerly the Canadian Museum of Civilization) especially were aware of their former shortcomings and were working to change the ways they depicted Indigenous peoples. "Over the past three decades, Canadian museums that used to tell the story of the nation's past with little regard for the histories of First Nations, Inuit, and Métis peoples have been slowly transforming. Although dialogue between museums and Aboriginal peoples has improved substantially since the 1980s, the broader debate continues over whose history is told and how it is interpreted."[85] Implicitly, the CMHR was criticized for soft-pedalling its treatment of residential schools. Given the deep controversies that exist regarding the history of the residential school system, it is perhaps not surprising that the CMHR was criticized by the Southern Chiefs Organization in Manitoba in June 2013, after media reports that the museum would not "label human rights violations against First Nations as genocide. From the perspective of the Southern Chiefs Organization, the museum was 'sanitizing the true history of Canada's shameful treatment of First Nations.'" The commissioners commented on the issue by segueing to discuss how museums should commemorate the 150th anniversary of Confederation in 2017. "The Commission believes that, as Canada's 150th anniversary approaches in 2017, national reconciliation is the most suitable framework to guide the commemoration of this significant historical benchmark in Canada's history." And they tied that point to a broader conviction, clearly one to which they were strongly attached, about the necessity to portray the past appropriately. "In the Commission's view, there is an urgent need in Canada to develop historically literate citizens who understand why and how the past is relevant to their own lives and the future of the country. Museums have an ethical responsibility to foster national reconciliation, and not simply tell one party's version of the past."[86]

The commission's preoccupation with the past and how it has been portrayed in Canada extended well beyond schools and museums. It also had a lot to say about the role of archives and official commemoration in moving towards reconciliation. Library and Archives Canada (LAC) was of particular interest to the commissioners because the TRC had had a legal battle with the federal government to gain access to LAC holdings as well as to other documents held by federal government departments. Commissioners pointed out that the United Nations had adopted a set of principles that instructed states on how "to satisfy their duty to guard against impunity from past human rights violations and prevent their reoccurrence." Victims' rights included their "right to know the truth about what happened to them and their missing family members. Society at large also has the right to know the truth about what happened in the past and what circumstances led to mass human rights violations." They called on LAC to embrace the UN approach to access to records of Indigenous peoples and on the federal government to fund a review by the Canadian Association of Archivists, in collaboration with Aboriginal people, of the degree to which archives in Canada conformed to UN principles about "Aboriginal peoples' inalienable right to know the truth about what happened and why, with regard to human rights violations committed against them in the residential schools."[87]

The TRC's *Final Report* also commented at length on commemoration, another aspect of a country's treatment of its history and something the Indian Residential Schools Settlement Agreement had dealt with at length. The commission reviewed its experience with the IRSSA's program of $20 million for commemoration. The projects the TRC recommended to Aboriginal Affairs for funding were "to be Survivor-driven," must "forge new connections that linked Aboriginal family and community memory to Canada's public memory and national history," and must "incorporat[e] Indigenous oral history and memory practices into the commemoration projects." It continued, "Unlike more conventional state commemorations, which have tended to reinforce Canada's story as told through colonial eyes," the projects the TRC had approved "challenged and recast public memory and national history."[88] In contrast, the commission was noticeably cool to the federal government's own national commemoration initiative, the stained glass window that Metis artist Christi Belcourt created for the Centre Block on Parliament Hill, simply stating that it "takes note" of the project.[89] It was similarly unimpressed with Canada's official commemorator, the Historic Sites and Monuments Board of Canada (HSMBC). Parks Canada, where HSMBC is housed, was criticized for not designating sites related to Aboriginal events after 1885 and for failing to act on a request in the mid-1990s to commemorate former residential schools. The *Final Report* recognized that a major barrier to undertaking commemoration that the commissioners thought appropriate was HSMBC's policies, including an emphasis on "commemorative integrity" that sometimes stood in the way of marking events that Indigenous people wanted. "Ultimately," the report said, "reconciliation requires a paradigm shift in Canada's national heritage values, policies, and practices which focus on conservation and continue to exclude Indigenous history, heritage values, and memory practices, which prioritize healing and the reclaiming of culture in public commemoration."[90]

Although history and commemoration were major concerns of the *Final Report*, they were not, of course, the only subjects that attracted the commissioners' attention. In its final volume, *Reconciliation*, where most of the their ninety-four recommendations were found, the

commissioners examined and made proposals on a wide range of topics affecting Aboriginal peoples. These included the United Nations
Declaration on the Rights of Indigenous Peoples, which Canada had
endorsed hesitantly and with reservations; "the Doctrine of Discovery"; the Royal Proclamation of 1763; treaties; a wide range of justice
and accountability issues (including the 2008 apology); and the Christian churches. At times, the report read like a revisiting of the final
report of the Royal Commission on Aboriginal Peoples. The TRC was
especially insistent on the importance of the UN declaration, which it
referred to repeatedly as a "framework for reconciliation."[91] Given the
notorious coolness of the Harper government towards the UN statement, recommendations concerning it clearly were not aimed, as Chief
Commissioner Sinclair noted on more than one occasion, only at the
government currently in office. Other recommendations that seemed
unlikely to attract support from the Conservative government called
on Ottawa "to restore and increase" funding for the Canadian Broadcasting Corporation and to adopt a new Royal Proclamation for reconciliation. Another recommendation was a call to the Roman Catholic
Church that, within one year, the pope apologize in Canada for the
church's role in residential schooling.[92] If the Truth and Reconciliation Commission was reporting for the future as well as the present,
as RCAP had in 1996, it ran the danger of having those of its recommendations that required federal government action be delayed, if not
thwarted indefinitely.

The labours of the TRC commissioners between 2009 and 2015 were pro-
digious and yielded an impressive set of accomplishments. The sheer
scale of their efforts, as they held seven national, two regional, and
seventy-seven community events was stunning. Over their term, they
"took part in nearly 900 separate events" organized by the commission
and many other agencies.[93] Throughout they had to contend with both
a recalcitrant federal government and, at times, elements among the
church entities that were parties to the settlement agreement. Their collective accomplishment was mind-boggling. Chief Commissioner Sinclair's promise to the Assembly of First Nations in July 2009 that he and
his fellow commissioners would go anywhere to meet with people who
had information to provide and were involved in the story of residential

schooling had not proved hollow. If the commissioners had, as Justice Sinclair himself acknowledged, faced scepticism when they took over in 2009, by their efforts, strong commitment, and force of personalities, they overcame the doubts. The mood among participants and the media coverage of the Ottawa closing event in June 2015 were convincing proof that the commission had established its credibility and won wide support for what it was doing.

The TRC's reports, especially the complex *Final Report* delivered in 2015, had a mixed reception. Two Winnipeg social scientists wondered why the commission had relied so heavily on survivors' accounts, "refusing to cast a wide net to capture the school experience of a random sample of attendees, despite a $60 million budget."[94] Their critique raised the issue of why the TRC had not conducted an extensive research program. One question that was asked about the commission's conclusions was whether it had got the balance between "truth" and "reconciliation" right. The commissioners' public statements and their reports placed the greater emphasis on what the survivors had told them, although some of that testimony also dealt directly with reconciliation and ways to achieve it. The TRC acknowledged that "reconciliation is going to take hard work. People of all walks of life and at all levels of society will need to be willingly engaged." Still, "this Commission remains cautiously optimistic."[95] Undoubtedly the labours and conclusions of the TRC are part of that initial work to grapple with the legacy of the past and advance towards reconciliation. While the scale of the commission's effort was impressive, some observers were less taken with the tone of the *Final Report* and the contents of the commission's calls to action: they complained that the history of residential schools had become an account that was largely about neglect and abuse, and that it was obvious that some of the commission's recommendations would not be implemented in the near term, if ever. In volume 6 of the *Final Report*, the TRC itself conceded the latter point:

As Commissioners, we understood from the start that although reconciliation could not be achieved during the TRC's lifetime, the country could and must take ongoing positive and concrete steps forward. Although the Commission has been a catalyst for deepening our national awareness of the meaning and potential of reconciliation, it will take many heads, hands, and hearts, working together, at all levels of society to maintain momentum in the years ahead. It will also take sustained political will at all levels of government and concerted material resources.[96]

The question hanging in the air at the conclusion of the TRC's work was whether the three commissioners had managed to create conditions for the passionate commitment of individuals, the genuine engagement of society, and the political will of governments that was required to bring about needed change.

Conclusion

As Canadians slowly began, over the past thirty years, to understand the reality of residential schools, the country has made modest progress towards reconciliation between Indigenous and other peoples. Beginning with the Christian churches that ran the schools on behalf of the government of Canada, a succession of agents and institutions have offered gestures of regret for the program that took Indigenous children from their home circle in an attempt to assimilate them and that provided a severely limited form of education. While the various churches were offering apologies, in the first half of the 1990s, the Canadian state opened up the question of the country's broader treatment of Indigenous peoples with the Royal Commission on Aboriginal Peoples (RCAP). After much investigative work, RCAP offered only a recommendation of a public inquiry as a solution to that question in its 1996 final report. In part because the federal government's response to RCAP was so limited, former residential school students turned to the courts to seek justice. But litigation would prove no more effective than church apologies or a royal commission recommendation, for the simple reason that the courts, like royal commissions, could not provide the acknowledgment of wrongdoing and the compensation for cultural loss that motivated much of the litigation. The evolution of litigation – from individual suits based on tort law, to an alternative dispute resolution program, and ultimately to the beginnings of class actions – testified to the impotence of the judicial system to produce what was needed. The Indian Residential School Settlement Agreement (IRSSA) delivered at least a portion of what school survivors sought and seemed to pave the way for some progress towards healing the nation's emotional wounds.

Since implementation of IRSSA began in September 2007, Canada has moved hesitantly and erratically towards the goal of reconciliation. The compensation programs under IRSSA, the Common Experience Payment and the Independent Assessment Process (IAP), were troubled by delays and other glitches, and often did not produce the gesture of contrition that many survivors sought. At best, the churches and government issued apologies to claimants at the end of successful IAP hearings. A more meaningful official gesture, at least temporarily, came in 2008, when Prime Minister Stephen Harper apologized in the House of Commons for the government's role in residential schooling. Even more was hoped for from the Truth and Reconciliation Commission (TRC), a creation of the settlement agreement, which began its work in earnest in 2009 after a failed attempt the previous year. The TRC's energetic and often imaginative approach to the execution of its mandate raised consciousness among the citizenry about the history of residential schools and offered hope for major progress towards reconciliation among survivors and their sympathizers. The commission delivered its substantial *Final Report* in 2015, which captured media attention and prompted some agencies of government across the land to move in the direction the TRC had recommended. Throughout this elaborate process, the question that hovered over the process of uncovering truth and promoting reconciliation was the attitude of the general public. Had the churches, the royal commission, the courts, and the Truth and Reconciliation Commission captured people's attention, convinced them that the history of their country contained a chapter on residential schools that was shameful, and enlisted some of them in a campaign to provide redress and healing of the divisions in Canadian society over the legacy of residential schools?

When the Christian churches began to react to the damage their residential schools had wrought, they did so at differing paces and with varied attitudes. They all had gone through a gradual process of consciousness raising since 1945 that shifted the emphasis of their work more towards social justice, thanks in part to international trends and in part to a growing awareness of their own complicity in the residential school story. But there were always differences in outlook among the churches. The United Church of Canada and the Presbyterian Church in Canada were the agencies most likely to respond to urgings that their policies on domestic issues such as residential schools and the role of Indigenous people within their own institution be reappraised and adjusted. Both denominations had an orientation towards social justice causes, and, from the 1970s onward, the United Church espe- cially was vigorous in pursuing issues such as redress on land claims and restraints on corporate action in remote, predominantly Aborigi- nal, regions of the country. The stances of the Anglicans and Roman Catholics on residential schools were discernibly different from those of the other two denominations. This difference arose, in large part, because the Anglicans and Catholics were the dominant religious insti- tutions in sub-Arctic and Arctic Canada, where the role of residential schools remained defensible after 1969, when the federal government began to phase out such schools. The continuing migratory economic activities of Dene and Inuit families meant that custodial schools for children whose parents were not sedentary could be justified longer than in the South. And, in the case of the Roman Catholics, the struc- ture of the denomination was a barrier to their taking decisive action to respond to revelations of problems with the residential schools. The United, Presbyterian, and Anglican Churches contained stronger sup- port for greater emphasis on social justice, though the Anglicans were somewhat constrained by internal resistance when it came to northern missions and schools. The Roman Catholics were held back because of their heavy "investment" in northern missions and their lack of a cen- tralized church structure.

Accordingly, at differing rates and with varied levels of enthusiasm, the churches began to grapple with the legacy of residential schools in the 1980s and 1990s. If their reaction could be criticized for being dilatory, it was at least more than the government of Canada or the Canadian population at large could claim. Although the churches that ran the schools could be criticized for how they had treated Indige- nous children, they at least were the minority of Canadians who cared enough about the welfare of Indigenous people to urge the government to provide schooling for their young and to contribute their own labour and money towards that process. Beginning in 1986 with an internally controversial apology for the way it had conducted missions to Aborigi- nal people, the United Church of Canada initiated the process of reflec- tion and apology. Its gesture was followed a few years later by a succes- sion of apologies from the other churches, which focused more specifi- cally on residential schools. In the spring of 1991, a National Meeting on Residential Schools, which was attended by some Canadian Catholic bishops, representatives of religious orders that had been involved in residential schooling, and some First Nations lay people, issued a statement of sorrow and regret. That summer, the Oblates of Mary Immaculate, the Roman Catholic missionary order that had run most of the Catholic schools, made their apology at the historic pilgrimage site of Lac Ste Anne, Alberta. The Roman Catholics were followed by the Anglicans in 1993 and the Presbyterians in 1994. Finally, in 1998, the United Church of Canada issued another apology, this time specifically for the denomination's role in residential schooling.

While these apologies were undoubtedly heartfelt, they could not provide solace to residential school survivors. The Catholic apologies came from specific agencies because the Catholics did not have a national structure; their individual dioceses were linked directly to Rome. In any event, the church apologies turned out to matter little to Native Canadians. The Truth and Reconciliation Commission noted in 2015 that, while many "survivors told us a great deal about how churches have affected their lives, and how, as adults, they may or may not practise Christianity, they seldom mentioned the churches' apologies or healing and reconciliation activities."[1]

Between 1992 and 1996, an agency of the federal state, the Royal Commission on Aboriginal Peoples, carried on the process of coming to grips with the legacy of residential schooling that the churches had begun. Created in response to the lengthy standoff at Oka, Quebec, in the summer of 1990, RCAP, under the leadership of co-chairs Georges Erasmus and René Dussault, canvassed the history and contemporary reality of Aboriginal communities. Its massive final report in 1996 constituted an extended exposé of the damage wrought by ill-advised government policies and the racism of the non-Aboriginal majority of Canada. Among the problems in the history of relations between Indigenous and other Canadians that the commission brought to light were the church-run residential schools. Incorporating both the commission's own original research and the findings of community hearings that it had held, the final report contained a hard-hitting chapter on the history of residential schools that left an indelible impression on anyone who read it. Unfortunately, the commissioners' recommendations were not effective in addressing the issues that they had uncovered. The steps they proposed tended to focus on reserve communities, home to only half of First Nations people, and they focused on initiatives, such as a massive and expensive overhaul of Canada's governance system, that were a non-starter in the small-government environment of the mid-1990s. As far as residential schools were concerned, RCAP recommended simply the appointment of "a public inquiry instructed to (a) investigate and document the origins and effects of residential school policies and practices respecting all Aboriginal peoples" and "fund establishment of a national repository of records and video collections related to residential schools."[2]

Although the federal government's response was as limited as the royal commission's program was grandiose, the long-term consequences of RCAP's work were substantial. In its lengthy survey of the history of Native-newcomer relations, the commission endorsed and popularized a revisionist history that had developed in the 1980s. In particular, scholarly historical writing on the Canadian government's Indian policy had revolutionized understanding of the purpose and nature of Ottawa's approach, at least among a limited academic audience. Earlier writing on Indigenous peoples, when it existed at all, had tended to emphasize their cultural incompatibility with the modern capitalist, industrialized world, and had portrayed federal government policies such as the treaties and creation of reserves in western Canada in the latter decades of the nineteenth century as benevolent in intent and far-sighted in nature. The reinterpretation of Indigenous, more especially First Nations, policy from the early 1980s onward instead demonstrated that First Nations had usually adjusted rapidly and effectively to economic change brought by newcomers, and that many of the economic and social ills that beset their communities were the result of misguided government policies. In this regard, of course, the residential schools and western reserve agricultural policies were prime examples. RCAP endorsement of this revisionist interpretation of Canadian history that portrayed government and church policies as incompetent at best and malevolent at worst was important.

The federal government responded to RCAP's final report with the publication of *Gathering Strength*. Two components of that volume would have a particularly lasting effect, one negative and the other extremely positive. Although the chief of the Assembly of First Nations (AFN), Ovide Mercredi, responded to RCAP with a call for the federal government to stop using the churches to shield itself on the residential school question and to apologize for its "policy of assimilation to destroy aboriginal languages, traditions and belief," Ottawa's response was muted.[3] The statement of reconciliation that Indian Affairs minister Jane Stewart delivered in January 1998 seemed to express profound personal regret, but it was received coolly by Aboriginal leaders. All but Phil Fontaine of AFN rejected it at the time, and Fontaine himself eventually came to agree that it was inadequate as an expression of government responsibility.

The positive lasting element of *Gathering Strength* was the government's commitment to provide $350 million dollars to establish the Aboriginal Healing Foundation (AHF). Under the leadership of chair Georges Erasmus, and executive director Dr Mike DeGagné, the AHF would have a profound impact. Although a reluctant Erasmus agreed to head it on the condition that his role would last only for six months of negotiations, he endured as board chair for the life of the foundation. The AHF would contribute massively in two areas until the government of Stephen Harper terminated its funding. First, it discharged its principal mandate, promoting healing among individuals and communities that had been blighted by exposure to residential schooling. It distributed funds to community healing initiatives and monitored the operation of therapeutic programs, in the process demonstrating that an Aboriginal-controlled organization could be efficient and effective. As well, the AHF continued the promotion of the revisionist history of residential schooling that RCAP had endorsed. Both in many AHF publications, and through a charitable agency that it sponsored, the Legacy of Hope Foundation, the depiction of residential schools as malevolent in their assimilative purpose and devastating in their impact on former students and their communities continued through the first fourteen years of the twenty-first century.

In the view of Aboriginal people, *Gathering Strength* responded inadequately to RCAP. The disappointment attending its release thus helped to usher in a new phase of the residential school saga in which the courts would become the dominant non-Aboriginal agency interacting with Indigenous people. The churches had offered their gestures after 1986, and a government-created royal commission had helped to focus attention on the malign legacy of residential schools in the mid-1990s. Beginning noticeably in 1998 and continuing to the middle of the next decade, the judiciary was the face of Canada's response to its troubled history in the schools.

For former students, there were several reasons to use tort law to press the federal government for compensation for the wrongs done them in the schools. Most obviously, successful litigation would make those who had authorized and operated residential schools accountable for their conduct. Such action would also provide some financial compensation for what the survivors had suffered in the schools. And, many hoped, litigation would make those responsible for the schools acknowledge the wrongs they had done and respond to former students. For such reasons, survivors initiated civil actions against the federal government. They and their lawyers focused on the state rather than naming both churches and the state as respondents for the simple reason that government, unlike the religious organizations, had "deep pockets," vast financial resources to pay compensation. Unfortunately, from the litigants' perspective, the federal government also had limitless resources with which to fight the legal actions. Ottawa's immediate response to a civil suit naming the government as respondent was to cross-sue the religious organization that had run the school the litigant had attended, thus complicating the legal action and delaying proceedings. For their part, the churches found the litigation phase of the residential school story harrowing for both material and spiritual reasons. Legal fees and compensation payments when the courts found them liable for damages severely strained their resources. During the 1998–2005 period, several Roman Catholic dioceses, the Oblate Province in the prairie west, and two Anglican dioceses, teetered on the edge of bankruptcy. The United Church of Canada was approaching insolvency when a large bequest granted it a reprieve. In addition, and often more important, the churches found the adversarial legal process emotionally draining. All the religious entities had been moving towards engagement with Indigenous peoples on social justice issues since the 1960s. Their preference was to work in solidarity with Indigenous people to achieve improvements in the treatment they received from governments, not to battle them in courtrooms.

All the parties eventually came to the realization that they had to find a better way than civil litigation to resolve issues related to the legacy of residential schools. Because the fact that litigation could not provide the relief that many sought quickly became apparent, by 2002–3 the three parties were discussing the adoption of an alternate dispute resolution mechanism that would eliminate the need for survivors to go through the wrenching cross-examination that was part of a standard civil action. In 2003, a dispute resolution (DR) process was developed, administered by a federal government agency and participated in by the churches and survivors, and their attorneys, that allowed former students to seek redress in a setting less bruising than the courts. While DR was undoubtedly an improvement over regular civil litigation, it, too, had deficiencies. It was extremely bureaucratic, with a long and complex application form, and procedural rules that required the adjudicators to probe the claimant's contentions about the experience of residential schooling. It was slow and it could not provide some of the forms of redress that many survivors desired. There was no provision for loss of language and culture, because Canadian civil law had not yet developed such a form of compensation. And, although there were impressive exceptions, such as the emotional feast and ceremony at Hazelton, BC, that brought closure to some of the First Nations people who had suffered in the United Church's Edmonton school, DR was not effective in restoring the victim's psychological health or in promoting reconciliation between the perpetrators and the sufferers.

By 2004, ironically at the point when DR was gathering steam and beginning to roll out decisions at an impressive rate, a consensus had developed among the Assembly of First Nations and the leadership of key federal departments (though not Indian and Northern Affairs) that a more comprehensive solution had to be sought. Indications that large-scale class actions, which litigated on behalf of thousands of former students at a time, would soon have their day in court provided the final push to move the parties to another set of negotiations. Over the reservations of some bureaucrats and in spite of the suspicion and reluctance of most of the church agencies, the search for a better process to deal with residential school claims began.

Throughout the litigation phase, forces were at work to strengthen the tendency that had been noticeable in the deliberations of the royal commission to see residential schools as solely a site of abuse. The Assembly of First Nations, the principal Aboriginal political organization that lobbied on residential school issues, always emphasized abuse, because that was the most effective way to rouse public opinion and get support for their campaigns. Not surprisingly, counsel for former students also responded to questions with talk of abuse, because it supported the actions they were pursuing. And members of the media, both print and electronic, also continued to focus on the schools as exclusively places of mistreatment, because they needed to tell a complex story as simply as they could and in a timely way. For such reasons, the litigation phase tended to solidify earlier tendencies to understand residential school history as only and always a history of abuse.

The Indian Residential Schools Settlement Agreement, which emerged from negotiations among former students, churches, and the federal government between 2004 and 2006, ushered in a new and decisive phase of the residential school saga. Among the many topics IRSSA tackled was a replacement for DR, the compensation process that many of the parties involved in the process viewed as unsatisfactory. Ironically, IRSSA simply continued DR under a new name, the Independent Assessment Process (IAP), and committed the federal government financially to support the adjudication mechanism and pay almost all of the compensation that adjudicators would award under IAP. But there were, of course, other important elements to the massive settlement agreement. Other components included compensation for all residential school survivors who could document their attendance at a recognized school, an allocation of funds for the Aboriginal Healing Foundation, $20 million for commemoration projects, and the creation of the Truth and Reconciliation Commission. The settlement agreement would prove to be the most expensive out-of-court resolution of a class action in Canada to that point.

Implementation problems dogged the IRSSA in every area and at every step. Even the money for the ongoing work of the Aboriginal Healing Foundation proved controversial when the Roman Catholic entities dragged their feet on providing the funds they were obligated to contribute, leading the AHF to take them to court. The commemoration program, though successful overall, was beset with problems, owing to the slow pace at which the TRC recommended projects and the way in which the Aboriginal Affairs department allocated funds. There could be no doubt, however, that enduring and influential markers of residential school history were created thanks to the commemoration component of the settlement agreement.

The IRSSA programs that compensated former students also experienced serious difficulties, in part because of the sheer number of survivors who made claims. Many would-be claimants were left thwarted and angry when they discovered that the schools they attended were not on the approved list negotiated by the parties to the IRSSA.

Although a small number of disgruntled former students succeeded in getting a handful of institutions added to the list, many more were left disappointed. The Common Experience Payment (CEP) that was to compensate for attendance and cultural loss was inundated with more than 100,000 claims, many of them complicated and time consuming. The requirement that claimants document their attendance at a recognized residential school caused enormous difficulties for many former students, in spite of efforts by church and government officials to assist them. Inevitably, the CEP left disappointment in its wake. Meanwhile, the Independent Assessment Process was, to a great extent, the victim of its own success. Successor to the dispute resolution system that had been in place from 2003 until the IRSSA was implemented in 2007, the IAP was simply overwhelmed when approximately three times the anticipated number of claimants came forward. Since all the IAP claims required a hearing by an adjudicator, completion of the IAP dragged on and was not completed until 2017. Inevitably, there were complaints about the application form, support for applicants, the adjudication process, and delays in rendering decisions. The additional complication created by litigation between the IAP and the Truth and Reconciliation Commission over access to the records of IAP hearings, which most claimants believed were to remain closed forever, was an additional source of distress for many claimants.

The litigation between the IAP and the TRC was a classic example of the clash of two worthy objectives – the TRC's desire to record residential school history as fully as possible and the IAP's belief that it was duty-bound to protect the privacy of claimants. The final stage – to date, at least – of the confrontation was a decision of the Ontario Court of Appeal in April 2016 that those claimants under the IAP who were still alive could decide over the next fifteen years whether they wished the record of their cases destroyed or transferred to the National Centre for Truth and Reconciliation that was created by the TRC.[4] The dispute is not necessarily over, though. The former executive director and then general counsel of the Truth and Reconciliation Commission, Tom McMahon, has argued in a paper titled "The Final Abuse of Indian Residential School Children: Deleting Their Names, Erasing Their Voices and Destroying Their Records without Their Consent" that the Court of Appeal decision is seriously flawed and should be reviewed by the Supreme Court of Canada.[5]

Like the CEP and the IAP, the Truth and Reconciliation Commission certainly had its share of problems. When the first trio of commissioners imploded spectacularly during the first few months of the commission's existence, there was concern that this key piece of the settlement agreement had been irreparably damaged. Although the parties to the IRSSA took an uncomfortably long time to do it, in 2009 they appointed three new commissioners, who would prove to be energetic, conscientious, sensitive, and effective. Chief Commissioner Murray Sinclair and Commissioners Marie Wilson and Wilton Littlechild succeeded impressively in areas where their predecessors had failed. Chief among their successes were political gains: with some exceptions, they succeeded in winning over parties who had created problems for the first TRC. They placated the demanding Assembly of First Nations by their promises and their efforts; they seemed to win friends among the badly rattled survivors; and, in spite of sometimes intemperate criticisms, they succeeded in working well with the Christian churches, which, as parties to the IRSSA, were indispensable partners in their work. The exception to that generalization was the Roman Catholic entities, which remained aloof at best and hostile at worst. The initial organizational and personnel problems the commission experienced were compounded by a time-consuming relocation to Winnipeg. If the commissioners did not establish a warm relationship with the federal government – and they would have damaged their credibility with survivors and the AFN if they had – they managed to work with Ottawa in spite of public differences. The TRC took the federal government to court over access to archival documents under federal control, but it was able to persuade the cabinet to grant an extra eighteen months and at least $6 million dollars more to carry its work to completion.

One factor in the Truth and Reconciliation Commission's ability to overcome the deficits it inherited and the challenges it created for itself was the success of the public events that it carried out. Obligated under the IRSSA to stage seven national events in two years, it began somewhat uncertainly and later gathered strength and more public support. The national events were accompanied by two regional gatherings and a large number of community events that appeased regional unhappiness at being passed over for a national event – as was the case with a regional event in Victoria that supported the National Event for British Columbia, which was held in Vancouver – and built grassroots support among Aboriginal peoples across the country. Attending all these meetings, not to mention private sessions with government, church groups, and organizations interested in the work of the commission, took a tremendous toll on the commissioners and staff. A comparison of pictures

9.1a The TRC commissioners at the beginning
of their labours, 2009

of the commissioners taken when they were appointed in 2009 and at
the closing national event in Ottawa in 2015 revealed the cost of inces-
sant travel, high-pressure meetings, and the strain of listening to hour
after hour of harrowing accounts by former students of their experience
in the schools.

Undoubtedly, the Truth and Reconciliation Commission will be
remembered principally for its published reports and its calls to action.
The interim report, *They Came for the Children* (2012); the summary version of its final report that it released at the TRC closing event in Ottawa
in June 2015, *Honouring the Truth, Reconciling for the Future*; and the massive six-volume *Final Report* issued in December 2015, all constitute the
commission's legacy, just as the 1996 final report of the Royal Commission on Aboriginal Peoples is the testament of that inquiry. Like
the RCAP final report, the TRC's reports combined a historical review,
symbolic gestures, and practical suggestions. Both the interim and final

9.1b ... and at the end, 2015.

reports of the TRC placed a strong emphasis on explaining the history that lay behind its inquiries and recommendations. In the case of residential schools, the TRC pointed out the flawed nature of the initiative that was present from the beginning and laid out the problems that Indigenous peoples, government, and churches encountered in its execution. Substandard classroom instruction and vocational training was accompanied by inadequate care and harsh discipline. The TRC, especially in its *Final Report*, which relied heavily on oral accounts that survivors provided at its hearings, laid out in great detail the multiple forms that abuse of students took. Although the commission took pains to explain that church-based school staff were often positively motivated and that some of them provided exceptional care for the children, the overall tenor of the reports was that the residential schools were principally sites of abuse.

The TRC's calls to action combined symbolic gestures and more concrete steps aimed at every level of government and most of the major agencies of civil society. The recommendations included both a call to repudiate the "Doctrine of Discovery" and an injunction to the federal government that it sign on fully to the United Nations Declaration on the Rights of Indigenous Peoples. The report urged the federal government to develop with Aboriginal leaders a Royal Proclamation of Reconciliation that would build on the Royal Proclamation of 1763 and its companion 1764 Treaty of Niagara, and would declare the link between Crown and Aboriginal peoples to be a nation-to-nation relationship. And it called on the pope, on behalf of the Roman Catholic Church, to deliver an apology for residential schools in Canada within one year of the publication of the *Final Report*. There were also many practical proposals in the areas of education and child care, along with an incongruous recommendation that urged the federal government to increase funding to the Canadian Broadcasting Corporation. As the former executive director of the Aboriginal Healing Foundation, Dr Mike DeGagné, has cogently argued, there are reasons for concern with the TRC recommendations. They are not well connected to the commission's mandate, they do not always flow logically from what survivors told the commissioners, and they rely too much on the work of other agencies, especially government, for implementation.[6]

Given the Truth and Reconciliation Commission's emphasis on history in explaining the corrosive relationship between Indigenous and other Canadians that had made the residential schools possible, it was not surprising that its calls to action devoted considerable attention to the past. The final report stated the commissioners' emphatic belief that "genuine reconciliation will not be possible until the broad legacy of the schools is both understood and addressed."[7] Key elements from the past that had potential to promote reconciliation were the treaties between Aboriginal peoples and the Crown. "If Canada's past is a cautionary tale about what not to do, it also holds a more constructive history lesson for the future. The Treaties are a model for how Canadians, as diverse peoples, can live respectfully and peacefully together on the lands we now share."[8] But, to advance towards reconciliation, Canada had to do more than acknowledge the past; it had to ensure that the history of the country was properly taught. To secure that objective, the TRC recommended a variety of steps, applying to all three levels of government, including providing better education for public servants and in schools on the history of Aboriginal peoples, ensuring that museums provided more and more balanced accounts of the history of the country, and making sure that archives, especially Library and Archives Canada, better serve Indigenous peoples. And, of course, the commissioners pushed strongly for financial support from the federal government for the National Centre for Truth and Reconciliation that had been part of their original mandate. What the commission said of Parks Canada and the country's official heritage commemoration programs applied more broadly: "Ultimately, reconciliation requires a paradigm shift in Canada's national heritage values, policies, and practices."[9]

The TRC's reports highlighted the question of how the residential school experience should be described. Although the chief commissioner sometimes flirted with calling the schools an instance of genocide, in the end the commission settled for referring to them as an example of cultural genocide. In doing so, the TRC stimulated a controversy over appropriate terminology.[10] Proponents of applying the term "genocide" point to the portion of the United Nations Convention on the Prevention and Prevention of the Crime of Genocide that refers to destroying "a national, ethnical, racial or religious group" by "forcibly transferring children of the group to another group."[11] They argue that the schools resulted in such a forcible transfer in their attempt to impose a Euro-Canadian identity on Aboriginal children. The problem with this argument is that residential schools housed only about one-third of status Indian children, and a smaller fraction of Métis children. Can such a social experiment be described as transferring a "racial ... group" to another people when so many others were not targeted? Moreover, it is demonstrable that many who went to residential school maintained their Aboriginal identity, albeit with difficulty. Under these circumstances, the use of an explosive term like "genocide" is socially dangerous: it can be a barrier to progress to reconciliation. Writing of the use of "genocide" in a different context in the 1980s, Plains Cree columnist Doug Cuthand argued, "'Genocide' is one of those loaded words that are thrown around a little too carelessly ... 'Genocide' is a very serious word, and to use it carelessly debases the language and cheapens it."[12]

In emphasizing history as a contributor to the problems in the relationship between Native and non-Native peoples, as well as a means to correct the problem, the TRC was consistent with the thirty-year history of Canada's pursuit of reconciliation. History had been at the heart of halting efforts of church and state to repair relations, beginning with the apologies in the 1980s and 1990s from the various churches and religious orders that had operated the residential schools. The role of the past had been even more prominent in the labours and final report of the Royal Commission on Aboriginal Peoples between 1992 and 1996. RCAP had adopted and popularized a revisionist history of state policy towards Indigenous peoples that had developed in the 1980s. Both implicitly and explicitly, the same interpretation of the past had been present in the work of the Aboriginal Healing Foundation and the Legacy of Hope Foundation (LHF). The AHF's publications took as a given the view that the policies of the government of Canada had harmed its relationship with Aboriginal peoples, and the LHF propagated the same view in the depiction of residential schooling that it put into its educational materials. And, as noted, the Truth and Reconciliation Commission was preoccupied with history, both the story of individual school students and the record of government and church actions, as it laid out its reports. What this sustained campaign amounted to, though this was not directly acknowledged, was to disrupt and replace a settler history myth about Canada that for a long time had whitewashed the country's understanding of its past.

The "settler" history that revisionists sought to dislodge was epitomized by a Heritage Minute dealing with the North West Mounted Police (NWMP) and Lakota chief Sitting Bull.[13] Set just north of the Saskatchewan-Montana border on 17 October 1877, the vignette recounts a negotiating meeting that was part of efforts by the United States to repatriate Sitting Bull, the victor of the Battle of the Little Big Horn the previous year. In the opening scene, U.S. Army general Terry is expostulating with NWMP commissioner James Macleod, pointing out how few Mounties Macleod had, compared to Terry's retinue. The American emphasizes that the Lakota are dangerous, but Macleod responds that they have kept the peace in Canada. The next scene, indoors, opens with American officers muttering darkly about the Lakota until Sitting Bull strides in. General Terry begins to tell Sitting Bull what terms President Hays is offering the Lakota to return to the United States. Sitting Bull, played by Graham Greene, interrupts the soldier, exclaiming, "The Grandmother's Medicine House is no place for lies. Not two more words. This country does not belong to you. We will stay here and keep the Grandmother's peace. She will let us raise our children. We do not want lies. These men, Walsh, Macleod, are the first white men who never lied to us." In an afterword, Macleod says, "I didn't know then that they would be starved out of Canada and back to the United States." Fade to black.

There is nothing historically incorrect in the content of this Heritage Minute. The meeting occurred, the strengths of the American and Canadian forces were strikingly different, and Sitting Bull did speak strongly in favour of staying in Canada. The Heritage Minute also acknowledged that the Canadian government worked assiduously, including using food as a weapon, to induce the Lakota chief and his followers to go back across the Medicine Line and remove an irritant from American-British-Canadian relations. But the tale also evokes tropes that are deeply embedded in Canadians' understanding of their history in relation to Native peoples: that, in the 1870s, the United States fought Native Americans in the West, in contrast to what happened north of the forty-ninth parallel, where treaties replaced warfare and red-coated mounted police took the place of blue-coated Long Knives; that Canadian officials, at least those on the ground, usually dealt honourably with Indigenous peoples, unlike Americans, who repeatedly breached the treaties they had negotiated; and so on.

The assumptions and expectations that the Heritage Minute plays to are part of what Paulette Regan has termed the "peacekeeper myth" of Canadian history. Dr Regan, holder of a doctorate in Aboriginal law and a mainstay of the Truth and Reconciliation Commission as a key staff member throughout its existence, has demonstrated how Canadians evince a smug, self-congratulatory attitude towards their past, and more especially to the history of Native-newcomer relations.[14] These same attitudes came to characterize school curricula. When Indigenous people were covered in the classroom, it was often in a patronizing or demeaning way, and usually within a framework that a trio of scholars from Queen's University has described as "nationalist self-congratulation."[15] It is the mindset – or, perhaps more accurately, assumption – that led a Canadian prime minister who had been immersed in debates over the history of residential schools and the United Nations Declaration on the Rights of Indigenous People to say flatly that Canada did not have an imperialist record. Speaking at a press conference following a G20 Summit in Pittsburgh on 25 September 2009, Stephen Harper said of Canada, "We also have no history of colonialism. So we have all of the things that many people admire about the great powers but none of the things that threaten or bother them."[16] This came from a leader with a keen interest in Canadian history who, during his time in office, promoted a particularly martial version of the nation's past and who published a hockey history. There is no reason to believe that Harper was being ironical or that he understood that, lacking irony, the words were ridiculous.

While Canadians' tendency towards smugness about themselves and their past is familiar ground, it is not as well known that, in Native history in particular, the Canadian state worked over many years to promote what can only be described as a "whitewashed" version of the past. The government of Canada – including those of all political stripes – from the 1870s onward built on an established attitude of moral superiority to the United States in Indian policy to promote its programs and defend itself from criticisms by the official opposition. A cartoon in the *Canadian Illustrated News* on 22 July 1876, less than four weeks after the Battle of the Little Big Horn and a month prior to the negotiation of Treaty 6 at Fort Carlton, Saskatchewan, spoke volumes. The cartoon was split into two panels, one supposedly depicting government-Native relations in the United States and the other the corresponding subject in Canada. South of the Medicine Line, whiskey traders debauched Native Americans, and sabre-wielding cavalry slew them; north of the international boundary, calm, commerce, and good feelings prevailed in a peaceful trading scene.[17] That Canadian governments exploited the self-satisfied assumptions embedded in the cartoon was soon confirmed. When the Alexander Mackenzie government referred to the recently concluded Treaty 6 in Parliament, it conceded that "some of the provisions of this treaty are of a somewhat onerous and exceptional character." But the ministry thought it best to ratify the agreement because "the Canadian policy is nevertheless the cheapest ultimately, if we compare the result with those of other countries; and it is above all a humane, just and Christian policy." To clinch the argument, it drew the now-familiar contrast: "Notwithstanding the deplorable war waged between Indian tribes in the United States territories, and the Government of that country, during the last year, no difficulty has arisen with the Canadian tribes living in the immediate vicinity of the scene of hostilities."[18] Yet, as a Canadian historian has demonstrated, in many ways the Americans implemented their western treaties with the Lakota more justly and humanely than did the dominion.[19]

From the 1870s on, the federal government routinely employed both images and text to advance its self-serving message about Canadian Indian policy. It had begun in British Columbia by commissioning photographers to record ethnographic details in Indian villages during the 1870s.[20] The introduction of the new technology of half-tone reproduction allowed the use of black-and-white images to accompany text in the 1890s. The Department of Indian Affairs (DIA) leapt at the opportunity to reinforce its self-laudatory message in annual reports with images that supposedly showed the positive results of a set of

9.2 Henri Julien, "Indian Policies of the United States and Canada," 1876.

beneficent policies. Between 1895 and 1905, the department's reports contained a total of 150 photographic images, fully 83 of which dealt with education. This selection included the famous Thomas Moore image of an Aboriginal child before and after attending Regina industrial schools. Thirty-two other illustrations that dealt with "farms and labour practices on reserves" documented the "success" of the DIA's agricultural policies.[21]

Closely related to the DIA's promotion of both its schooling and farming policies was a model village initiative it began in 1901. At the instigation of Indian Commissioner William Graham, and with the enthusiastic cooperation of Kate Gillespie (later Motherwell), principal of the Presbyterian File Hills Boarding School, and Father Joseph Hugonnard, OMI, principal of the Qu'Appelle Indian Industrial School, the department created the File Hills Colony on the Peepeekeesis Reserve in Saskatchewan. Young couples who, in many cases, had been encouraged by their principals to get married as they left the residential school, moved onto the colony, where they received encouragement, equipment, and oversight from the department. Because a nearby town was on a railway line to Regina, DIA officials frequently took visitors to the colony to show them the living proof of their policies' success. Official visitors included more than one governor general and at least one prime minister, accompanied, of course, by reporters. Yet, the memories of colony residents indicate that the cultural hothouse was not the thorough assimilator the department thought it was.[22]

The Department of Indian Affairs also strove to shape favourable public perceptions of its policies by other means in the early twentieth century. In 1906, it commissioned Amelia McLean Paget to interview a number of elderly Plains First Nations people to collect their memories before they were lost. Paget was a mixed-descent woman who had been captured by Wandering Spirit's warriors at Fort Pitt, Saskatchewan, in 1885, and later married Frederick Paget, an employee in the Winnipeg office of the DIA. She produced a manuscript on the Plains people, which was then taken over by Duncan Campbell Scott of the DIA. Scott handled all the discussions on editorial and related matters with the publisher and chose the illustrations for *Peoples of the Plains*. The published volume provided a sympathetic portrait of Plains culture without commenting negatively on Indian Affairs policies – several of which targeted that culture – and their impact.[23]

Indian Affairs bureaucrats worked steadily to promote the DIA's image in the United States as well. Canadian propagandists dealt with a receptive audience, as had been demonstrated in 1869, when a report of the House of Representatives' Committee on Indian Affairs concluded a report on Canadian policy by saying that Canada "'will be known in history as having striven to do justice to the aborigines ... They have so far founded their empire or dominion upon the principles of humanity and true civilization.'" Canadian officials reinforced this rosy view at every opportunity. Canadians spoke to the annual conference of the influential Friends of the Indian Conference, a lobbying organization, at Lake Mohonk, New York, several times. In 1900, missionary Egerton Ryerson Young told the Americans that Canadians "have no Indian question. We get along very nicely with our Indians." Twelve years later, the deputy minister of Indian Affairs, Frank Pedley, delivered a self-congratulatory address on the department, and his successor, Duncan Campbell Scott, underlined the message at Lake Mohonk in 1914 and 1916. Among other things, Scott pointed out to the eager American audience that Canadians did not take much interest in Indian affairs, unlike their southern neighbours. According to historian Hana Samek, Scott said that in Canada "the public was content to let government and religious bodies deal with native people."[24]

Scott's second appearance at Lake Mohonk led to a review of Canadian practice by Frederick H. Abbott, secretary of a citizens' committee that monitored American Indian policy. The result of Abbott's seven-week survey in Canada was a 150-page report entitled *The Administration of Indian Affairs in Canada*, which lauded the DIA and its partners. It praised the consolidation of statutory Indian policy in a single act, the reliance on a nonpartisan civil service that avoided upheavals after elections, the work of the Mounted Police, and the close cooperation between the missionary churches and Ottawa.[25] The Abbott report had little direct impact on American policy, but it established the practice of journeying to Ottawa to see how Indian policy should be crafted. Less than twenty years later, the executive secretary of another lobbying group, the American Indian Defense Association, and a future Bureau of Indian Affairs official spent time with the DIA and produced three highly laudatory journal articles about Canada's Indian administration.[26] Canadians believed what a J.W. Bengough cartoon had claimed earlier: "What Uncle Sam doesn't know about governing a nation would fill several volumes – and we have the books." Behind the cartoon's Uncle Sam perusing a volume in the library was a shelf of books with titles such as *Canada's Civil Service System, Canada's Banking System*, and *Canada's Indian Administration System*.[27]

OUR FREE LIBRARY.

What Uncle Sam doesn't know about governing a nation would fill several volumes—and we have the books.

9.3 "Our Free Library," 1899, manifests Canadian superiority.

Thus, by the interwar period a deeply embedded view of how the Canadian government treated First Nations portrayed Canada and Canadians as beneficent, kindly, and effective. Since shortly after Confederation the government of Canada had laboured energetically to portray its policies as wise and beneficial. This depiction, in fact, built on already established assumptions of Canadian superiority in Indian policy that were widespread. Judging by the reaction of Americans who took an interest in the DIA, the Canadian efforts were successful. Generations of both American Indian Affairs bureaucrats and members of the Friends of the Indian movement agreed that Canada dealt honourably with the Indigenous population. A similar pattern of bureaucratic promotion that focused just on Canadian treaty-making also fed the stream of admiration for the Canadian government's policy. Beginning with publications by two treaty commissioners from the 1870s, Alexander Morris and David Laird, and continuing with an article in a popular American journal by D.C. Scott on Treaty 9, an interpretation of the post-Confederation treaties as generous, far-sighted, and helpful was advanced.[28]

Against such a background of effective pro-government propaganda, it was not surprising that the first major historical work that examined treaties and Indian policy in western Canada also came to positive conclusions about the government's treatment of First Nations. George Stanley's *The Birth of Western Canada: A History of the Riel Rebellions*, published in 1936, was tilted in the government's favour by the author's theoretical approach. A disciple of the Frederick Jackson Turner school, Stanley saw the clashes between Indigenous groups in the West and the national government as "the manifestation in Western Canada of the problem of the frontier, namely the clash between primitive and civilized peoples." Stanley's section on the numbered treaties of the 1870s, characterized as "The Indian Problem: The Treaties," contained no fewer than nine citations of Alexander Morris's book on treaty-making, seven of parliamentary *Sessional Papers,* and three from Colonial Office records.[29] Not surprisingly, Stanley's depiction of the Canadian government's treaty-making was generally positive. The greater problem was that Stanley's interpretation of early dominion policy in the West remained dominant for almost half a century. The study's scope was so large and descriptions so detailed that few saw any reason to challenge its findings or investigate the topics he had traced lightly with greater thoroughness. It was not, in fact, until John Tobias's influential article "The Subjugation of the Plains Cree" in 1983 that Stanley's positive portrayal was uprooted in academe. A vigorous and sweeping revision of historical understanding of Canadian Indian policy was then developed by English-language historians through the rest of the 1980s and the 1990s that served as a foundation for the major historical framing of the final report of the Royal Commission on Aboriginal Peoples in 1996.

Most Canadians do not believe their governments' policies dealing with Aboriginal people have been misguided or pernicious. An exception – possibly a temporary exception – to this generalization is the history of residential schools, the dark side of which has received an enormous amount of attention in recent years. A Leger Marketing survey of some

1,500 people via web panel in June 2015 revealed that a striking 83 per cent of respondents agreed or strongly agreed with the statement, "I am proud of the history of Canada." That total was composed of provincial and regional tallies that ranged from a low of 76 per cent in British Columbia to a high of 89 per cent in Alberta.[30] Because the Canadian public has not been convinced that the country's history contains much that is negative, including Native peoples, Canadians often do not connect individually with revelations of residential school abuse and other forms of governmental mistreatment in the past.

Historians who revolutionized their profession's understanding of governmental treatment of First Nations and Métis over the last thirty years have not succeeded in spreading their findings beyond the ivory tower to the public square. The responsibility for this shortcoming lies with the historians themselves. It is not that Canadians are uninterested in their history. The enormously successful scholarly military historian Tim Cook has noted that the people whom he encounters long to know more about their history. But, he argues, those Canadians are not attracted by academics' writings, which are often dense, obscure, and riddled with jargon and theory incomprehensible to the general public. He notes, too, that, among the most successful historians of Canada writing in English, are journalists such as Richard Gwyn and Charlotte Gray.[31] Bruce Walsh, the director of the University of Regina Press, who has enjoyed enormous commercial success with some of his titles in 2015 and 2016, observes that "the academy stopped communicating to everybody but non-specialists ... Therefore the audience for the books became much smaller."[32] There is a crying need to unseat the "settler myth" so carefully propagated for a century and a half, but academic historians are unlikely to be the researchers who will accomplish the necessary task. Don Jackson, a key figure in the movement of alumni of Shingwauk residential school for the last thirty-five years, points out that reconciliation requires that both parties become better informed about how relations got so bad.[33] Louise Halfe, a Cree poet and residential school survivor, makes a similar point when she argues that the country needs dialogue. Native people, she says, need to know they don't have a monopoly on pain, and non-Natives have to learn about their history of being perpetrators.[34]

The lack of knowledge about the past and its problems among the citizenry in general complicates the task of building support for reconciliation. If Canadians do not understand the deep roots of contemporary problems afflicting Native peoples, they are unlikely to pay attention to efforts to deal with those difficulties. Writing for an Aboriginal Healing Foundation publication, the former co-director of research for RCAP and researcher and writer for the AHF, Marlene Brant Castellano, noted that "consensus that residential school experience was injurious in itself, and not just in instances of physical and sexual abuse, is shared by only a small proportion of Canadian citizens, in contrast to the view of most First Nations, Inuit, and Métis people."[35] An Environics Research Group poll conducted for the TRC and Indian Residential Schools Resolution Canada reported in 2008 that knowledge of the Indian Residential Schools Settlement Agreement was "fairly low," with four in ten aware of the Common Experience Payment, and half that number or fewer knowing about other elements of the settlement.[36] In the Leger Marketing survey mentioned above, most Canadians were proud of their country's history, but half of those polled did not know or preferred not to answer when asked specifically what made them feel most proud.[37] Lacking an awareness of the historic roots of contemporary problems, Canadian political leaders have not felt voters' pressure to grapple publicly with Aboriginal issues. As two leading land claims researchers have observed, "the Parliament of Canada has neither sponsored nor carried out a full debate on the role, rights, and place of Aboriginal peoples in Canada." Apart from Aboriginal people and a few sympathetic academics and interest groups, "there is virtually no political constituency demanding that the Government of Canada or the provincial and territorial governments remain true to and fully and generously implement the treaties."[38]

It is imperative that Canadians break the hegemony of the settler myth because a huge task must be undertaken if Canada is to move in the direction of reconciliation between Indigenous and immigrant peoples. In addition to the running sore of residential schooling, which the Truth and Reconciliation Commission uncovered and began to lance, there is a broad range of problems that must be addressed effectively before Canadians can come together. Some of these are familiar issues, such as murdered and missing Aboriginal women or vast numbers of Aboriginal children in the state's care – issues that have been in the news a great deal in recent years. Problems in the funding of on-reserve schools and in substandard housing and drinking water on many reserves are also well known. It is striking that a federal general election that began a scant two months after release of the summary final report of the TRC and lasted eleven weeks was notable for not addressing Aboriginal peoples' issues in any meaningful way. Liberal leader Justin Trudeau promised to implement all ninety-four of the TRC's recommendations, and both his Liberals and the New Democratic Party made commitments directly to First Nations on issues such as education funding and an inquiry into missing and murdered Aboriginal women. But, over all, Aboriginal issues were, to use the phrase Stephen Harper used to describe his own attitude towards missing and murdered women, below the radar of the Canadian public. There is no chance the country will make progress towards reconciliation until Canadians summon the political will that will lead to action on familiar issues, as well as a vast range of others lurking in the background. And these other issues are major ones: over one thousand unresolved First Nations claims, more than sixty groups mired in treaty negotiations under the British Columbia Treaty Commission process that has been in place for over twenty years and yielded only four new treaties to the summer of 2016. In addition, there are other regions, such as Atlantic Canada and far northern Quebec, where territorial treaties have never been negotiated and Aboriginal title continues unimpaired.

To its credit, the Trudeau government that took office late in 2015 tried to advance the cause of reconciliation. It committed itself to dealing with Indigenous peoples on a "nation-to-nation basis," and in 2016 it took action on some key issues the TRC had addressed. In May it announced that it would remove the qualifications on Canada's endorsement of the United Nations Declaration on the Rights of Indigenous People and settled out of court a class action launched by former students of residential schools in Newfoundland and Labrador that had been left out of the IRSSA, and in August it launched the inquiry into murdered and missing Indigenous women after an extensive, intense period of consultation.[39] These actions were a good beginning, but they will not be enough.

Canadians cannot approach reconciliation thinking that fine words, amicable gestures, and a few measures in line with TRC calls to action are enough. First Nations want their claims settled and many are interested in concluding treaties. Until Canada moves effectively to meet their desires, the country lacks the measures of social justice for Native peoples that are a precondition for progress towards reconciliation. University of Calgary law professor Kathleen Mahoney, a key player in the creation of the IRSSA, tells a story from South Africa about "Tabo" and "Mr. Smith," from the black majority and white minority respectively, who were brought together in an attempt at reconciliation. Smith had taken Tabo's cow from him, destroying his livelihood and impoverishing his family. In the South African Truth and Reconciliation Commission process, Smith apologized and Tabo accepted the statement. "They hugged, they kissed, and they had a cup of tea together and even shared a few jokes." When Smith was leaving, "Tabo asked, 'Mr. Smith, what about the cow?'" Replied Smith, "'Tabo, you are messing up this thing about reconciliation, it has nothing to do with the cow.'"[40] Canadians have to discuss and act to restore justice about "that cow" and not simply engage in noble and well-intentioned talk. As James Bartleman, former lieutenant-governor of Ontario and a member of the Chippewas of Mnjikaning First Nation, has explained, "There can be no true reconciliation and Canada cannot claim it is a just and equal society unless economic and social equality is accorded to Aboriginal people."[41]

The cause of reconciliation is not hopeless; there are encouraging signs of individual and local initiatives designed to bring about reconciliation on a small scale. One of the most moving is the story of a non-Native Roman Catholic clergyman being adopted by an Anishnaabe residential school survivor who had attended an Oblate residential school in northwestern Ontario. During a historic meeting of survivors with Pope Benedict XVI in 2009, Tobasonakwut, a former student as well as a former Anishnaabe chief, met the archbishop of Winnipeg, Jim Weisgerber. The archbishop had been a member of the executive of the Canadian Conference of Catholic Bishops for several years and had invited Phil Fontaine to address the plenary assembly of bishops in September 2008. Weisgerber and Tobasonakwut hit it off, and their friendship grew over the next few years. Tobasonakwut began to attend Mass occasionally and ask the archbishop to bless him. The survivor decided that he wished to make a personal gesture of reconciliation that involved Weisgerber, and he arranged for them to meet for lunch. When, at that meeting, the former chief handed the archbishop tobacco, the latter realized that something important was coming, but he was stunned when Tobasonakwut asked to adopt him. Tobasonakwut explained that his language did not have a word for reconciliation but that his people's custom of adoption was a means to promote better relations. Weisgerber accepted the invitation, and a ceremony that took place at Thunderbird House in Winnipeg saw the archbishop being adopted by Tobasonakwut and his brother, Fred Kelly, as well as by Phil Fontaine, who had earlier been adopted by Tobasonakwut, and his brother Bert.

The archbishop's four new brothers each gave him a feather, and he gave each of them a rosary. Weisgerber and Tobasonakwut and the latter's family remained close thereafter. The cleric attended a Sun Dance with Tobasonakwut and his family, and both were at the canonization of Mohawk Kateri Tekakwitha in Rome in 2012. The archbishop was with Tobasonakwut's family and prayed with them as the old chief lay dying.[42]

Other local reconciliation initiatives are more collective. In June 2011, the Halifax public school board responded to a demand of Mi'kmaq people, led by activist Daniel Paul, who objected to the commemoration of Edward Cornwallis, the founder of Halifax, in the name of a junior high school. As well as overseeing the establishment of the Nova Scotia capital in 1749, in the same year Cornwallis had issued a scalp proclamation that encouraged people to turn in the scalps of Mi'kmaq for a Crown payment. In 2011, the school board removed Cornwallis's name from the school,[43] although a dispute continues over a statue of Cornwallis in the city. In Ontario, many people responded to a poignant story about Charlie Hunter, a student at the Oblate-run Fort Albany St Anne's residential school who drowned in 1974 while trying to save a fellow student who had fallen through the ice. Residential school officials had arranged to have Charlie buried in Moosonee, 515 kilometres from his home community of Peawanuck. After Charlie's story ran in the *Toronto Star* in March 2011, a flood of donations, estimated at more than $21,000, came into the newspaper to meet the cost of his burial closer to home. On 9 August 2011, Charlie Hunter's remains were reinterred in his and his surviving parents' home community.[44]

In Saskatchewan, a church group that had no direct connection with residential schools engaged in another reconciliation venture related to land stolen from a First Nation by the Crown. The followers of Chief Young Chipewyan, who had agreed to Treaty 6 in 1876, did not, for a variety of reasons, take up their reserve for many years. As waves of immigrants seeking farmlands arrived in the region after 1896, the federal government simply cancelled the reserve and made the lands available for homesteading. The descendants of Mennonites who were part of a bloc settlement that took in the purloined lands eventually became aware that their farms were located on a former reserve. Through the Mennonite Central Committee Saskatchewan, they engaged in discussions with descendants of Young Chipewyan's community and members of the local Lutheran congregation to, in the words of one of the leaders of the initiative, "talk about our mutual efforts to work at this outstanding land issue." In August 2006, the three parties signed a covenant of solidarity, and they have continued to work together to achieve a satisfactory settlement of the Young Chipewyan claim.[45] Whether or not the First Nation will ever get compensation for its loss of territory, a version of reconciliation will have been achieved. But will reconciliation without restoration of "that cow" be true reconciliation?

There are hopeful signs in initiatives at the individual and local level that have the potential to maintain the momentum behind the reconciliation movement: cities declaring a Year of Reconciliation: provincial and territorial governments committing to overhauling school curricula to include material on residential schools and treaties to educate children about the Canadian past; the small gestures between survivor and priest or usurper and dispossessed, or even between charitable non-Natives and a grieving family. If enough of these actions develop and spread, they could create the popular support for large-scale state measures that will redress the hard, material wrongs that stand in the way of reconciliation. Should that blissful day ever come, Canada will be able to advance meaningfully towards the goal of reconciliation.

Notes

Introduction: "We Did Not Hear You"

1 Jim Sinclair interview, North Bay, ON, 28 June 2010.
2 "Apology to First Nations Peoples 1986," www.united-church.ca/beliefs/policies/1986/a651 (accessed 31 May 2013). See also the *United Church Observer*, Oct. 1986, 6, 8–13.
3 Unless otherwise noted, the individual apologies are taken from the useful compendium that appears in Janet Bavelas, *An Analysis of Formal Apologies by Canadian Churches to First Nations*, Centre for Studies in Religion and Society, University of Victoria, Occasional Paper No. 1, July 2004, 20–5, www.uvic.ca/psyc/bavelas/2004/ChurchApol.pdf (accessed 2 July 2013).
4 Archbishop Michael Peers, primate, to the National Native Convocation of the Anglican Church, Minaki, ON, 6 Aug. 1993, cited in Carling Beninger, "The Anglican Church of Canada: Indigenous Policies, 1946–2011," (MA thesis, Trent University 2011), 128–9. I am indebted to Ms Beninger, who kindly provided me with a copy of her thesis.
5 Letter from the Rev. Laverne Jacobs, coordinator, Aboriginal Ministries, Feb. 2006, www.united-church.ca/aboriginal/relationships/letter (accessed 31 May 2013). See also Donna Sinclair, "Of Course We Forgive You," *United Church Observer*, Oct. 1986, 10.
6 In the United Church, a conference is a subdivision of the national church. The United Church is organized into congregations, presbyteries (groups of congregations), conferences (usually geographical groupings of presbyteries), and the General Council.
7 All Native Circle Conference, Response to the 1986 Apology, 1988 www.united-church.ca/aboriginal/Relationships/response (accessed 31 May 2013).

1. The Churches Apologize

1 For a summary of the New France experience, see J.R. Miller, *Shingwauk's Vision: A History of Native Residential Schools* (Toronto: University of Toronto Press 1996), chaps 1 and 2.

2 J. Fingard, "The New England Company and the New Brunswick Indians, 1786–1826: A Comment on the Colonial Perversion of British Benevolence," *Acadiensis* 1, 2 (spring 1972): 29–42.

3 Miller, *Shingwauk's Vision*, chap. 3.

4 Library and Archives Canada (LAC), MG 26 A, Sir John A. Macdonald Papers, vol. 91, 35428, N.F. Davin, "Report on Industrial Schools for Indians and Half-Breeds," confidential, 14 March 1879, 12–15.

5 Miller, *Shingwauk's Vision*, chaps 4 and 5.

6 *Minutes of the General Council of Indian Chiefs and Principal Men, Held at Orillia, Lake Simcoe Narrows, on the Proposed Removal of the Smaller Communities, and the Establishment of Manual Labour Schools* (Montreal: Canada Gazette 1846), 1–5 (copy in Baldwin Room, Toronto Reference Library).

7 For First Nations' attitudes to schooling in treaty-making in the 1870s, see J.R. Miller, *Compact, Contract, Covenant: Aboriginal Treaty-Making in Canada* (Toronto: University of Toronto Press 2009), chap. 6.

8 "Report of the Special Commissioners Appointed on the 8th of September, 1856, to Investigate Indian Affairs in Canada," *Journals of the Legislative Assembly of the Province of Canada*, vol. 16, appendix 21, 1858, unpaginated.

9 Miller, *Shingwauk's Vision*, 251–68; John S. Milloy, *A National Crime: The Canadian Government and the Residential School System, 1879 to 1986* (Winnipeg: University of Manitoba Press 1999), 169–71.

10 Miller, *Shingwauk's Vision*, 184–99.

11 Noel Dyck, *What Is the Indian "Problem"? Tutelage and Resistance in Canadian Indian Administration* (St John's: ISER Books 1991), 31.

12 Robert W. Mardock, "Indian Rights Movement until 1887," and Hazel Whitman Hertzberg, "Indian Rights Movement, 1887–1973," in *Handbook of North American Indians*, vol. 4, *History of Indian-White Relations*, ed. Wilcomb E. Washburn (Washington: Smithsonian Institution 1988), 303–4 and 305–11.

13 Hana Samek, *The Blackfoot Confederacy: A Comparative Study of Canadian and U.S. Indian Policy* (Albuquerque: University of New Mexico Press 1987), 9. Scott was speaking to the annual conference of Friends of the Indians at Lake Mohonk, NY.

14 Miller, *Shingwauk's Vision*, 133–4 and 137–40; Milloy, *A National Crime*, 77, 90–1, and 101–2. Some idea of the mindset of Indian Affairs senior bureaucrats about the conditions in the schools can be discerned from the cool observation by another deputy minister in 1916 that "it is quite within the mark to say that fifty per cent of the children who passed through these schools did not live to benefit from the education which they had received therein." D.C. Scott, "Indian Affairs, 1867–1912," in *Canada and Its Provinces*, edited by A. Shortt and A.G. Doughty (Toronto: Glasgow, Brook & Company 1914), 7: 615.

15 Miller, *Shingwauk's Vision*, 382

16 Ibid., 384

17 Wallace Havelock Robb, "Indian Leaders Encouraged to Press Claims for Justice," *Globe and Mail*, 7 June 1944, quoted in Scott Sheffield, *The Red Man's on the Warpath: The Image of the "Indian" and the Second World War* (Vancouver: UBC Press 2004), 99–100; "The Poet's Walk of Abbey Dawn," *Kingston Whig Standard*, 17 March 2015, www.thewhig.com/2015/03/17/the-poets-walk-of-dawn (accessed 18 July 2016). Robb's career as a poet was drawn to my attention by one of the readers for the University of Toronto Press.

18 J.H. Blackmore, in Canada, Special Joint Committee of the Senate and the House of Commons [on] the Indian Act (SJC), *Minutes of Proceedings and Evidence* 2 (1947): 1673, 10 June 1947.

19 This summary is based on the excellent analysis by Jayme K. Benson, "Different Visions: The Government Response to Native and Non-Native Submissions on Education Presented to the 1946–9 Special Joint Committee of the Senate and the House of Commons" (M.A. thesis, University of Ottawa, 1991). My thanks to Jayme for providing me with a copy of his study.

20 SJC, *Minutes of Proceedings and Evidence* 2 (1947): 952, 8 May 1947

21 Father Plourde, OMI, to H.A. Alderwood, 4 June 1946, in Benson, "Different Visions," 49–50.

22 SJC, *Minutes of Proceedings and Evidence* 2 (1947): 1498, 29 May 1947.

23 Miller, *Shingwauk's Vision*, 381.

24 SJC, *Minutes of Proceedings and Evidence* 2 (1948): 186–90, Final Report, 22 June 1948. The brief recommendation on "The Operation of Indian Schools" appears on 188.

25 Miller, *Shingwauk's Vision*, 390.

26 Benson, "Different Visions," 59–60.

27 General Synod Archives GSA), GS 75–103, box 22, file 6 (1961), Henry G. Cook, Superintendent's Report to the Board of Management, 30 May 1961.

28 Miller, *Shingwauk's Vision*, 391–2.
29 See George Manuel and Michael Posluns, *The Fourth World: An Indian Reality* (Don Mills, ON: Collier-Macmillan 1974).
30 *A Survey of the Contemporary Indians of Canada: Economic, Political, Educational Needs and Policies*, 2 vols. (Ottawa: Indian Affairs Branch 1966–7). Key recommendations included the following: "7. Indians should be regarded as 'citizens plus'; in addition to the normal rights and duties of citizenship, Indians possess certain additional rights as charter members of the Canadian community"; and "1. Integration or assimilation are not objectives which anyone else can properly hold for the Indian. The effort of the Indian Affairs Branch should be concentrated on a series of specific middle range objectives, such as increasing the educational attainments of the Indian people, increasing their real income, and adding to their life expectancy." *Survey of the Contemporary Indians*, 1:13.
31 GSA, 75–103, box 20, file 2, item #18, Trevor Jones, Report to M.S.C.C. Executive Committee, 26 May 1964.
32 Carolyn Purden, "Church Exits from Historic Field," *Canadian Churchman* 96, no. 5 (May 1969): 17. For the muted Anglican reaction in general, see Carling Beninger, "The Anglican Church of Canada: Indigenous Policies, 1946–2011" (M.A. thesis, Trent University, 2012), 19–21.
33 Beninger, "Anglican Church," 23–4, 27–30.
34 Charles E. Hendry, *Beyond Traplines: Does the Church Really Care? Towards an Assessment of the Work of the Anglican Church of Canada with Canada's Native Peoples* (Toronto: Anglican Church of Canada 1969).Hendry's background included theological studies. See "Man Who Challenged Church to Change Is United Layman," *Canadian Churchman* 96, no. 5 (May 1969): 6.
35 Hendry, *Beyond Traplines*, 80.
36 Ibid., 80–1.
37 Ibid., 86.
38 Ibid., 91.
39 Ibid., 91–2.
40 Sandra Beardsall, "'And Whether Pigs Have Wings': The United Church in the 1960s," in *The United Church of Canada: A History*, ed. Don Schweitzer (Waterloo, ON: Wilfrid Laurier University Press 2012), 112. On the evolution of the United Church's approach to evangelism and social service in general, see Phyllis D. Airhart, *A Church with the Soul of a Nation: Making and Remaking the United Church of Canada* (Toronto: McGill-Queen's University Press 2014), esp. chaps 8 and 9.
41 Joan Wyatt, "The 1970s: Voices from the Margins," in Schweitzer, *The United Church*, 128, 133–4.

42 Trent University Archives (TUA), 95-006, Indian-Eskimo Association of
Canada fonds, Biography/History, www.trentu.ca/library/archives/95-006
.htm (accessed 11 July 2013).

43 Vancouver School of Theology Archives, Administrative History, Aboriginal
Rights Coalition fonds, https://www.memorybc.ca/aboriginal-rights
-coalition-fonds;rad (accessed 11 July 2013).

44 "Canadian Churches Are Forming New Partnerships," *Canadian Churchman*
102, no. 5 (May 1976): 12.

45 Miller, *Compact,* 257–63. The agreement was also the first comprehensive
(Aboriginal title) claim settlement reached under a claims resolution process
that the federal government had created in 1973–4 in the aftermath of the
Supreme Court of Canada decision in *Calder.*

46 Beninger, "Anglican Church," 53–5.

47 J.R. Miller, *Skyscrapers Hide the Heavens: A History of Indian-White
Relations in Canada,* 3rd ed. (Toronto: University of Toronto Press 2000),
368–70.

48 Beninger, "Anglican Church," 57–8.

49 See the 1984 pamphlet issued by the churches, *You Can Help Write the Next
Chapter in Canada's History,* cited in http://home.istar.ca~arc/english/
new_cov_e.html (accessed 4 July 2013).

50 Miller, *Compact,* 177–9, 184–5.

51 Aboriginal Rights Coalition, "A New Covenant," http://home.istar.ca~arc/
english/new_cov_e.html (accessed 4 July 2013).

52 Beninger, "Anglican Church," 58–61.

53 GSA, "Native Program Planned," *Anglican Journal* 118, no. 3 (March 1992): 3.
The *Anglican Journal* had earlier been titled *Canadian Churchman.*

54 See, for example, sundry documents in United Church of Canada Archives
(UCA), Series 2, Records of the General Secretary 1972–, box 25-13, Native
Ministries, 1978–88.

55 "Canadian Churches Have Their Own Racism," *Observer,* Sept. 1980, 17.

56 St Andrew's College Library, Saskatoon, United Church of Canada, *30th
General Council Record of Proceedings, August 6th–August 7th Morden,
Manitoba 1984,* 100, 416–17.

57 UCA, Series 2, Records of the General Secretary, 1972–, 91.162C, General
Council Minutes, Memo from Helga Kutz-Harder, 28 August 1986.

58 "Formation of the All Native Circle Conference (1987)," www.united
-church.ca (accessed 15 July 2013).

59 UCA, 2.001C, General Council Records, Series II, Minutes of Executive and
Sub-Executive, Minutes of 19–22 March 1985; Jim Sinclair interview, North
Bay, ON, 28 June 2010.

60 See http://www.united-church.ca/, cited in Janet Bavelas, *An Analysis of Formal Apologies by Canadian Churches to First Nations*, Occasional Paper No. 1, Centre for Studies in Religion and Society, University of Victoria, 19, www.uvic.ca/psyc/bavelas/2004/ChurchApol.pdf (accessed 2 July 2012); Bill Phipps interview, Calgary, 20 April 2010.

61 Phil Fontaine interview, Winnipeg, 20 March 2015.

62 Statement by the National Meeting on Indian Residential Schools, March 1991, in Bavelas, *Analysis of Formal Apologies*, 20.

63 "Homily Presented at Lac Ste. Anne, Alberta, 24 July 1991" and "An Apology to the First Nations of Canada by the Oblate Conference of Canada," *Western Oblate Studies* 2 (1992): 253–8 and 259–62. The quotations are from 255 (homily) and 259, 260, and 262 (apology); the emphasis is in the original.

64 "An Apology to the First Nations of Canada by the Oblate Conference of Canada," in Bavelas, *Analysis of Formal Apologies*, 21.

65 "A Message from the Primate to the National Native Convocation," Minaki, ON, 6 Aug. 1993, in Bavelas, *Analysis of Formal Apologies*, 22–3.

66 GSA, GS2010–10, box 1, file 1, Sacred Circle 1993 – Minaki Lodge, Evaluation of National Native Convocation 1993, shows that few Aboriginal delegates commented on the apology. Of those who did, one said it was the thing s/he liked second least; another said the apology was the second most likable thing about the gathering in his/her opinion.

67 Andrew Wesley interview, Toronto, 12 Dec. 2013.

68 "Our Confession," in Bavelas, *Analysis of Formal Apologies*, 24–5.

69 Rev. Laverne Jacobs, coordinator, Aboriginal Ministries, United Church of Canada, "Letter from the Rev. Laverne Jacobs," Feb. 2006, www.united -church.ca (accessed 25 April 2008); Donna Sinclair, "Of Course We Forgive You," *United Church Observer*, Oct. 1986, 10.

70 Moderator Bill Phipps's apology "for its complicity in the Indian Residential School System," in Bavelas, *Analysis of Formal Apologies*, 26.

71 Phipps interview.

72 Moderator's Message "A Letter on the 20th Anniversary of the Apology to First Nations," www.united-church.ca (accessed 16 July 2013). According to Will Kunder, who, along with Elders Murray Whetun and Floyd Steinhauer, was present at the Aboriginal Consultation in 2005, "stories were told and additional stones cemented to the Cairn" at that time. Jim Sinclair to J.R. Miller, 28 Feb. 2014. I am grateful to Jim Sinclair and Will Kunder for providing this additional information about the event.

2. The State Investigates

1 The history of Oka-Kanesatake and the land dispute are summarized in J.R. Miller, "Great White Father Knows Best: Oka and the Land Claims Process," *Native Studies Review* 7, no. 1 (1991): 23–51.
2 Ibid., 28–36.
3 Ibid., 42–3.
4 J.R. Miller, *Skyscrapers Hide the Heavens: A History of Indian-White Relations in Canada*, 3rd ed. (Toronto: University of Toronto Press 2000), 383–4.
5 For a brief summary of the deficiencies of the specific claims-resolution process between 1974 and the early 1990s, see Miller, "Great White Father," 39–41.
6 The link between Oka and the creation of RCAP was heavily emphasized in the opening section of an RCAP-sponsored DVD on the commission's work: *No Turning Back* (National Film Board in association with RCAP 1996).
7 Brian Dickson to Brian Mulroney, 2 Aug. 1991, in RCAP, *The Mandate: Royal Commission on Aboriginal Peoples – Background Documents* (N.p., 1991), unpaginated. The impressive list of the more than sixty people Dickson consulted is in Appendix 1 of the document. Those consulted consisted principally of Aboriginal leaders, government officials and politicians, and members of the legal profession.
8 Order in Council 1991-1597 (P.C. 1991-1597), 26 Aug. 1991, Schedule 1; in *The Mandate*.
9 NFB-RCAP, *No Turning Back.*
10 Brief biographies of the commissioner are in RCAP, *Report of the Royal Commission on Aboriginal Peoples*, vol. 1, *Looking Forward, Looking Back* (Ottawa: RCAP 1996), 703–5 (hereafter *Looking Forward*). During a conversation prior to the taping of a television program in 1991, Georges Erasmus told me that he had not attended a residential school. His father had, he said, but, because of his experience, he had insisted that his children not go to residential school.
11 Allan Blakeney, *An Honourable Calling: Political Memoirs* (Toronto: University of Toronto Press 2008), 217–18.
12 Ibid., 220.
13 RCAP, *Integrated Research Plan* (Ottawa: RCAP, July 1993), 2. The list of commissioned papers is in Appendix D, 59–64.
14 Ibid., 16. The other special study in the same category "is a set of life histories that will describe the experiences of Aboriginal individuals and families over the century." These studies never were published by the commission.

15 *Integrated Research Plan*, 27.

16 RCAP, *Looking Forward*, 236.

17 *Integrated Research Plan*, 27–8.

18 Ibid., 28. None of these projected volumes was published.

19 RCAP, *Public Hearings: Overview of the First Round* (Ottawa: RCAP Oct. 1992), 1, 62. The overviews of the public consultations and follow-up documents designed to report on the previous round and help shape presentations for future rounds were prepared for the commission by Ginger Group Consultants, which was headed by former Ontario New Democratic Party leader Michael Cassidy.

20 United Church of Canada Archives (UCA), series 2, 2003.166c Records of the General Secretary 1972, box 13-1 S64 1987–98, John Siebert to Stan McKay et al., 23 March 1993, re: Canim Lake Residential School Event, 8–9 March 1993, point 4.

21 Ibid.

22 University of Saskatchewan Archives, Royal Commission on Aboriginal Peoples hearing transcripts, Port Alberni, BC, 20 May 1992.

23 David MacDonald interview, Toronto, 18 Feb. 2009.

24 RCAP, *Public Hearings: Overview of the First Round*, 18–19. Ms Brooks was executive director of Anduhyuan, a shelter for Aboriginal women in Toronto, Ontario. Ibid., 19.

25 Ibid., 19–20.

26 RCAP, *Public Hearings: Overview of the Second Round* (Ottawa: RCAP 1993), 1.

27 RCAP, *Public Hearings. Discussion Paper 2: Focusing the Dialogue* (Ottawa: RCAP 1993), v. This discussion paper was intended to prompt those who participated in the next round to frame their presentations along particular lines.

28 RCAP, *Public Hearings: Overview of the Second Round*, 49.

29 Ibid., 50.

30 Ibid.

31 Library and Archives Canada (LAC), RG33, 1997–98 089, RCAP Fonds, vol. 124, file 6014–1, memorandum from Kim Scott, senior policy analyst, to Residential School Strategy Committee members, directors, 16 Nov. 1992, "re: Residential School Strategy."

32 Ibid.

33 NFB-RCAP, *No Turning Back*.

34 Ibid.

35 Denise G. Réaume and Patrick Macklem, "Education for Subordination: Redressing the Adverse Effects of Residential Schooling," unpublished paper for RCAP, June 1994. A copy of this paper was supplied to me by

John Siebert, who in 1994 was working on behalf of the United Church of Canada. J. Siebert to J.R. Miller, 18 Dec. 1996.

36 LAC, RG33 1997–98 089, vol. 175, files 7402–4.1, 7402–5.1, 7402–7.1 (vol. 1 and 2), and 7402-8.1.

37 Initially there was a third research assistant, but he did not last a month. Interview with John Milloy, Peterborough, ON, 25 Nov. 2015.

38 LAC, RG 33 1997–98 089, vol. 175, file 7402–2, "Residential School Study – Design," various dates in 1993. See in particular J.S. Milloy to Dara Culhane, 13 April 1993 and attachment. Milloy interview.

39 LAC, RG 33 1997–98 089, vol. 175, file 7402–2, "Residential School Study – Design," J.S. Milloy to Dara Culhane, 13 April 1993.

40 Milloy interview. Milloy recounted that he had been informed that Erasmus told the Indian Affairs minister that he would go to the prime minister if necessary to get the documents Milloy wanted.

41 RCAP, *Public Hearings. Exploring the Options: Overview of the Third Round* (Ottawa: RCAP 1993), co-chairs' preface, v.

42 Ibid., 1.

43 Ibid., 4.

44 Ibid., 2.

45 Ibid., 4.

46 Ibid., 10.

47 Ibid., 3.

48 RCAP, *Toward Reconciliation: Overview of the Fourth Round* (Ottawa: RCAP 1994), 1, 31 (ARC), and Appendix 1, "Special Consultation with the Historic Mission Churches," 83–9. Archbishop Exner's comments are 83–4.

49 Ibid., 37.

50 Ibid., 34–5.

51 Ibid., 37.

52 RCAP, *Choosing Life: Special Report on Suicide among Aboriginal People* (Ottawa: RCAP 1995) and *Treaty Making in the Spirit of Co-existence: An Alternative to Extinguishment* (Ottawa: RCAP 1995).

53 RCAP, *The Right of Aboriginal Self-Government and the Constitution: A Commentary* (Ottawa: RCAP 1992), preface.

54 Ibid., 13.

55 Ibid., 31.

56 Ibid., 34.

57 RCAP, *Partners in Confederation: Aboriginal Peoples, Self-Government, and the Constitution* (Ottawa: RCAP 1993); René Dussault, "Aboriginal Autonomy? It's Already Guaranteed," *Globe and Mail*, 7 Sept. 1993.

58 *Partners in Confederation*, 49.

59 UCA, Series 2, Records of the General Secretary 1972–, Acc. No. 2003,16c
box/file 13–2 S64, Residential Schools 1995–99, Brief to the Royal
Commission on Aboriginal Peoples by the United Church of Canada,
8–9 Nov. 1993,

60 RCAP, *Looking Forward*.

61 James Walker, quoted in J.R. Miller, "Bringing Native People in from the
Margins: The Recent Evolution and Future Prospects of English-Canadian
Historiography on Native-Newcomer Relations," *Reflections on Native-
Newcomer Relations: Selected Essays* (Toronto: University of Toronto Press
2004), 14. On historiography down to the 1970s, see 13–18.

62 G.F.G. Stanley, *The Birth of Western Canada*, 2nd ed. (Toronto: University of
Toronto Press 1961), 206.

63 John L. Tobias, "Canada's Subjugation of the Plains Cree, 1879–1885" and
"Protection, Civilization, Assimilation: An Outline History of Canada's
Indian Policy," in *Sweet Promises: A Reader on Indian-White Relations in
Canada*, ed. J.R. Miller (Toronto: University of Toronto Press 1991), 212–40
and 127–44. "Subjugation" was first published in the *Canadian Historical
Review* in 1983, and "Protection" in 1976 in an anthropology journal.

64 Brian Titley, *A Narrow Vision: Duncan Campbell Scott and the Administration
of Indian Affairs in Canada* (Vancouver: UBC Press 1986).

65 Olive P. Dickason, *Canada's First Nations: A History of Founding Peoples from
Earliest Times* (Toronto: McClelland & Stewart 1992); Miller, *Skyscrapers
Hide the Heavens*; and Arthur J. Ray. *I Have Lived Here since the World Began:
An Illustrated History of Canada's Native Peoples* (Toronto: Key Porter 1996).

66 RCAP, *Looking Forward*, 243–4.

67 *Looking Forward, Looking Back*, chap. 10, "Residential Schools," 333–409.
The recommendations appear on 385–6.

68 RCAP, *Report of the Royal Commission on Aboriginal Peoples*, vol. 2,
Restructuring the Relationship, part 1, 106.

69 Ibid., 166.

70 Ibid., 168.

71 Ibid., 167.

72 MacDonald interview.

3. The State Responds

1 United Church of Canada Archives (UCA), Series 2, Records of the General
Secretary 1972–, Acc No. 2003.16C, Box/File 12–15 W64 Aboriginal Rights
Coalition – Project North 1989–98, memo from John Siebert, co-chair of ARC,
to ARC executive, 28 March 1994 re meeting with Ron Irwin, 22 March 1994.

2 Ghislain Otis, "The Impact of the Royal Proclamation of 1763 on Quebec: Then and Now," in *Keeping Promises: The Royal Proclamation of 1763, Aboriginal Rights, and Treaties in Canada*, ed. Terry Fenge and Jim Aldridge (Montreal and Kingston: McGill-Queen's University Press 2015), 70–3.

3 RCAP, *Final Report of the Royal Commission on Aboriginal Peoples*, vol. 5, *Renewal* (Ottawa: RCAP 1996), 34–46; René Dussault, "Reconciliation: The Only Way Forward to Fair and Enduring Coexistence," in *Response, Responsibility, and Renewal: Canada's Truth and Reconciliation Journey*, ed. Gregory Younging, Jonathan Dewar, and Mike DeGagné (Ottawa: Aboriginal Healing Foundation 2009), 32. The "dead on arrival" comment came from Harry Swain, deputy minister of INAC 1987–92 in his *Oka: A Political Crisis and Its Legacy* (Vancouver and Toronto: Douglas & McIntyre 2010), 168–9.

4 Shawn Tupper interview, Ottawa, 9 June 2008.

5 CBC News, "Red Road Forward: What Happened at Gordon's," 26 Feb. 2010, http://www.cbc.ca/news/canada/saskatchewan/red-road -forward-what-happened-at-Gordon's? (accessed 5 June 2014).

6 Tupper interview, 9 June 2008. Tupper led the INAC unit working on the residential school portion of the government response to the RCAP final report from January 1997 to January 1998.

7 Scott Serson interview, Ottawa, 21 Jan. 2010. See also Scott Serson, "Reconciliation: For First Nations This Must Include Fiscal Fairness," in Younging et al., *Response, Responsibility, and Renewal*, 150–2.

8 Serson interview.

9 Government of Canada, *Gathering Strength: Canada's Aboriginal Action Plan* (Ottawa: INAC 1997), http://www.ahf.ca/downloads (accessed 6 June 2014), unpaginated. This account is also based on my viewing of the minister's statement on television on 7 January 1998.

10 *Gathering Strength*, emphasis in original.

11 Ibid.

12 Serson interview.

13 *Gathering Strength*. As of 2016, Manitoba is the only jurisdiction other than Saskatchewan to have a treaty commission. In Ontario, nothing has occurred, despite a recommendation in May 2007 of the Linden Commission Report on the death of Dudley George at Ipperwash Park in 1995 to create a treaty commission.

14 See http://www.collectionscanada.gc.ca/webarchives/20051228184255/ http://www.ainc-inac.gc.ca/gs/chg_e.html, quoted in Wayne Spear, *Full Circle: The Aboriginal Healing Foundation and the Unfinished Work of Hope, Healing and Reconciliation* (Ottawa: Aboriginal Healing Foundation 2014), 16.

15 University of Saskatchewan Archives (USA), transcripts of RCAP hearings, Phil Fontaine, Fort Garry Place, Winnipeg, 22 April 1992

16 See www.cbc.ca/gsa?q=Phil+Fontaine%2C+The Journal%2C+Oct.+1990 (accessed 3 Nov. 2014). See also Phil Fontaine, "A Preface," in Spear, *Full Circle*, xi-xii

17 USA, Transcripts of RCAP hearings, Charlie Cootes, Port Alberni, 20 May 1992. The allusion to payment for not building helicopters referred to the fact that the Chrétien-led Liberals had campaigned against the Mulroney government's decision to spend lavishly on new helicopters for the armed forces. Once elected in 1993, the Liberal government cancelled the order for helicopters and had to pay a large sum in compensation to the firm that was building them.

18 Phil Fontaine interview, Winnipeg, 20 March 2015.

19 Ibid.

20 *Vancouver Province*, 8 Jan. 1998, in UCA, Series 2, Records of the General Secretary 1971–, Acc. No. 2003.166C, Box 12-15 S64, Willie Blackwater to Brian Thorpe, 8 Jan. 1998.

21 Janet Bavelas, *An Analysis of Formal Apologies by Canadian Churches to First Nations*, Occasional Paper No. 1, Centre for Studies in Religion and Society, University of Victoria, web.uvic.ca/psyc/bavelas/2004ChurchApol (accessed 11 June 2014).

22 Tupper interview, 9 June 2008.

23 RCAP, *Report of the Royal Commission on Aboriginal Peoples*, vol. 1, Looking Forward, Looking Back (Ottawa: RCAP 1996), 385.

24 *Gathering Strength*, 5.

25 www.innovation.ca (accessed 13 April 2015).

26 Spear, *Full Circle*, 14.

27 The foundation's creation was dated 31 March 1998 to meet the requirement Treasury Board imposed of starting to use the $350 million allocated to it by the end of the 1997–8 fiscal year, but a public launch did not take place until early May.

28 Georges Erasmus, in Spear, *Full Circle*, 41; Fontaine interview.

29 Spear, *Full Circle*, 18–19.

30 Ibid., 19–24.

31 See www.nipissingu.ca/about-us/newsroom/Pages/Nipissing-installs -Dr.-Mike-Degn%C3% (accessed 5 Nov. 2014). See also Spear, *Full Circle*, 44–5.

32 Mike DeGagné interview, Ottawa, 28 May 2009.

33 Spear, *Full Circle*, 45.

34 DeGagné interview.

35 DeGagné interview; Spear, *Full Circle*, 43–59, the DeGagné quotation is at 45.
36 DeGagné interview.
37 www.ahf.ca (accessed 28 May 2013).
38 Spear, *Full Circle*, 36–9.
39 Tupper interview, 9 June 2008.
40 Remarks at an Aboriginal Healing Foundation book launch, University of British Columbia Aboriginal House of Learning, 11 Aug. 2014.
41 Gilbert Oskaboose, "The Aboriginal Healing Foundation: A Nest of Maggots," http://www.firstnations.com/oskaboose/nest-of-maggots.htm, (accessed 24 Nov. 2008).
42 Frances Widdowson, "The Aboriginal Healing Foundation boondoggle," *National Post*, 17 Dec. 2009, http://blogs.mtroyal.ca/fwiddowson/tag/aboriginal-healing-foundation (accessed 17 Oct. 2014). The currently posted version omits the phrase "the most significant non-aboriginal player," the author having deleted it after being corrected publicly.
43 *National Post*, 9 Jan. 2010.
44 Auditor General of Canada, *2005 February Status Report of the Auditor General of Canada*, chapter 4, "Accountability of Foundations," http://www.oag-bvg.ca/internet/docs/20050204ce.pdf, cited in Institute on Governance, *A Legacy of Excellence: Best Practices Board Study – Aboriginal Healing Foundation* (Ottawa: Institute on Governance 2009), 31.
45 IOG, *A Legacy of Excellence*, 13.
46 Ibid., 20, 25 (ethics); 17–18 (Aboriginal values). See also Mike DeGagné, "Administration in a National Aboriginal Organization: Impacts of Cultural Adaptations," *Canadian Public Administration* 51, no. 4 (Dec. 2008): 659–72.
47 IOG, *A Legacy of Excellence*, 17.
48 Ibid., 22–3, 25, 27, 33–4, and 37–8.
49 Maegan Hough, "Personal Recollections and Civic Responsibilities: Dispute Resolution and the Indian Residential Schools Legacy" (LLM thesis, University of Victoria, 2014), 103. I am grateful to Ms. Hough, who kindly provided me with a copy of her thesis.
50 IOG, *A Legacy of Excellence*, 8–10.
51 DeGagné interview.
52 IOG, *A Legacy of Excellence*, 9.
53 DeGagné interview.
54 IOG, *A Legacy of Excellence*, 29.
55 A useful list of many of the AHF publications to 2010 can be found at http://archives.algomau.ca/main/node20177 (accessed 16 Dec. 2014). See also Hough, "Personal Recollections," 103.
56 DeGagné interview.

57 http:archives.algomau.ca/main/node20177 (accessed 16 Dec. 2014).

58 Amy Bombay, *Origins of Lateral Violence in Aboriginal Communities: A Preliminary Study of Student-to-Student Abuse in Residential Schools* (Ottawa: Aboriginal Healing Foundation 2014).

59 Remarks at Aboriginal Healing Book Launch, UBC, 11 Aug. 2014. DeGagné had said on other occasions that Angeconeb was highly influential in the work of the AHF (personal observation).

60 All three were published by the Aboriginal Healing Foundation, Ottawa. Respectively, they were edited by Marlene Brant Castellano, Linda Archibald, and Mike DeGagné; Gregory Younging, Jonathan Dewar, and Mike DeGagné; and Ashok Mathur, Jonathan Dewar, and Mike Degagné.

61 Shelagh Rogers, Mike DeGagné, Jonathan Dewar, and Glen Lowry, eds. *Speaking My Truth: Reflections on Reconciliation and Residential School*, "Book Club edition" (Ottawa: Aboriginal Healing Foundation 2012).

62 Shelagh Rogers interview, Gabriola Island, BC, 22 April 2014.

63 Conversation with Mike DeGagné, Ottawa, 2 Nov. 2012.

64 Rogers interview.

65 Mike DeGagné, remarks at AHF book launch, UBC, 11 Aug. 2014.

66 The origins, evolution, and contributions of the LHF are explained well in Spear, *Full Circle*, 163–71.

67 Trina Cooper-Bolam interview, Ottawa, 27 Aug. 2015. Cooper-Bolam was a long-serving member of the LHF staff, acting for a considerable period as its executive director.

68 Although some of the LHF's materials are out of print, all are downloadable from the foundation's website, www.legacyofhope.ca (accessed 19 Dec. 2014).

69 Cooper-Bolam interview.

70 Mike DeGagné, remarks at AHF book launch.

4. The Bench Adjudicates

1 This quotation comes from a summary of comments at an "exploratory dialogue" among survivors, churches, and government at Kamloops, BC, 29–30 September 1998, in Canada, *Reconciliation and Healing: Alternative Resolution Strategies for Dealing with Residential School Claims* (Ottawa: Minister of Indian Affairs and Northern Development 2000), 67. I am grateful to Doug Ewart, a participant at the exploratory dialogues and the principal compiler of the summary of statements, for providing me with a copy of this volume. See also Glenn Sigurdson, *Vikings on a Prairie Ocean* (Winnipeg: Great Plains Publications 2014),

290–3. I am grateful to Mr Sigurdson for bringing this valuable volume to my attention.

2 David Russell interview, Vancouver, 19 May 2010. Russell was in the Vancouver Office of Indian Affairs. The person in Ottawa he telephoned about sponsoring a ceremony was Shawn Tupper.

3 Canada, *Reconciliation and Healing*, 4, 41, and 44.

4 Both these quotations come from a summary of comments at the exploratory dialogue at Kamloops, 29–30 September 1998, in Canada, *Reconciliation and Healing*, 6, 18. Concerning the comment on the painful nature of legal proceedings, see ibid., 18. On the other hand, a minority opinion among survivors was that resorting to litigation, in spite of its difficulty and pain, was "a source of pride and a sense of empowerment. Used to being on the opposite end of the justice system [they] now are in charge of actions against the Crown." Ibid., 32. See also Ted Hughes interview, Victoria, 3 June 2013, in which he spoke of a former Kuper Island school student who was profoundly grateful that he had been heard and compensated, and who wrote to let Hughes know of his gratitude: [name withheld] to Hughes, 8 April 2008. Copy provided by Mr Hughes. For an excellent explanation of why Canadian tort law was incapable of providing justice to survivors who had suffered abuse, see Bruce Feldthusen, "Civil Liability for Sexual Assault in Aboriginal Residential Schools: The Baker Did It," *Canadian Journal of Law and Society* 22, no. 1 (2007), esp. 61, 79, and 87–90.

5 When I attended meetings between the Office of the Treaty Commissioner for Saskatchewan and community leaders and Elders at Fort Qu'Appelle in September 1997, I heard a number of Elders describe the devastation caused by the compensation money that arrived after Starr's conviction. The federal government had compensated victims because when Starr was at the Gordon school it was administered by the government.

6 Canada, *Reconciliation and Healing*, 59; interview with George M. Thomson, Ottawa, 20 Jan. 2010. Mr Thomson had been deputy minister of justice, 1994–8, and then special advisor to the minister of justice for about eighteen months.

7 Thomson interview.

8 Thomson interview; Canada, *Reconciliation and Healing*, 86.

9 This account is based on the Thomson and Ewart interviews, as well as *Reconciliation and Healing*. Doug Ewart interview, Toronto, 19 Feb. 2009. Ewart was an adviser to the federal deputy minister of justice during this period.

10 Sigurdson, *Vikings*, 290–3.

11 Doug Ewart noted how critically important Chief Robert Joseph and Maggie Hodgson were to the success of the dialogues; Ewart interview.

12 Ibid.; David Iverson interview, Kingston, 19 March 2010.

13 Canada, *Reconciliation and Healing*, 84. This account of the dialogues is based on the Ewart and Thomson interviews, and on *Reconciliation and Healing*.

14 Sigurdson, *Vikings*, 293; Sigurdson interview.

15 Maggie Hodgson interview, Dead Man's Flats, AB, 10 March 2015.

16 Chief Robert Joseph interview, North Vancouver, 12 Aug. 2015.

17 Canada, *Reconciliation and Healing*, 29.

18 Ibid., 92; also, 95: "There is a lack of trust and bargaining in good faith, especially by the churches, which continue to use words such as 'frivolous' in disputing claims and rely on limitation periods and are lobbying politicians for changes to limitations acts."

19 Ewart interview; Presbyterian Church in Canada Archives (PCA), 2003-1086-1-2, Exploratory Dialogues, 1998–9, "A Report on the Victim/Witness Support Service of a Multiple Child Sexual Abuse Court Trial in Inuvik, Northwest Territories, August 1998" (n.p.), 16 Oct. 1998.

20 Canada, *Reconciliation and Healing*, 17, 31.

21 Ewart interview; Canada, *Reconciliation and Healing*, 11.

22 Canada, *Reconciliation and Healing*, 94.

23 Ibid., 19.

24 Ibid., 34.

25 Ibid., 76.

26 Ibid., 105.

27 Ibid., 14, 28.

28 Ibid., 22.

29 Ibid., 37.

30 Ibid., 91.

31 Ibid., 100, 101. The speaker was referring to pilot ADR projects, which were expected to be developed following the dialogues.

32 Ibid., 101, 92.

33 Ibid., 93.

34 Ewart interview; Canada, *Reconciliation and Healing*, 69.

35 Canada, *Reconciliation and Healing*, 100, 102.

36 PCA, 2003-1-86-1-2, Ecumenical Working Group on Residential Schools [EWGRS], Aug.–Dec. 1999, Rev. Ian Morrison's notes of meeting of 20 Dec. 1999; ibid., 2007-1067-1-5, EWGRS, 2004, Daniel B. Konkin to file 2424.010, 20 June 2004, reporting meeting with Mario Dion, Shawn Tupper, Chief Adjudicator Ted Hughes et al., 10 June 2004. The latter report indicated

that ten pilot projects had been initiated, but only eight were still active in June 2004.

37 Canada, *Reconciliation and Healing*, 106–14.

38 Ibid., 98. See also Stephen Kendall interview, Toronto, 27 Feb. 2015.

39 Thomson interview; Tupper interview; Ewart interview. In an interview in Toronto on 18 Feb. 2009, former member of Parliament and United Church minister David MacDonald reported a conversation around 1998–2000 with an official in the federal Office of the Interlocutur for Métis and Non-Status Indians that revealed the bureaucrat completely misunderstood the United Church's financial position.

40 PCA, file 2011-1016-1-2, Church-Canada meetings 2001–2003, Bud Smith, Chancellor of Diocese of Cariboo, to Jim Boyles, 14 Nov. 2001. Smith was responding to a government press release, 29 Oct. 2001, "Federal Government Takes Steps to Speed Up Resolution of Abuse Claims at Indian Residential Schools." Ellie Johnson interview, Oakville, ON, 20 Feb. 2009, emphasized the anxiety that Anglican workers at Church House felt because of the financial situation.

41 *Anglican Journal*, June 2000, www.anglicanjournal.com (accessed 9 March 2015).

42 *Saskatoon StarPhoenix*, 25 Feb., 2000. The doctor had left US$14 million to relatives when he died in 1954. When all the recipients had passed away in turn over the next forty-five years, the United Church was the residual legatee of the remainder of the estate.

43 PCA, 2003-1086-1-3, EWGRS, 2000, memo from Roman Catholic representative Gerry Kelly, 27 April 2000, concerning meeting with Pelletier.

44 Ewart interview. Dr Stagg was the second and longest serving deputy minister of IRSRC.

45 According to Catholic representative Peter D. Lauwers: PCA, file 2011-1016-1-2, Peter D. Lauwers to Catholic Task Group, 5 Dec. 2001.

46 J.R. Miller, "The Alberni Residential School Case: Blackwater v Plint," *Indigenous Law Bulletin* [Australia] 5, no. 2 (2001): 20–1. See also http://www.courts.govbc.ca/jdb-txt/SC/01/09/2001BCSC0997.htm (accessed 13 Aug. 2001).

47 Herb Gray to editor, *Anglican Journal*, Oct. 2001, www.anglicanjournal.com/archives (accessed 30 Jan. 2015).

48 PCA, file 2011-1016-1-1, (copy) Marlene Catterall to Rev. James T. Hurd, 3 Dec. 2001.

49 Ibid., notes from meeting with Tony Macerollo, 11 March 2002.

50 PCA, 2011-1016-1-3, Archbishop Michael Peers to Herb Gray, 10 Sept. 2001. The primate is the top representative of the Anglican Church, akin to the position of moderator in the Presbyterian or United Church.

51 A twenty-nine-page report (twenty pages of analysis; nine of the polling instrument) is found under a cover memo from the Office of Indian Residential Schools Resolution Canada to Anglican Archdeacon Jim Boyles, 7 Sept. 2001, in PCA, file 2011-1016-1-3.

52 PCA, file 2011-1016-1-3, notes of ecumenical group's caucus, 11 Sept. 2001.

53 Interview with Jim Boyles, Toronto, 25 Feb. 2015. Boyles was general secretary, the highest appointed official, of the Anglican Church.

54 Ewart interview.

55 Interview with Bill Phipps, Calgary, 20 April 2010. Phipps, a former lawyer, was moderator in 1997–2000.

56 Interview with David Iverson, Kingston, ON, 9 March 2010.

57 The complicated story of the St Andrew's congregation's activities from 1995 to 1998 is thoroughly covered in Julianne Kasmer, "The Quest for Hope and Healing: A History of the Residential School Apology from St. Andrew's United Church in Port Alberni, BC, May 6, 1997" (unpublished research paper, ThM degree program, Vancouver School of Theology, 2007). I am most grateful to Ms. Kasmer for providing me with a copy of her paper and to Brian Thorpe for telling me of its existence.

58 Email from Smith to Julianne Kasmer, 26 Oct. 2006, in Kasmer, "The Quest for Hope," 29.

59 Kasmer, "The Quest for Hope," 44–8.

60 Phillip Spencer and Foster Freed, column in *PQ [Parksville-Qualicum] News*, n.d., in ibid., 84.

61 Phipps interview; UCA, accession 2003, 164C JGER Richard Chambers Files – Native Ministries, box 7-14, circular letter from Moderator to "Dear Friends," 10 Nov. 1998.

62 UCA, accession 2002, 046C, box 6, file 9, "Ki-ke-win aka Ron Hamilton," to Bill Phipps, 6 Nov. 1998.

63 Interview with Rev. Brian Thorpe, Vancouver, 18 May 2010.

64 Interview with John Siebert, Kitchener, ON, 7 July 2009.

65 Thorpe interview.

66 Siebert interview.

67 Phipps interview.

68 Brian Thorpe, "A Loss of Innocence: The United Church Coming to Terms with the Legacy of the Residential Schools," *Ecumenism*, no. 155 (Sept. 2004), 21. I am grateful to Brian Thorpe for supplying me with a copy of this article. If anything, the tension was worse in Prince Rupert, where the second stage of the trial took place in 1999, than it was earlier in Nanaimo. Thorpe interview.

69 Phipps interview.

70 Sinclair interview.
71 Thorpe interview.
72 UCA, accession 2002, 046C, box 6, file 9, Port Alberni Appeal 1998–9,
    David S. Hooper to Bill Phipps, 7 Sept. 1998. Hooper, who was chair of the
    board of St Andrew's Church in Port Alberni, said that he had attended
    the feast and apology in May 1997: "Since that time, there has been
    disappointment, confusion, even anger, due to events beyond our control –
    Trial in Nanaimo, Appeal, the national church's position."
73 Miller, "Alberni Residential School Case."
74 Ewart interview.
75 Ibid.; Shawn Tupper interview, Ottawa, 9 Sept. 2008; Fred Kaufman,
    "Searching for Justice: An Independent Review of Nova Scotia's Response
    to Reports of Institutional Abuse," Jan. 2002, www.gov.ns.ca/just
    (accessed 21 April 2015). See also Fred Kaufman, *Searching for Justice: An
    Autobiography* (Toronto: University of Toronto Press and the Osgoode
    Society for Canadian Legal History 2005), 281–7.
76 Ewart interview.
77 This account is based on the following sources: Paulette Regan, "An
    Apology Feast in Hazelton: A Settler's Unsettling Experience," chap. 8
    of *Unsettling the Settler Within: Indian Residential Schools, Truth Telling,
    and Reconciliation in Canada* (Vancouver: UBC Press 2010); Truth and
    Reconciliation Commission [TRC], *Final Report*, vol. 6, *Canada's Residential
    Schools: Reconciliation* (Montreal and Kingston: McGill-Queen's University
    Press and TRC, 2015), 73–4; Keith Howard, "No More to Wander," and
    David Wilson, "Serving Justice outside the Courts," both in *Observer*,
    June 2004, 20–4 and 24–5; Shawn Tupper interview, 9 Sept. 2008, and text
    of government of Canada apology provided by Tupper; Brian Thorpe
    interview; and the following materials provided by Brian Thorpe: memo
    from Brian Thorpe, "Inviting the Chiefs: Apology Feast to the Gitxsan";
    memo Brian Thorpe to Residential Schools Steering Committee, "Hazelton
    ADR"; Brian Thorpe, "Transformation in the Encounter: Reflections on
    a Dispute Resolution Process," *Touchstone* 24, no. 2 (1 May 2006): 17–25;
    email message from Brian Thorpe to Jamie Scott, David MacDonald,
    Cynthia Gunn, Jim Sinclair, and Lynn Mdaki, 7 Sept. 2004 re "Continuing
    Our Healing Journey – Edmonton." I have chosen not to refer to the
    Hazelton feast as a potlatch because its proceedings deviated too much
    from those of a potlatch and because the hosts were non-Natives.
78 Brian Thorpe, "Inviting the Chiefs: Apology Feast to the Gitxsan"
    (unpublished memo). This item was kindly provided by Mr Thorpe.
79 Ibid.

80 Regan, *Unsettling the Settler*, 196.
81 Howard, "No More to Wander," 23.
82 Email from Brian Thorpe to Jamie Scott, David MacDonald, Cynthia Gunn, Jim Sinclair, and Lynn Mdaki, 7 Sept. 2004.
83 Akivah Starkman, *The Independent Assessment Process: Reflections* (n.p.: Author 2014), 25. I am grateful to Dr Starkman, who provided me with a copy of his informative report.
84 Ewart interview.
85 Interview with Jamie Scott, Ottawa, 11 Sept. 2010.
86 Hughes interview.
87 "Dispute Resolution Model for Indian Residential School Abuse Claims," part of a Form Filler Toolkit DVD provided by David Russell of Aboriginal Affairs, Vancouver, 19 Aug. 2010. As well, see summary of an interview with David Russell, Vancouver, 19 May 2010. I am grateful to David Russell for his assistance. Ewart interview.
88 Hughes interview.
89 Starkman, *Independent Assessment Process*, 28.
90 Ewart interview. See also "Ottawa Launches Dispute Settlement Program," *Globe and Mail*, 7 Nov. 2003, in which complaints about the lack of redress for loss of culture and language were expressed, and federal minister Ralph Goodale pointed out that Canadian courts had never awarded damages for such losses.
91 Scott interview.
92 Russell interview; Hodgson interview.
93 PCA, 2007-1067-1-6 EWGRS 2005, email, Mario Dion to Aboriginal Working Caucus members and church representatives, 13 May 2005.
94 Ewart and Thomson interviews; Shawn Tupper, "Alternative Resolution System Humane Way to Settle Claims," *Saskatoon StarPhoenix*, 4 March 2005. Tupper was responding to a column critical of DR by regular First Nations columnist Doug Cuthand, ibid., 18 Feb. 2005.
95 "Statement of Reconciliation – Learning from the Past," part of the Form Filler Toolkit.

5. The Parties Negotiate

1 Kathleen Mahoney interview, Calgary, 14 May 2009. Dr Mahoney had notified the chair of the meeting, former Supreme Court justice Frank Iacobucci, about what they were going to do.
2 Doug Ewart interview, Toronto, 19 Feb. 2009.
3 David Russell interview, Vancouver, 19 May 2010; Form Filler Toolkit supplied by David Russell.

4 Presbyterian Church in Canada Archives (PCA), 2007-1067-5-4, Aboriginal Healing Foundation, transcription of column, 6 March 2004, p. 7.

5 Ewart interview.

6 Dan Ish interview, Saskatoon, 10 June 2013.

7 PCA, 2011-1016-1-14, Ecumenical Working Group on Residential Schools (EWGRS), 2003-4, National Chief, Assembly of First Nations, Phil Fontaine to Mario Dion, 3 Oct. 2003.

8 Ibid., and Dion to Fontaine, 22 Oct. 2003.

9 "Feds Appeal $1,500 Residential Award to Elderly Women," *Saskatoon StarPhoenix*, 14 Sept. 2008.

10 PCA, 2007-1067-1-6, EWGRS, 2005, e-mail Ian Morrison to Working Group, 16 March 2005.

11 House of Commons Standing Committee on Aboriginal Affairs and Northern Development, Standing Committee, "Study," Evidence, 15 Feb. 2005, cited in Paulette Regan, *Unsettling the Settler Within: Indian Residential Schools, Truth Telling, and Reconciliation* (Vancouver: UBC Press 2010), 128–31 and 262nn38, 39. Adjudicator's awards could be appealed if they compensated actions that fell outside those specified in the DR procedure. Interview with Mario Dion, Ottawa, 2 Nov. 2012.

12 Jim Sinclair interview, North Bay, 10 June 2013.

13 Interviews with two experienced adjudicators under the DR program whose names are withheld at their request. The incident in which a claimant insisted there was nothing more to tell was described by Ish in his interview.

14 Canada, *Reconciliation and Healing: Alternative Resolution Strategies for Dealing with Residential School Claims* (Ottawa: Indian Affairs and Northern Development 2000), 107–13

15 Kathleen Mahoney, "Whither Reconciliation?" paper presented to the University of Toronto Law School Conference Assessing the Indian Residential Schools Litigation and Settlement Processes, 17–18 Jan. 2013. I am grateful to Dr Mahoney for providing me with a copy of her presentation.

16 Meagan Hough, "Personal Recollections and Civic Responsibilities: Dispute Resolution and the Indian Residential Schools Legacy" (LLM thesis, University of Victoria, 2014), 110.

17 Mahoney, "Whither Reconciliation?"

18 Ibid.

19 Dion interview.

20 Ibid.

21 Mahoney, "Whither Reconciliation?" Dr Mahoney noted that she drafted the report with the assistance of some of her students, Mahoney to J.R. Miller, 6 Feb. 2015.

22 Assembly of First Nations, "Report on Canada's Dispute Resolution Plan to Compensate for Abuses in Indian Residential Schools" (n.p. 2004), 13. I am grateful to Dr Mahoney for providing a digital copy of the report.

23 Ibid., 14.

24 Ibid., 18–19 and 3. The reference to compensation for language and culture loss appears in the executive summary, 3.

25 Ibid., 36.

26 Dion interview.

27 Ibid.

28 Mahoney, "Whither Reconciliation?"

29 Daphne A. Dukelow, ed., *The Dictionary of Canadian Law*, 4th ed. (Toronto: Carswell 2011), 202. The residential schools abuse class actions were representative class actions, in which the action is brought by "persons asserting a common right, and even where those persons may have been wronged in their individual capacity." The other type of class action is a derivative class action, in which an entity to which a number of claimants belong suffers damage.

30 "Supreme Court Clears Way for Schools Class Action," *Saskatoon StarPhoenix*, 13 May 2005.

31 Andy Scott interview, Fredericton, 1 Nov. 2012. The dismissal of the funding of the accord as written on the back of a napkin came from Inky Mark, a Manitoba Conservative MP.

32 Andy Scott interview.

33 Dion interview. Dion noted that McLellan had attended the reception following the signing on 30 May 2005 with pleasure and had stayed for two hours. He said that he thought that if he could convince McLellan to adopt a new approach, the government would be able to convince voters that it was necessary and appropriate.

34 Phil Fontaine interview, Winnipeg, 20 March 2015.

35 Ewart interview.

36 Thomson interview. In his interview, Ewart also complained that the costs of developing DR were considered, rather than just the cost of running it. "The process takes too long and its administration costs are disproportionately high in comparison with the amount of awards paid out" (AFN, "Report on Canada's Dispute Resolution Plan," 2), and "the current caseload is estimated to take another 53 years to conclude at a cost of $2.3 billion in 2002 dollars, *not* including the value of the actual settlement costs" (ibid., 6). Also on these points, Dion interview.

37 Shawn Tupper interview, Ottawa, 13 Nov. 2008.

38 www.torys.com/en/people/iacobucci-the-honourable-frank (accessed
    10 Feb. 2015).
39 In his interview, Mario Dion referred to sixty-five lawyers at the talks.
    Kathleen Mahoney referred to eighty lawyers being involved in her
    summary of events in 2013 in "Whither Reconciliation?"
40 Dion interview.
41 Chief Robert Joseph interview, North Vancouver 12 Aug. 2015.
42 Ewart interview.
43 Dion interview.
44 Andy Scott interview.
45 Ewart interview.
46 Thomson interview.
47 Interview with Pierre Baribeau, Montreal, 28 Nov. 2011.
48 Jamie Scott interview, Ottawa, 11 Sept. 2010.
49 According to Jamie Scott, he and others brought survivors into the talks
    at the second table. He supplemented information in his interview by an
    email: Jamie Scott to Jim Miller, 19 Aug. 2016.
50 Mahoney interview; Mahoney, "Whither Reconciliation?"; and
    Lucianna Ciccocioppo, "Conference Took Stock of Canada's Indian
    Residential Schools Settlement Agreement," University of Toronto
    Faculty of Law website, www.law.utoronto.ca (accessed 21 Feb. 2013).
    In her interview, Professor Mahoney stressed the importance of advice
    from people involved in the Irish industrial schools inquiry and
    settlement to avoid legalism wherever possible. At the University of
    Toronto Law School conference in 2013 she was quoted as saying that
    the decision not to seek subpoena powers for the TRC "was based
    on the counsel of Aboriginal advisers because the survivors were not
    interested 'in an adversarial approach,' which subsequently led to the
    disintegration" of South Africa's Truth and Reconciliation Commission
    in the 1990s.
51 Email, Jamie Scott to Jim Miller, 19 Aug. 2016.
52 Dion interview.
53 Ciccocioppo, "Conference Took Stock."
54 Fontaine interview.
55 Baribeau interview. Baribeau was the chief negotiator for the Catholic
    entities.
56 Warren K. Winkler, "Access to Justice: Personal Reflections," Silas E. Halyk,
    Q.C. Visiting Scholar in Advocacy Lecture, College of Law, University of
    Saskatchewan, 18 Jan. 2016, personal observation.
57 Baribeau interview.

58 PCA, 2011–1016–2-3, EWGRS, 2007, Alexander Pless, IRSRC, to Alexander D. Petingill and John S. Page, n.d.

59 IRSSA, s 4.06 (f), /http://www.residentialschoolsettlement.ca/English .html (accessed 13 Feb. 2015).

60 Akivah Starkman, *The Independent Assessment Process: Reflections* (n.p.: Author 2014), 102.

61 IRSSA, s. 4, "Implementation of This Agreement."

62 Ibid., preamble, items E, F.

63 David MacDonald interview, Toronto, 18 Feb. 2009. MacDonald, a United Church minister and former member of Parliament, acted as the church's Ottawa lobbyist on residential school matters.

64 IRSSA, ss. 3.02–3.06.

65 Dion interview.

66 IRSSA, ss.5.01 and 5.02.

67 Ibid., ss. 5.04–5.09; also Schedule L.

68 I was corrected publicly by Chief Fontaine at a training session for new adjudicators under the Independent Assessment Process in Calgary in November 2009 when I said during my presentation that language and culture loss were not compensated by the settlement agreement. A senior INAC official who was close to the residential school file agreed with Fontaine that the Common Experience Payment was meant in part to compensate for cultural loss. Shawn Tupper interview, Ottawa, 9 June 2008.

69 Ewart interview. Former deputy minister Mario Dion referred to Ewart as "the scientist" who designed the IAP. Dion interview.

70 IRSSA, s. 6, and Schedule D, Independent Assessment Process.

71 Kathleen Keating interview, Vancouver, 8 July 2015.

72 IRSSA, Schedule D.

73 Ibid., Schedule N, ss. 153–4, and Schedule N, Mandate of the Truth and Reconciliation Commission, ss. 11–12.

74 Ibid., 53–4 and Schedule N s. 2(l).

75 Ibid., Schedule N, s. 3(g) 68–9.

76 Ibid., Schedules E and F.

6. Implementing the Indian Residential Schools Settlement Agreement

1 Indian Residential Schools Settlement Agreement (IRSSA), s. 3, www .residential schoolsettlement.ca (accessed 24 March 2015).

2 Andrew Wesley interview, Toronto, 21 Nov. 2013.

3 IRSSA, Schedule O-3 and Schedule B.

4 Wayne Spear, *Full Circle: The Aboriginal Healing Foundation and the Unfinished Work of Hope, Healing and Reconciliation* (Ottawa: Aboriginal Healing Foundation 2014), 212–13. The complex story of Schedule O-3 and the Catholic entities' dealings with the AHF and government is on 209–16.

5 Ibid., 214–15.

6 Ibid., 214.

7 Ibid., 216.

8 Ibid., 214–16.

9 "Legal Misstep Lets Catholic Church Off Hook for Residential Schools Compensation," *Globe and Mail*, 17 April 2016, www.globeandmail.com (accessed 18 April 2016).

10 *Fontaine v. Saskatchewan (Attorney General)*, 2015 SKQB 220 16 July 2015. I would like to thank Greg Wurzer of the University of Saskatchewan Law Library for helping me obtain a copy of this ruling.

11 "Ottawa Killed Appeal of Settlement Ruling," *Globe and Mail*, 21 April 2016.

12 Nora Saunders, general secretary, United Church of Canada, to editor, *Globe and Mail*, 30 April 2016; and Colin R. Johnson, Archbishop of Toronto, Anglican Church of Canada, to editor, *Globe and Mail*, 4 May 2016.

13 Gerry Kelly interview, Ottawa, 9 Sept. 2010.

14 *Reconciliation and Healing: Alternative Resolution Strategies for Dealing with Residential School Claims* (Ottawa: Indian and Northern Affairs Canada 2000), 22.

15 Ibid., 37.

16 Ibid., 100.

17 Phil Fontaine interview, Winnipeg, 20 March 2015.

18 IRSSA, Schedule J, Commemoration Policy Directive.

19 Trina Cooper-Bolam interview, Ottawa, 27 Aug. 2015.

20 "Commemoration," Aboriginal Affairs and Northern Development website, www.aadnc-aandc.gc.ca/eng/ 1370974213551/1370974338097#nat (accessed 24 March 2015).

21 This account has benefited from Trina Cooper-Bolam's "Healing Heritage: New Approaches on Commemorating Canada's Indian Residential School System" (MA thesis, Carleton University 2014) and an interview with Trina Cooper-Bolam, Ottawa, 27 Aug. 2015. Cooper-Bolam notes (p. 105) that 45 per cent of projects had a healing component. I am grateful to Ms Cooper-Bolam for providing me with a copy of her thesis.

22 "Spotlight: The Royal Winnipeg Ballet," *Globe and Mail*, 1 Oct. 2014, www.rwb.org/who-weare/history/ (accessed 26 March 2014). Between 21 and 30 March 2016, the ballet was performed in Brandon, Regina, Saskatoon, and Kelowna. Program for *Going Home Star: Truth and Reconciliation*, Saskatoon, 23 March 2016.

23 Marsha Lederman, "Art Installation Will Let Canadians Bear Witness to Dark Era of Residential Schools," *Globe and Mail*, 10 Sept. 2014, www.theglobeandmail.com (accessed 11 Sept. 2014).

24 Ibid., and related articles Marsha Lederman, "A Monument to Both Tragedy and Healing," *Globe and Mail*, 17 May 2014, and "Symbolic Meaning," *Canada's History* (April–May 2016), 16–17.

25 Personal observation of Witness Blanket, University of Regina, 19 Feb. 2015. Many of the comments in the visitors' book were highly emotional. See also Marsha Lederman, "Artist Creates Epic Monument to Canada's Residential Schools," *Globe and Mail*, 17 May 2014.

26 I had a limited role in advising on the project early in its development. Email, Sylvia Smith to J.R. Miller, 5 Jan. 2008, enclosing proposal; Miller to Smith, 6 Jan. 2008; and Smith to Miller 6 Jan. 2008 (emails in author's possession).

27 Aboriginal Affairs and Northern Development Canada release, www.aadnc-aandc.gc.ca/eng/1332859355145/1332859433503, and transcript of AANDC video of remarks by minister John Duncan, "Future Location of Stained Glass Artwork," www.aadnc-aandc.gc.ca/eng/1320333022635/1320333157758 (both accessed 24 March 2015).

28 *Reconciliation and Healing*, 7.

29 Ibid., 43.

30 Information on the Common Experience Payment program is found at 22–3 and 43–9 of the settlement agreement and in Schedule I (Trust Agreement) of the Settlement Agreement.

31 Common Experience Payment, www.aadnc-aandc.gc.ca/eng/11000100015594/100100015 (accessed 27 April 2015).

32 Settlement Agreement, s. 5, entitled "Common Experience Payment," 43–9.

33 Madeleine Dion Stout and Rick Harp, *Lump Sum Compensation Payments Research Project: The Circle Rechecks Itself* (Ottawa: Aboriginal Healing Foundation 2007), xi.

34 Justice Murray Sinclair interview, Winnipeg, 30 March 2015.

35 Ibid.

36 Aboriginal Affairs and Northern Development Canada, "Statistics on the Implementation of the Indian Residential Schools Settlement Agreement," http://www.aadnc-aandc.gc.ca/eng/1315320539682/1315320692192 (accessed 27 July 2016). At the time of writing, the latest statistics available on the site were to 31 March 2016. The site also indicated that there were then five applications in progress at the initial stage, and seventeen more at the NAC appeal stage.

37 Employment and Social Development, "Evaluation: Delivery of the Common Experience Payment," http://www.esdc.gc.ca/eng/publications/evaluations/service_canada (accessed 27 March 2015). Caroline Davis interview, Kingston, ON, 19 March 2010. Ms Davis, who oversaw the financial aspects of the settlement agreement for the government, conceded later that "we were swamped." She got more help in to deal with the backlog, but the process was still slow.

38 "Common Experience Payment" instructions and application form, http://www.servicecanada.gc.ca/eforms/forms/gc-mp5419(2012-0! (accessed 27 March 2015)

39 Indian Residential Schools Resolution Canada, "Common Experience Payment Process and Validation," 20 June 2007, 8. The copy I used was obtained from the Shingwauk Project Archive at Algoma University. I would like to thank the hard-working people in charge of the Shingwauk Project, Ed Sadowski, Don Jackson, and Krista McCracken for assistance in this and many other matters.

40 Ibid., 10.

41 Aboriginal Healing Foundation, transcripts of interviews, transcript A8-404. I would like to thank Jonathan Dewar, then research director at the AHF, for facilitating my research in the anonymized transcripts of the interviews for the AHF's analysis of lump-sum payment compensation programs.

42 Ibid., A5-103. This informant was seventy-two.

43 Ibid., A4-108. See also T6-802, a twenty-four-year-old First Nation woman.

44 Ibid., T6-203. This man, though he was compensated for fewer years of attendance than he thought he was entitled to, nonetheless considered the CEP "a positive, I bought a car and my wife takes it to work, so I think it was alright."

45 Ibid., A-905.

46 Ibid., T6-208.

47 Ibid., A-907.

48 Ibid., T5-104.

49 Susie Jones interview, Wallaceburg, ON, 17 Oct. 2011.

50 AHF transcripts, A5-105.

51 Ibid., S4-501.

52 Ibid., S4-501.

53 Ibid., A5-106.

54 Ibid., A4-03.

55 Ibid., A4-09.

56 Ibid., A2-202. This informant was fifty years of age.
57 Ibid., S4-508.
58 Ibid., T6-819.
59 Ibid., T6-809.
60 Ibid., A-906.
61 Ibid., S6-831.
62 Ibid., S4-509.
63 Ibid., A4-03 (the same woman who said "Fuck you!" to the Health Canada help line woman).
64 Ibid., T6-810.
65 Ibid., A4-11.
66 Ibid., T6-826.
67 Ibid., T3-513.
68 *Saskatoon StarPhoenix*, 19 Dec. 2012 (reprint of a *Winnipeg Free Press* story).
69 AHF transcripts, T6-821.
70 Ibid., A4-14.
71 Ibid., T6-803.
72 Ibid., A4-516.
73 Ibid., S4-626.
74 Ibid., S4-510.
75 Ibid., A4-09.
76 Ibid., A8-401.
77 Ibid., T12-304.
78 Ibid.A-903.
79 Ibid., T12-306.
80 IRSSA, Schedule D, Part III (o) "Privacy," ii. See also Akivah Starkman, *Independent Assessment Process: Reflections* (n.p.: Author 2014), 118.
81 Doug Ewart interview, Toronto, 19 Feb. 2009; Dion interview, Ottawa, 2 Nov. 2012. Mario Dion, deputy minister of Indian Residential Schools Residential Canada, was a strong advocate of a comprehensive settlement of all issues associated with residential schools.
82 Starkman, *Independent Assessment Process*, 29–30, 71n106, and 80; IRSSA, Schedule D, Part III, Assessment Process Outline.
83 IRSSA, Schedule D, Part II (Compensation Rules) (charts), pp. 3–6, and Part III (e) (Procedure [adjudicator powers]).
84 Adjudication Secretariat Statistics, from 19 Sept. 2007 to 31 Jan. 2016, http://iap-pei.ca/information/stats-eng.php (accessed 16 March 2016).
85 IRSSA, Schedule D, Part III: (c) (Safety and Support); (i) (Solemnity); (j) (Setting).

86 Starkman, *Independent Assessment Process*, 25. Chief Adjudicator Dan Ish also observed that adopting a plausible link as the test cut down on the length of hearings and length of transcripts. Dan Ish interview, Saskatoon, 10 June 2013.

87 IRSSA, Schedule D, Part III (r) (IAP Oversight Committee).

88 *Globe and Mail*, 26 and 29 Feb. 2016. The recently elected Liberal government ordered a review of the issue once the legal tactic and its impact became known.

89 Starkman, *Independent Assessment Process*, 35, 45, and 84; Adjudication Secretariat Statistics from September 19, 2007 to December 31, 2015, http://iap-pei.ca/information/stats-eng.php (accessed 20 Jan. 2016).

90 Adjudication Secretariat Statistics about the IAP. Since not all claims resulted in a full 15 per cent award of fees to the claimants' lawyers, the overall totals must be approximate. Similarly, the adjudication secretariat does not break down the number of claims settled, rejected, and withdrawn, making it impossible to be precise about the number of claims actually resolved. Indigenous Affairs, "Statistics on the Implementation of the Indian Residential Schools Settlement," www.aadnc- aandc.gc.ca/eng/1315320539682/1315320692192 (accessed 27 July 2016). At the time of writing, the latest statistics were to 31 March 2016. Letter of Chief Adjudicator Dan Shapiro to editor, *Saskatoon StarPhoenix*, 10 May 2016.

91 Starkman, *Independent Assessment Process*, 84–9.

92 Ibid., 35, 42.

93 Ibid., 99.

94 Full disclosure: I was a paid speaker on the history of residential schools for most of the adjudicator training sessions, going back to the first one under dispute resolution; and in 2011, through the kindness of Chief Adjudicator Dan Ish, I was permitted to sit in on the week of training. In some cases, my description of adjudicator training is based on notes I made during the 2011 session.

95 Starkman, *Independent Assessment Process*, 47–8; Deputy Chief Adjudicator Rodger Linka's remarks at adjudicator training session, 24 Aug. 2011. Starkman, a former executive director of the IRSAS, said that the organization was in " a perpetual state of organization-building" because of such requirements.

96 Starkman, *Independent Assessment Process*, 43.

97 Elder Roland Duquette, adjudicator training session, 22 Aug. 2011. In fact, one of the deputy chief adjudicators, Delia Opekekew, was a First Nation woman.

98 Dan Shapiro at adjudicator training, 23 Aug. 2011.
99 Comments of Dan Shapiro, Rodger Linka, and Deputy Chief Commissioner Kaye Dunlop, 24 Aug. 2011.
100 Reported by Chief Commissioner Dan Ish, 26 Aug. 2011.
101 "Many Reactions to Schools Litigation," www.cbc.ca/news/Canada/ Saskatchewan/many-reactions-to, 30 Jan. 2015 (accessed 12 Nov. 2015).
102 AHF transcripts, T6-807.
103 APTN National News, "Outgoing Chief Adjudicator Criticizes Lawyers in Residential School Compensation Process," http://aptn.ca.news/2013 /03/11outgoing-chief-adjudicator-criticizes-lawyers-in-residential -school-compensation-process (accessed 20 Jan. 2016).
104 The following account is based on Starkman, *Independent Assessment Process*, 77–9 and 98–9; and *Fontaine v. Canada (Attorney General)* in the British Columbia Supreme Court, 2012 BSC 839, www.caselaw.canada.globe24h .com/0/0/british-columbia/2012/06/05/fontaine-v-canada-attorney -general-2012-bcsc-839.shtml (accessed 23 April 2015), at 154, 166–8.
105 *Fontaine v. Canada (Attorney General)*, 2012 BSC 839, at 154 and 166–8.
106 Starkman, *Independent Assessment Process*, 111.
107 Irene Fraser interview, Millet, AB, 4 May 2015.
108 APTN, "Outgoing Chief Adjudicator."
109 *Globe and Mail*, 25 Feb. 2008.
110 AHF transcripts, S4-503.
111 Ibid., S4-501.
112 Ibid., S6-844.
113 Ibid., T3-502.
114 Ibid., T6-813.
115 Ibid., T4-416.
116 Ibid., T12-304.
117 Ibid., S4-505.
118 Ibid., T4-601.
119 Ibid., T4-418.
120 Ibid., A8-03.

7. Truth and Reconciliation

1 Text of Prime Minister Harper's Apology, 11 June 2008 (hereafter, Harper Apology), www.fns.bc.ca/pdf/TextofApology.pdf (accessed 8 Jan. 2009).
2 Truth and Reconciliation Commission, *Final Report*, vol. 6, *Canada's Residential Schools: Reconciliation* (Montreal and Kingston: McGill-Queen's University Press 2015), 81.

3　Melissa Nobles, *The Politics of Official Apologies*, (Cambridge: Cambridge University Press 2008), x. See also Robert R. Wyeneth, "The Power of Apology and the Process of Historical Reconciliation," *Public Historian* 23, no. 3 (summer 2001): 33, 38. I am grateful to Dr Merle Massie, who kindly drew this article to my attention.

4　Nobles, *Official Apologies*, 71–2.

5　Royal Commission on Aboriginal Peoples, *Final Report*, vol. 1, *Looking Forward, Looking Back* (Ottawa: RCAP 1996).

6　Stuart Macintyre and Anna Clark, eds., *The History Wars* (Melbourne: Melbourne University Press 2004).

7　Quoted in ibid., 1, 3.

8　Stuart Macintyre, "The History Wars," *Sydney Papers* (winter/spring 2003): 77–83, http:www.kooriweb.org/foley/resources/pdfs/198.pdf (accessed 27 May 2015). It is worth noting that historian Geoffrey Blainey coined the terms "black armband history" and "three cheers"; he criticized the former but admitted that he had identified with the latter.

9　See, for example, Donald Wright, *Donald Creighton: A Life in History* (Toronto: University of Toronto Press 2015).

10　Interview with Tom Flanangan, Calgary, 8 Sept. 2009.

11　Interview with Phil Fontaine, Winnipeg, 20 March 2015.

12　"No Residential School Apology, Tories Say," *Globe and Mail*, 27 March 2007, www.theglobeandmail.com (accessed 30 March 2007).

13　Bill Curry, "House Apologizes to Residential School Students," *Globe and Mail*, 2 May 2007.

14　Speech from the Throne, press release, 16 Oct. 2007, www.sft-ddt.gc.ca/eng/index.asp (accessed 6 May 2008).

15　Interview with David MacDonald, Toronto, 18 Feb. 2009; Bill Curry and Brian Laghi, "Mounting Sense of Urgency Was Apology's Catalyst," *Globe and Mail*, 13 June 2008, A4. Maher Arar was a Canadian who had been surreptitiously transported with Canadian help by the Americans to a Middle East country, where he was tortured.

16　Fontaine interview.

17　Sue Bailey, "MP Retracts Radio Remarks," *Globe and Mail*, 13 June 2008, A4.

18　The ceremony appears in Canada, Parliament, House of Commons, *Debates*, 11 June 2008 (hereafter *Debates*), 6849–57.

19　Harper Apology. The phrase belonged to Capt. Richard Pratt, the director of a large residential school in Carlisle, Pennsylvania, in the late nineteenth century.

20　Ibid.; *Debates*, 6849–52.

21　*Debates*, 6851 (Dion), 6852–53 (Duceppe), and 6853–54 (Layton).

22 *Debates,* 6854–55 (Fontaine), 6855–56 (Brazeau), 6856 (Simon), 6856 (Chartier), and 6856–57 (Jacobs).

23 "Voices," *Ottawa Citizen,* 12 June 2008, A4.

24 Caroline Alphonso, "A Childhood Taken Away – 'It's Just a Bunch of Words,'" *Globe and Mail,* 12 June 2008, A8.

25 "Survivors Respond," *Ottawa Citizen,* 12 June 2008, A5.

26 Bill Curry, "Lengthy Battle for Public Apology," *Globe and Mail,* 11 June 2008, A5.

27 Andrew Wesley interview, Toronto, 21 Nov. 2013.

28 Omar El Akkad, 'School-abuse Apology Widely Backed," *Globe and Mail,* 14 June 2008. An MA thesis described the apology as "robust and full" and found that it was positively received by a small sampling of media outlets that the author consulted. Michael Boldt Radmacher, "Squaring the Circle Game: A Critical Look at Canada's 2008 Apology to Former Students of Indian Residential Schools" (MA thesis, University of Victoria 2010), 58 and 72–7.

29 Aboriginal Healing Foundation (AHF) transcripts, L8-301.

30 Remarks of a seventy-one-year-old First Nations woman, AHF transcripts, T4-606.

31 AHF transcripts, T4-614.

32 Ibid., T6-205.

33 Ibid., T12-309.

34 Ibid., S4-629. Other positive comments include those of a fifty-nine-year-old status Indian woman (S6-827) and of a Métis husband and wife, he seventy-two and she sixty (T5-104 and T5-105, respectively). The man (preferred Dion's remarks to Harper's.

35 Ibid., T6-809.

36 Remarks by a fifty-three-year-old male status Indian, ibid., T6-826.

37 Remarks by a sixty-five-year-old female status Indian, ibid., A5-106.

38 Remarks by a sixty-year-old female status Indian, ibid., T4-405.

39 Remarks by a sixty-six-year-old female status Indian, ibid., T12-304.

40 Ibid., AHF transcripts, A-908. For other examples of suspicion that Harper was not sincere, see the remarks of a forty-eight-year-old status Indian woman (T3-505) and, a sixty-one-year-old status Indian woman (T4-401).

41 Ibid., T12-308.

42 Ibid., S4-622.

43 Ibid., A2-211.

44 Ibid., T4-618.

45 Ibid., A04-19; see also a First Nations woman, age unspecified, S6-835.

46 Ibid., A4-06.

47 Remarks by a forty-eight-year-old status Indian man, ibid., T6-810.

48 Ibid., S6-838.

49 Remarks by a fifty-two-year-old status woman, ibid., T6-801. For similar examples, see the remarks by a forty-eight-year-old male status Indian (S4-631), a fifty-seven-year-old status woman (S6-833); and, and a fifty-year-old status Indian man (T3-502).

50 Remarks by a twenty-four-year old status Indian woman, AHF transcripts, T6-802.

51 Remarks by a fifty-year-old Inuk woman, ibid., K8-309.

52 Ibid., S4–501.

53 From a Canadian Press roundup of opinion reproduced in a blog kept by Rarihokwats four_arrows@canada.com, 30 June 2008. I am grateful to Rarihokwats for providing this and other information about First Nations issues.

54 AHF transcripts, A8-407.

55 Remarks by a sixty-year-old status Indian man, ibid., T6-817.

56 Ibid., A4-10.

57 Mark Gibney, Rhoda E. Howard-Hassmann, Jean-Marc Coicaud, and Niklaus Steiner, eds., *The Age of Apology: Facing Up to the Past* (Philadelphia: University of Pennsylvania Press, 2008).

58 *Debates*, 12 June 2008, 6885.

59 Akivah Starkman, *The Independent Assessment Process: Reflections* (n.p.: Author 2014), 37.

60 Gloria Galloway, "Government Used Technical Argument to Disqualify Residential School Claims," *Globe and Mail*, 3 Feb.; and Gloria Galloway, "Ottawa to Review Tactics in Abuse Claims," *Globe and Mail*, 4 Feb. 2016.

61 Interview with Murray Sinclair, Winnipeg, 30 March 2015. It is Senator Sinclair's view that, had the apology been conveyed to the bureaucracy effectively, the TRC would have had more fruitful relations with bureaucrats.

62 Canada, Aboriginal Affairs and Northern Development Canada, "Canada's Statement of Support on the United Nations Declaration on the Rights of Indigenous Peoples," 12 Nov. 2010, http:www.aadnc-aandc .gc.ca/eng/1309374239861/130937546142 (accessed 12 June 2015).

63 Cartoon in *Saskatoon StarPhoenix*, 13 June 2008; repeated 2 Jan. 2009, A9.

64 Kim Stanton, "Canada's Truth and Reconciliation Commission: Settling the Past?" *International Indigenous Policy Journal* 2, no. 3 (Aug. 2011): 1, 4. I am grateful to Dr Stanton for informing me about her work on the TRC.

65 Ibid., 4.

66 Interview with Jamie Scott, Ottawa, 11 Sept. 2010. Scott also observed that the values statement concerning the commission embodied principles of restorative justice.

67 Indian Residential Schools Settlement Agreement (IRSSA), preamble (B) and (c), http://www.residentialschoolsettlement.ca/settlement.html (accessed 13 Feb. 2015).

68 Ibid., s. 7.01(2).

69 IRSSA, Schedule N, s. 1.

70 Jennifer Llewellyn, "Bridging the Gap between Truth and Reconciliation: Restorative Justice and the Indian Residential Schools Truth and Reconciliation Commission," in *From Truth to Reconciliation: Transforming the Legacy of Residential Schools*, ed. Marlene Brant Castellano, Linda Archibald, and Mike DeGagné (Ottawa: Aboriginal Healing Foundation 2008), 186.

71 IRSSA, Schedule N, s. 1.

72 Ibid., s. 2 (q).

73 Ibid., s. 2 (b), (c), (f), and (h).

74 Kathleen Mahoney interview, 14 May 2009; Lucianna Ciccocioppo, "Conference Took Stock of Canada's Indian Residential Schools Settlement Agreement," University of Toronto Law website, www.law.utoronto.ca (accessed 21 Feb. 2013).

75 IRSSA, Schedule N, s. 9.

76 Ibid., s. 3 (a) and (d).

77 Ibid., 4 (d) (oral traditions); 11 (all relevant documents)

78 Ibid., s. 11.

79 Ibid., s. 12.

80 Personal observation. I met with Watts and Harrison on 9 June 2008. Helen Harrison to Bob Watts, Paulette Regan, and Seetal Sunga, 27 May 2008. My account of the short life of the first TRC is also informed by the following interviews: Helen Henderson, Ottawa, 31 March 2016; Marianne MacLean, Ottawa, 2 May 2016; and Alex Maass, Gatineau, QC, 3 May 2016.

81 IRSSA, Schedule N, s. 6 (ii) (Secretariat).

82 Ibid., s. 7.

83 Ibid., s. 14 (Budget and Resources).

84 Ibid., s. 5 (Membership).

85 Helen Harrison apprised me of this development at an informal meeting we had 9 Sept. 2008.

86 "Justice Harry S. LaForme Resigns as Chair of the Indian Residential Schools Truth and Reconciliation Commission," Report by CNW Group,

http://www.newswire.ca/en/release/archive/October2008/20/c7708
.html (accessed 20 Oct. 2008).

87 Maass interview. Ms Maass worked intensively on the missing children
project.

88 Bill Curry and Joe Friesen, "Commission to Probe Graves at School Sites,"
Globe and Mail, 27 Oct. 2008, http://www.theglobeandmail.com/news/
national/commission-to-probe-graves-at-school-sites/article1064906/
(accessed 27 Oct. 2008); Harrison interview.

89 Sinclair interview, 30 March 2015.

8. The Truth and Reconciliation Commission

1 Murray Sinclair speech to AFN, Calgary, 22 July 2009, Indian and Northern
Affairs Canada transcript supplied by Catherine Twinn, 18 Sept. 2009.

2 Truth and Reconciliation Commission (TRC), "Meet the Commissioners,"
www.trc.ca (accessed 30 June 2015).

3 John Ibbitson, "A Challenge for Canada," *Globe and Mail*, 6 June 2015.

4 Because of her honorary doctorate, she was often referred to as Dr Marie
Wilson: "Meet the Commissioners."

5 "Meet the Commissioners"; personal observation.

6 Justice Murray Sinclair interview, Saskatoon, 23 June 2015.

7 Sinclair speech to AFN, 22 July 2009.

8 Ibid.

9 TRC, "The First Six Months," www.trc-cvr.ca/new.html, (accessed
8 Jan. 2010).

10 Personal observation, Toronto, 11 Dec. 2009,

11 Personal experience; I served on the SSHRC board in 1998–2005.

12 TRC press release, "TRC Opens New Office, Appoints New Executive
Director," www.trc-cvr.ca/news.html (accessed 8 Jan. 2010); Sinclair public
lecture, 11 Dec. 2009.

13 The comment re difficulty was made at a public lecture, 11 Dec. 2009, and
that about the additional expense is from the Sinclair interview, 23 June 2015.

14 TRC, "TRC Opens New Office."

15 Indian Residential Schools Settlement Agreement, Schedule N, s. 10 (A)
(National Events) (i) www.residentialschoolsettlement.ca (accessed 13
Feb. 2015).

16 Interview with Kim Murray, executive director of TRC, Winnipeg, 25
Nov. 2014.

17 Personal observation; the dawn fire ceremony was particularly disheartening
on the wet days.

18 TRC, "Northern National Event," information for Inuvik national event, www.trc.ca, (accessed 14 June 2011).

19 Although the commission stated that the "box will travel with the TRC to all of its seven National Events throughout Canada," in fact it was not present in Winnipeg and made its first appearance later. Personal recollection. At the Winnipeg national event, I made an invited Gesture of Reconciliation and placed the text of my remarks into the hands of Commissioners Littlechild and Wilson, who put it into a simple black box. TRC, "Bentwood Box," 20 March 2013, www.trc.ca (accessed 2 July 2015). See the contrary version in TRC, *Final Report of the Truth and Reconciliation Commission of Canada. Volume One: Summary: Honouring the Truth, Reconciling for the Future* [hereafter *Summary Final Report*] (Toronto: Lorimer 2015), 271.

20 Andy Scott interview, Fredericton, 1 Nov. 2012.

21 Personal observation, Edmonton, 28 March 2014.

22 Shelagh Rogers interview, Gabriola Island, BC, 2 April 2014.

23 Through the kindness of Tom McMahon of the commission staff, I was able to tour the private statement gathering area at the Edmonton national event when it was not in use. The unnamed videographer who was on hand when I was there answered questions about his experience, offering that the job could be stressful.

24 Ruth Cameron interview, Saskatoon, 22 July 2015.

25 Ry Moran interview, Winnipeg, 10 Sept. 2014, and by telephone, 8 Oct. 2014.

26 Personal observation, Halifax, 28 Oct. 2011. Information about friction is based on statements made to me by people close to the Halifax event who would prefer to remain anonymous.

27 Sinclair interview, 23 June 2015. Justice Sinclair said that Jon Gerrard, an expert on avian subjects, had told him that an eagle had never been known to fly over downtown Winnipeg in anyone's memory.

28 Personal observation; Patrick White, "National Events Attract Large Crowds," *Globe and Mail*, 23 Sept. 2013. The TRC claimed 70,000 participated.

29 Personal observation, Edmonton, 27 and 28 March 2014.

30 Chief Commissioner Sinclair said (23 June 2015) that the Ottawa Police Service estimated that 10,000–12,000 participated in the walk. The *Ottawa Citizen*, by contrast, reported 3,000 participants (1 June 2015).

31 Diane Munier, "The Voice of the Bell," *Kairos Canada*, www.kairoscanada .org/dignity-rights/indigenous-rights/the-voice-of-the-bell (accessed 22 July 2015). This item was kindly provided by Dr Donald B. Smith, Professor Emeritus of History, University of Calgary.

32 Personal observation, Halifax, 27 Oct. 2011.

33 These comments are based on personal observation at the events in Winnipeg, Halifax, Saskatoon, Vancouver, Edmonton, and Ottawa.

34 John Milloy interview, Peterborough, ON, 25 Nov. 2015.

35 Marianne McLean interview, Ottawa, 2 May 2016; Helen Henderson interview, Ottawa, 31 March 2016.

36 Milloy interview.

37 Bill Curry, "Research Director Resigns from Truth Commission," *Globe and Mail*, 12 July 2010.

38 Ibid.

39 Murray interview.

40 "Statistics on the Implementation of the Indian Residential Schools Settlement Agreement" (to 31 March 2015), www.aadnc-aandc.gc.ca/eng/1315320539682/1315320692 (accessed 16 Nov. 2015). For the Métis view, see www.metisnation.ca/index.php/news/metis-residential-and-day-school-survivors-great (posted 16 June 2013; accessed 16 Nov. 2015).

41 Sinclair interview, 23 June 2015.

42 IRSSA, Schedule N, s. 11, (Access to Relevant Information), www.residentialschoolsettlement.ca (accessed 13 Feb. 2015).

43 "Catholic Church Reluctant to Release Residential School Records," *Globe and Mail*, www.globeandmail.com 6 April 2010 (accessed 6 April 2010).

44 TRC researcher John Milloy, who heard Sinclair's complaints about archives often, thought he was referring only to the Roman Catholics. Milloy interview.

45 McLean interview.

46 Sinclair interview, 25 Nov. 2014.

47 Gloria Galloway, "Debate Over Crucial Documents Delays Reconciliation Deal," *Globe and Mail*, 22 Dec. 2012.

48 *Fontaine v. Canada (Attorney General)*, ONSC 684, especially at 83 (LAC) and 94–99 (impacts), 30 Jan. 2013. A copy of the ruling was kindly provided by Tom McMahon. McMahon to author 31 Jan. 2013.

49 Sinclair interview, 25 Nov. 2014 and 30 March and 23 June 2015; Murray interview. See also the comment of John Milloy, TRC research director, 2009–10, in "Doing Public History in Canada's Truth and Reconciliation Commission," *Public Historian* 35, no. 4 (Nov. 2013): 3–6. I am grateful to Professor Milloy for providing me with a copy of his article.

50 IRSSA, Schedule N, s. 1 (a) and (b) (Goals); see also s. 10 (A) (f) (National Events).

51 Moran interview. Moran was director of statement gathering.

52 TRC, *The Survivors Speak: A Report of the Truth and Reconciliation of Canada* (n.p.: TRC 2015), 1.

53 Henderson interview.

54 Personal observation, Halifax, 28 Oct. 2011.

55 TRC, *What We Have Learned: Principles of Truth and Reconciliation* (n.p.: TRC [2015]), 119–20.

56 Pierre Baribeau interview, Montreal, 28 Nov. 2011.

57 Lea Meadows interview, Calgary, 27 July 2015. Ms Meadows's parents were both missionaries in United Church residential schools in northern Manitoba. She said that for both her grandmother and her mother, attending residential school was "a positive life-changing event."

58 Alison Norman interview, Toronto, 1 March 2016.

59 *The Survivors Speak* contains 203 pages of text.

60 Ronald Niezen, *Truth and Indignation: Canada's Truth and Reconciliation Commission on Indian Residential Schools* (Toronto: University of Toronto Press 2013), esp. 151, 155.

61 Personal observation at and following national events in Winnipeg, Halifax, Saskatoon, Vancouver, Edmonton, and Ottawa.

62 These comments are based on personal observation at the five national events I attended.

63 Ruth Cameron interview

64 Personal observation, Halifax, 26 Oct. 2011.

65 See Andrew Woolford, *This Benevolent Experiment: Indigenous Boarding Schools, Genocide, and Redress in Canada and the United States* (Winnipeg: University of Manitoba Press 2015), 15, concerning "trauma drama" and Matt James's comments on "residential schools syndrome" trope in his "A Carnival of Truth? Knowledge, Ignorance and the Canadian Truth and Reconciliation Commission," *International Journal of Transitional Justice* (2012): 16–17.

66 Schedule N, s. 8(b) (interim report, and s. 3 (g), (h) (final report).

67 TRC, *They Came for the Children: Canada, Aboriginal Peoples, and Residential Schools* (Winnipeg: TRC 2012); *Final Report of the Truth and Reconciliation Commission of Canada. Volume One: Summary: Honouring the Truth, Reconciling for the Future* [hereafter *Summary Final Report*] (Toronto: Lorimer 2015); and the six volumes of the final report – TRC, *The Final Report of the Truth and Reconciliation Commission of Canada*: volume 1, *Canada's Residential Schools: The History, Part 1, Origins to 1939* [hereafter *History, Part 1*] and *Canada's Residential Schools: The History, Part 2, 1939 to 2000* [hereafter *History, Part 2*]; volume 2, *Canada's Residential Schools: The Inuit and Northern Experience* [hereafter *Inuit*]; volume 3, *Canada's Residential Schools: The Métis Experience* [hereafter *Métis*]; volume 4, *Canada's Residential Schools: Missing Children and Unmarked Burials*

[hereafter *Missing Children*]; volume 5, *Canada's Residential Schools: The Legacy* [hereafter *Legacy*]; and volume 6, *Canada's Residential Schools: Reconciliation* [hereafter *Reconciliation*]. All six volumes were published in English and French by McGill-Queen's University Press in 2015. The five Indigenous languages were Cree, Dené, Inuktitut, Mi'kmaq, and Ojibwe. *Manitoulin Expositor*, 23 Dec. 2015, www.manitoulin.ca/2015/12/23 (accessed 10 Feb. 2016).

68 *Summary Final Report*, 117, 127, points out that there were good school staff.

69 See, for example, the introduction to the section "The Attack on Children" in *History, Part 1*, 162.

70 For example, *History, Part 2*, 416–17.

71 *History, Part 1*, 711, stressed that "there were many qualified and experienced people working in the schools"; *History, Part 2*, between 300 and 301, an illustration of a teacher that noted that "many residential school staff members were drawn to the work by a desire to teach and 'improve the world'"; and *History, Part 2*, ch. 14, "The Staff Experience: 1940–2000," 493–550.

72 *They Came for the Children*, 86.

73 *Summary Final Report*, 8.

74 *Legacy*.

75 *History, Part 1*, 7.

76 Chinta Puxley, "Residential Schools 'an Act of Genocide,'" *Globe and Mail*, 18 Feb. 2012. Sinclair had also used similar language in a question-and-answer session on a program in the CBC Television's series *The 8th Fire*, www.cbc.ca/doczone/episodes David B. MacDonald, "Genocide in the Indian Residential Schools: Canadian History through the Lens of the UN Genocide Convention," in *Colonial Genocide in Indigenous North America*, ed. Andrew Woolford, Jeff Benvenuto, and Alexander Laban Hinton (Durham, NC: Duke University Press 2014), 623.

77 On Beverley McLachlin's speech, see Sean Fine, "Chief Justice Says Canada Attempted 'Cultural Genocide' on Aboriginals," *Globe and Mail*, 29 May 2015.

78 *Reconciliation*, 11.

79 Ibid., 17.

80 Ibid., 4.

81 Ibid., 19.

82 Ibid., 21.

83 Ibid., 119.

84 Ibid., 121–2 (calls to action 62 and 63).

85 Ibid., 134.
86 Ibid., 136–7.
87 Ibid., 143–5 (calls to action 69 and 70).
88 Ibid., 183.
89 Ibid., 186–7.
90 Ibid., 188–91 (quotation on 191). See also Trina Cooper Bolam, "Healing Heritage: New Approaches on Commemorating Canada's Indian Residential School System" (unpublished MA thesis, Carleton University, 2014), esp. 48–9 and 55–8; and interview with Trina Cooper-Bolam, Ottawa, 27 Aug. 2015. I am grateful to Ms Cooper-Bolam for providing me with a copy of her thesis. Disclosure: I am the Saskatchewan representative on the HSMBC.
91 *Reconciliation*, 28 (calls to action 43 and 44).
92 Ibid., new Royal Proclamation (calls to action 45–7); papal apology (no. 58; CBC funding (no. 84).
93 *Summary Final Report*, 25, 32.
94 Hymie Rubenstein and Rodney Clifton, "Truth and Reconciliation Report Tells a 'Skewed and Partial Story' of Residential Schools," *National Post*, 22 June 2015 (accessed 15 Aug. 2016). Although the authors were commenting on the *Summary Final Report* of June 2015, the same criticism applied to the larger final report issued later that year.
95 *Reconciliation*, 221, 209.
96 Ibid., 4.

Conclusion

1 *The Final Report of the Truth and Reconciliation Commission of Canada*, vol. 6, *Canada's Residential Schools: Reconciliation* (Montreal and Kingston: McGill-Queen's University Press 2015), 101 (hereafter *Reconciliation*).
2 In this chapter, only quotations and other points that had not previously been referenced will be documented.
3 Art Babych, "Government Using Churches as Scapegoats, Says Mercredi," *Canadian Catholic News*, 16 Dec. 1996. This item was kindly provided by John Siebert of the United Church, who received it from Gerry Kelly, the Roman Catholics' point man on residential school matters.
4 *Fontaine v. Canada (Attorney General)*, Ontario Court of Appeal, 4 April 2016, *Globe and Mail*, 5 April 2016.
5 Tom McMahon, "The Final Abuse of Indian Residential School Children: Deleting Their Names, Erasing Their Voices and Destroying Their Records without Their Consent," unpublished paper dated 15 July 2016 that was

kindly supplied by Mr McMahon. Tom McMahon to Jim Miller, 18 July 2016.

6 Mike DeGagné, "The Truth and Reconciliation Commission Recommendations," remarks delivered at the University of British Columbia House of Learning on 16 Sept. 2015 and to the Centre for Policy Alternatives, Ottawa, 19 Nov. 2015, speaking notes. I greatly appreciate Dr DeGagné's generous sharing of his speaking notes with me.

7 *The Final Report of the Truth and Reconciliation Commission of Canada*, vol. 5, *Canada's Residential Schools: The Legacy* (Montreal and Kingston: McGill-Queen's University Press 2015), 8.

8 *Reconciliation*, 34.

9 Ibid., 191.

10 David B. MacDonald, "Genocide in the Indian Residential Schools: Canadian History through the Lens of the UN Genocide Convention," in *Colonial Genocide in Indigenous North America*, ed. Alexander Woolford, Jeff Benvenuto, and Alexander Laban Hinton (Durham, NC: Duke University Press 2014); Alexander Woolford, *This Benevolent Experiment: Indigenous Boarding Schools, Genocide, and Redress in Canada and the United States* (Winnipeg: University of Manitoba Press 2015); Conrad Black, "Canada's Treatment of Aboriginals Was Shameful, but It Was Not Genocide," *National Post*, 6 June 2015, www.nationalpost.com (accessed 15 Aug. 2016).

11 United Nations Convention on the Prevention and Punishment of the Crime of Genocide, 1948, s. (e).

12 Doug Cuthand, "Make It a Fight Worth Having," *Tapwe: Selected Columns of Doug Cuthand* (Penticton, BC: Theytus Books 2005), 8. I am grateful to one of the readers for the University of Toronto Press, who drew this work to my attention.

13 https://www.historicacanada.ca/content/heritage-minutes/sitting-bull-o April 2017).

14 Paulette Regan, *Unsettling the Settler Within: Indian Residential Schools, Truth Telling, and Reconciliation in Canada* (Vancouver: UBC Press 2010).

15 Anne Godlewska, Jackie Moore, and C. Drew Bednaser, "Cultivating Ignorance of Aboriginal Realities," *Canadian Geographer* 54, no. 4 (2010): 426.

16 "Harper in Denial at G20: Canada Had 'No History of Colonialism'," www.Rabble.ca, 28 Sept. 2009 (accessed 11 April 2016).

17 *Canadian Illustrated News*, 22 July 1876, 56, Library and Archives Canada (LAC), C064475.

18 Canada, House of Commons, *Debates*, 8 Feb. 1877, 3, Speech from the Throne.

19 Jill St Germain, *Broken Treaties: United States and Canadian Relations with the Lakotas and the Plains Cree, 1868–1885* (Lincoln: University of Nebraska Press 2009).

20 Carol J. Williams, *Framing the West: Race, Gender, and the Photographic Frontier in the Pacific Northwest* (New York: Oxford University Press, 2003), 51; Dan Savard, *Images from the Likeness House* (Victoria: Royal British Columbia Museum 2010), 83–97.

21 Angela Wanhalla, "State-Sponsored Photography and Assimilation Policy in Canada and New Zealand," in *Within and Without the Nation: Canadian History as Transnational History*, ed. Karen Dubinsky, Adele Perry, and Henry Yu (Toronto: University of Toronto Press 2015), 92–101 and 107–9.

22 Sarah Carter, "Demonstrating Success: The File Hills Farm Colony," *Prairie Forum* 16, 2 (fall 1991): 157–83; J.R. Miller, *Shingwauk's Vision: A History of Native Residential Schools* (Toronto: University of Toronto Press 1996), 358; Eleanor Brass, *I Walk in Two Worlds* (Calgary: Glenbow-Alberta Institute 1887); and Eleanor Brass, "The File Hills Ex-Pupil Colony," *Saskatchewan History* 6, 2 (spring 1953): 66–9.

23 Sarah Carter, "The 'Cordial Advocate': Amelia McLean Paget and *The People of the Plains*," in *With Good Intentions: Euro-Canadian and Aboriginal Relations in Colonial Canada*, ed. Celia Haig- Brown and David A. Nock (Vancouver: UBC Press 2006), 212–21.

24 Hana Samek, *The Blackfoot Confederacy, 1880–1920: A Comparative Study of Canadian and U.S. Indian Policy* (Albuquerque: University of New Mexico Press 1987), 6, 8–9.

25 Ibid., 9–10.

26 Allan G. Harper, "Canada's Indian Administration: Basic Concepts and Objectives [*sic*]," *America Indigena* 5, no. 2 (April 1945): 119–32; "Canada's Indian Administration: The 'Indian Act,'" *America Indigena* 6, no. 2 (April 1946): 297–314 and "Canada's Indian Administration: The Treaty System," *America Indigena* 7, no. 2 (April 1947): 13–48. Samek, *Blackfoot Confederacy*, 188n38.

27 J.W. Bengough, "Our Free Library" (cartoon), *Toronto Globe*, 26 Jan. 1899, LAC, Mikan 2955996, reference number R13244-162-5-E.

28 Arthur J. Ray, Jim Miller, and Frank Tough, *Bounty and Benevolence: A History of Saskatchewan Treaties* (Montreal and Kingston: McGill-Queen's University Press 2000), 204–6.

29 G.F.G. Stanley, *The Birth of Western Canada: A History of the Riel Rebellions*, reprints in Canadian History edition (1936; Toronto: University of Toronto Press 1960), contents and 430–1.

30 Leger Marketing survey commissioned by the Association for Canadian Studies and distributed by the ACS by email on 30 Sept. 2015.

31 Dr Cook's observations, which are not new, were made at a book promotion event in Saskatoon on 16 Oct. 2015.

32 Bruce Walsh, "Standing Out in the World of Scholarly Publishing," *University Affairs* April 2016, 12–13. Mr Walsh mentioned that one of his University of Regina Press titles, James Daschuk's *Clearing the Plains*, has sold more than 18,500 copies.

33 Don Jackson interview, Sault Ste Marie, ON, 26 June 2010.

34 Louise Halfe interview, Saskatoon, 9 Jan. 2011.

35 Marlene Brant Castellano, "A Holistic Approach to Reconciliation: Insights from Research of the Aboriginal Healing Foundation," in *From Truth to Reconciliation: Transforming the Legacy of Residential* Schools, ed. Marlene Brant Castellano, Linda Archibald, and Mike DeGagné (Ottawa: AHF 2008), 386.

36 Environics Research Group, *Final Report: 2008 National Benchmark Survey*, cited in Kim Stanton, "Canada's Truth and Reconciliation Commission: Settling the Past?" *International Indigenous Policy Journal* 2, no. 3 (2011): 7.

37 Association for Canadian Studies (ACS) email release, 15 Oct. 2015. Those aspects of Canada that made respondents most proud were "Multiculturalism (i.e. Immigration policies, openness to cultures)," 10%; "Peacekeeping (i.e. Humanitarian missions)," 9%; and "Peace (i.e. no social strife, civil war, unilateral engagement)," 6%. Another release from ACS on 30 November 2015 reported that, for those who acknowledged there were events in Canadian history that made them ashamed, 35% cited "Treatment of Aboriginals" and "Indian residential schools" (16%) specifically. Shame for residential school was highest in the four western provinces (ranging from 21% in Alberta to 28% in Manitoba and Saskatchewan) and lowest in Quebec (9%). ACS email release, 30 Nov. 2015.

38 Terry Fenge and Jim Aldridge, eds., *Keeping Promises: The Royal Proclamation of 1763, Aboriginal Rights, and Treaties in Canada* (Montreal and Kingston: McGill-Queen's University Press, 2015), "In Conclusion," 195–6, 197.

39 National Inquiry into Missing and Murdered Indigenous Women and Girls, www.aadnc aandc.gc.ca/eng/1448633299414/144863350146 (accessed 12 April 2017); and inquiry website www.mmiwg-ffada.ca (accessed 12 April 2017).

40 Kathleen Mahoney, "Whither Reconciliation," paper presented at the University of Toronto conference Assessing the Indian Residential Schools Litigation and Settlement Process,' 17–18 Jan. 2013. Substantially the same

talk, retitled, "The Indian Residential School Settlement: Is Reconciliation
Possible?" became available at www.ablawg.ca/2013/06/26/the-indian
-residential-school-settlement-agreement-is-reconciliation-possible
(accessed 30 Nov. 2015).

41 James Bartleman, "The Importance of Truth Telling in a Just Society,"
quoted in Stanton, "Canada's Truth and Reconciliation Commission," 13.

42 Archbishop James Weisgerber interview, Regina, 3 April 2014; Wab Kinew,
The Reason You Walk (Toronto: Viking 2015), 89–91, 210–11, 245–6, and 256.

43 Jim Guild, "History Revisited," *Globe and Mail*, www.theglobeandmail.
com, 25 June 2011 (accessed 12 April 2017).

44 Krista McCracken, "Returning Home: Repatriation and Missing Children,"
Active History, www.activehistory.ca/2011/03; "Star Readers Rally to Bring
Charlie Hunter Home," www.thestar.com/new/canada/article/953851
(accessed 9 Sept. 2015). *The Toronto Star* story was kindly forwarded to
me by Ed Sadowski, then a worker in The Shingwauk Project at Algoma
University. Ms McCracken is also associated with that project.

45 Leonard Doell to Jim Miller, e-mail, 7 Feb. 2012. I have been briefed about
this initiative, which the Mennonites call "Aboriginal Neighbours," by Mr
Doell on several occasions. As well, Mr Doell facilitated my viewing of a
documentary, *Reserve 107: Reconciliation on the Prairies* (Rebel Sky Media)
that deals with the movement, Leonard Doell to Jim Miller, 30 Jan. 2016.

Bibliography

Primary Sources

Archival Sources

General Synod Archives (Anglican Church of Canada)
GS75-103, Series 2: Committees, Series 2-15, Indian and Eskimo Residential
Schools and Indian Schools Administration 1906–68, box 20, file 2, and
box 22, file 6, 1961
GS 2010-10, Partnerships: Indigenous Ministries, box 1, 1993–2004, and box
2, 2003–7
Library and Archives Canada (LAC)
RG 10, Records of the Department of Indian Affairs
RG33, Records of the Royal Commission on Aboriginal Peoples
Presbyterian Church in Canada Archives (PCA)
Acts and Proceedings [of the General Assembly]
1992-1256-2-10, Aboriginal Rights Coalition (ARC), Residential Schools,
1990–92
1998-1003-39-4, General Board of Missions/Board of World Missions,
Committee Minutes, Indian Task Force 1973–80
1998-1008-87-17, General Board of Missions/Board of World Missions,
Research and Planning, Native People – Reassessment Project 1977–80
1998-1003-87-19, General Board of Missions/Board of World Missions,
Research and Planning, Project North 1975–80
1998-1003-69-6, General Board of Missions/Board of World Missions,
Administrative Correspondence, Indians 1956–76
2003-1086-1-2, Exploratory Dialogues, 1998–99, "A Report on the Victim/
Witness Support Service of a Multiple Child Sexual Abuse Court Trial in
Inuvik, Northwest Territories, August 1998," 16 Oct. 1998

2003-1086-1-2, Ecumenical Working Group on Residential Schools (EWGRS), Aug.–Dec. 1999; EWGRS, 2000; 1-4, 1999

2003-1067-1-1, Life and Mission Agency, EWGRS, 1998–99; 1-2, 1999; 1-3, EWGRS, 2000

2006-1023, Healing and Reconciliation Initiative

2007-1067--1, EWGRS, 2000; 1-2, EWGRS, 2001; 1-3, EWGRS, 2002; 1-4, EWGRS, 2003; 1-5, EWGRS, 2004; 1-6, EWGRS, 2005

2007-1067-5-1, Aboriginal Healing Foundation (also 5-2, 5-3, 5-4, 5-5, 5-6)

2009-1039-1-1, Healing and Reconciliation Design Team, part 1 (2004–5)

2009-1039-1-2, Healing and Reconciliation Design Team, part 2

2011-1016-1-1, 1-2, and 1-3, Principal Clerk/Assembly Office, box 1, Residential School Files, Church-Canada meetings 2001–3

2011-1016-1-6, Principal Clerk/Assembly Office, Residential Schools, Church-Canada Working Group, Apportionment, Viability and Ability, 2001

2011-1016-1-8, Principal Clerk/Assembly Office, Residential Schools, Working Groups – Ecumenical 2001

2011-1016-1-12, Principal Clerk/Assembly Office, Residential Schools, Leaders' Tour, 2008

2011-1016-1-14, Principal Clerk/Assembly Office, Residential Schools, 1-14 EWGRS, 2003–4

2011-1016-2-2, EWGRS, 2006; 2-3, 2007

St Andrew's College Library, Saskatoon

Shingwauk Project Archives, Algoma University. "Common Experience Payment Process and Validation," 20 June 2007

Trent University Archives

Indian-Eskimo Association of Canada fonds (online)

United Church of Canada. *General Council Records of Proceedings*

United Church of Canada Archives (UCA)

Accession no. 2.001C, General Council Minutes,

Accession no. 2002, 046C, box 6, file 9 (Port Alberni case); file 10, Indian Residential Schools Correspondence, 1998–99, Bill Phipps material re apology

Accession no. 2003, 164C JGER, Richard Chambers files

Accession no. 82.001C, Minutes of General Council Executive, 1984–86; 82.001, 35-2 Minutes, 1986–88

Accession no. 91.162C, Series 2, Records of the General Secretary

Box 7-7RR, C13, All Native Circle Conference

Box 7-14, E60, Native Ministries: ANCC Healing Fund – Working File, 1971, 1993–2002

Box 7-15, file E60

Box 7-16, Correspondence, 1998

Box 8-3, Residential Schools

Series 2, accession no. 2003.166C, Records of the General Secretary, 1972– ;
    13-1 S64, Native 1987–98; 13–2 S64, Residential Schools, 1995–99; 17-17
    S64, Healing Fund Minutes

University of Saskatchewan Archives, Royal Commission on Aboriginal
    Peoples, hearing transcripts

Vancouver School of Theology Archives, Aboriginal Rights Coalition fonds,
    www.vst.edu/vst/people/staff/archives

Published Primary Sources

Aboriginal Healing Foundation. *Directory of Residential Schools in Canada.* Rev.
    ed. Ottawa: Author 2007.

Blakeney, Allan. *An Honourable Calling: Political Memoirs.* Toronto: University
    of Toronto Press 2008.

Brant Castellano, Marlene, Linda Archibald, and Mike DeGagné, eds. *From
    Truth to Reconciliation: Transforming the Legacy of Residential Schools.* Ottawa:
    Aboriginal Healing Foundation 2008.

Canada. "Federal Government Takes Steps to Speed Up Resolution of Abuse
    Claims at Indian Residential Schools." Press release, 29 Oct. 2001.

– *Gathering Strength: Canada's Aboriginal Action Plan.* Ottawa: Indian and
    Northern Affairs Canada, 1997.

– *Reconciliation and Healing: Alternative Resolution Strategies for Dealing with
    Residential School Claims.* Ottawa: Indian Affairs and Northern Development
    2000.

– Parliament. House of Commons. *Debates.* 8 February 1877 [on Treaty 6].

– Parliament. House of Commons. *Debates.* 11 June 2008 [Harper apology].

– Parliament. Senate. Special Joint Committee of the Senate and the House
    of Commons [on] the Indian Act. *Minutes of the Proceedings and Evidence*
    (1946–48).

Chansonneuve, Deborah. *Reclaiming Connections: Understanding Residential
    School Trauma among Aboriginal People: A Resource Manual.* Ottawa:
    Aboriginal Healing Foundation 2005.

Dion Stout, Madeleine, and Rick Harp. *Lump Sum Compensation Payments
    Research Project: The Circle Rechecks Itself.* Ottawa: Aboriginal Healing
    Foundation 2007.

Dion Stout, Madeleine, and Gregory Kipling. *Aboriginal People, Resilience and the Residential School Legacy*. Ottawa: Aboriginal Healing Foundation 2003.

Dukelow, Daphne A., ed. *The Dictionary of Canadian Law*. 4th ed. Toronto: Carswell 2011.

Graham, John, and Laura Mitchell. *A Legacy of Excellence: Best Practices Board Study – Aboriginal Healing Foundation*. Ottawa: Institute on Governance 2009.

Hendry, Charles E. *Beyond Traplines: Does the Church Really Care? Towards an Assessment of the Work of the Anglican Church of Canada with Canada's Native Peoples*. Toronto: Anglican Church of Canada 1969.

Kaufman, Fred. *Searching for Justice: An Autobiography*. Toronto: University of Toronto Press and the Osgoode Society for Canadian Legal History 2005.

Kinew, Wab. *The Reason You Walk*. Toronto: Viking Penguin Random House 2015.

Legacy of Hope Foundation. *Where Are the Children? Healing the Legacy of the Residential Schools*. Ottawa: Legacy of Hope Foundation 2003.

– *100 Years of Loss: The Residential School System in Canada. Teacher's Guide*. Ottawa: Legacy of Hope Foundation 2011.

Mathur, Ashok, Jonathan Dewar, and Mike DeGagné, eds. *Cultivating Canada: Reconciliation through the Lens of Cultural Diversity*. Ottawa: Aboriginal Healing Foundation 2011.

Minutes of the General Council of Indian Chiefs and Principal Men, Held at Orillia, Lake Simcoe Narrows, on the Proposed Removal of the Smaller Communities, and the Establishment of Manual Labour Schools. Montreal: Canada Gazette Office 1846.

Phipps, Bill. *Cause for Hope: Humanity at the Crossroads*. Kelowna, BC: Copper House 2007.

"Report of the Special Commissioners Appointed on the 8th of September, 1856, to Investigate Indian Affairs in Canada., *Journals of the Legislative Assembly of the Province of* Canada. Vol. 16, appendix 21, 1858.

Rogers, Shelagh, Mike DeGagné, Jonathan Dewar, and Glen Lowry, eds. *Speaking My Truth: Reflections on Reconciliation and Residential School*. Book Club edition. Ottawa: Aboriginal Healing Foundation 2012.

Royal Commission on Aboriginal Peoples. *Choosing Life: Special Report on Suicide among Aboriginal People*. Ottawa: RCAP 1995.

– *Integrated Research Plan*. Ottawa: RCAP 1993.

– *The Mandate: Royal Commission on Aboriginal Peoples – Background Documents*. N.p. 1991.

– *Partners in Confederation: Aboriginal Peoples, Self-Government, and the Constitution*. Ottawa: RCAP 1993.

– *Public Hearings. Discussion Paper 1: Framing the Issues*. Ottawa: RCAP 1992.

– *Public Hearings. Discussion Paper 2: Focusing the Dialogue*. Ottawa: RCAP 1993.
– *Public Hearings: Overview of the First Round*. Prepared for the Commission by Michael Cassidy, Ginger Group Consultants. Ottawa: RCAP 1992.
– *Public Hearings: Overview of the Second Round*. Prepared for the Commission by Michael Cassidy, Ginger Group Consultants. Ottawa: RCAP 1993.
– *Public Hearings. Exploring the Options: Overview of the Third Round*. Ottawa: RCAP 1993.
– *Public Hearings. Toward Reconciliation: Overview of the Fourth Round*. Ottawa: RCAP 1994.
– *Report of the Royal Commission on Aboriginal Peoples*. 5 vols. Ottawa: RCAP 1996.
– *The Rights of Aboriginal Self-Government and the Constitution: A Commentary*. N.p. 1992.
– *Sharing the Harvest: The Road to Reliance. Report of the National Round Table on Aboriginal Economic Development and Resources*. Ottawa: RCAP 1993.
– *Treaty Making in the Spirit of Co-Existence: An Alternative to Extinguishment*. Ottawa: RCAP 1995.
Scott, D.C. "Indian Affairs, 1867–912."In *Canada and Its Provinces*, edited by A. Shortt and A.G. Doughty. Toronto: Glasgow, Brook & Company 1914.
Sigurdson, Glenn. *Vikings on a Prairie Ocean*. Winnipeg: Great Plains Publications 2014.
Starkman, Akivah. *The Independent Assessment Process: Reflections*. N.p.: Author 2014.
Swain, Harry. *Oka: A Political Crisis and Its Legacy*. Vancouver and Toronto: Douglas & McIntyre 2010.
Thorpe, Brian. Thorpe, Brian. "Inviting the Chiefs: Apology Feast to the Gitxsan." Unpublished memo in author's possession.
– "A Loss of Innocence: The United Church Coming to Terms with the Legacy of the Residential Schools." *Ecumenism* no. 155 (Sept 2004).
– "Transformation in the Encounter: Reflections on a Dispute Resolution Press." *Touchstone* 24, no. 2, 1 (May 2006).
Truth and Reconciliation Commission. *Final Report of the Truth and Reconciliation Commission of Canada. Volume One Summary: Honouring the Truth, Reconciling for the Future*. Toronto: Lorimer 2015.
– *Final Report of the Truth and Reconciliation Commission of Canada*. Vol. 1. *Canada's Residential Schools: The History. Part 1. Origins to 1939; Canada's Residential Schools. The History. Part 2, 1939 to 2000*. Montreal and Kingston: McGill-Queen's University Press 2015.
– *Final Report of the Truth and Reconciliation Commission of Canada*. Vol. 2. *Canada's Residential Schools The Inuit and Northern Experience*. Montreal and Kingston: McGill-Queen's University Press 2015.

– *Final Report of the Truth and Reconciliation Commission of Canada. Vol. 3. Canada's Residential Schools: The Métis Experience.* Montreal and Kingston: McGill-Queen's University Press 2015.
– *Final Report of the Truth and Reconciliation Commission of Canada. Vol. 4. Canada's Residential Schools: Missing Children and Unmarked Burials.* Montreal and Kingston: McGill-Queen's University Press 2015.
– *Final Report of the Truth and Reconciliation Commission of Canada. Vol. 5., Canada's Residential Schools: The Legacy.* Montreal and Kingston: McGill-Queen's University Press 2015.
– *Final Report of the Truth and Reconciliation Commission of Canada. Vol. 6. Canada's Residential Schools: Reconciliation.* Montreal and Kingston: McGill-Queen's University Press 2015.
– *They Came for the Children: Canada, Aboriginal Peoples, and Residential Schools.* Winnipeg: TRC 2012.
Younging, Gregory, Jonathan Dewar, and Mike DeGagné, eds. *Response, Responsibility, and Renewal: Canada's Truth and Reconciliation Journey.* Ottawa: Aboriginal Healing Foundation 2009.

Newspapers and Periodicals

Anglican Journal. See also *Canadian Churchman.*
Canada's History, April–May 2016
Canadian Churchman. See also *Anglican Journal.*
Globe and Mail
National Post
Ottawa Citizen
Presbyterian Record
StarPhoenix (Saskatoon)
United Church Observer
Western Oblate Studies

Interviews

All interviews were conducted by the author. In addition to the interviews that are listed below, I also had the benefit of interviews with four other informants who requested anonymity. Also included in this category are remarks and conversations as noted.

Pierre Baribeau, Montreal, 28 Nov. 2011
Jim Boyles, Toronto, 25 Feb. 2015

Ruth Cameron, Saskatoon, 22 July 2015
Trina Cooper-Bolam, Ottawa, 27 Aug. 2015
Caroline E. Davis, Kingston, ON, 19 March 2010
Mike DeGagné, Ottawa, 28 May 2009; conversation during a breakfast
    meeting, Ottawa, 2 Nov. 2012; remarks at AHF book launch, UBC, 11 Aug.
    2014 (personal observation); "The Truth and Reconciliation Commission
    Recommendations," remarks delivered at the University of British
    Columbia House of Learning on 16 Sept. 2015 and to the University of
    Ottawa Centre for Policy Alternatives, 19 Nov. 2015 (copy in author's
    possession)
Mario Dion, Ottawa, 2 Nov. 2012
Doug Ewart, Toronto, 19 Feb. 2009
Tom Flanagan, Calgary, 8 Sept. 2009
Phil Fontaine, Winnipeg, 20 March 2015; Edmonton, 28 Sept. 2016
Irene Fraser, Millet, AB, 4 May 2015
Louise Halfe, Saskatoon, 9 Jan. 2011
Helen Harrison, Ottawa, 31 March 2016
Maggie Hodgson, Dead Man's Flats, AB, 10 March 2015
Shirley Horn, Sault Ste Marie, ON, 29 June 2010
Ted Hughes, Victoria, 3 June 2013
Dan Ish, Saskatoon, 10 June 2013
David Iverson, Kingston, ON, 19 March 2010
Don Jackson, Sault Ste Marie, ON, 26 June 2010
Ellie Johnson, Oakville, ON, 20 Feb. 2009
Susie A. Jones, Wallaceburg, ON, 17 Oct. 2011
Chief Robert Joseph, North Vancouver, 12 Aug. 2015
Kathleen Keating, Vancouver, 8 July 2015
Gerry Kelly, Ottawa, 9 Sept. 2010
Stephen Kendall, Toronto, 27 Feb. 2015
David MacDonald, Toronto, 18 Feb. 2009
Marianne McLean, Ottawa, 2 May 2016
Alex Maass, Gatineau, QC, 3 May 2016
Kathleen Mahoney, Calgary, 14 May 2009
Lea Meadows, Calgary, 27 July 2015
John S. Milloy, Peterborough, ON, 25 Nov. 2015
Ry Moran, Winnipeg, 10 Sept. and 8 Oct. 2014; and Saskatoon, 2 Feb. 2015
Kim Murray, Winnipeg, 25 Nov. 2014
Alison Norman, Toronto, 1 March 2016
Bill Phipps, Calgary, 20 April 2010
Shelagh Rogers, Gabriola Island, BC, 22 April 2014

David Russell, Vancouver, 19 May 2010
Andy Scott, Fredericton, 1 Nov. 2012
Jamie Scott, Ottawa, 11 Sept. 2010 . Jamie Scott to Jim Miller, 19 Aug. 2016 re
    negotiations for Settlement Agreement
Scott Serson, Ottawa, 21 Jan. 2010
John Siebert, Kitchener, ON, 7 July 2009
Jim Sinclair, North Bay, ON, 28 June 2010
Justice Murray Sinclair, Winnipeg, 25 Nov. 2014 and 30 March 2015;
    Saskatoon, 23 June 2015; public lecture, University of Toronto Law School,
    11 Dec. 2009 (personal observation)
George Thomson, Ottawa, 20 Jan. 2010
Brian Thorpe, Vancouver, 18 May 2010
Tupper, Shawn, Ottawa, 9 June 2008, 9 Sept. 2008, and 13 Nov. 2008
Archbishop James Weisgerber, Regina, 3 April 2014
Rev. Andrew Wesley, Toronto, 21 Nov. and 12 Dec. 2013

Web Sources

Aboriginal Rights Coalition. "A New Covenant." http://home.istar.ca arc/
    English/new_cov_e.html (accessed 4 July 2013).
– *You Can Help Write the Next Chapter in Canada's History.* http://home.istar.ca
    arc/English/new_covenant_e.html (accessed 4 July 2013).
APTN. "Outgoing Chief Adjudicator Criticizes Lawyers in Residential School
    Compensation Process." http://aptnnews.ca/2013/03/11/outgoing-chief
    -adjudicator-criticizes-lawyers-in-residential-school-compensation-process/
    (accessed 20 Jan. 2016).
Assembly of First Nations. "Report on Canada's Dispute Resolution Plan to
    Compensate for Abuses in Indian Residential Schools." N.p. 2004, http://
    epub.sub.uni-hamburg.de/epub/volltexte/2009/2889/pdf/Indian_
    Residential_Schools_Report.pdf (accessed 12 April 2016).
Bavelas, Janet. *An Analysis of Formal Apologies by Canadian Churches to First
    Nations.* Centre for Studies in Religion and Society, University of Victoria,
    Occasional Paper no. 1, July 2004 www.uvic.ca/psyc/bavelas/2004/
    ChurchApol.pdf (accessed 2 July 2013).
Canada. Aboriginal Affairs and Northern Development. "Canada's Statement
    of support on the United Nations Declaration on the rights of Indigenous
    Peoples." https://www.aadnc-aandc.gc.ca/eng/1309374407406/130937445
    8958#a2 (accessed 12 June 2015).
– "Commemoration." www.aadnc-aandc.gc.ca/eng/1100100015635/110010
    0015636 (accessed 24 March 2015).

– "Common Experience Payment." www.aadnc-aandc.gc.ca/eng/11000100015594/100100015 (accessed 27 April 2015).
– "Future Location of Stained Glass Artwork." Remarks by Minister John Duncan. www.aadnc-aandc.gc.ca/eng/1332859355145/1332859433503 and www.aadnc-aandc.gc.ca/eng/1320333022635/1320333157758 (accessed 24 March 2015).
– Indian Residential Schools Settlement Agreement. http://www.residentialschoolsettlement.ca/settlement.html (accessed April 2017).
– Speech from the Throne. 16 Oct. 2007. www.sft-ddt/gc/caemgomdex/asp (accessed 8 Feb. 2013).
– "Statistics about the IAP." www.aadnc-aandc.gc.ca/eng/1315320539682/1315320692 (accessed 16 Nov. 2015 and 27 July 2016).
– "Statistics on the Implementation of the Indian Residential Schools Settlement Agreement." www.aadnc-aandc.gc.ca/eng/1315320539682/1315320692192 (accessed 10 Nov. 2015; 31 March and 27 July 2016).
Canada. Employment and Social Development. "Evaluation: Delivery of the Common Experience Payment." www.esdc.gc.ca/eng/publications/evaluations/service_canada (accessed 27 March 2015).
Canada. Service Canada. "Common Experience Payment" instructions and application form. www.servicecanada/gc/ca/eforms/forms/gc-mp5419 (2012-01 (accessed 27 March 2015).
CBC. Interview with Phil Fontaine. 2 Oct. 1990. www.cbc.ca/gsa?q=Phil-Fontaine%w2C+The Journal%2C_Oct._1990 (accessed 3 Nov. 2014).
– "Red Road Forward: What Happened at Gordon's." 26 Feb. 2010. http://www.cbc.ca/news/canada/saskatchewan/red-road-forward-what-happened-at-Gordon's? (accessed 5 June 2014).
Ciccocioppo, Lucianna. "Conference Took Stock of Canada's Indian Residential Schools Settlement Agreement." University of Toronto Law website, www.law.utoronto.ca (accessed 21 Feb. 2013).
CNW Group. http://www.newswire.ca/en/release/October2008/20/c7708.html (accessed 20 Oct. 2008)
Duncan, John. "Future Location of Stained Glass Artwork." Video of remarks by the minister. www.aadnc-aandc.gc.ca/eng/1332859355145/1332859433503 and www.aadnc-aandc.gc.ca/eng/1320333022635/1320333157758 (both accessed 24 March 2015).
Four_arrows@canada.com A compilation of Aboriginal-related press items compiled and distributed by Rarihokwats (accessed 6 Aug. 2013)
Harper apology. www.fns.bc.ca/pdf/TextofApology.pdf (accessed 8 Jan. 2009)
Harper statement re lack of imperial history www.reuters.com/Article2C (accessed 12 Oct. 2015)

Historica. Heritage Minutes. www.historica-dominion.ca/content/heritage
    _minutes.si (accessed 12 Oct. 2015).

Indian Residential Schools Adjudication Secretariat. "Adjudication Secretariat
    Statistics from September 19, 2007 to January 31, 2016." http://iap-pei.ca/
    information/stats-eng.php (accessed 16 March 2016).

Kairos Canada. "The Voice of the Bell." http://www.kairoscanada.org/the
    -voice-of-the-bell-by-diane-munier (accessed 22 July 2015).

Kaufman, Fred. "Searching for Justice: An Independent Review of Nova
    Scotia's Response to Reports of Institutional Abuse." Jan. 2002. www.gov
    .ns.ca/just (accessed 21 April 2015).

Macintyre, Stuart. "The History Wars." *Sydney Papers,* winter/spring 2003,
    77–83. http://www/koorieweb/org/foley/resources/pdfs/198.pdf
    (accessed 27 May 2015).

Mahoney, Kathleen. "Whither Reconciliation?" Paper presented to University
    of Toronto Law School Conference Assessing the Indian Residential Schools
    Litigation and Settlement Processes, 17–18 Jan. 2013. www.ablawg.ca/2013/
    06/26/the-indian-residential-school-settlement-agreement-is-reconciliation
    -possible (accessed 30 Nov. 2015).

McCracken, Christa, "Returning Home: Repatriation and Missing Children."
    Active History, 24 Aug. 2011, http://activehistory.ca/tag/charlie-hunter/
    (accessed 9 Sept. 2015).

Oskaboose, Gilbert. "The Aboriginal Healing Foundation: A Nest of
    Maggots." www.firstnations.com/oskaboose/nest-of-maggots.htm
    (accessed 24 Nov. 2008).

Truth and Reconciliation Commission. "Bentwood Box." www.trc.ca (accessed 7
    July 2015).

– "The First Six Months." www.trc.ca (accessed 8 Jan. 2010).

– "Meet the Commissioners." www.trc.ca (accessed 30 June 2015).

– "Northern National Event." www.trc.ca (accessed 14 June 2011).

– "TRC Opens New Office, Appoints New Executive Director." www.trc.ca
    (accessed 8 Jan. 2010).

United Church of Canada. "All Native Circle Conference, Response to the
    1986 Apology." 1988. www.united-church.ca/aboriginal/Relationships/
    response (accessed 31 May 2013).

– "Apology to First Nations Peoples," 1986, www.united.church.ca/beliefs/
    policies/1986/a651 (accessed 31 May 2013).

– "Formation of the All Native Circle Conference, 1987." www.united-church
    .ca (accessed 15 July 2013).

– "A Letter on the 20th Anniversary of the Apology to First Nations."
    Moderator's message. www.united-church.ca (accessed 16 July 2013).

– www.cbc.ca/news/Canada/Saskatchewan/many-reactions-to 30 Jan. 2015
   (accessed 12 Nov. 2015)
www.nipissingu.ca/about-us/newsroom/Pages/Nipissing-installs-Dr.-Mike=
   Degn%C3 (accessed 5 Nov. 2014)
www.torys.com/en/people/iacobucci-the-honourable-frank (accessed
   10 Feb. 2015)

Secondary Sources

Books

Airhart, Phyllis D. *A Church with the Soul of a Nation: Making and Remaking the United
   Church of Canada*. Montreal and Kingston: McGill-Queen's University Press 2014.
Attwood, Bain. *Telling the Truth about Aboriginal History*. Crows Nest, Australia:
   Allen & Unwin 2005.
Barkan, Elazar, and Alexander Karn, eds. *Taking Wrongs Seriously: Apologies
   and Reconciliation*. Stanford, CA: Stanford University Press 2006.
Bombay, Amy, with Kim Matheson and Hymie Anisman. *Origins of Lateral
   Violence in Aboriginal Communities: A Preliminary Study of Student-to-Student
   Abuse in Residential Schools*. Ottawa: AHF 2014.
Curthoys, Ann, Ann Genovese, and Alexander Reilly. *Rights and Redemption:
   History, Law and Indigenous People*. Sydney, Australia: University of New
   South Wales Press 2008.
Cuthand, Doug. *Tapwe: Selected Columns of Doug Cuthand*. Penticton, BC: Theytus
   Books 2005.
Dickason, Olive P. *Canada's First Nations: A History of Founding Peoples from
   Earliest Times*. Toronto: McClelland & Stewart 1992.
Dyck, Noel, *What Is the Indian "Problem"? Tutelage and Resistance in Canadian
   Indian Administration*. St John's: ISER Books 1991.
Fenge, Terry, and Jim Aldridge, eds. *Keeping Promises: The Royal Proclamation
   of 1763, Aboriginal Rights, and Treaties in Canada*. Montreal and Kingston:
   McGill-Queen's University Press 2015.
Gibney, Mark, Rhoda E. Howard-Hassmann, Jean-Marc Coicaud, and Niklaus
   Steiner, eds. *The Age of Apology: Facing Up to the Past*. Philadelphia: University
   of Pennsylvania Press 2008.
Hawthorn, Harry, et al. *A Survey of the Contemporary Indians of Canada. Economic,
   Political, Educational Needs and Policies*. 2 vols. Ottawa: Indian Affairs Branch
   1966–67.
Krog, Antjie. *Country of My Skull: Guilt, Sorrow, and the Limits of Forgiveness in
   the New South Africa*. New York: Three Rivers Press 1998.

Macintyre, Stuart, and Anna Clark, eds. *The History Wars*. Rev. ed. Melbourne: Melbourne University Press 2004

Manuel, George, and Michael Posluns. *The Fourth World: An Indian Reality*. Don Mills, ON: Collier-Macmillan 1974.

Miller, J.R. *Compact, Contract, Covenant: Aboriginal Treaty-Making in Canada*. Toronto: University of Toronto Press 2009.

– *Shingwauk's Vision: A History of Native Residential Schools*. Toronto: University of Toronto Press 1996.

– *Skyscrapers Hide the Heavens: A History of Indian-White Relations in Canada*. 3rd ed. Toronto: University of Toronto Press 2000.

– ed. *Reflections on Native-Newcomer Relations: Selected Essays*. Toronto: University of Toronto Press 2004.

– ed. *Sweet Promises: A Reader on Indian-White Relations in Canada*. Toronto: University of Toronto Press 1991.

Milloy, John S. *A National Crime: The Canadian Government and the Residential School System, 1879 to 1986*. Winnipeg: University of Manitoba Press 1999.

Niezen, Ronald. *Truth and Indignation: Canada's Truth and Reconciliation Commission on Indian Residential Schools*. Toronto: University of Toronto Press 2013.

Nobles, Melissa. *The Politics of Official Apologies*. Cambridge: Cambridge University Press 2008.

Posel, Deborah, and Graeme Patterson, eds. *Commissioning the Past: Understanding South Africa's Truth and Reconciliation Commission*. Johannesburg: Witswaterand University Press 2002.

Quinn, Joanna R., ed. *Reconciliation(s): Transitional Justice in Postconflict Societies*. Montreal and Kingston: McGill-Queen's University Press 2009.

Ray, Arthur P. *I Have Lived Here since the World Began: An Illustrated History of Canada's Native Peoples*. Toronto: Key Porter 1996.

Ray, Arthur P., Jim Miller, and Frank Tough, *Bounty and Benevolence: A History of Saskatchewan Treaties*. Montreal and Kingston: McGill-Queen's University Press 2000.

Regan, Paulette. *Unsettling the Settler Within: Indian Residential Schools, Truth Telling, and Reconciliation in Canada*. Vancouver: UBC Press 2010.

St Germain, Jill. *Broken Treaties: United States and Canadian Relations with the Lakotas and the Plains Cree, 1868–1885*. Lincoln: University of Nebraska Press 2009.

Samek, Hana. *The Blackfoot Confederacy: A Comparative Study of Canadian and U.S. Indian Policy*. Albuquerque: University of New Mexico Press 1987.

Savard, Dan. *Images from the Likeness House*. Victoria: Royal British Columbia Museum 2010.

Schweitzer, Don, ed. *The United Church of Canada: A History*. Waterloo, ON: Wilfrid Laurier University Press 2012.

Sheffield, Scott. *The Red Man's on the Warpath: The Image of the "Indian" and the Second World War*. Vancouver: UBC Press 2004.

Sinclair, Donna. *Crossing Worlds: The Story of the Woman's Missionary Society of the United Church of Canada*. Toronto: United Church Publishing House, 1992.

Spear, Wayne. *Full Circle: The Aboriginal Healing Foundation and the Unfinished Work of Hope, Healing and Reconciliation*. Ottawa: AHF 2014.

Stanley, G.F.G. *The Birth of Western Canada: A History of the Riel Rebellions*. 1936; 2nd ed. Toronto: University of Toronto Press 1961

Teitel, Ruti G. *Transitional Justice*. Oxford: Oxford University Press 2000.

Titley, Brian. *A Narrow Vision: Duncan Campbell Scott and the Administration of Indian Affairs in Canada*. Vancouver: UBC Press 1986.

Williams, Carol J. *Framing the West: Race, Gender, and the Photographic Frontier in the Pacific Northwest*. New York: Oxford University Press 2003.

Woolford, Alexander. *This Benevolent Experiment: Indigenous Boarding Schools, Genocide, and Redress in Canada and the United States*. Winnipeg: University of Manitoba Press 2015.

Woolford, Alexander, Jeff Benvenuto, and Alexander Laban Hinton, eds. *Colonial Genocide in Indigenous North America*. Durham, NC: Duke University Press 2014.

Wright, Donald. *Donald Creighton: A Life in History*. Toronto: University of Toronto Press 2015.

Articles and Book Chapters

Brass, Eleanor. "The File Hills Ex-Pupil Colony." *Saskatchewan History* 6, 2 (spring 1953): 66–69.

Buur, Lars. "The South African Truth and Reconciliation Commission: A Technique of Nation-State Formation., In *States of Imagination: Explorations of the Postcolonial State*, edited by Thomas Blom Hansen and Finn Stepputat, 149–81. Durham, NC: Duke University Press 2001.

Carter, Sarah. "The 'Cordial Advocate': Amelia McLean Paget and the People of the Plains." In *With Good Intentions: Euro-Canadian and Aboriginal Relations in Colonial Canada*, edited by Celia Haig-Brown and David Nock, 199–228. Vancouver: UBC Press 2006.

– "Demonstrating Success: The File Hills Farm Colony." *Prairie Forum* 16, 2 (fall 1991): 157–83.

Corntassel, Jeff, and Cindy Holder. "Who's Sorry Now? Government Apologies, Truth Commissions, and Indigenous Self-Determination in

Australia, Canada, Guatemala, and Peru." *Human Rights Review* 9 (2008): 465–89.

Dube, Siphiwe. "Aporia, Atrocity, and Religions in the Truth and Reconciliation Commission of Canada. In *Mixed Blessings: Indigenous Encounters with Christianity in Canada*, edited by Tolly Bradford and Chelsea Horton, 145–63. Vancouver: UBC Press 2016.

Feldthusen. Bruce. "Civil Liability for Sexual Assault in Aboriginal Residential Schools: The Baker Did It." *Canadian Journal of Law and Society* 22, no. 1 (2007): 133–72.

Fingard, Judith. "The New England Company and the New Brunswick Indians, 1786-1826: A Comment on the Colonial Perversion of British Benevolence." *Acadiensis* 1, 2 (spring 1972): 29–42.

Godlewska, Anne, Jackie Moore, and C. Drew Bednaser. "Cultivating Ignorance of Aboriginal Realities." *Canadian Geographer* 54, no. 4 (2010): 417–40.

Harper, Allan G. "Canada's Indian Administration: Basic Concepts and Objetives [sic]." *America Indigena* 5, no. 2 (April 1945): 119–32.

– "Canada's Indian Administration: The Indian Act." *America Indigena* 6, no. 2 (April 1946): 297–314.

– "Canada's Indian Administration: The Treaty System." *America Indigena* 7, no. 2 (April 1947): 129–48.

Hertzberg, Hazel Whitman. "Indian Rights Movement, 1887–1973." In *Handbook of North American Indians*. Vol. 4. *History of Indian-White Relations*, edited by Wilcomb E. Washburn, 301–4. Washington, DC: Smithsonian Institution 1988.

James, Matt. "A Carnival of Truth? Knowledge, Ignorance and the Canadian Truth and Reconciliation Commission." *International Journal of Transitional Justice* (2012): 1–23.

Llewellyn, Jennifer J., "Restorative Justice in Transitions and Beyond: The Justice Potential of Truth-Telling Mechanisms for Post-Peace Accord Societies." In *Telling the Truths: Truth Telling and Peace Building in Post-Conflict Societies*, edited by Tristan Anne Borer, 83–113. Notre Dame, IN: University of Notre Dame Press 2006.

Mardock, Robert W. "Indian Rights Movement until 1887." *Handbook of North American Indians*. Vol. 4. *History of Indian-White Relations*, edited by Wilcomb E. Washburn, 302–4. Washington, DC: Smithsonian Institution 1988.

Miller, J.R. "The Alberni Residential School Case: Blackwater v Plint." *Indigenous Law Bulletin* [Australia] 73 (2001).

– "Great White Father Knows Best: Oka and the Land Claims Process." *Native Studies Review* 7 (1991): 23–51.

Milloy, John S. "Doing Public History in Canada's Truth and Reconciliation Commission." *Public Historian* 35, no. 4 (Nov. 2013): 10–19.

Payne, Carol. "Through a Canadian Lens: Discourses of Nationalism and Aboriginal Representation in Government Photographs." In *Canadian Cultural Poesis: Essays on Canadian Culture*, edited by Garry Sherbert, Annie Gérin, and Sheila Petty, 421–42. Waterloo, ON: Wilfrid Laurier University Press 2006.

"Standing Out in the World of Scholarly Publishing," *University Affairs*, April 2016.

Stanton, Kim. "Canada's Truth and Reconciliation Commission: Settling the Past?" *International Indigenous Policy Journal* 2, no. 3 (2011): 1–18.

Wanhalla, Angela. "State-Sponsored Photography and Assimilation Policy in Canada and New Zealand." *Within and Without the Nation: Canadian History as Transnational History*, edited by Karen Dubinsky, Adele Perry, and Henry Yu, 91–114. Toronto: University of Toronto Press 2015.

Theses, Dissertations, and Other Unpublished Secondary Sources

Beninger, Carling. "The Anglican Church of Canada: Indigenous Policies, 1946–2011." MA thesis, Trent University, 2011.

Benson, Jayme K. "Different Visions: The Government Response to Native and Non-Native Submissions on Education Presented to the 1946-49 Special Joint Committee of the Senate and the House of Commons." MA thesis, University of Ottawa, 1991.

Cooper Bolam, Trina. "Healing Heritage: New Approaches on Commemorating Canada's Indian Residential School System." MA thesis, Carleton University, 2014.

Hough, Maegan. "Personal Recollections and Civic Responsibilities: Dispute Resolution and the Indian Residential Schools Legacy." LL.M. thesis, University of Victoria, 2014.

Kasmer, Julianne. "The Quest for Hope and Healing: A History of the Residential School Apology from St. Andrew's United Church in Port Alberni, BC, May 6, 1997." ThM [formerly MTh] course research paper, Vancouver School of Theology, 2007.

Radmacher, Michael Boldt. "Squaring the Circle Game: A Critical Look at Canada's 2008 Apology to Former Students of Indian Residential Schools." MA thesis, University of Victoria, 2010.

Rhéaume, Denise G. and Patrick Macklem, "Education for Subordination: Redressing the Adverse Effects of Residential Schooling." Report for RCAP.

Stanton, Kim Pamela. "Truth Commissions and Public Inquiries: Addressing Historical Injustices in Established Democracies." JDS dissertation, University of Toronto, 2010.

Illustration Credits

Index

(Page numbers in italics indicate photographs.)

problem of survivors of schools
not on IRSSA list, 148, 227,
251–2; as RCAP research topic, 55;
Roman Catholics exempted from,
201–2; suggestions for in AFN
report, 132; through DR, 127, 130;
as topic at RCAP hearings, 51, 53;
and troubles implementing CEP,
160–3, 181, 299n37
Congress of Aboriginal Peoples, 81
Conservative Party of Canada,
135, 138
constitutional talks, 29–30, 59–60
Coon Come, Matthew, 59
Cootes, Charlie, 77
Cornwallis, Edward, 270
Corporation of Catholic Entities
(CCE), 142, 153–5, 201–2, 226, 231
Cotler, Irwin, 135
courts, 134, 141–2, 178–9, 229. *See
also* litigation of residential schools
covenants, 29–30
Cree, 59
Crosby, Douglas, 35
cultural genocide, 235–6, 257
culture/language loss: and ADR
pilot projects, 108, 116; in AFN
report, 132; argument over in
setting up AHF, 82, 86; and CEP,
160, 296n68; and DR, 127, 130;
and exploratory dialogues, 100;
and IAP, 144; litigation for, 99;
and new ADR process, 122; and
question of liability for, 108; in
residential schools, 15–16
Cuthand, Doug, 257

Daniels, Harry, 78
Davin, Nicholas, 13
Davis, Caroline, 299n37

decolonization, 23, 24–7, 30–1, 245
DeGagné, Mike: and AHF, 82–4, *83*,
85, 90, 94; and Catholic financial
obligation, 153; on G. Valaskakis,
91; on lateral violence, 91; Native
criticism of, 86–8; and S. Rogers,
92; on TRC recommendations, 256
Department of Indian Affairs:
and AHF, 86; cuts grants to
schools during Depression,
18; feelings about churches,
107; and Hawthorn Report,
23–4; inside view of residential
schools, 275n14; investigations
into residential schools, 18; in
litigation, 98; and Oka, 43; policy
of integrated schooling, 21–3,
276n30; and RCAP, 66, 69–70;
role of in revised history of
western treaties, 64; whitewashing
Canada's Indian policy, 260–5.
See also Department of
Indian Affairs and Northern
Development (DIAND); Indian
and Northern Affairs Canada
(INAC)
Department of Indian Affairs and
Northern Development (DIAND),
55–6, 73–4
Dewar, Jonathan, 91
DeWolfe, Mark, 230
Dickson, Brian, 45
Dion, Mario, 131, 133, 137, 138, 144
Dion, Stéphane, 194
dispute resolution (DR): attempts
to fix, 130–3; defenders of, 136,
294n36; deficiencies of, 126–30,
249–50; expense of, 135; failure
forces government to negotiate
IRSSA, 125–6; as part of IRSSA,